AF724989

A Taste for Luxury in Early Modern Europe

A Taste for Luxury in Early Modern Europe

Display, Acquisition and Boundaries

Edited by Johanna Ilmakunnas and Jon Stobart

BLOOMSBURY ACADEMIC
LONDON • NEW YORK • OXFORD • NEW DELHI • SYDNEY

BLOOMSBURY ACADEMIC
Bloomsbury Publishing Plc
50 Bedford Square, London, WC1B 3DP, UK
1385 Broadway, New York, NY 10018, USA

BLOOMSBURY, BLOOMSBURY ACADEMIC and the
Diana logo are trademarks of Bloomsbury Publishing Plc

First published in Great Britain 2017
Paperback edition published 2018

Copyright © Johanna Ilmakunnas, Jon Stobart and Contributors, 2017

Johanna Ilmakunnas and Jon Stobart have asserted their right under the
Copyright, Designs and Patents Act, 1988, to be identified as Editors of this work.

Cover image: *The Officers' Mess or The Remains of a Lunch*, 1763,
Jean-Baptiste Simeon Chardin / Bridgeman Images

All rights reserved. No part of this publication may be reproduced or
transmitted in any form or by any means, electronic or mechanical,
including photocopying, recording, or any information storage or retrieval
system, without prior permission in writing from the publishers.

Bloomsbury Publishing Plc does not have any control over, or responsibility for,
any third-party websites referred to or in this book. All internet addresses given
in this book were correct at the time of going to press. The author and publisher
regret any inconvenience caused if addresses have changed or sites have
ceased to exist, but can accept no responsibility for any such changes.

A catalogue record for this book is available from the British Library.

ISBN: HB: 978-1-4742-5823-4
PB: 978-1-3500-9487-1
ePDF: 978-1-4742-5824-1
eBook: 978-1-4742-5825-8

Names: Ilmakunnas, Johanna, 1974– editor of compilation. |
Stobart, Jon,1966– editor of compilation.
Title: A taste for luxury in early modern Europe : display, acquisition and
boundaries / edited by Johanna Ilmakunnas and Jon Stobart.
Description: London ; New York : Bloomsbury Academic, an imprint of
Bloomsbury Publishing Plc, 2017. | Includes bibliographical references and index.
Identifiers: LCCN 2016051196| ISBN 9781474258234 (hardcover) |
ISBN 9781474258241 (PDF) | ISBN 9781474258258 (ePub)
Subjects: LCSH: Europe—History—1648–1789. | Europe–History—1789–1815. |
Luxuries—Europe—History. | Aesthetics—Social aspects–Europe—History.|
Material culture—Europe—History. | Consumption
(Economics)—Europe—History. | Social status—Europe—History. |
Europe—Social life and customs. | Europe—Economic conditions. | BISAC:
HISTORY / Europe / General. | HISTORY / Modern / 18th Century. | HISTORY /
Social History. | HISTORY / Modern / 19th Century.
Classification: LCC D273.5 .T37 2017 | DDC 940.2—dc23 LC record available at
https://lccn.loc.gov/2016051196

Typeset by RefineCatch Limited, Bungay, Suffolk

To find out more about our authors and books visit
www.bloomsbury.com and sign up for our newsletters.

Contents

Figures

Tables

Contributors

Bruno Blondé (ORCID 0000-0002-2118-799X) is a full professor at the Centre for Urban History and the Urban Studies Institute of the University of Antwerp. His major research interests include the history of transportation, economic growth and social inequality, material culture and consumption of the early modern Low Countries. With Ilja Van Damme he is writing a new synthesis on the material culture of Antwerp in the sixteenth to the eighteenth centuries.

Kerry Bristol (ORCID 0000-0001-9844-8919) is an architectural historian interested in the history and historiography of British and Irish architecture between *c.*1600 and *c.*1840. She is a senior lecturer in the School of Fine Art, History of Art and Cultural Studies at the University of Leeds where she has taught country house studies since 1999. She is currently researching a book on the Winns of Nostell.

Alida Clemente (ORCID 0000-0003-1065-6858) is a lecturer and assistant professor of economic history at the University of Foggia. She graduated in social history at the 'Orientale' University of Naples in 1997 and she obtained her PhD in economic history at the University of Bari in 2003. She has published on urban and regional economic history of the Mediterranean between the seventeenth and the nineteenth centuries, with special regard to fisheries, migration, social assistance, maritime trade and luxury consumption. Her main publications include *Il mestiere dell'incertezza: La pesca nel Golfo di Napoli tra XVIII e XX secolo* (Guida, 2005) and *Il lusso 'cattivo': Dinamiche del consumo nella Napoli del Settecento* (Carrocci, 2011).

Natacha Coquery is a professor of modern history at the University of Lyon 2, senior member of the Institut universitaire de France (2014–2019). Specializing in history consumption and retail in Paris in the eighteenth century, her current research focuses on the luxury market during the French Revolution. Her publications include *Le commerce du luxe: Production et circulation des* *objets précieux du Moyen Âge à nos jours* (edited with Alain Bonnet, Mare et Martin, 2015), 'Luxury and Revolution: selling textiles in Revolutionary France', in *Selling Textiles in the Long Eighteenth Century*, ed. Jon Stobart and Bruno Blondé (Palgrave Macmillan, 2014) and 'Selling China and India in Eighteenth-Century Paris', in *Goods from the East, 1600–1800: Trading Eurasia*, ed. Maxine Berg (Palgrave Macmillan, 2015).

Veerle De Laet holds a PhD in history (University of Antwerp, Centre for Urban History, 2009) and conducted research at the crossroads of art and economic history at the universities of Antwerp, Leuven, Bordeaux and Rotterdam. Private art, luxury consumption and cultural exchanges at the early modern Netherlandish art market are the main topics of her expertise and publications. Currently she is director and publisher at Leuven University Press, an international publishing house affiliated with the University of Leuven.

Kristóf Fatsar (ORCID 0000-0003-2317-8015) has been lecturing on the history and conservation of gardens and designed landscapes for nearly two decades and is an Advisory Member of the ICOMOS-IFLA International Scientific Committee on Cultural Landscapes. He has an MSc in Landscape Architecture (Budapest, 1994) and another Master's in Heritage Conservation from the Catholic University of Leuven, Belgium (1996). He earned his PhD in 2001 with a dissertation on Baroque gardens of Hungary. Currently a Senior Lecturer in Landscape Architecture at Writtle University College (Essex, UK), he also holds a professorship at the Faculty of Landscape Architecture and Urbanism in Budapest.

Ulla Ijäs (ORCID 0000-0002-2066-6104) completed her PhD thesis at the School of History, Culture and Arts Studies at the University of Turku, in June 2015. Her research interests include merchant houses in the eighteenth and nineteenth centuries, merchant networks, migration, towns, gender and consumption. Currently, she is working at the University of Helsinki in the Faculty of Law.

Johanna Ilmakunnas (ORCID 0000-0003-0746-5129) is acting as professor of Finnish history at the University of Turku. Her research interests include material culture, consumption, lifestyle, credit, work and leisure, gender and elites in eighteenth-century Sweden and France. Her publications include a major study of the lifestyle of Swedish eighteenth-century aristocracy *Ett ståndsmässigt liv: Familjen von Fersens livsstil* (SLS and Atlantis, 2012) and *Early Professional Women in Northern Europe, c. 1650 to the 1850s* (Routledge, forthcoming – edited with Marjatta Rahikainen and Kirsi Vainio-Korhonen).

Yme Kuiper holds the chair Historic Country Houses and Estates at the Faculty of Arts, University of Groningen and is emeritus professor historical anthropology at the same university. He co-edited *Nobilities in Europe in the Twentieth Century* (Peeters, 2015) and *Buitenplaatsen in de Gouden eeuw* [Country Houses in the Golden Age: The Richness of Country Life in the Dutch Republic] (Verloren, 2015). His inaugural address is published as 'The Rise of the Country House in the Dutch Republic' in *The Country House: Material Culture and Consumption*, eds Jon Stobart and Andrew Hann (Historic England, 2016).

Sofia Murhem (ORCID 0000-0001-9071-8689) is a lecturer and Associate Professor at the Department of Economic History, Uppsala University. Her main research areas include post-war Swedish and European industrial relations and regulations, consumption, second-hand retailing (auctions and pawnbroking), credit and marketing from the eighteenth century onwards. Together with associate professor Göran Ulväng she is running a project on the Swedish church as a financier of the agrarian revolution from 1750 to 1850.

Michael North is professor and chair of modern history at the University of Greifswald, Honorary Doctor of the University of Tartu and director of the International Graduate Program 'Baltic Borderlands'. His publications include *Art Markets in Europe, 1400-1800* (Ashgate, 1998 – together with David Ormrod), *Material Delight and the Joy of Living: Cultural Consumption in Germany in the Age of Enlightenment* (Ashgate, 2008), *Artistic and Cultural Exchanges between Europe and Asia 1400–1900* (Ashgate, 2010), *The Expansion of Europe, 1250–1500* (Manchester University Press, 2012), *Mediating*

Netherlandish Art and Material Culture in Asia (Amsterdam University Press, 2014 – together with Thomas DaCosta Kaufmann) and *The Baltic: A History* (Harvard University Press, 2015).

Astrid Pajur (ORCID 0000-0002-0121-7346) is a PhD candidate in early modern history at the University of Uppsala in Sweden. Her dissertation explores clothing, clothing culture and related social phenomena – including inventory-making, bequests and conflicts concerning clothes – in seventeenth-century Tallinn, Estonia.

Nadia Fernández-de-Pinedo (ORCID 0000-0001-6708-1480) is a senior lecturer at the Universidad Autónoma de Madrid. She completed undergraduate and doctoral degrees at the Universidad del País Vasco and a postdoctoral research project at the University of Warwick. Her work covers a wide range of consumption and distribution networks including eighteenth and nineteenth-century Spanish and Atlantic history. She participates in a number of cross-disciplinary projects and she is a member of the Global History Network and the Group of Innovation, Business and Commerce. There, she has embarked on several projects for examining technology transfer processes, institutions, fabric distribution and material culture. Her previous publications include *Circuits of Knowledge: Foreign Technology and Transnational Expertise in Nineteenth-century Cuba* (Palgrave Macmillan, 2016 – together with David Pretel) and 'Distribution of English Textiles in the Spanish Market at the Beginning of the Eighteenth Century' (*Revista de Historia Económica*, 31, 2013 – with Emiliano Fernández-de-Pinedo).

Marie Steinrud (ORCID 0000-0002-9350-7622), PhD, is a cultural historian at Stockholm University. Her research interests cover elites, identities, gender and manifestations of power. She is currently working on a research project about ironmasters in Sweden between 1700 and 1900, focusing on how the ironmasters built a common identity during this period. Her publications include her thesis *Den dolda offentligheten: Kvinnlighetens sfärer i 1800-talets högreståndskultur* [Hidden Publicity: Female spheres in the nineteenth-century Swedish Nobility] (Carlssons, 2008), journal articles and book chapters on ironmasters and their manifestations of power, elite status, elite women's lives and experiences in eighteenth-century and early nineteenth-century Sweden, as well as masculine ideals within nineteenth-century upper-class culture.

Jon Stobart (ORCID 0000-0002-9771-4741) is professor of history at Manchester Metropolitan University. His research interests range across the practices, spaces and materiality of retailing and consumption, mostly in eighteenth-century England. Most recently, he has focused on the country house as a site and nexus of consumption. His publications on this include *The Country House: Material Culture and Consumption* (Historic England, 2016 – edited with Andrew Hann) and *Consumption and the Country House* (Oxford University Press, 2016 – co-authored with Mark Rothery). He is currently working on a project on Comfort and the Country House with Marie-Curie Fellow, Cristina Prytz.

Corinne Thépaut-Cabasset (ORCID 0000-0003-0361-1491) is a Marie Sklodowska-Curie research fellow at the Centre for Textile Research (CTR)/SAXO Institute, University of Copenhagen (Denmark) on a project entitled 'Dressing the New World: The Trade and the Culture of Clothing in the Spanish colonies (1500–1800)'. She has previously worked at the Palace of Versailles, where she was principal investigator for several publications and exhibitions projects. In 2010–2013, she was postdoctoral research fellow at the Victoria and Albert Museum London, working on the project 'Fashioning the Early Modern: Creativity and Innovation in Europe 1500–1800' funded by Humanities in the Research Area (HERA), investigating creativity and innovation that lay behind the creation and spread of fashionable goods in early modern Europe. Her publications reflect the various topics she carried out for her research on dress and textile. They all explore, from different perspectives, the ways in which archival sources interact with objects-based studies.

Göran Ulväng (ORCID 0000-0002-2907-8982) is a research fellow and associate professor at the Department of Economic History at Uppsala University. His research has mainly focused on changes in agriculture, household and work organization, material culture (houses and inventories) and consumption (auctions, pawnbroking) in the countryside and towns during the eighteenth, nineteenth and twentieth centuries, with a specific focus on the manorial economy, consumption and material culture. Together with associate professor Sofia Murhem he is running a project on the Swedish church as a financier of the agrarian revolution from 1750 to 1850.

Acknowledgements

The idea for a collection of essays on luxury across Europe was first raised at the tenth European Social Science Conference 2014 in Vienna, where we organized two sessions entitled 'A Taste for Luxury, *c.* 1750–1850'. The first focused on Sweden, Finland and Russia and the second on France, Spain and Britain. The aim of these sessions was to offer comparative perspectives on the meaning and articulation of taste and luxury in different parts of Europe. They allowed us to explore how these terms were contingent on local economic and cultural circumstances, but also how they were drawn together through the movement of goods and through shared ideals and practices, especially of a cosmopolitan elite. Reflecting on the sessions, we quickly realized that there were geographical and conceptual gaps in the picture that had emerged. As a result, we sought out papers that offered us a view from Germany, the Low Countries and Italy, and asked contributors to think about questions of agency and the usefulness of broader concepts, most notably Jan de Vries's notion of old and new luxury. The result is this volume which, we feel, offers the reader both a series of fascinating case studies and a framework for understanding the relationship between taste and luxury during this crucial period in European history.

We wish to thank all the contributors to the volume for their engagement with the project, and the anonymous readers for their invaluable comments. We would also like to thank Emma Goode and Rhodri Mogford at Bloomsbury Publishing for their expertise and help in bringing the project to fruition.

Johanna Ilmakunnas's work for the volume has been carried out with the support of the project 'Diligent aristocracy: Nobility, service and work in Sweden from the Great Northern War to the Napoleonic Wars' (266059), funded by the Academy of Finland.

Display, Acquisition and Boundaries of Luxury and Taste

Johanna Ilmakunnas and Jon Stobart

The image on the cover of this volume, *The Officers' Mess or The Remains of a Lunch,* painted by Jean Baptiste Siméon Chardin in *c.* 1763 visualizes some of the key issues of luxury and taste during the long eighteenth century. The small still life (38 × 46 cm) depicts a table on which the remains of a lunch are left in a serving room. There is a sugarloaf, bread, cheese and pâté, fruits, decanters of vinegar and oil, and jars of compote. A large porcelain tureen with a decorated knob, a porcelain dish and a small silver vessel are placed on the table, and a white linen towel in the middle of the table catches the eye. To the right of the serving table there is another table, small and painted red, on which a sugar bowl and two teacups of Chinese porcelain are placed.[1] Together, these objects and commodities suggest the global dimension as well as the comfort and pleasures of everyday luxury. As such, they encapsulate perfectly our concerns in this book: the nature of taste and luxury, the acquisition of luxurious goods and the shifting meaning of these objects as they moved across spatial and social boundaries.

Thinking about luxury

Many of the things illustrated in Chardin's painting had been expensive novelties in the seventeenth century, beyond the means of most European households, but they were more widely consumed by the middle decades of the eighteenth century, even by those of very limited means.[2] Contemporary commentators were alive to this spreading consumption of luxury, Daniel

Defoe noting of Britain that 'the Way of Living [is] large, luxurious, vain and expensive'. Moreover, Defoe was clear about the mechanisms that allowed this change: the rich would take the best wines, spices, tea, linens, muslins and so on, but there were cheaper versions of all these goods readily accessible to those of lesser means.[3] The same was also true of a wide range of manufactures; from ceramics and snuff-boxes to buttons, ribbons and fans. Such goods were made in various materials and styles in order to suit consumers across the social scale. Producers and merchants created endless new products to meet the growing markets for luxury and semi-luxury goods, and they used skilful marketing strategies to sell their wares.[4]

That everyone could have their own slice of luxury raises two important issues. The first is that luxury was relative rather than absolute; it was contingent on time, place and spending power, and on cultural and political norms. An object or a material luxurious for a shopkeeper was neat and simple for a gentleman; extravagant use of silver and gold was ostentatious luxury for an aristocrat, but a necessity in the display of sovereign power. Definitions of luxury are thus dependent upon the consumer as well as the commodity or, as Maxine Berg puts it, they are 'shaped by public structures of meaning and private experience' which were mutually constitutive.[5] The second issue, and closely related to this public–private nexus, is that luxury had considerable moral, social and economic significance in the seventeenth and eighteenth centuries. Across Europe there was an ongoing, but shifting debate about the characteristics of luxury goods and the ways in which these impacted upon society and economy.[6] To summarize these very briefly, there was a gradual move away from seeing luxury as harmful to the national economy and towards a view that it formed the bedrock of economic growth. Through much of the seventeenth century, mercantilist understandings of the economy blamed luxury for draining away resources as money was spent on unnecessary imported goods. Starting with Mandeville, political economists increasingly viewed luxury, and consumption more generally, as an economic stimulus and an employer of the poor. A parallel debate on the morality of luxury critiqued elite excess, which was often associated with foreignness (especially French) and effeminacy, but the real focus for censure was the poor. This was partly because, as John Sekora in particular has argued, luxury was seen as breeding indolence and crime amongst the lower orders, and partly because the spread of luxury broke down traditional markers of social distinction.[7]

This debate has informed much of the historiography on consumption, framing discussions about the relationship between consumption and economic development, the shifting character and definition of luxury goods, and the motivations underpinning luxury consumption.[8] In casting consumption as the central plank of industrial capitalism, Werner Sombart explained the rise of luxury in psychological, sensual and ultimately sexual terms. Yet individual gratification is a poor explanation for the rise of luxury consumption, even in the rarefied atmosphere of court society. Norbert Elias's reading of a court-based aristocracy offers a more sociological basis for luxury consumption, courtiers being obliged to spend in accordance with their rank.[9] There is a parallel here with the prescriptions of sumptuary legislation and with the 'old luxury' identified by Jan de Vries as a marker of status which relied on 'grandeur and exquisite refinement' in order to distinguish the elite from other social groups. In contrast, 'new luxury' was socially inclusive and revolved around notions of comfort, pleasure and sociability, and encouraged civilized communication.[10] It was characteristic of the new urban middling sorts who, by implication, felt less need to emulate the luxury spending and lifestyles of the old elite. There are problems with this neat alignment of luxury spending and social groups, not least the mutual exclusivity implied for the two modes of behaviour. However, the refinement of luxury as comfort and decency has been picked up in the work of John Crowley and Woodruff Smith, who respectively argue for an increasing search for physical comfort and social respectability as leitmotifs in eighteenth-century consumption.[11]

Defining taste

If luxury is a mutable concept, then taste is even more difficult to define and delimit. It is often viewed as a means of refining luxury and moderating the ostentation of straightforward displays of wealth through material possessions. In this sense, taste was critically important in distinguishing those of rank and breeding from the rest of society; indeed, it became central to elite identity.[12] Thus we see London's *Beau Monde* being characterized by Lord Chesterfield as possessing a certain 'je ne scay quoy [*sic*] ... which other people of fashion acknowledge'.[13] For Chesterfield, good taste was an innate quality of the elite, closed to others by birth, rank and dignity. In reality, however, it could be learned; indeed, the cultivation of taste formed a central element of the education of elite men and women. It was carefully nurtured from early childhood both within the family and in social circles, social life being a central arena for refining as well as displaying one's good taste. For men, tutors, private schools, university and especially the Grand Tour were both a vehicle for enculturation and a means of refining behaviour, manners and taste. For women, these same qualities were acquired from governesses, drawing, music and dancing masters, as well as social visiting.[14] This process of learning was especially true of new money, which had to be educated in the choice, display and use of goods in order to develop the manners, deportment and good taste that formed what Thorstein Veblen has called 'the voucher of a life of leisure'.[15] The importance of education in cultivating taste and thus cementing status distinctions is central to Pierre Bourdieu's analysis of the persistence of class divisions in post-war France, where the metropolitan elite perpetuated their privilege through the educational opportunities afforded by the *Grand Écoles* and through the cultivation of cultural capital. This involved the construction of a set of tastes that were very different from those of the lower orders and often involved a Kantian aesthetic, i.e. a preference for 'difficult' things that were less immediately accessible and pleasurable. For Bourdieu, this was a conscious strategy of social reproduction through cultural distinction – an idea that resonates with many eighteenth century elite practices.[16]

Taste also has other meanings, however, most importantly in terms of the bundling of goods, practices and manners into a set 'type' that has specific and distinct characteristics. [17] More usually, though, taste in this sense is seen in national terms: notably Italian, French and English/British. Taste was linked to national qualities well before the rise of nationalism and nation states in the nineteenth century; indeed, the building of a national identity had begun early in France, where good taste was considered quintessentially French. From the seventeenth century onwards, Louis XIV deliberately constructed the image of France as a power state, in which French culture and taste played a significant role. The production of high quality engravings and books ensured the wide dissemination of the idea of French taste as the most exquisite in Europe.[18]

Thus, during the second half of the seventeenth century, the image of sophisticated French taste was embedded to the European imagination of luxury and taste. Obviously, this carefully cultivated image represented only one strand of what was a complex and fluid concept. Didier Massieu discusses the rivalry between French and English taste in the eighteenth century, the subject having evoked an abundance of contemporary commentators to argue over whether English or French manners, products and gastronomy were supreme.[19] The rivalry was symbolic, but impacted on real political, cultural and economic spheres, in which the two countries became more serious rivals in the course of the eighteenth century. In a broader European context, Italian taste has perhaps been most closely linked to the Grand Tour and its idealization of classicism and Renaissance artistic achievements – a view that looked backwards, rather than drawing on contemporary society.

The key quality of taste has thus always been its ability to mark distinctions, whether social, cultural, political or national.[20] Much the same could be said of luxury. In the course of history, taste and luxury have been important tools for separation, differentiation and power; they have created influential and enduring boundaries between social groups and countries. However, individuals or groups who possessed the means to define and shape 'good taste' have also possessed considerable power to define their societal place and the opportunities to increase or consolidate their own power, both in the material world of producing, distributing and consuming luxuries and at a more immaterial level of cultural and political competence.

Luxury and taste: some unanswered questions

Luxury and taste are thus familiar, perhaps even over-familiar, ideas in the historiographies of consumption; and yet there are many aspects of both that remain under-explored. First, whilst we know that displays of luxury and their refinement through taste lie at the heart of attempts to display wealth and status, we understand less well the ways in which luxury and taste were constructed and delineated in particular places. It is easy to observe that luxury is a relative term, but much more difficult to say what this meant when it came to defining luxury or taste in different parts of Europe. What was permitted and what was not; what constituted 'good taste', and how important was novelty and tradition in shaping ideas of luxury and taste? More fundamentally, what was the role of economics, culture and the law in these processes? Second, recent years have seen a growing interest in the processes of acquiring goods, particularly the luxuries and novelties bought from metropolitan retailers.[21] This work has rightly placed considerable emphasis on the reputation and kudos of particular tradesmen and women, and the emergence of distinct zones of elite shopping, both of which helped to define the parameters of rank and taste. But how did consumers, even amongst the elite, know what to buy? What defined particular goods as tasteful or luxurious? Are these qualities that were attached to the goods or to the retailers who sold them? On a more practical level, how did consumers ensure that the goods they were acquiring (or getting others to purchase on their behalf) were tasteful? Third, and implicit in the above, is the question of the boundaries of luxury and especially taste. Much has been written on this in an aesthetic and material sense: the discernment of the connoisseur and collector, the ignorant ostentation of the nouveaux riches, the excesses of the macaroni, and so on. Equally, contemporaries and historians alike are alive to social boundaries and the anxiety created by transgression of these distinctions.[22] But what of geographical boundaries: how were they bridged or transgressed by luxury goods and cultures of taste? Here, there is a growing body of work on the impact of Eastern goods, although variations in their reception and meaning in different European countries has received rather less attention.[23] Intra-European transfers are seldom discussed: what did French taste or English goods, for example, actually mean when they were transferred to Spain or Sweden; and what happened to notions of luxury and taste when society, politics or economies were transformed, through revolution or reform?

This book attempts to address some of these questions and, in doing so, revise our understanding of the link between taste, luxury and identity both at a personal and national level. Its various surveys and case studies of consumption practices, material culture, political economy and retail marketing offer new readings of luxury and taste; fresh perspectives on the processes of acquiring commodities and the ways in which these helped to define them as tasteful or luxurious objects, and a more nuanced picture of the practices and experiences of luxury. They are arranged into three broad sections: displaying taste and luxury; making and acquiring taste; and crossing boundaries of taste and luxury. Readers may thus choose to explore one or more of these organizing themes. However, there are a number of key ideas that run through the whole volume and which draw together chapters, time and places, and which offer the reader a different route through the book and the worlds of luxury and taste.

Key ideas

It is something of a truism to say that both luxury and taste are relative and contingent, their meaning varying over time and space. However, the reasons for and processes of changing tastes are too rarely given the attention that they deserve. The introduction of novel goods, either through overseas trade or industrial innovation, is well recognized as a stimulus for new forms of consumption. This point is brought out in several of the chapters in this volume, Murhem and Ulväng, for example, demonstrating in Chapter 10 the retailing of porcelain in Stockholm how a taste for Chinese porcelain impacted on ways of selling as well as the homes of wealthy, and not so wealthy, citizens. Here, it was traded goods that drove change; elsewhere, the ability of the individual to bring home exotic items was instrumental in shaping their domestic environment, as with the wealthy Dutch nabob studied by Kuiper in Chapter 4.[24] New wealth, of course, brought greater capacity for luxury consumption and the nabob has long been recognized as a problematic figure, disrupting traditional hierarchies of wealth and status and established norms of taste.[25] More generally, political change could form important moments of transition in taste. Pinedo and Thépaut-Cabasset in their study of imported goods in Bourbon Madrid (Chapter 11), and Clemente in her analysis of luxury and taste in eighteenth-century Naples (Chapter 3) both show how the introduction of a new ruling house could transform taste, especially amongst the elite. In contrast, in discussing the Parisian market during the Terror of the 1790s (Chapter 14), Coquery demonstrates that even an event as traumatic as the French Revolution could leave some expressions of taste and the demand for certain luxuries largely unchanged, although the power of political idealism swept others aside.

In as much as it represents the replacement of one set of material and cultural values with another, we might see this as an extreme version of the kind of process modelled by Jan de Vries.[26] His ideas of a transition between old and new luxury are adopted in many of the chapters. Pajur, for example, uses it to frame her analysis of sumptuary laws, social order and propriety in seventeenth-century Tallinn (Chapter 1), whilst Ijäs argues that the ideals of new luxury engendered particular consumption choices amongst the merchant elite of nineteenth-century Vyborg (Chapter 13). A fuller and more explicit engagement comes in the chapter by Blondé and De Laet, who argue for the Southern Netherlands cities of Brussels and Antwerp (Chapter 2) that transition between the two was partial and far from linear: material aspects of new luxury were found amongst both established and new elite groups, whilst the emerging elites adopted many of the trappings of old luxury to bolster their status. These arguments are echoed in Clemente's chapter, which highlights divisions within the established elite of Naples where old and new luxury marked political as well as status groups.

Geographically, elite ideas of taste and luxury are often seen as being characterized by a pan-European cosmopolitanism – a shared culture that helped to draw together Europe's aristocracy and distinguish them from the lower orders.[27] The European was mixed and enriched by an exoticism that might be strikingly bold, as with the black servants brought home from India by returning nabobs like Sichtermann who came back to Groningen after a career with the Dutch East India Company (see Kuiper, Chapter 4). But it was increasingly internalized and domesticated, as is apparent from the consumption of Chinese wallpapers and porcelain by Lord Leigh in England; ironmasters in rural Sweden, such as Per Reinhold Tersmeden, and wealthy shoppers in Stockholm (see Stobart, Chapter 7; Steinrud, Chapter 9; and Murhem and Ulväng, Chapter 10).[28] Despite this, what emerges over and over again are the barriers and resistance to any notion of transnational taste. These were most obviously expressed in the restrictions introduced by many countries to protect domestic industries from luxuries being imported from other countries, especially France. As Clemente notes of Naples, for example, a taste for such goods was recognized as being deeply problematic for local craftsmen. However, as Pajur makes clear for seventeenth-century Tallinn (Chapter 1), sumptuary laws could also play a powerful role in shaping local identities by marking in material terms differences with people coming in from other countries or cities.

In Tallinn's sumptuary laws, cosmopolitanism came into direct conflict with localism. More generally, there was an ongoing tension between the national and the transnational, often seen in the pan-European influence of French and later English taste.[29] The powerful influence of French taste is discussed in broad terms by Clemente, who sees it as an important aspect of the ebb and flow of cultural and political power in eighteenth-century Naples. This intimate binding of taste and politics also comes through Ilmakunnas's analysis of the role of envoys and ambassadors in conveying taste and transporting luxury goods from France to Sweden (Chapter 12). In this instance, French goods spoke of power, luxury and the economic and social 'reach' of the consumer; being able to afford and access French luxuries told of their owner's status. In the homes of the elite of Brussels and Antwerp, French goods perhaps held less of a political charge, but they remained important markers of status (see Blondé and De Laet), just as they were in many country houses in England. Here, though, there were tensions born of political conflict, patriotism and prohibitions. These sometimes led to consumers seeking goods on the grey market, as we see in Bristol's discussion of the shopping habits of Sabine Winn of Nostell Priory (Chapter 8); but French styles more often were internalized and re-imagined through the practices of craftsmen such as Chippendale. The confidence with which English taste was deployed at home grew alongside the country's expanding influence across Europe. Clemente notes its growing influence in Naples, where English taste formed a conscious counterpoint to French taste and, in some ways, its natural successor as economic and political power swayed towards England from the middle decades of the eighteenth century. The march of English taste across Germany and into Scandinavia is familiar enough, although the depth and range of influence carried by English styles and English goods is brought out fully in North's analysis of the German fashion journal *Journal des Luxus und der Moden* (Chapter 5) and Ijäs's discussion of the consumption practices of merchants in the Finnish port of Vyborg in the nineteenth century (Chapter 13). In both contexts, English meant modernity and social progressiveness. What is perhaps more surprising is Coquery's assertion that demand for English goods and tastes in Revolutionary France remained high, at least until the start of the Reign of Terror in the autumn of 1793 (Chapter 14).

Despite the undoubted importance of political and economic power in exerting cultural influence, it would be mistaken to see these changes as a simple reflection of two superpowers competing for cultural supremacy. As North's discussion makes clear, French and English taste also represented different social values, especially in relation to luxury; it was no accident that the established and aristocratic elite favoured the former, whilst the emergent urban bourgeoisie aligned themselves with the latter.[30] Indeed, it is possible to read the ideals and cultural contexts of old and new luxury in these two national systems of taste. And yet, however alluring they might be, these simple dichotomies are problematic. For one thing, the precise meaning of French and English was highly complex. They might refer to tastes or goods directly imported from France or England, an important aspect in supplying the wealthy Swedish, Finnish and Flemish consumers studied by Ilmakunnas, Ijäs, and Blondé and De Laet respectively; but these same consumers were also acquiring locally produced goods in the French or English style or, more loosely, local interpretations of what French or English taste might look like. As Ilmakunnas notes, for example, French servants may have been brought over from France, but they might equally be French trained or simply French-speaking. Moreover, other national tastes were also being asserted, a practice seen most directly in the construction of national costumes. In 1778, Gustav III launched the national Swedish dress, both praised and criticized, and mainly worn by courtiers and civil servants.[31] Similar attempts in Germany were perhaps less successful, although North notes the ownership of clothes that broadly conform to published ideals. Equally, wealthy elites might simply reject the fashionable modernity represented by international taste, as with Prince Esterházy's retention of his formal gardens at Süttör, despite the rising fashion for English landscape gardens (see Fatsar, Chapter 6).

The way that North links the rhetoric of journals with the reality of people's wardrobes highlights the important materiality of taste and luxury. These were ideals and concepts, but they were, in the end, expressed in tangible objects and spaces. Maxine Berg argues that the physical characteristics of luxuries were important in defining them as such; indeed, luxury was a visceral experience that appealed to all of the senses.[32] Refining this sensuality through taste often had the effect of privileging the visual, outward appearance being central to assessments of people, their social worth, integration into the community, wealth and status, political allegiance, and so on. Clemente makes this point most clearly in relation to Naples, but it also comes out in Sabine Winn's concern with her clothing (see Bristol), the importance of appropriate clothing and specifically the Dorpat costume in Tallinn (Pajur), and the significance of wig ownership in Brussels and Antwerp (Blondé and De Laet). With each of these, the material qualities of the goods were important. Pajur details the specific cloth, colour and cut of clothing that sumptuary laws prescribed to each layer of society, making it quite clear that luxury – or its absence – was marked in clearly visible and unambiguous material terms. Pinedo and Thépaut-Cabasset also emphasize the importance of different grades and colours of cloth, and their differential acquisition by various groups within mid-eighteenth-century Madrid where high status was marked by the ownership of the finest imported cloths.

Importantly, they also note that these textiles might be used to adorn the home as well as the body, reminding us that the domestic realm was an important venue and showcase for taste and luxury. In many ways, this is familiar ground,[33] but the manifold constructions and expressions of taste in the domestic realm have yet to be fully explored. In this volume, Stobart highlights the importance of coordinated schemes and the often-protracted process of creating an appropriately tasteful backdrop to domestic life in the English country house. More fragmented, but equally telling, is the picture painted by Steinrud of the houses of wealthy and titled owners of ironworks in Sweden. Here, it is some of the small details that are telling: the arrangement of chinaware or the flowers in the garden. For the super-rich, the materiality of luxury could be extensive and costly, as with the showy frontage for the townhouse of the Dutch nabob, Sichtermann, and his huge collection of armorial porcelain (Kuiper), or the extensive landscaped grounds of Prince Esterházy in Hungary (Fatsar). Yet in both instances, these were tempered by refined taste: a gallery of old masters and musical patronage respectively. What is particularly striking is that taste and luxury could interact differently in different parts of an elite consumer's life. Two things are important in this. The first is that taste was not necessarily something that was or could be expressed equally in all aspects of spending. Thus, as Fatsar demonstrates,

Prince Esterházy's taste in art perhaps fell short of his taste in music – an imbalance which calls into question easy assumptions of the innate 'good taste' of the nobility.[34] The second is that the location and setting of luxury was significant in shaping its impact. Blondé and De Laet demonstrate this in relation to the display of paintings in the homes of the elite in Brussels and Antwerp, their gradual relocation into more private spaces being linked to changing genres and motivations. Stobart shows how assembling more luxurious goods together in different rooms at Stoneleigh Abbey could mark important distinctions, even between ostensibly similar spaces like guest bedrooms.

What also comes out through Stobart's analysis, and are apparent in many other chapters, are the practical and logistical challenges facing even wealthy consumers: learning taste and acquiring luxury was a difficult process involving lots of hard work. For many consumers, this meant bringing goods over long distances, a process which almost invariably involved engaging the help of intermediaries. Quite apart from the practicalities of communicating and transferring payment, this meant that the purchaser was reliant upon someone else to exercise taste and judgement, be it Swedish nobles drawing on diplomats in Paris (Ilmakunnas), rural ironmasters using family members in Stockholm (Steinrud) or Vyborg merchants seeking help from business partners in England (Ijäs). These proxy shoppers, as Claire Walsh has called them, were important sources of consumer intelligence as well as consumer goods,[35] but most wealthy consumers, even in relatively remote locations, also gathered information from a variety of other sources. Steinrud's bachelor ironmaster and Kuiper's returning nabob both visited the homes of their friends and neighbours, picking up decorative ideas appropriate to their tastes and purses, whilst the Stockholm elite visited shops for inspiration as well as goods (see Murhem and Ulväng). Bristol shows that Sabine Winn, isolated in West Yorkshire, was reduced to scouring the newspaper advertisements, although, as Coquery makes clear, these could remain an important source of consumer intelligence even in the most challenging times. Journals formed an increasingly important source of guidance, a development that North explores in detail, although readers needed to interpret the polemic with some care. Indeed, the perils faced by even wealthy consumers meant that the ideals of taste were sometimes compromised by the exigencies of the immediate situation, as

Stobart demonstrates in relation to the ways in which Lord Leigh dealt with some poor-quality furniture supplied from London.

Finally, there are the pleasures to be gained from luxurious and tasteful goods. The sensual nature of luxury, highlighted by Werner Sombart and reiterated by Maxine Berg, is too easily forgotten; but we need to remember that luxury and taste – indeed, consumption more generally – was not all about appearance and identity.[36] Physical pleasure could be gained from food, as the Swedish nobles with their French-trained cooks no doubt appreciated, as did the wealthy patriarchs drinking chocolate in Madrid (Ilmakunnas and Pinedo and Thépaut-Cabasset); flowers could fill the air with fragrant smells (Steinrud), and music could captivate and transport the listener, especially when it was of the quality produced by Joseph Haydn (Fatsar). Equally important were the emotional responses elicited by even quite modest luxuries such as the ribbons and lace bought by Sabine Winn or the English dog acquired by the Hackmans in Vyborg (Bristol and Ijäs).

Taken together, then, the chapters in this volume offer fresh insights into the nature of luxury and taste by drawing together case studies from across Europe. They reveal the nuances and complexities of luxury and taste as they played out in particular local settings, but also demonstrate how each place is set within the context of broader Europe-wide and even global processes. Indeed, one of the key threads running through each chapter is the importance of interconnections and interchange. We see this in the cultural currency of French and English taste; the long-distance flows of goods between merchants and to individual consumers, and the influx of goods from Atlantic colonies and the Orient. This returns us to Chardin's painting of *The Officers' Mess* and highlights the cosmopolitanism of elite consumption. Does internationalization of taste imply a single culture of consumption, shared by elites across Europe? Whilst there are many common elements, many of which we have outlined above, the answer to this question appears to be no. Two things cut across and disrupted any homogeneity of purpose and expression. First is the varied nature of the elite, which included landed gentry, titled nobility and royal courts, but also merchants, wealthy burghers and colonial servants. These social groups may have shared a desire to distinguish themselves from other sections of society and, as consumers, possessed a 'reach' that allowed them to acquire a range of goods beyond the means of others; but they were far from homogeneous in their wealth, tastes or material culture. Second, consumption, taste and luxury were situated in particular political, economic and social contexts that shaped the parameters within which individuals and groups could operate. This is not to fragment human experience into a series of unconnected episodes, but rather to emphasize the relational and contingent nature of taste and luxury, and thus to challenge universal and normative understandings of consumption and identity. Place and context mattered because it formed the active setting in which goods were acquired, owned, displayed and utilized: English goods, for instance, meant something different to the citizens of revolutionary Paris, merchants in Vyborg, courtiers in Naples and landowners in Warwickshire. We need to be just as sensitive to these differences as we are of the integrative power of global trade.

Notes

1 Jean Baptiste Siméon Chardin, *La Table d'office, ou les Débris d'un déjeuner*, *c*. 1763. Oil on canvas, 38 × 46 cm. Musée du Louvre, Paris, M.I.1040.

2 Anne E. C. McCants, 'Exotic Goods, Popular Consumption, and the Standard of Living: Thinking about Globalization in the Early Modern World,' *Journal of World History* 18 (2007), 433–62; see also Martin Bruegel, 'A Bourgeois Good? Sugar, Norms of Consumption and the Labouring Classes in Nineteenth-Century France', in *Food, Drink and Identity: Cooking, Eating and Drinking in Europe Since the Middle Ages*, ed. Peter Scholliers (Oxford and New York: Berg, 2001), 99–118; Philippe Meyzie, *L'alimentation en Europe à l'époque moderne* (Paris: Armand Collin, 2010); Craig Muldrew, *Food Energy and the Creation of Industriousness: Work and Material Culture in Agrarian England, 1550–1780* (Cambridge: Cambridge University Press, 2011).

3 Daniel Defoe, *A Plan of the English Commerce* (London, 1728), 144, 166.

4 See Natacha Coquery, *Tenir Boutique à Paris au XVIIIe Siècle: Luxe et Demi-Luxe* (Paris: Éditions du Comité Historique et Scientifique, 2011); Maxine Berg, *Luxury and Pleasure in Eighteenth-Century Britain* (Oxford: Oxford University Press, 2005); Carolyn Sargentson, *Merchants and Luxury Markets: The Marchands Merciers of Eighteenth-Century Paris* (London: Victoria and Albert Museum, 1996).

5 Berg, *Luxury and Pleasure*, 31.

6 For useful summaries, see: Christopher Berry, *The Idea of Luxury: A Conceptual and Historical Investigation* (Cambridge: Cambridge University Press, 1994); *Consumers and Luxury: Consumer Culture in Europe, 1650–1850*, eds Maxine Berg and Helen Clifford (Manchester: Manchester University Press, 1999); *Luxury in the Eighteenth Century: Debates, Desires and Delectable Goods*, eds Maxine Berg and Elizabeth Eger (London: Palgrave Macmillan, 2003), 7–27; *Luxury and Gender in European Towns, 1700–1914*, eds Deborah Simonton, Marjo Kaartinen and Anne Montenach (London: Routledge, 2015).

7 John Sekora, *Luxury: The Concept in Western Thought, Eden to Smollett* (Baltimore: Johns Hopkins University Press, 1977); see also Leif Runefelt, *Att hasta mot undergången: Anspråk, flyktighet, förställning i debatten om konsumtion i Sverige 1730–1830* (Lund: Nordic Academic Press, 2015).

8 See, for example: Berg, *Luxury and Pleasure*.

9 Werner Sombart, *Luxury and Capitalism* (Ann Arbor: University of Michigan Press, 1967); Norbert Elias, *The Court Society* (Oxford: Blackwell, 1983).

10 Jan de Vries, *The Industrious Revolution* (Cambridge: Cambridge University Press, 2006), 44.

11 John Crowley, *The Invention of Comfort: Sensibilities and Design in Early-Modern Britain and Early America* (Baltimore: Johns Hopkins University Press, 2001); Woodruff Smith, *Consumption and the Making of Respectability, 1600–1800* (London: Routledge, 2002).

12 Didier Masseau, *Une histoire du bon goût* (Paris: Perrin, 2014), 23; see also Thorstein Veblen, *The Theory of the Leisure Class: An Economic Study in the Evolution of Institutions* (New York and Basingstoke: Palgrave Macmillan, [1899] 1912).

13 Hannah Greig, *The Beau Monde: Fashionable Society in Georgian London* (Oxford: Oxford University Press, 2013), 3.

14 See Henry French and Mark Rothery, *Man's Estate: Landed Gentry Masculinities, 1660–1900* (Oxford: Oxford University Press, 2012), 85–184; Greig, *Beau Monde*, 36–47.

15 Veblen, *Theory of the Leisure Class*, 49. See also Berg, *Luxury and Pleasure*, 39–43.

16 Pierre Bourdieu, *Distinction: A Social Critique of the Judgement of Taste* (London: Routledge and Kegan Paul, 1984); for a useful critique, see M. Savage, 'Status, lifestyle and taste', in *The Oxford Handbook of the History of Consumption*, ed. Frank Trentmann (Oxford: Oxford University Press, 2012), 557–67.

17 See, for example, Nicola Pickering, 'Mayer Amschel de Rothschild and Mentmore Towers: Displaying 'le goût Rothschild', in *The Country House: Material Culture and Consumption*, eds Jon Stobart and Andrew Hann (Swindon: Historic England, 2016), 185–96.

18 *A Kingdom of Images: French Prints in the Age of Louis XIV, 1660–1715*, eds Rémi Mathis, Vanessa Selbach, Louis Marchesano and Peter Fuhring (Los Angeles: Getty Research Institute, 2015).

19 Masseau, *Une histoire du bon goût*, 114–119.

20 Bourdieu, *Distinction*; Masseau, *Une histoire du bon goût.*

21 See, for example, Linda Levy Peck, *Consuming Splendor: Society and Culture in Seventeenth-Century England* (Cambridge: Cambridge University Press, 1995); Claire Walsh, 'Shops, Shopping and the Art of Decision Making in Eighteenth-Century England', in *Gender, Taste and Material Culture in Britain and North America*, eds John Styles and Amanda Vickery (New Haven: Yale University Press, 2006), 151–77; Coquery, *Tenir boutique à Paris;* Johanna Ilmakunnas, 'The Luxury Shopping Experience of the Swedish Aristocracy in Eighteenth-Century Paris,' in *Luxury and Gender in European Towns, 1700–1914*, eds Deborah Simonton, Marjo Kaartinen and Anne Montenach (London: Routledge, 2015), 115–31.

22 See Penelope Corfield, 'The Rivals: Landed and Other Gentlemen,' in *Land and Society in Britain, 1700–1914*, eds Negley Harte and Roland Quinault (Manchester: Manchester University Press, 1996).

23 For a rare comparative analysis, see *The Spinning World: A Global History of Cotton Textiles, 1200–1850*, eds Giorgio Riello and Prasannan Parthasarathi (Oxford: Oxford University Press, 2009).

24 See also the various case studies produced by the project East India Company at Home: http://blogs.ucl.ac.uk/eicah/case-studies-2/

25 Stephanie Barczewski, *Country Houses and the British Empire, 1700–1930* (Manchester: Manchester University Press, 2014), 136–164.

26 De Vries, *Industrious Revolution*, 44–45, 57–58.

27 Gonthier Louis Fink, 'Cosmopolitisme,' in *Dictionnaire européen des Lumières*, dir. Michel Delon (Paris: Quadridge/PUF, 2007), 320–323.

28 Emile de Bruijn, 'Consuming East Asia: Continuity and Change in the Development of Chinoiserie', in *The Country House: Material Culture and Consumption*, eds Jon Stobart and Andrew Hann (Swindon: Historic England, 2015), 95–104.

29 See, for example, William H. Sewell, 'The Empire of Fashion and the Rise of Capitalism in Eighteenth-Century France', *Past and Present* 206 (2010), 81–120.

30 See also Michael North, *'Material Delight and the Joy of Living': Cultural Consumption in the Age of Enlightenment in Germany*. Trans. by P. Selwyn. (Aldershot and Burlington VT: Ashgate 2008) and Karin Wurst, *Fabricating Pleasure: Fashion, Entertainment, and Cultural Consumption in Germany, 1780–1830* (Detroit: Wayne State University Press, 2005).

31 Lena Rangström, *Kläder för tid och evighet: Gustaf III sedd genom sina dräkter* (Stockholm: Livrustkammaren, 1997), 165–177; Aileen Ribeiro, *Dress in Eighteenth-Century Europe, 1715–1789* (New Haven and London: Yale University Press, 2002), 196–201.

32 Berg, *Luxury and Pleasure*, 37–38.

33 See, for example, Leora Auslander, *Taste and Power: Furnishing Modern France* (Berkeley: University of California Press, 1996); Amanda Vickery, *Behind Closed Doors: At Home in Georgian England* (New Haven: Yale University Press, 2009).

34 Cf. Masseau, *Une histoire du bon goût.*

35 Walsh, 'Shops, shopping'.

36 See Berg, *Luxury and Pleasure*, 37–8.

Part One

Displaying Taste and Luxury

1

The Fabric of a Corporate Society: Sumptuary Laws, Social Order and Propriety in Early Modern Tallinn

Astrid Pajur*

September 1636 was an eventful month for Alhard Bondel, a gymnasium teacher in Tallinn (known as Reval at the time). Not only did he get married, he also got fined, placed under house arrest and almost fired from his job. The reason? Shortly after the wedding, his wife had donned her so-called 'Dorpat costume', along with a hat made of sable fur, and gone to the Sunday sermon in St Olaf's church. Interestingly, the sumptuary law had explicitly forbidden the 'Dorpat costume' in 1631 but it also stated that if a woman already owned one she could retain it in order to avoid expenses associated with acquiring new clothes. The town council was dismayed by this transgression on her part and informed Bondel that his wife was not to appear in public in her 'Dorpat costume' without risk of serious consequences. He was also summoned for a face-to-face discussion concerning his wife's attire, which he ignored, and as a result of his continued absence the town council threatened to relieve him of his duties as a teacher and fined him the hefty sum of 200 *Reichsthaler*. Evidently, he agreed to acquire a new wardrobe for his wife after three months of resistance. He did, however, ask for a time extension as it was bound to be costly.[1]

* I would like to thank Beverly Tjerngren, Jonas Lindström and Mikael Alm as well as the editors of this volume for their helpful advice and insightful comments on the draft manuscript.

Indeed, the 'Dorpat costume' must have been one hell of a get-up, provoking such outrage from the town council that they spent considerable time and energy trying to rein in one gymnasium teacher and his defiant wife. This case vividly illustrates the obsession in early modern society with order and ordering, appropriateness and the cobbler sticking to his last. In a society where dress was intended to demonstrate its wearer's position in the social system, unrecognizability was seen as a serious threat.[2] If one could not be instantly recognized by external appearance, then how was everybody else supposed to know who that person was, where he/she placed in the social hierarchy and how he/she stood in relation to others?

In confining the consumption of specific commodities to the elites, and thus enforcing rigid status structures, early modern sumptuary legislation was a means to ensure that a person's outer appearance reflected his or her station in society.[3] Not only did it curtail the consumption of luxury goods – including luxury goods of foreign origin, fine apparel, fabrics and accessories – sumptuary legislation also regulated gift-giving and public events, such as weddings and funerals.[4] Having peaked in the seventeenth century, the blurring of social classes and redefinition of luxury led to the demise of sumptuary legislation in the eighteenth century, even though a few countries, such as Sweden and Russia, continued issuing them.[5] In Tallinn, eight clothing regulations from the beginning of the seventeenth century until 1706 have been preserved. The length and detail of these regulations varies considerably, ranging from a few pages to around twenty. Although it is possible to discern between an introductory part, the main body of the document and a concluding section, both how detailed the regulations are and the various issues they deal with vary greatly. On some occasions the legal provisions of the regulations are numbered, on other occasions (mostly from 1690 onwards), the whole text is a continuous prose.

The exclusivity of sumptuary laws reminds us of the concept 'old luxury' used by Jan de Vries to describe luxury in pre-commercial societies. This kind of luxury was essential in maintaining the established order, often associated with extravagant and unrestrained consumption at princely and episcopal courts and fraught with moral danger.[6] In the eighteenth century, however, luxury debates moved beyond these concerns; luxury consumption, generated by urban societies rather than courts, was understood to be beneficial for economic development and increasingly associated with comfort and pleasure rather than grandeur or exquisite refinement.[7] Such consumption was ideally supposed to be more frugal and based on a regular self-examination of whether one needed something or was indulging in gratuitous conspicuous consumption.[8]

In studies of eighteenth-century consumer behaviour, taste is usually considered as a counterpoint to excessive luxury consumption. Taste provided a set of limits to exuberance and sensuality that were 'formulated in terms of an aesthetic of balance and order'.[9] More importantly, taste radically redefined ideas about status and individuals' use of goods to express status.[10] However, as I argue in this chapter, in the preceding century taste was closely connected to norms of propriety and knowing one's place within the established order. This has also been called the pattern of maintaining order, whereby dress, food and housing could serve as status objects that helped to bolster the social order. Importantly, the motivation behind sumptuary laws that saw a correspondence between legitimate distribution of power in society and wearing attire appropriate for a particular social class was recognized by people at all social levels, not just the elite.[11] As the story of Alhard Bondel's wife demonstrates, knowing what to wear and when to wear it was crucial to navigating seventeenth-century society. Unrecognizability was tasteless because it was inappropriate.

It has been often suggested that luxury and taste were relative and contingent upon the goods that were consumed and who consumed them.[12] This chapter will take as its point of departure the same notion and tease out the various ways in which luxury and taste were constructed and delineated in sumptuary legislation emanating from seventeenth-century Tallinn. The first part will discuss who was and was not addressed in sumptuary laws and thus understood to be part of the framework of luxury consumption. The second part will examine the ways that the boundaries of luxury and taste were defined in sumptuary legislation and to what extent they were congruent with one's social position. This discussion will be facilitated by an examination of the three main modes of differentiation in early modern costume – form, fabric and colour. Unfortunately, the scarcity of visual sources detailing clothing practices in seventeenth-century Tallinn inevitably means that the discussion remains somewhat theoretical.

Who issued sumptuary legislation?

During the seventeenth century, sumptuary legislation in Tallinn was issued by the town council, the highest judicial, legislative and executive power in the lower town, which was governed autonomously from the upper town on the Dome Hill, the seat of Swedish royal power.[13] The council consisted of four burgomasters and fourteen councillors elected for life, usually from amongst the senior members of the Great Guild. Personal requirements to become a member of the town council included being born to free married parents (that is, to parents who were not serfs), impeccable reputation and ownership of land within the town. Artisans and people who produced their goods through manual labour were not considered suitable to hold a position within the council.[14]

The town council imagined itself at the top of the social hierarchy, exempt from the boundaries drawn in sumptuary legislation, and explicitly stated so at the beginning of every clothing regulation.[15] Until the 1690 regulation the wording remained virtually unchanged and should therefore be quoted in full:

> Because it cannot be confirmed that in his costume, any member of the town council conducts himself [as if he was] above his social standing but it is rather felt that each of them would prefer to dress in a poor and lowly habit, if only they would not be required to honour the city, the council and their status; consequently, less reformation is necessary for this social standing.[16]

Sumptuary legislation did not apply to the town council because its members were on top of the social hierarchy and could not dress inappropriately to their social standing. The regulations did not demand that they *had* to wear a velvet hat but not doing so would have shown a lack of taste because they were, after all, town councillors. The office together with the accompanying social standing demanded appropriate manifestation; had they worn a simple habit, nobody would have taken them seriously – this was so-called righteous or necessary luxury.[17] Thus, as the case of Alhard Bondel and his wife illustrates, the town council as the small and exclusive social elite was a major agent in the luxury and taste negotiations. Through issuing sumptuary legislation they established the boundaries of luxury for different social groups and consequently established and upheld the norms for taste and propriety.

Who did the sumptuary legislation address?

Let us now consider the complex issue of which social groups sumptuary legislation addressed and who was supposed to adhere to it. As the seventeenth century progressed, clothing regulations became more elaborate and began to distinguish between an increasing number of social groups in Tallinn. This envisioned system reached its apex in the regulation of 1665 with the following social hierarchy: first and at the top was the town council, also included in the regulations of 1631 and 1639; then members of the Great Guild with their wives and daughters as well as members of the Brotherhood of the Blackheads, who were mentioned in all of the regulations until 1665; then members of St Canute's Guild with their wives and daughters, also referred to as higher or distinguished artisans in the regulations of 1631 and 1639; then members of St Olaf's Guild with their wives and daughters, also referred to as lower or common artisans in the earlier regulations; finally servants who were distinguished as a group from the first clothing regulation onwards.[18] Children were also part of the regulations but only to the extent that their costume was required to make visible their parents' position in the social hierarchy.[19]

The only group that is visible in the clothing regulations during the whole century is servants. By no means treated as a homogenous group, the laws distinguished between maidservants, wet-nurses and male house-servants. Female servants were regulated significantly more than male house-servants: for example, in addition to the garments and fabrics that were allowed for them, the 1665 regulation also included a long list of forbidden items with the harshest documented punishment of the whole century, namely confiscation of the item and imprisonment.[20] Even though by 1690 the elaborate social system had all but disappeared, the regulation of female servants remained in place with the motivation that was very much the same as it had been before – servant girls and housemaids were dressing themselves arrogantly and even dared to ape the young ladies they were serving.[21] Dressing above their rank was inappropriate for the servants because it posed a threat to the social order. This confirms that the boundaries of luxury – that is, what was appropriate for whom – corresponded to the boundaries of social order.

Sumptuary legislation issued in Tallinn during the seventeenth century was concerned with men and women roughly to the same extent and both were subject to regulation throughout the whole century.[22] Whereas men had access to public roles and their social status was to a great extent connected to their occupation, it is clearly visible from the sumptuary laws that women's social position derived entirely from their fathers or husbands.[23] As the century progressed, the more marked the differentiation between women based on their husbands' social position became. Whereas in the earliest regulation wives and daughters of guildsmen were treated together as a group and distinguished from servants, in 1665 all three guilds were separated with the wives and daughters of St Olaf's Guild being referred to as *Weiber* and *Töchter* and the wives and daughters of the Great Guild as well as St Canute's Guild members more honourably as *Frawen* and *Jungfern*.[24] Thus, what a woman could wear was directly connected to her father's or her husband's social and professional status and to which corporation they belonged.

The most striking difference between the regulations concerning male and female costume is the distinction between local and foreign costume in women's clothing during the first half of the century.[25] According to the earliest regulation women of foreign origin who had married into Tallinn could retain their usual dress to avoid the expense of getting an entirely new costume. It was also specified that the fabrics of their costume could not be more expensive than G*ewandt, Röselschen,* says, woollen camlet, Turkish and coarser grosgrain.[26] Additionally, the furs, precious metals and the fabrics their clothes were made of could not be of higher value than what was stipulated for the so-called 'Reval costume'.[27] Their daughters, on the other hand, were obliged to adopt the costume of Tallinn. It was also explicitly made clear that the women who had so far dressed according to the traditional Reval fashion could not adopt a new foreign fashion.[28] It is interesting that such explicit distinction in the clothing regulations only touched upon female clothing.

In 1631, this foreign fashion was termed 'Dorpat costume' and appears to have acquired certain characteristic traits that the town council attempted to regulate.[29] Included in this attire were round hats made of sable fur, knitted stockings, some type of high shoes, shoe ribbons made of silk and shoe-roses, most likely some kind of decoration, all of which were forbidden. In addition, only bracelets with average-sized corals were allowed and trimmings with pearls were only allowed on Sundays and other festive occasions.[30] Though some of its wearers surely originated from Dorpat (now known as Tartu), it is unlikely that everyone from Tartu wore this type of costume, and equally unlikely that all who wore it came from Tartu. Rather, it seems to have been a general label for all the foreign and undesirable elements in female costume. Since there are no visual sources that certainly depict the 'Dorpat costume' it is impossible to establish how such a term came into existence, from where its wearers originated, whether it actually had specific characteristic features, and whether these features remained the same or changed over time.

That these concerns about foreignness were not unfounded is explicitly manifested in the sumptuary legislation through the presence of foreign fabrics, accessories and designs.[31] Items such as Bremen skirts, Polish gloves, Swedish hats and Polish slitted hats appear, as well as fabrics such as Venetian lace, French silk and Turkish grosgrain.[32] It is likely that fabrics were named by the place of production, but what made a slitted hat or a pair of gloves Polish,

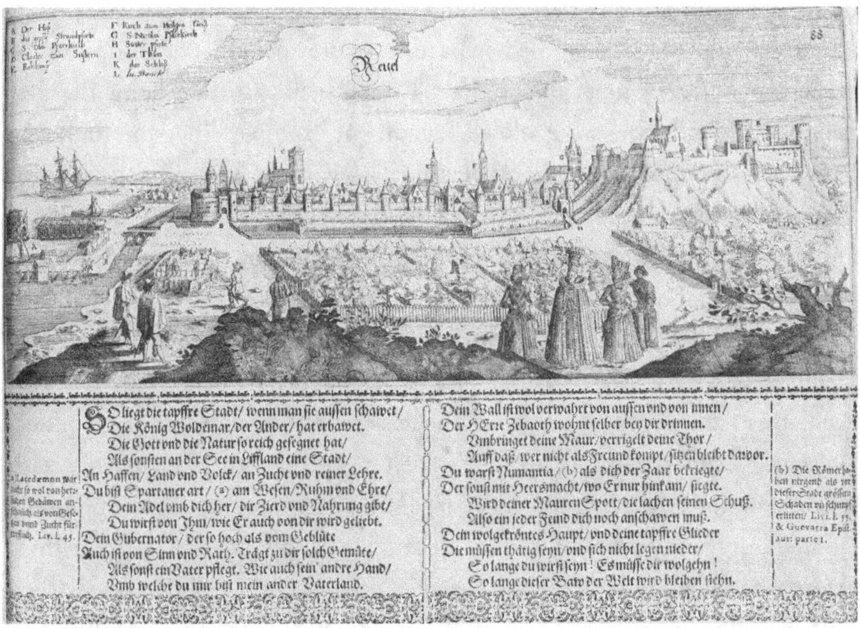

Figure 1.1 Panorama of Tallinn with four women in the foreground from Adam Olearius's *Offt begehrte Beschreibung Der Newen Orientalischen Reise* (Schleswig, 1647). Olearius was in Tallinn for several months in 1636, making the women's costumes arguably contemporaneous with the sumptuary debates of the 1630s. Unfortunately, it is unknown whether they represent the 'Reval costume' or the 'Dorpat costume'.

© Herzog August Bibliothek Wolfenbüttel: 263.1 Hist. 2°.

be it a specific regional design or fabric, is impossible to know. Although comparisons can be drawn with other parts of Europe, visual sources from Tallinn are scarce and it is ultimately difficult to know what costume in early modern Tallinn looked like. And, apart from the discourse about foreignness in clothing regulations, it is also hard to know if and to what extent distinction between local and foreign costume was visible. But the presence of foreign designs, fabrics and garments reveals that, even in a peripheral place like early modern Tallinn, sartorial practices did not develop in isolation from the rest of the world; rather, they were in constant interaction with fashion elsewhere.

It is generally agreed that sumptuary legislation was often unsuccessful in regulating people's clothing practices and as the unfortunate story of the gymnasium teacher Bondel and his wife reveals, the issue of the 'Dorpat costume' remained highly problematic. Even though the town council would have liked to see women wearing only the 'Reval costume' so that there would be a 'respectable alikeness' amongst them, already in 1639 they were forced to admit that the 'Dorpat costume' had become so prevalent that banning it would be accompanied by great difficulties.[33] Consequently, certain items that had been forbidden before were allowed again. For example, since the round fur hats were so popular that no other kind was worn it was difficult to forbid them entirely, but permission to wear them was granted only to the wives of Great Guild members.[34] The 1639 clothing regulation also conceded that bracelets could be worn according to the wearer's liking, either with corals or reasonably gilded, and that trimmings with pearls could be worn all the time.[35]

It has been suggested that luxury and foreignness have been associated with each other from the earliest times.[36] The discourse of foreignness in sumptuary legislation with regards to women's costume reveals that during the early modern period it was an important part of the contexts of luxury and propriety. Contemporaries understood that clothing was by no means something external to the body, which could be taken off and put back on as one wished. Rather, clothes were seen to 'mould a person and materialize identity'.[37] By defining foreignness in and through sartorial practices, the town council also defined what was recognizable, or in other words, what was tasteful and appropriate.[38] If a person's social standing could not be recognized by their external appearance, 'it would break the fundamental connection between dress and person.'[39]

Of course, it is obvious that the term 'every social class' ideally subject to regulation was extremely problematic as in reality the regulations only included members of the four corporations with their families and servants. The representatives of the town community or *Gemeinde*, consisting of the Great Guild and the two artisan guilds and excluding the merchant journeymen from the Brotherhood of the Blackheads, participated in town politics and the town council, at least in theory, had to take its opinion into account when adopting legislation and deciding other matters.[40] What about all the other people? Only in the 1665 regulation is reference made to an in-between group, namely the town council servants who, together with their wives and children, were supposed to dress and conduct themselves like members of St Olaf's Guild.[41] Thus, their position in the social hierarchy is likened to that of the lower artisans and their families.

The clothing regulations issued by the town council were meant to apply to everybody.[42] But apart from the above-mentioned instance, various other groups of people such as clergy, teachers and medical staff, but also the lowest artisans and daily labourers were omitted from the regulations. Legislation concerning costume is relatively clear when it comes to members of the four corporations, their wives and daughters, and servants, and occasionally gives a few guidelines with regards to apprentices, children and town council servants with their families. However, they say nothing about how the majority of the inhabitants of Tallinn were expected to dress.

The anatomy of appearances

Let us now turn to how one's position in the social hierarchy discussed above determined what the appropriate framework for sartorial expression was to be. During the early modern period 'the sumptuary order' could be established in three different ways: through colour, fabric and form. This distinction, however, is analytical and in reality all three were at work simultaneously.[43]

Contrary to what has been suggested in previous research, colour as an important marker for social distinction was not one of the concerns in sumptuary legislation.[44] Red, the sign of majesty, status and wealth, was mentioned only in the earliest regulation, where it was stated that wives of guildsmen were allowed hats made of red velvet.[45] Black, often the colour of the upper ranks and symbolizing values like loyalty and constancy, was mentioned a few times during the seventeenth century: in the earliest regulation, maidservants and wet-nurses were only allowed hats made of black *Wande*; the 1631 regulation stated that artisans' wives and daughters could have skirts of black says or *Wande*; the 1696 regulation allowed women to wear black silk coats lined with lace not wider than a hand.[46] The most detailed provision regarding colour instead concerns servants. In 1639, male servants could be dressed at most in Russian *Wandt* which could not be red, green or blue.[47] Beyond these scattered examples, colour as a social marker appears to not have been a concern for the town council to the same extent as it was in the rest of Europe.

In contrast, fabric was crucial in order to make a person recognizable to everyone else. With the exception of certain fabrics, such as silk and velvet which remained exclusive during the whole century due to their cost and foreign origin, the regulations generally stated the most expensive fabric from which a garment could be made, depending both on the wearer's social position and the occasion, be it Sunday or a feast or wedding day.[48] The clothing regulation of 1639 illustrates this best. Members of the Great Guild and the Brotherhood of the Blackheads could have clothes of caffa and on Sundays and festive days they could wear doublets made of damask or satin.[49] For members of St Canute's Guild all kinds of silk fabrics such as velvet, caffa, damask and satin were completely forbidden. They were, however, allowed to use coarser materials such as *Florett*, *Gewand*, grosgrain, *Türksch* and *Vierdrat*. For members of St Olaf's Guild it was merely stated that they could wear clothes made of simple coarse fabrics with no added decorations.[50] Thus, the lower down one moved on the social hierarchy, the lower the quality of the fabric became.

Silk, like velvet, remained an exclusive fabric and items such as silk skirts and silk aprons were generally forbidden for women.[51] The only exceptions were usually made for the more distinguished women, such as wives and daughters of town councillors or merchants on festive days and wedding days, and even then they were only allowed to wear coarser silk fabrics such as silk grosgrain, camlet and terzenel.[52] The 1665 regulation stated that wives and daughters of Great Guild members should wear skirts made of woollen fabric and *Lacke* but not scarlet and without any golden ribbons or laces.[53] Wives and daughters of better artisans were allowed to wear a skirt and a jacket made of coarser woollen fabric such as *Lacken*, says, *Türkschen* or grosgrain; on wedding and other festive days they could wear skirts made of taffeta or terzenel without any trimmings.[54] Those of lesser artisans were only allowed to wear skirts made of coarse wool material such as *Lacke, Mageir*, says, *Bohmseide, Uberkiker* or *Rash.*[55] Here also the social hierarchy of women, so intimately connected to the hierarchy of their fathers and husbands, is visible through the decreasing quality of the garment's material.

Based on the different kinds of permitted fabrics mentioned in the regulations, the number of fabrics was relatively similar both in the upper and the lower ends of the social hierarchy. Thus, social hierarchy was ideally to be visualized and made legible through the decreasing quality of the fabric and not the range or choice allowed. By establishing the most expensive fabric a garment could be made of, sumptuary legislation also defined where the boundaries between luxury and necessity for various social groups ran. Precisely because one's true self and external appearance were supposed to correspond, it was of utmost importance that a fabric was worn tastefully and in an appropriate social context.[56] For a distinguished town councillor velvet fabric was a necessity, signifying propriety and legitimacy. However, when worn by a lower artisan, it carried negative connotations of inappropriateness, unrecognizability and illegitimacy.

Form in costume comprised the cut or the design of the garment as well as decorative accessories/applications on the garment and the body; both elements were important ways of making a distinction between people of higher and lower standing.[57] Rapidly changing styles and 'modish dress' was at the heart of fashion with its values of change and novelty, its flexibility abolishing distinction and threatening the social *status quo*.[58] However, in Tallinn, differentiation by cut was rare. There are only a few occasions when the design of the garment is mentioned, such as in 1639 when it was stated about the women's 'Dorpat costume' that the neckline on a jacket could not be too steep.[59] Here the concern appears to have been not so much with potential social confusion but rather the usual argument of the 'sin of vanity' and immorality in women's costume.[60]

While cut was of no concern for the town council, accessories were an integral part of both male and female costume and all kinds of ribbons, trimmings, hooks, belts and jewellery were regulated carefully during the whole century. In the 1665 regulation, there was a long list of accessories forbidden to members of the Great Guild and merchant journeymen: belts embroidered with gold, silver and pearls; luxurious trimmings with gold, silver and various other threads; all kinds of trimmings in French fashion; golden and silver laces, braids and bows or the same items woven through with golden or silver thread; hat ribbons with gold, silver and pearls. Better artisans were allowed to wear only one ribbon as a coat decoration and lower artisans were presumably allowed none.[61] Even though it would seem to go without saying that everything forbidden to members of the Great Guild was also forbidden to everyone else, this condition was explicitly mentioned in the regulation, presumably with the understanding that 'everyone else' meant men of lower social status and not, for example, the town councillors.[62]

Why all this fuss about accessories and not at all about the cut or the colour of the garment? Simply put, clothing was costly during the early modern period and such accessories provided a way of reinventing and renewing one's wardrobe relatively cheaply. It has been suggested that 'fashion change itself was most easily and inexpensively registered in accoutrements – via ribbons, handkerchiefs, and headgear. Accessories allowed a woman to re-trim an old dress for the fraction of the cost of making a new gown.'[63] Even such small alterations to one's costume might have made the crucial difference between shabby and stylish. Additionally, 'the more added value any piece of clothing had [. . .] beyond the basic user value, the more exclusive they appeared, and the more status they inferred on their wearer.'[64] The 'use value' of a coat without golden trimmings might have been the same as that of a coat with golden trimmings but the latter's 'status value' was incomparably higher.

Conclusion

To conclude, this chapter has attempted to establish the cultural contexts for luxury and taste in a corporatist early modern society through examining how they were defined and negotiated in sumptuary legislation. Rather than analysing luxury and taste within the contexts of comfort and convenience, this article has argued that, in a seventeenth-century society concerned with maintaining the established order, they should be seen within the context of propriety. Sumptuary legislation, which established and upheld the framework for luxury as well as the norms for the proper sartorial expression of one's social standing, was issued by the town council, who also formed the town's social elite. Below them were members of the Great Guild with their wives and children, followed by members of St Canute's Guild with their wives and children, followed by members of St Olaf's Guild with their wives and children, followed by servants. Although such structure had been lost in clothing regulations by 1690, the most basic differentiation between non-servants and servants remained in place during the whole century. At the same time there were also people, such as clergy, teachers, medical staff and daily labourers, who were also expected to maintain the norms of propriety, yet completely excluded from the clothing regulations.

In Tallinn, the use of sumptuary laws to regulate appearance was primarily concerned with the quality of fabrics and various accessories. Certain expensive and exclusive fabrics, such as velvet and silk, were only considered appropriate for a very limited circle of people, such as senior members of the Great Guild and their wives, in limited quantities, for example on coat lapels, and only on special occasions, such as public festivities. As a rule, the regulations specified the most expensive fabric that was permitted for every social group and the lower down one moved on the social scale, the poorer the quality of acceptable fabrics became. Where accessories were concerned, these were an important way to renew one's outfit without having to change all the individual garments and consequently remained one of the main concerns throughout the whole century. Thus, sumptuary legislation established the contexts of luxury and propriety that were dependent on a person's position within the social hierarchy. People outside the social elite were restricted by ever-narrowing parameters within which to express themselves through dress. While a velvet coat was well within the bounds of propriety for a town councillor, and might even have been considered a necessity, such a garment would have been wildly inappropriate for an artisan, whose options regarding fabric and form were strictly limited by the laws.

Seventeenth-century sumptuary legislation was also highly preoccupied with foreign influences in costume, so much so that a tangible line was drawn between what was considered local and what was considered foreign.

Foreignness had from the earliest times been linked with luxury in its more negative sense and concerns surrounding it were by no means unique to early modern Tallinn. Foreignness in clothing was inappropriate and showed a lack of taste precisely because it was unrecognizable. Even though foreign costume was regulated only with regards to women, it is evident from other legislation that there was ample cause for concern when it came to men's costume. Neither was this concern some abstract discussion that the councillors held in the stuffy halls of the town council; on the contrary, the townspeople also perceived that foreignness in costume could rend the fabric of society to such a degree that they felt driven themselves to rend quite literally the offending items from the unfortunate wife of Alhard Bondel.

Notes

1 Tallinn City Archives (hereafter TLA) collection 230 *Der Revaler Magistrat*, inventory 1 no. Bp5 *Stadtschule, Gymnasium, Buchdruckerei*, 'Alhard Bondels Streit mit dem Rat', 37–38. For the 1631 clothing regulation, see TLA collection 190 *Archiv der St. Kanutigilde*, inventory 1 no. 2 *Resolutione/n/von Heerme/istern/und Könige Lit. A*, 397. A version of this story has also been narrated in Gotthard von Hansen, *Geschichtsblätter des revalschen Gouvernements-Gymnasiums zu dessen 250jährigen Jubiläum am 6. Juni 1881* (Reval: Verlag von Franz Kluge, 1881), 12–14.

2 Daniel Roche, *The Culture of Clothing: Dress and Fashion in the Ancien Régime* (Cambridge: Cambridge University Press, 1996), 39.

3 Maxine Berg and Elizabeth Eger, 'Introduction', in *Luxury in the Eighteenth Century: Debates, Desires and Delectable Goods*, eds Maxine Berg and Elizabeth Eger (Basingstoke: Palgrave Macmillan, 2003), 8. Despite there being a number of local studies, some more and some less dated, on the phenomenon of sumptuary legislation, the limited scholarship has led to claims that sumptuary laws have been chronically understudied. See Ulinka Rublack, *Dressing Up: Cultural Identity in Renaissance Europe* (Oxford: Oxford University Press, 2010), 265; Alan Hunt's *Governance of the Consuming Passions: History of Sumptuary Law* (Basingstoke: Palgrave Macmillan, 1996) is the only work to systematically examine early modern sumptuary laws in Western Europe; however, its serious limitation is that it only uses literature translated into English. In what is now Estonia, sumptuary laws appear to have been of interest to scholars of Baltic German origins in the later nineteenth century. See Eduard Pabst, 'Beiträge zur Sittengeschichte Revals',

Archiv für die Geschichte Liv-, Esth- und Curlands, volume 1 (Reval: Verlag von Franz Kluge, 1857), 197–241; Wilhelm Stieda, 'Eine Revaler Rathsverordnung wider den Luxus bei Hochzeiten', *Beiträge zur Kunde Ehst-, Liv- und Kurlands* 3 (Reval: Verlag von Franz Kluge, 1887), 78–88.

4 Rublack, *Dressing* Up, 266–7; Catherine Kovesi Killerby, *Sumptuary Law in Italy 1200–1500* (Oxford: Oxford University Press, 2010), 2; Carolina Brown, 'Den vita lyxen: Spetsar i 1700-talets visuella och materiella kultur', in *Det svenska begäret: Sekler av lyxkonsumtion*, eds Paula von Wachenfeldt and Klas Nyberg (Stockholm: Carlsson Bokförlag, 2015), 81.

5 Christopher Berry, *The Idea of Luxury: A Conceptual and Historical Investigation* (Cambridge: Cambridge University Press, 1994), 82; Marjatta Rahikainen and Kirsi Vainio-Korhonen, 'Manlig och kvinnlig lyx: Överflödsförordningar och modeartiklar', in *Det Svenska begäret: Sekler av lyxkonsumtion*, eds Paula von Wachenfeldt and Klas Nyberg (Stockholm: Carlsson Bokförlag, 2015), 29.

6 Jan De Vries, 'Luxury in the Dutch Golden Age in Theory and Practice', in *Luxury in the Eighteenth Century: Debates, Desires and Delectable Goods*, eds Maxine Berg and Elizabeth Eger (Basingstoke: Palgrave Macmillan, 2003), 41.

7 De Vries, 43. For an exploration of old and new luxury patterns in consumption in early modern Brussels see the chapter by Blondé and De Laet in this volume.

8 Rublack, *Dressing Up*, 272.

9 Woodruff D. Smith, *Consumption and the Making of Respectability, 1600–1800* (London and New York: Routledge, 2002), 81.

10 Grant McCracken, *Culture and Consumption: New Approaches to the Symbolic Character of Consumer Goods and Activities* (Bloomington: Indiana University Press, 1990), 17–19.

11 Smith, *Consumption and the Making of Respectability*, 35–6.

12 On this issue see also the chapter by Ilmakunnas and Stobart in this volume.

13 Karsten Brüggemann and Ralph Tuchtenhagen, *Tallinna Ajalugu*, trans. T. Vassiljeva and K. Kaugver (Tallinn: Varrak, 2013), 99.

14 Ernst Gierlich, *Reval 1621 bis 1645: von der Eroberung Livlands durch Gustav Adolfs biszum Frieden von Brömsebro* (Bonn: Kulturstiftung der deutschen Vertriebenen, 1991), 24.

15 TLA.190.1.2, 394; TLA collection 230 *Der Revaler Magistrat*, inventory 1, no. Bs7 *Kleider-, Hochzeits-, Kindtauf-, Begräbnis- u.s.w. Ordnungen 1497–1738*, f. 318r; TLA collection 191 *Revaler Kaufmanns- Oder Grosse Gilde*, inventory 1 no. 19 *Armen-Ordnung, Rewidierte Ordnung des allgemeinen Gottes-Kastens. Kasten-Ordnungen, Kleider-Ordnungen*, f. 86v.

16 TLA.191.1.19, f. 86v. *Weilen nicht zu befinden, das sich Jemand innerhalb Rahts vber seinen Standt in Kleidung verhalte besondern viellmehr erspüret wird, dass ein*

Jedweder sich lieber in schlechtern vnd gerinern Habit, kleiden würde, wan Er solches nicht der Stadt, dem Raht-Stuhl vnd seinem stande zu Ehren dan vnd wan thun muste; Alss hat dieser Standt insoweit destoweiniger reformation nötigh.

17 Maria Hayward, *Rich Apparel: Clothing and the Law in Henry VIII's England* (Farnham: Ashgate, 2009), 22.

18 TLA.190.1.2, 387–92. Brotherhood of the Blackheads united merchant journeymen and unmarried merchants of mainly German origin. Unlike the three other guilds they did not participate in town politics. St Canute's Guild united better artisans, such as goldsmiths, bakers, milliners and painters and St Olaf's Guild united lower artisans, such as butchers, furriers, carpenters and stonemasons. See Paul Johansen and Heinz von zur Mühlen, *Deutsch und Undeutsch in mittelalterlichen und frühneuzeitlichen Reval* (Köln: Böhlau Verlag, 1973), chapter 4.

19 TLA.190.1.2, 396; TLA.230.1.Bs7, f. 320r; TLA.191.1.19, f. 88r.

20 TLA.191.1.19, f. 92v.

21 *Generale Kleiderordnung von 1691* in *Archiv für die Geschichte Liv-, Est- und Kurlands*, volume 1 (Reval: Verlag von Franz Kluge, 1857), 239; Estonian Historical Archives (hereafter EAA), collection 1002 *Viljandi magistraat*, inventory 1 no. 14 *Samelband von Ordnungen der Städte Riga, Pernau, Reval und andere. Teils Drucksachen und Kopien*, f. A3r.

22 Compare this, for example, to Henrician sumptuary legislation, which did not concern itself with women at all, and the sumptuary legislation of Renaissance Italy, which was almost solely concerned with regulating women. In seventeenth-century Sweden, which at the time also included Tallinn, both men and women were subject to regulation, even though this had not been the case until 1644, see Eva Andersson, 'Foreign Seductions: Sumptuary Laws, Consumption and National Identity in Early Modern Sweden', *Fashionable Encounters: Perspectives and Trends in Textile and Dress in the Early Modern Nordic World*, eds Tove Engelhart Mathiassen et al., (Oxford: Oxbow Books, 2014), 16; For sumptuary legislation and luxury in seventeenth-century Sweden, see Håkan Möller, *Lyx och mode i stormaktstidens Sverige* (Stockholm: Atlantis, 2014); for the eighteenth century see Leif Runefelt, *Att hasta mot undergången: Anspråk, flyktighet förställning i debatten om konsumtionen i Sverige 1730–1830* (Lund: Nordic Academic Press, 2015), chapter 8 and also chapter by Murhem and Ulväng in this volume.

23 Hunt, *Governance of the Consuming Passions*, 129.

24 TLA.191.1.19, f. 89r, f. 90v, f. 91v.

25 On foreignness in sumptuary legislation see also Andersson, 'Foreign Seductions', 15–31.

26 *Gewandt* (also *Wandt, Wande* in the regulations) – a woollen fabric; I have not found a description of *Röselschen* but it was presumably a fabric of similar value.

Liselotte Eisenbart, *Kleiderordnungen der deutschen Städte zwischen 1350 und 1700: Ein Beitrag zur Kulturgeschichte des deutschen Bürgertums* (Göttingen: Musterschmidt, 1962), 125.

27 TLA.190.1.2, 388.

28 TLA.190.1.2, 389.

29 TLA.190.1.2, 399–400.

30 TLA.190.1.2, 400.

31 On foreign, especially French, influences elsewhere in Europe see also the chapters by Clemente, Fernandez de Pinedo and Thépaut-Cabasset, and Ilmakunnas in this volume.

32 TLA.230.1.Bs7, f. 320v, p. 322v; EAA.1002.1.14, f. A3r.

33 TLA.190.1.2, 396–7.

34 TLA.230.1.Bs7, f. 321r.

35 TLA.190.1.2, 400; TLA.230.1.Bs7, f. 322v; TLA.230.1.Bs7, f. 322r.

36 Berg and Eger, 'Introduction', 8.

37 Rublack, *Dressing Up*, 138.

38 According to Alan Hunt, there is ground for suggesting that most people accepted appearential order as not only natural but also desirable. See Hunt, *Governance of the Consuming Passions*, 117.

39 Andersson, 'Foreign Seductions', 26.

40 Gierlich, *Reval 1621 bis 1645*, 41.

41 TLA.191.1.19, f. 90v.

42 Johansen and von zur Mühlen, *Deutsch und Undeutsch in mittelalterlichen und frühneuzeitlichen Reval*, 291; TLA.191.1.19, f. 93r. The 1665 regulaton explicitly stated that everybody, whether they were citizens, had business in Tallinn or were in somebody's employment had to adhere to the regulation.

43 Roche, *The Culture of Clothing*, 39–40; Hayward, *Rich Apparel*, xv; Mikael Alm, 'Making a Difference: Sartorial Practices and Social Order in Eighteenth-Century Sweden', *Costume* 51 (2016), 8.

44 Regarding colour see for example Beverly Lemire, 'Second-hand Beaux and "red-armed Belles": Conflict and the Creation of Fashions in England, c. 1660–1800', *Continuity and Change* 15 (2000), 397; Hayward, *Rich Apparel*, 96.

45 TLA.190.1.2, 391. On red colour, see also Rublack, *Dressing Up*, 97–101.

46 TLA.190.1.2, 392; TLA.190.1.2, 399; EAA.1002.1.14, f. A3r.

47 TLA.230.1.Bs7, f. 318v.

48 TLA.191.1.19, f. 87r. Exceptions could be made for the senior members of the Great Guild and other older and more respectable citizens but also for their wives and daughters. For example, the 1665 regulation stated that the aldermen and senior members of both the Great Guild and Brotherhood of Blackheads as well

as other respectable older citizens of Tallinn could wear doublets and jackets made of silk on Sundays and other festive days but other fabrics such as velvet, plush and brocade remained forbidden.

49 TLA.230.1.Bs7. f. 319v.

50 TLA.230.1.Bs7. f. 320r. *Florett* – light woven fabric; *Türksch* – a mixed cloth of wool produced in Turkey; *Vierdrat* – low-value stronger woollen fabric. Eisenbart, *Kleiderordnungen der deutschen Städte zwischen 1350 und 1700*, 124, 128, 131.

51 TLA.230.1.Bs7, f. 323r; TLA.190.1.2, 389, 398.

52 TLA.190.1.2, 398. TLA.230.1.Bs7, f. 320v. Terzenel (also *Tercionell*) – silk fabric from the city of Tours. Eisenbart, *Kleiderordnungen der deutschen Städte zwischen 1350 und 1700*, 128.

53 TLA.191.1.19, f. 89r. *Lacke* – general term for woollen cloth. See 'laken' in *Deutsches Wörterbuch von Jacob Grimm und Wilhelm Grimm* (Leipzig: Verlag von S. Hirzel, 1885).

54 TLA.191.1.19, f. 91r.

55 *Mageir* – coarse woollen fabric; *Bohmseide* – woven cotton fabric; *Uberkiker* – woollen fabric; *Rash* – light woollen fabric named after the Dutch town where it was initially produced. Eisenbart, *Kleiderordnungen der deutschen Städte zwischen 1350 und 1700*, 123, 126–7.

56 Gerhard Jaritz, 'Social Groupings and the Languages of Dress in the Late Middle Ages', *The Medieval History Journal* 3 (2000), 247.

57 Alm, 'Making a Difference', 7. On form as a way of making a distinction, see also Hayward, *Rich Apparel*, 41; Roche, *The Culture of Clothing*, 39.

58 Roche, *The Culture of Clothing*, 41.

59 TLA.230.1.Bs7, f. 321v.

60 Hayward, *Rich Apparel*, 22.

61 TLA.191.1.19, f. 86–7.

62 TLA.191.1.19, f. 87v–88r.

63 Amanda Vickery, 'Mutton Dressed as Lamb? Fashioning Age in Georgian England', *Journal of British Studies* 52 (2013), 880.

64 Alm, 'Making a Difference', 20. For the concepts of 'use value' and 'status value', see Gudrun Andersson, 'A Mirror of Oneself: Possessions and the Manifestation of Status among a Local Swedish Elite, 1650–1770', *Cultural and Social History* 3 (2006), 24.

2

New and Old Luxuries Between the Court and the City: A Comparative Perspective on Material Cultures in Brussels and Antwerp, 1650–1735

Bruno Blondé and Veerle De Laet

New and old luxuries

When Neil McKendrick postulated a prosperous interdependence between economic growth, social equity and consumer emancipation in the eighteenth century, the last not only required the economic ability to consume but also the political and moral freedom to do so;[1] hence the importance given to the study of the cultural mindset behind consumption. As a result of this shift in research focus, luxury debates entered at the heart of the historiography of consumption, initially framed in a Cold War narrative of freedom and abundance.[2] For many historians the eighteenth-century luxury debates marked an era of transition to material modernity. Not coincidentally this transition was paralleled by swift changes in material culture and consumption patterns.[3] Bernard Mandeville in particular was credited with a pivotal role in the changing discourse on the reassessment of the benefits of consumption. What previously had been perceived as 'vicious' he transformed into something beneficial for society at large. Today the ruptures between the ideological framework for consumption in the eighteenth century and that of the 'material renaissance' in Italy are considered less pronounced than previously has been claimed.[4] Firmly rooted in medieval and classical philosophy, concepts such as 'magnificence' and especially 'splendour' provided moral sanction for conspicuous consumption as early as the fifteenth century.[5] And while, conversely, it is true that consumer anxieties still loomed large in renaissance Italy,[6] this was also the case in the seventeenth and eighteenth centuries – in Brabant and Brussels as well as Italy.[7] Many a seventeenth-century commentator firmly disputed the vices of new fashion and changing luxury models which clearly illustrates how rapid changes in material life provoked moral and cultural anxieties in this era. Fear of blurred social boundaries became a popular and powerful topos[8] next to the moral and sexual nervousness that accompanied the imported 'frivolous' French fashion.[9]

These frictions, Jan de Vries argues, were deeply rooted in 'an old discourse' that no longer applied to the reality of contemporary practices. Indeed, he describes the consumer changes of the seventeenth and eighteenth centuries in a dichotomous transition model from 'new' to 'old' luxuries. Whereas the old luxury model was geared towards leisure and conspicuous consumption of elites in socially skewed societies, the new luxury model was not necessarily preoccupied with social distinction, but instead appealed to a larger set of values such as comfort and pleasure. Moreover, the new luxuries were enjoyed and fostered by larger groups in society than ever before. In his search for the origins of this 'new luxury model', de Vries arrives in the Northern Netherlands where a bourgeois model of consumption (one that differed markedly from the old luxury model) emerged in the seventeenth century. The latter, characterized by patronage, still was in force in the urban economies of Flanders and Brabant, the urban core of the Southern Netherlands.[10]

This article takes de Vries' claims concerning the 'old luxury' model in the urban economies of the Southern Netherlands as its point of departure. Our challenge is not so much to test them, but rather to tap into the old intellectual discussion on the forces that shape behavioural and consumer changes. While a plethora of authors have pointed to the court as a major civilizing force,[11] others forcefully defended the thesis that urban societies delivered the most dynamic contribution to changing repertoires of behaviour and material culture in the early-modern period.[12] The exercise is a challenging one. Similar consumption and material culture patterns, as we will argue below, may serve different social and cultural purposes; similar objects can be found in different consumer models, whilst carrying different and context-depending cultural and social meanings. Sources are far from generous in documenting these often-subtle cultural differences. On top of that, chronological distinctions and social identifications are not always as clear as historians would like them to be. Therefore, the conceptual difference between 'old' and 'new luxuries' is hard to evidence; yet we will not refrain from using de Vries' thesis as the intellectual starting point of our exploration, not least because it enables us to clearly phrase our questions about the social forces behind changing consumer patterns.

It is exactly this social dimension of luxury consumption that we would like to highlight in this chapter on seventeenth- and early eighteenth-century Brussels and Antwerp. Here both consumer logics came together and acted upon one another in the second half of the seventeenth and the early eighteenth century, a period marked by critical consumer transitions in the Southern Netherlands.[13]

Brussels, a capital city in comparative contrast[14]

Antwerp and Brussels were by far the two most prominent towns of Brabant in the eighteenth century.[15] Demographically and economically Brussels surpassed Antwerp, formerly the commercial metropolis and still a major producer of luxury products for the larger part of the seventeenth century. In the course of this century both towns had shifted places at the top of the urban hierarchy, a shift that was mainly due to the capital and courtly functions of Brussels. Although foreign visitors described the Brussels court as one of secondary importance, it effectively fulfilled capital functions that attracted wealthy residential elites who contributed to an aristocratic local culture having strong economic and cultural linkage effects on Brussels society at large.[16] However, it was more than a court town: residential elites dovetailed with a variety of rich middling sorts, including many shopkeepers. Brussels owed its income more to the provisioning of goods and services – its central place functions – whereas Antwerp relied more heavily upon its commercial and industrial base. Indeed, the hierarchical difference between the two cities is clear from the buying strategies of richer households in Antwerp: even though Antwerp was dotted with numerous *fashion shops,* for example, the richest and most prominent Antwerp households headed to Brussels boutiques for their specialist luxury purchases.[17]

Antwerp elites entered noble ranks as families gradually withdrew from commerce, yet they were still considered *arriviste* by contemporary high nobility. Hence, when an anonymous member of the high nobility turned to Antwerp in search of a bride, Jacomo de Pret explained to him that it would be very difficult to find an appropriate partner in Antwerp. After all, living patterns (*la manière de vivre*) are quite different in Antwerp, he argued, even though the city was located very close to Brussels. Antwerpers, according to de Pret, even educated their children with a certain mistrust for courtly life.[18] When, on another occasion, the count of Calenberg enquired about the possibility of selling luxury furniture in Antwerp, the same Jacomo de Pret replied that he had looked around for some possible buyers for his table and mirror, but that it would be very difficult to find an appropriate one. The furniture for sale was more appropriate for Brussels clients, de Pret thought, because Antwerpers usually did not invest so explicitly in conspicuous furniture.[19] In general the Brussels elite is thought to have spent at least three times as much on luxury compared to their Antwerp peers.[20] Table 2.1 further evidences the social and economic causes and consequences of the cultural differences between both cities. Overall, among the cities included in this table, Brussels monopolized almost 60 per cent of the residential potential, whereas Antwerp accounted for only 30 per cent of the rentier households in Brabant, employing on average a smaller number of domestic staff as well. While Brussels and Nijvel counted more residential families than expected, on the basis of their demographic weight, the other towns included in Table 2.1 were

Table 2.1 Rentier households in Brabantine towns, 1755

	% population	% rentier households	Ratio rentier households/ population	Average number of domestic staff employed
Brussel	39	58	1.5	4.03
Antwerpen	33	29.3	0.9	3.13
Leuven	11	4.1	0.4	3.3
Nijvel	4	6.9	1.7	2.1
Tienen	3	1.3	0.4	1.25
Turnhout	6	0.3	0.1	2
Waver	2	0	0	0
Herentals	2	0	0	0

Source: Blondé, *Economie met verschillende snelheden*, 96.

less successful in attracting wealthy burghers. In sum, much can be gained from a comparison of expenditure and luxury patterns in the two most prominent central places of the Southern Low Countries. Both towns were gifted with extremely rich elites, but the consumer cultures apparently differed markedly between the two cities. Conspicuous consumption loomed large in Brussels, as a consequence of its capital status; Antwerpers, by contrast, never lost sight of their mercantile background.

Luxury patterns in an era of critical transition: Brussels and the 'new luxuries'?

In this chapter, mainly probate inventory evidence is used to describe consumer patterns, the introduction of innovations and material culture changes. All probate inventories examined for Antwerp and Brussels stem from notary records. These documents, primarily drawn up for the purpose of safeguarding family inheritance after the death of a parent, are rarely found among the poor because the act of drawing up inventories was a costly exercise. Ideally, complementary sources are needed in order to define and refine social categories, and to socially contextualize the consulted inventories.[21] Unfortunately, the Brussels and Antwerp city archives lack such auxiliary alternatives, nor do the Brabantine inventories themselves contain valuations by sworn assessors. These deficiencies have forced us to devise our own criterion for assigning relative socio-economic standing to those whose inventories we analyse: the number of rooms listed.[22] Although this is merely a proxy for movable wealth and social rank, it has an obvious rationale, and it supplies a hierarchical ranking in line with those typically found in material culture studies of goods ownership. Furthermore, our samples of probate inventories are distributed quite evenly among the different categories by number of rooms. Categories I and II comprise a socially mixed category, including (among others) the working poor, a heterogeneous collection of individuals ranging from single women in religious orders to a servant, a grave maker, a tailor and a shoemaker, as well as an army captain and a nobleman of modest means.[23] Amongst the last group was Pedro Casco Archiascisuch: a member of an important central council, his domestic horizon was limited to the one room he rented in the house of Peeter Huysman. Residents living in two or three rooms, categories III and IV, contain middle-groups: retailers and some professionals, plus an over-representation of successful master craftsmen, such as bakers, brewers, bleachers, hatters and so on. Category V covers representatives of the upper middle classes and some who belonged to the urban elites. Category VI includes richly decorated urban dwellings, occupied by the urban upper crust.

Quite often, seventeenth-century Dutch art is taken as a major proxy of the new luxuries as 'elite patronage gave way to a market economy' for a bourgeois clientele.[24] It is also the starting point in our analysis. For the Dutch Republic product and process innovations are generally believed to have substantially contributed to the widening social reach of paintings.[25] An inquiry into the Brabantine luxury market at the end of the seventeenth century, however, reveals that the contrast between the Dutch bourgeois market and the Brabantine patronage was much less sharp than often postulated.[26] In Brabant too, paintings were spread among all layers of urban inventory testators. Actually, sixteenth-century Antwerp product and process innovations need to be credited for having given rise to a consumer model in which, eventually, the large majority of the urban populace owned several paintings.[27] By the end of the seventeenth century, middle-class testators in both Brussels and Antwerp owned rather impressive collections of paintings (Table 2.2).[28] The bourgeois nature of this market is also amply reflected in the shift in tastes in favour of

Table 2.2 Median number of paintings by social category, in Brussels and Antwerp probate inventories

	Brussels		**Antwerp**	
	1670/1690	1720/1730	1680	1730
I	2.5	4	0	6
II	13	18	5.5	3
III	10	20	14	12
IV	24	23	23	16
V	24	22	31	30
VI	54	37	79	24

Note: I – 1 room; II – 2–3 rooms; III – 4–7 rooms; IV – 8–11 rooms; V – 12–15 rooms; VI – 16 rooms or more.

Source: Probate inventory database Antwerp (Bruno Blondé), probate inventory database Brussels (Veerle De Laet).

landscapes and genre paintings which met the needs of bourgeois clients and gained enormously in popularity. Meanwhile, the religious zeal of the Counter-Reformation did not prevent paintings representing devotional themes from losing in popularity at home: both in Antwerp and Brussels, the art market was characterized by a process of secularization.[29] The general tendency was for a more decorative, democratized display of paintings: representative rooms gradually declined in importance for displaying paintings throughout the seventeenth century, as pictures were increasingly hung in backstage and upstairs rooms.[30] Hence, at the start of the eighteenth century, conspicuous consumption was far from the only reason for people to acquire and decorate their homes with works of art.

Obviously, it would take too long to develop similar arguments for all the other new luxuries that are often considered pivotal for the advent of a new consumer pattern in the eighteenth century, but the particular importance of sugar and hot drinks in these processes leads us to trace these innovations.[31] While a culture of hot drinks was largely spread among courtly elites in the early eighteenth century, the first innovators of hot drinks in late seventeenth-century Brussels were to be found out of court, among the middling sort of people.[32] In contrast to what one might expect, the Brussels nobility – for reasons that are yet unclear – was surprisingly reluctant to embrace this new culture. By 1730, if we note the presence rather than counting the number of items, the large majority of inhabitants in both Brussels and Antwerp owned at least a couple of the utensils required to prepare and serve hot drinks (see Table 2.3).

Table 2.3 Median ownership of coffee and tea utensils in Brussels and Antwerp, by social category, 1730

	Brussels	**Antwerp**
I	0	2
II	1	1
III	2	3
IV	2	2
V	3	2
VI	7	5

Note: I – 1 room; II – 2–3 rooms; III – 4–7 rooms; IV – 8–11 rooms; V – 12–15 rooms; VI – 16 rooms or more.

Source: Probate inventory database Antwerp (Bruno Blondé), probate inventory database Brussels (Veerle De Laet).

These and other findings essentially reveal a consumer pattern that runs remarkably parallel to the one described by de Vries for the seventeenth-century Northern Netherlands. In the Southern Netherlands too, broad middling layers of people animated the production of semi-luxuries that were accessible beyond the confines of courtly and urban elites. These then appealed to a variety of consumer aspirations that went far beyond the motivations of conspicuous consumption.

Luxury patterns in an era of critical transition: the ambiguity of 'new' and 'old luxuries'

Thus far, our analysis could be used to provide evidence of the populuxe nature of several key consumer innovations and their close connection to the urban middling layers as a dynamic group of consumers. Yet, it seems wise to stress how much the ownership of paintings and hot drinks utensils was still socially unevenly distributed. Richer burghers both in Antwerp and Brussels were inclined to own significantly more utensils for hot drinks than did their poorer co-citizens. Still more important were the qualitative differences in the materials that were used and the decorative schemes that were applied to consumer durables for citizens with different social backgrounds. The Brussels courtly elite, although late in appropriating the new hot drinks culture, quickly outstripped social competitors in both the quantity and quality of their possessions, as illustrated by the conspicuously refined silver, Japanese porcelain and silver-gilded crystal tableware they commanded at the start of the eighteenth century. By adding heraldic devices to these already precious table sets and displaying them in a well-considered way in central halls and main reception rooms, the Brussels nobility unmistakeably appropriated the new culture into its own social vocabulary.[33] A similar observation can be made for the paintings that were introduced above as proxies for the bourgeois nature of the art market in the Southern Low Countries. While a widespread tendency towards a shared decorative use of paintings among the middling layers of society can hardly be denied, simultaneously art lovers and connoisseurs built up prestige by acquiring large collections that testified to a learned cultural background and sophisticated cultural taste.[34] When Albertus Piermans, nobleman and secretary of the Council of Estate, died in Brussels in 1727, he left no fewer than 125 paintings, of which thirty-three were attributed to named artists.[35] Owing to the number and overall quality of these paintings, the entire collection was separately inventoried and subsequently auctioned.[36] It is reasonable to suppose that, not only the wealth of his collection, but also its use in social interactions with other art lovers amongst his peers served the purpose of social distinction. In fact, it seems safe to argue that old luxuries in the eighteenth century had lost little of their social and economic potential. This holds true in the first place for noble households that derived part of their social status from adhering to an old luxury pattern, one reflecting the patina of history.[37] Paradoxically enough, in Paris, The Hague or Brussels, eighteenth-century noble families were sometimes relatively slow in appropriating some new luxuries and this holds true especially for members of the lower nobility.[38] While urban middling groups were keen to use textiles, such as cotton, for wall hangings, the Brussels nobility adhered much longer to Oudenaarde or Brussels tapestries and gilt leather wall hangings – a feature also noted for the British aristocracy by Stobart in his chapter in this volume.[39] Clearly, the idea of tradition and lineage was of crucial importance for the nobility. Even when they turned to novelties and new luxuries, all noblemen still owed much of their prestige to key positional goods such as tapestries, lavishly decorated silverware, hunting scenes, (family) portraits and the application of heraldic devices on household goods of different kinds.[40] This is not to say that high noblemen failed to invest in novelties. On the contrary, the language of fashion was theirs and they certainly welcomed exotic or at least 'foreign' novelties such as Turkish carpets, Italian adornments, Chinese or Japanese porcelain, English furniture and clothing of the latest French fashion.[41] Yet, it is important to ascertain how much of this fashionable consumption was inspired by the logic of old luxury. This can easily be demonstrated by looking at the vocabulary used in the inventories to describe silver objects. A textbook example of old luxury, silverware was described in terms such as 'fashionable' and 'according to the latest fashion'. Thanks to its potential for re-melting and re-styling, silverware appealed both to the volatile consumer climate of the eighteenth century and at the same time borrowed from an old luxury consumer logic: these were items of both conspicuous consumption and a safe investment.[42] Hence, while Brabant middle-class households increasingly met with difficulties in investing in silverware, noble families may even have intensified this particular urge for conspicuous consumption. The silver-gilded toilet mirror of *douairière* baroness d'Geemberck, who died in 1732, is another vivid example of the way in which fashionable novelties were appropriated by urban elites through adding a touch of old luxury refinement.[43] This old luxury consumer model also continued to appeal to lower (non-noble) social groups, in a manner somewhat akin to classic emulation-like consumption. Francois Vandenhecke, for instance, a Brussels tapestry weaver and official purveyor to the court, almost usurped a heraldic vocabulary. Although he was never officially ennobled, heraldic devices were prominently placed in the *salet*, the main reception room of his Brussels dwelling, emphasizing his personal prestige and privileged position.[44] Particularly in Antwerp, where most noble families stemmed from a mercantile background and were only recently ennobled, a clear tendency to invest in old luxuries can be discerned among the newly ennobled.[45] A remarkable increase in the ownership of luxury horses, one of the most costly and extravagant manifestations of conspicuous consumption, can be witnessed in the eighteenth century.[46] In Brussels too, rich burgher families applied for ennoblement in this period and it is hardly surprising that this new nobility invested in a material culture that managed to translate these social aspirations.[47] Outside the nobility, commoners freely borrowed from a noble life style, as also can be illustrated by the example of Albertus Piermans (d. 1727), secretary of the Council of Estate, who owned an impressive collection of no less than 130 pieces of silverware, a countryside castle near Brussels, a coach and two black coach horses. The material world with which he surrounded himself testifies to a distinct lifestyle and undimmed noble aspirations. At least two books in his library seem to have served this purpose as well. He owned a copy of *L'honneste homme ou l'art de plaisir a la court* as well as a book entitled *L'education des princes*.[48] By buying prominent and refined silverware, applying heraldic symbols and borrowing from the vocabulary of hunting, state officials and even some master craftsmen easily moved between the urban middling layers and the members of the Brussels high society with whom they mingled, associated and frequently interacted.

Navigating between the logic of old and new luxury

While the boundaries between social groups were less clear-cut than is often thought, something similar is true for the boundaries between old and new luxuries themselves. For obvious reasons, the periwig can be seen as a strategic symbol for the old consumer luxuries that were stimulated by the dramatic upsurge of French fashion in the late seventeenth century.[49] Given their potential for social distinction, it hardly comes as a surprise that Brussels noblemen and court-related testators had wigs recorded in their probate inventories. All in all, wigs were rather rare items of clothing apparel, both in Brussels and in Antwerp, taking into account that our statistics might run the risk of under registration. In the second half of the seventeenth century, wigs were the prerogative of Brussels inventory testators connected to court life or holding high social positions, even when they occupied rather modest dwellings. Paulo Vits, for instance, a councillor of the *Rekenkamer,* owned a periwig which he could combine with a whole series of luxurious and refined garments.[50] Unmistakably, the Antwerp elites lagged far behind in this respect. In the decades that followed, wigs evolved into a more modest piece of clothing that could also be worn by members of the urban middling sorts, such as the Brussels master slater and bachelor, Thomas Kreus, who died in 1725.[51] This is amply reflected in the 1730 figures that demonstrate a relatively strong incidence of periwigs among all layers of society (Table 2.4). By this date, Antwerp probate inventory testators included a bargeman and a priest as well

Table 2.4 Percentage of households with periwigs, Brussels and Antwerp

	Brussels		**Antwerp**	
Social category	1670–1690	1720–1730	1680	1730
I	0	30	0	5
II	27	14	0	0
III	7	15	0	17
IV	6.25	33	0	21
V	0	0	0	7
VI	0	14	20	71

Note: I – 1 room; II – 2-3 rooms; III – 4–7 rooms; IV – 8–11 rooms; V – 12–15 rooms; VI – 16 rooms or more.

Source: Probate inventory database Antwerp (Bruno Blondé), probate inventory database Brussels (Veerle De Laet).

as some shopkeepers. At that time, the wig had lost most of its noble exclusivity, but had also transformed into a much less conspicuous form.

In sum, the consumer changes in the era under study mirror the capability of durable goods and behavioural codes to smoothly move between various social circles and to carry highly varying symbolic meanings. Next to this first observation, our sample of inventories also shows how new and old luxuries were simultaneously present in the households of the high nobility, the urban nobility, the state officials and even those of successful craftsmen.

Conclusions

The tentative conclusions of this exploration of consumer models within Brussels and Antwerp society mirror the social and economic picture that was drawn of both cities at the start of this chapter. Even though Brussels was a court city of lesser importance, the presence of several major central institutions pulled important residential elites into town. Courtly life significantly contributed to the urban economy and society, and Brussels was a city with a distinct conspicuous consumer culture. Yet the growing importance of the courtly elites was not at odds with the presence of strong urban middling layers with a substantial discretionary income. On the contrary, through their provisioning of the capital city and its elites, these middling groups managed to prosper. Unsurprisingly then, our analysis confirms the importance of bourgeois consumer patterns for the quick arrival and general spread of new luxuries in Brabantine society. In fact, as the example of painting ownership demonstrates, the Southern Low Countries already had a long-established tradition in innovation through product and process innovations that dialectically interfered with the consumer patterns and preferences of the urban middle classes, who can safely be considered as a more or less autonomous force of consumption. As such, Brabant cities were far ahead of the Northern Netherlands in fostering a middle-class consumer culture geared towards new luxuries.

Not only were new luxuries older than suggested by Jan de Vries in his account of consumer practices in the seventeenth-century Northern Netherlands, old luxuries proved remarkably resilient as well. Moreover, the boundaries between new and old luxuries were far from clear, which makes any straightforward dichotomy misleading.[52] The popularity of new luxuries, for example, did not prevent the elites in both towns from continuing to invest in old luxuries. Most tellingly, new luxuries were often appropriated by elites in a way that fitted into the consumer logic of the leisure class and its old luxury vocabulary. Conversely, existing old luxuries such as silverware and wigs were culturally adapted to eighteenth-century consumer preferences by their continuous refashioning. Nor did the success of new luxuries discourage middling sorts of people from selectively investing in models of old luxury which were held in high esteem. In short, boundaries between social groups and consumer patterns were blurred and permeable. At first sight, the myriad of mental frictions arising from a variety of consumer innovations in the seventeenth and eighteenth centuries as revealed in contemporary legislation and literature seems to lack any coherence. Contemporary moralists thus can be blamed for framing the 'consuming' problem in an inappropriate, anachronistic way. However, as this chapter has highlighted, their reactions were no less complex than the consumer changes that provoked their fear and moral anger. Indeed, in the late early-modern period new and old luxuries and their complex accompanying mentalities did not follow a chronological stage model. Rather, they co-existed, overlapped, competed, shaped mixed models and forms, and migrated between groups and individuals; much as they continue to do today. Whilst not denying the intellectual importance of Jan de Vries' model, our analysis – like that of Clemente in her chapter on Naples – reveals that this approach probably has a conceptual rather than a historical value.

Notes

1 Neil McKendrick, John Brewer and John Harold Plumb, *The Birth of a Consumer Society: The Commercialisation of Eighteenth-Century England* (London: Europa Publications Limited, 1982).

2 Frank Trentmann, 'Introduction', in *The Oxford Handbook of the History of Consumption*, ed. Frank Trentmann (Oxford: Oxford University Press, 2012).

3 Maxine Berg and Helen Clifford, *Consumers and Luxury: Consumer Culture in Europe 1650–1850* (Manchester: Manchester University Press, 1999); Maxine Berg and Elizabeth Eger, 'The Rise and Fall of the Luxury Debates', in *Luxury in the*

Eighteenth Century: Debates, Desires and Delectable Goods, eds Maxine Berg and Elizabeth Eger (Basingstoke: Palgrave Macmillan, 2003).

4 Bruno Blondé and Wouter Ryckbosch, 'In "Splendid Isolation": A Comparative Perspective on the Historiographies of the "Material Renaissance" and the "Consumer Revolution"', *History of Retailing and Consumption* 1:2 (2015), 105–24.

5 Evelyn Welch, 'Public Magnificence and Private Display: Pontano's "De Splendore" and the Domestic Arts', *Journal of Design History* 15 (2002), 211–27.

6 Patricia Allerston, 'Consuming Problems: Worldly Goods in Renaissance Venice', in *The Material Renaissance*, eds Michelle O'Malley and Evelyn Welch (Manchester: Manchester University Press, 2007), 11–47.

7 Jan de Vries, 'Luxury in the Dutch Golden Age in Theory and Practice', in *Luxury in the Eighteenth Century: Debates, Desires and Delectable Goods*, eds Maxine Berg and Elizabeth Eger (Basingstoke: Palgrave Macmillan, 2003), 41–56; Simon Schama, *The Embarrassment of Riches: An Interpretation of Dutch Culture in the Golden Age* (New York: Random House, 1987).

8 Such as in Erycius Puteanus, (Honorius van den Born), *Sedigh Leven: Dagelyckx Broodt (1639). Ingeleid, uitgegeven en toegelicht door H. Dehennin* (Gent, 1999), 117, number XCII and in Jan De Grieck, *De Sotte Wereldt ofte den waeren Af-druck der Wereldtsche Sotttigheden. Alles tot onderrichtinge der feylen, ende ghebreken des menschen leven* (Brussels, 1682).

9 Harald Deceulaer, *Pluriforme patronen en een verschillende snit: Sociaal-Economische, institutionele en culturele transformaties in de kledingsector in Antwerpen, Brussel en Gent, 1585–1800* (Amsterdam: Stichting Beheer IISG, 2001), 167–93.

10 Jan de Vries, *The Industrious Revolution: Consumer Behavior and the Household Economy, 1650 to the Present* (Cambridge: Cambridge University Press, 2008).

11 See, for example, Norbert Elias, *The Civilizing Process: The Development of Manners: Changes in the Code of Conduct and Feeling in Early Modern Times*, trans. Edmond Jephcott (Oxford: Blackwell, 1978).

12 Jacques Le Goff, *La civilisation de l'occident médiéval* (Paris, 1964), 365–67.

13 Bruno Blondé and Ilja Van Damme, 'Retail Growth and Consumer Changes in a Declining Urban Economy, Antwerp (1650–1750)', *The Economic History Review* 63:3 (2010), 638–63.

14 The following paragraph is entirely based upon the following publications which can be consulted for methodological considerations and extensive source references. Bruno Blondé, 'Disparities in the Development of the Brabantine Urban Network: Urban Centrality, Town-Countryside Relationships, and Transportation Development', in *Recent Doctoral Research in Economic History*, ed. Clara Eugenia Núnez (Madrid: Universidad nacional de educacion a distancia,

1998), 41–52; Bruno Blondé and Raymond Van Uytven, 'De smalle steden en het Brabantse stedelijke netwerk in de Late Middeleeuwen en de Nieuwe Tijd', *Lira Elegans* 6 (1996), 129–82; Bruno Blondé, *Een economie met verschillende snelheden: ongelijkheden in de opbouw en de ontwikkeling van het Brabantse stedelijke netwerk (ca. 1750–ca. 1790)* (Brussels: Paleis der Academiën, 1999).

15 Raymond Van Uytven, 'Brabantse en Antwerpse centrale plaatsen (14de–19de Eeuw)', in *Het stedelijk netwerk in België in historisch perspectief (1350–1850): Een statistische en dynamische benadering* (Brussels: Gemeentekrediet, 1992), 29–79.

16 Blondé, *Economie met verschillende snelheden*, 98–101.

17 Herman Coppens and Karel Degryse, 'Levenswijze en consumptiepatroon van een Antwerps adellijk gezin: De huishoudboeken van Charles Bernard Van De Werve De Vorselaer (1764–1786)', in *Een kompas met vele streken: studies over Antwerpen, scheepvaart en archivistiek aangeboden aan Dr. Gustaaf Asaert ter gelegenheid van zijn 65ste verjaardag*, eds Gustaaf Asaert, Griet Maréchal and Marijke Hoflack, *Archiefkunde* (Antwerp: Vlaamse vereniging voor bibliotheek-, archief- en documentatiewezen, 1994), 52–73.

18 Karel Degryse, *De Antwerpse fortuinen: kapitaalsaccumulatie, -investering en rendement te Antwerpen in de 18de eeuw.*, vol. 88, *Bijdragen tot de geschiedenis* (2005), 182. '. . . les partis tells qu'on les souhaite sont assez rares, et quoy-que nous ne sommes éloignées que de huit lieues de Brusselles, la maniere de vivre est fort différente. On y eleve les enfans dans une certaine prevention contre les cours, et en leur procurantun etablissement on suit ordinairement l'ancien systeme: si vis nubere, nube pari [. . .].'

19 Degryse, *De Antwerpse fortuinen*, 183. 'Je me suis informé dans le discours, s'il n'y auroit pas ici quelquie amateur pour acheter la belle table et miroir de feue madame la marquise de Pasquale, mais on croyeit generalement que non, qu'elle est plus propre pour Brusselles que pour Anvers, ou un particulier ne se sert pas de meubles aussi riches et distingués.'

20 Karel Degryse, 'The Aristocratization of the Antwerp Mercantile Elite (17th–18th Centuries)', in *Entrepreneurs and Entrepreneurship in Early Modern Times: Merchants and Industrialists within the Orbit of the Dutch Staple Market*, eds Clé Lesger and Leo Noordegraaf (Den Haag: Stichting Hollandse Historische Reeks, 1995), 38; Degryse, *De Antwerpse fortuinen*, 183–85; Roger De Peuter, *Brussel in de achttiende eeuw: Sociaal-economische structuren en ontwikkelingen in een regionale hoofdstad* (Brussels: VUB press, 1999), 48–9.

21 Thera Wijsenbeek-Olthuis, *Achter de gevels van Delft: Bezit en bestaan van rijk en arm in een periode van achteruitgang (1700–1800)* (Hilversum: Verloren, 1987).

22 In her study of Brussels' inventories Veerle De Laet opted for a composite index, reflecting the number of rooms, the quality of beds, as well as copperware and

linen ownership. For comparative purposes, however, we have chosen to align the results of this study on the methodology used for studying Antwerp inventories. Veerle De Laet, *Brussel binnenskamers: Kunst- en luxebezit in het spanningsveld tussen hof en stad, 1600–1735, Studies Stadsgeschiedenis* (Amsterdam: Amsterdam University Press, 2011), 49–59.

23 Veerle De Laet, 'At Home in Seventeenth-Century Brussels: Patterns of Art and Luxury Consumption in Private Households', in *Embracing Brussels. Art and Culture in the Court City, 1600–1800*, eds Katlijne Van der Stighelen et al. (Turnhout, 2013) 15–17.

24 De Vries, 'Luxury in the Dutch Golden Age,' 55; de Vries, *The Industrious Revolution*, 55–6; Michael North, 'Art and Commerce in the Dutch Republic,' in *A Miracle Mirrored: The Dutch Republic in European Perspective*, eds Karel Davids and Jan Lucassen (Cambridge: Cambridge University Press, 1995), 284–302; Michael North, *Art and Commerce in the Dutch Golden Age* (New Haven: Yale University Press, 1997).

25 John Michael Montias, *Le Marché De L'art Aux Pays-Bas: XVe–XVIIIe Siècles* (Paris: Flammarion, 1996); John Michael Montias, 'Socio-Economic Aspects of Netherlandish Art from the Fifteenth To the Seventeenth Century: A Survey', *The Art Bulletin* 72:3 (1990), 358–73; John Michael Montias, 'The Influence of Economic Factors on Style', *De Zeventiende Eeuw. Cultuur in de Nederlanden in interdisciplinair perspectief* 6 (1990), 49–57; North, *Art and Commerce in the Dutch Golden Age*; *Art Markets in Europe, 1400–1800*, eds Michael North and David Ormrod (Aldershot: Ashgate, 1998).

26 Bruno Blondé, 'Art and Economy in Seventeenth- and Eighteenth-Century Antwerp: A View from the Demand Side', in *Economia E Arte Secc. Xiii–Xviii: Atti Delle Trenteessima Settimana Di Studi, 30 Aprile–4 Maggio 2000* (Firenze, 2002), 379–91; De Laet, 'At Home in Seventeenth-Century Brussels', 11–20.

27 Bert Hendrickx, 'Het schilderijenbezit van de Antwerpse burger in de tweede helft van de zestiende eeuw: een socio-economische analyse' (MA thesis, Katholieke Universiteit Leuven, 1997); Maximiliaan Martens and Natasja Peeters, 'Paintings in Antwerp Houses (1532–1567),' in *Mapping Markets for Paintings in Europe, 1450–1750*, eds Neil De Marchi and Hans J. Van Miegroet, *Studies in European Urban History, 1100–1800* (Turnhout: Brepols, 2006), 35–53; Carolien De Staelen, 'Spulletjes en hun betekenis in een commerciële metropool: Antwerpenaren en hun materiële cultuur in de zestiende eeuw' (PhD thesis, University of Antwerp, 2007); Filip Vermeylen, *Painting for the Market: Commercialization of Art in Antwerp's Golden Age*, vol. 2, *Studies in European Urban History* (Turnhout: Brepols, 2003); Filip Vermeylen, 'The Commercialization of Art: Painting and Sculpture in Sixteenth-Century

Antwerp', in *Early Netherlandish Painting at the Crossroads: A Critical Look at Current Methodologies*, ed. Maryan W. Ainsworth (New Haven: Yale University Press, 2001), 46–61.

28 These figures can withstand comparison with statistics that were collected for Dutch towns such as Amsterdam, Delft and 's-Hertogenbosch by John Michael Montias, 'Works of Art in a Random Sample of Amsterdam Inventories', in *Economic History and the Arts*, ed. Michael North (Köln: Böhlau, 1996), 78; Veerle De Laet, 'Schilderijenconsumptie in de marge van de Republiek: Smaak en voorkeur in het Bossche interieur van de zeventiende en de achttiende Eeuw', *Tijdschrift voor Sociaal-Economische Geschiedenis* 3:4 (2006), 49.

29 De Laet, 'At Home in Seventeenth-Century Brussels', 13–14; De Laet, *Brussel Binnenskamers*, 207–10.

30 De Laet, *Brussel binnenskamers*, 220–2.

31 Sidney W. Mintz, *Sweetness and Power: The Place of Sugar in Modern History* (New York: Penguin Books, 1985), 267; Anne McCants, 'Exotic Goods, Popular Consumption, and the Standard of Living: Thinking About Globalization in the Early Modern World', *Journal of World History* 18 (2007), 173; Carole Shammas, *The Pre-Industrial Consumer in England and America* (Oxford: Clarendon, 1990); Bruno Blondé and Wouter Ryckbosch, 'Arriving to a Set Table: The Integration of Hot Drinks in the Urban Consumer Culture of the Eighteenth-Century Southern Low Countries', in *Goods from the East, 1600–1800: Trading Eurasia*, eds Maxine Berg et al. (Houndmills: Palgrave Macmillan, 2015), 309; Jon Stobart, *Sugar and Spice: Grocers and Groceries in Provincial England, 1650–1830* (Oxford: Oxford University Press, 2013).

32 De Laet, *Brussel binnenskamers*, 183: De Laet, 'At Home in Seventeenth-Century Brussels', 14–15.

33 John Styles, 'Product Innovation in Early Modern London', *Past and Present* 168 (2000), 124–170; De Laet, *Brussel binnenskamers*, 193–5.

34 Bert Timmermans, *Patronen van patronage in het zeventiende-eeuwse Antwerpen: Een elite als actor binnen een kunstwereld* (Amsterdam: Aksant, 2008); B. Timmermans, 'Een elite als actor op de kunstscène: Patronen van het mecenaat in het zeventiende-eeuwse Antwerpen,' *Bijdragen tot de Geschiedenis* 83 (2000), 35–55; Z. Z. Filipczak, *Picturing Art in Antwerp, 1550–1700* (Princeton: Princeton University Press, 1987); H. Vlieghe, 'The Fine and Decorative Arts in Antwerp's Golden Age', in *Urban Achievement in Early Modern Europe: Golden Ages in Antwerp, Amsterdam and London*, eds Patrick O'Brien et al. (Cambridge: Cambridge University Press, 2001), 173–185; De Laet, 'At Home in Seventeenth-Century Brussels', 17–18.

35 De Laet, *Brussel binnenskamers*, 213.

36 State Archives Brussels, Notariaat Generaal van Brabant, notary N. J. J. Tollenaers, microfilm 752994.

37 Grant McCracken, *Culture and Consumption: New Approaches to the Symbolic Character of Consumer Goods and Activities* (Bloomington: Indiana University Press, 1990); Koen De Vlieger-De Wilde, 'Adellijke levensstijl: Dienstpersoneel, consumptie en materiële leefwereld van Jan Van Brouchoven en Livina De Beer, Graaf en Gravin Van Bergeyck (ca. 1685–1740)' (MA thesis, KUL, 2003), 119–21.

38 Lorna Weatherill, *Consumer Behaviour and Material Culture in Britain, 1660–1760* (London: Routledge and Kegan Paul, 1988), 168, made a similar observation for the English gentry; Thera Wijsenbeek-Olthuis, 'Noblesse Oblige: Material Culture of the Nobility in Holland', in *Private Domain, Public Inquiry: Families and Life-Styles in the Netherlands and Europe, 1550 to Present*, eds Anton Schuurman and Pieter Spierenburg (Hilversum, 1996), 118–21.

39 De Laet, *Brussel binnenskamers*, 184, 191–5.

40 De Laet, *Brussel binnenskamers*, 148.

41 De Laet, *Brussel binnenskamers*, 193.

42 Inneke Baatsen and Bruno Blondé, 'Zilver in Antwerpen: drie eeuwen particulier zilverbezit in context', in *Zilver in Antwerpen: De handel, het ambacht en de klant*, ed. Leo De Ren (Leuven: Peeters, 2011), 95–125; De Laet, *Brussel binnenskamers*, 191–2.

43 State Archives Brussels, Notariaat Generaal Brabant, notary L. Le Clerck, microfilm 746333.

44 De Laet, *Brussel binnenskamers*, 113; State Archives Brussels, Notariaat Generaal van Braban, notary G. vander Borcht, microfilm 782291.

45 Bruno Blondé, 'Conflicting Consumption Models? The Symbolic Meaning of Possessions and Consumption Amongst the Antwerp Nobility at the End of the Eighteenth Century', in *Fashioning Old and New: Changing Consumer Preferences in Europe (Seventeenth–Nineteenth Centuries)*, eds Bruno Blondé et al. (Turnhout: Brepols, 2009), 61–79.

46 Bruno Blondé, 'Indicatoren van het luxeverbruik? Het paardenbezit en de conspicuous consumption te Antwerpen in de 17e en de 18e eeuw', *Bijdragen tot de Geschiedenis* 84 (2001), 497–512.

47 De Laet, *Brussel Binnenskamers*, 186–9.

48 State Archives Brussel, Notariaat Generaal van Brabamt, notary N. J. J. Tollenaere, microfilm 752994.

49 Ilja Van Damme, 'Middlemen and the Creation of a "Fashion Revolution": The Experience of Antwerp in the Late Seventeenth and Eighteenth Centuries', in *The Force of Fashion in Politics and Society: Global Perspectives from Early Modern to Contemporary Times*, ed. Beverly Lemire (Farnham: Ashgate, 2010), 21–39; Bruno

Blondé, Laura Van Aert and Ilja Van Damme, 'According to the Latest and Most Elegant Fashion: Retailing Textiles and Changes in Supply and Demand in Seventeenth- and Eighteenth-Century Antwerp', in *Selling Textiles in the Long Eighteenth Century: Comparative Perspectives from Western Europe*, eds Jon Stobart and Bruno Blondé (London: Palgrave Macmillan, 2014), 138–59.

50 De Laet, *Brussel binnenskamers*, 171, 187–9.

51 Michael Kwass, 'Big Hair: A Wig History of Consumption in Eighteenth-Century France', *American Historical Review* 111:3 (2006), 630–58; De Laet, *Brussel binnenskamers*, 171.

52 For very similar conclusions see also Linda Levy Peck, *Consuming Splendor: Society and Culture in Seventeenth-Century England* (Cambridge: Cambridge University Press, 2005), 13, 346–59.

3

Luxury and Taste in Eighteenth-Century Naples: Representations, Ideas and Social Practices at the Intersection Between the Global and the Local

Alida Clemente

Cosmopolitanism and the decor of everyday life

In 1790, the Marquis of Tufo Pasquale Piatti died. His nephew, the inheritor of his estate, wanted to make sure that he had complied with the legal trust (*fideicommissum*) established by his grandfather. The court provided an inventory of his goods in order to compare it with the one that had been drawn up in 1732, upon the grandfather's death.[1] In that year, the large palace was decorated with a profusion of gilt-framed religious paintings, high-value decorative textiles such as damasks and velvets, mirrors, and furniture in ebony. The ornamental emphasis was mostly placed on Baroque-style silver collections, sacred precious objects and some *chinoiserie*. After sixty years, the same palace had taken on a somewhat different appearance. Some of the rooms were decorated with wall coverings of 'English paper' and the furniture was enriched with new elements such as a couch, a *trumeau*, several games tables and 'stoves of England'. But what catches the eye is the amazing quantity of such 'tasteful' items as snuffboxes, series of small paintings, statuettes, clocks, porcelain cornucopias, flower vases of English, Chinese and Japanese porcelain, mythological figurines and a centrepiece from the 'King's factory'. Finally, in the dining room, we find in place of the common copper cookware some services of English and Florentine porcelain, including cups for coffee and hot chocolate, and glasses for punch.

The Piatti family was a beneficiary of feudal revenues, but it originally belonged to a supranational merchant class whose members, during the seventeenth century, were the main promoters of global tastes.[2] Moreover, Pasquale was not a typical absentee lord,[3] for he did not neglect productive investment. He also attended academies and theatres and had contacts in the loftiest Neapolitan intellectual milieu.[4] In short, he was an example of the refined elite that was shaped by the rich social life of the capital city; where academies, theatres, clubs and salons emerged from court society to become in the second half of the century the essential ingredients of a public sphere made up of aristocrats, intellectuals and professional bourgeoisie.[5]

Distinguishing features of this new elite's taste included exoticism and neo-classicism in the design of their furnishings, the collecting of antiquities, a fascination with new materials, the cult of music and theatre.[6] In short, according to most scholars of history of art and material culture, the Neapolitan high society finally became 'European'.[7] It aligned itself with the dominant fashions and tastes of a cosmopolitan elite, consisting of diplomats, merchants, scholars and travellers of the Grand Tour who shaped, in the enlightened eighteenth century, a kind of 'International' of taste.

Historians have generally associated the spread of taste as a form of self-representation that is distinct from old luxury with the fading of the courteous sociability and the emergence of a society of individuals.[8] Indeed, the interweaving of the cosmopolitan *beau monde* with Baroque court society, which belatedly developed in Naples as a result of the new absolutist policy of the Bourbons, emphasizes the complexities of this very unequal urban society. In actual fact, the internationalism of taste became a social distinguishing character in eighteenth-century Naples alongside the rise of a real court society. At a later stage, the criticism of the Old Regime emerged as a result of the fascination that foreign models of social life and institutions exercised on the local progressive intellectuals. Thus, the second feature of the Neapolitan context was the strong political meaning that refined taste assumed both as a tool of celebration of power, and later as a tool for contesting the social *status quo*.

French courtly taste and 'emulative' absolutism

From the late 1730s, Naples was marked by two seemingly inconsistent processes:[9] on the one hand, its transformation into a centre of belated absolutism which tended to produce national identity and social consensus; on the other, the intensification of cultural and economic globalization processes. The establishment of an independent kingdom, ratified in 1734 by Charles of Bourbon's ascent to the throne, started a phase in which the assertion of political autonomy took on visible representative forms, by making the city an *imago regni*.[10] Producing identity and social consensus went hand in hand with the monarchy's international affirmation in competing on stylistic and artistic grounds within the European arena by using goods as semiophores of absolute power. Thus, after centuries of cultural peripherality, Naples entered its European season.[11] Within a short time, Charles of Bourbon built the largest theatre in Europe and his 'little Versailles' in Caserta. He founded porcelain factories in the Chinese style, crystal factories in the Venetian style, and tapestry and precious stones factories, all by carefully choosing and attracting foreign skilled artisans.[12] He promoted the patronage of arts and the archaeological excavations by fostering the central role which Naples played in the tourist market.[13] French fashion became the official style of the Bourbon court, in line with developments elsewhere in Europe.[14] The lavish wardrobe of the king, as well as wigs and various luxuries, were produced by French artisans.[15] The sovereign's promotion of that intangible surplus value that underpinned the empire of French fashion only amplified an ongoing market tendency.[16] Indeed, French silks and other fineries had already invaded the Neapolitan market in the 1730s.[17] Against the backdrop of the *Pacte de Famille*, the growth of commercial traffic led to the city merchants who imported goods and promoted their social value through the Masonic circles, the court and aristocratic salons.[18] The members of the French nation, also including many Genevans, who were the major importers of luxuries and textiles – Liquier, Teissier, Combe and later Meuricroffe, to mention the most important – were active in promoting new forms of urban sociability.[19] The paradox of the Bourbons' policy of aesthetic grandeur was that the adoption of foreign styles had the effect of finally downgrading local production and guilds. Indeed, this decline was already under way as a result of an increasing international division of labour which pushed the Kingdom's economy in a commercial semi-periphery.[20] The growing complementarities between the French and Neapolitan economies especially contributed to the devaluing of locally produced finished silk, an area in which Naples had excelled in the previous centuries, when it exported fashion abroad.[21] The aesthetic internationalism of the court also contributed to creating a distance between the powerful and the common people, who looked sceptically at the elite's changing fashions. Not surprisingly, they even became the object of ridicule:

> Where have we ever seen / such a hideous and ugly thing / which amazed / all the people/ By following the French way and fashion /they let their country's own fashion die / These ladies / who come out / You well understand me / I don't need to explain it/ they have good reasons for adopting the French-style / otherwise Mssr. Freemason / might punish them [. . .].[22]

In 1783, there were many satires of this kind circulating in the popular squares of Naples. The object of the mockery was the French bias of the 'brainless' nobles, victims of their capricious ladies. The people clearly attributed the inconstancy of fashion to the influence of foreigners, as well as Jews and 'Freemasons', which were conflated as active players in an alien cosmopolitan space. Paradoxically, they even feared the extinction of the old luxury practices, for they served a dual function. Firstly, they made immediately visible social status in the representative public sphere through a shared and recognizable code.[23] Secondly, by enabling the circulation of wealth, they ensured that noble excesses would promote the survival of artisans and shopkeepers and the large plebeian universe employed in service activities. Thus, the ladies who dressed and made their way along the Strada Nuova in the French style were blamed for leaving the people to die.[24] Anti-cosmopolitan topics were repeated in the satirical compositions that the craft guilds disseminated through posters and leaflets during masquerades for the carnival. Here, the city guilds mercilessly mocked new social practices, such as French cuisine, the Tuscan language, the use of wigs, caps, neckties and pocket watches, as they were considered to be objects without any intrinsic value.[25] Even the coffeehouses, which were generally operated by foreigners, were attacked as a place of unnecessary discussions on incomprehensible political matters, in which social identities mixed, subverted and threatened the *status quo*.[26] The people opposed to the changing fashions the traditional ideas of luxury and charity as distributive virtues. Moreover, French taste was also identified with an elitist consumption that could not be emulated, both because of its variability and its prohibitive expense. Still, showy luxury was not entirely unattainable in the city of the court, where luxurious items circulated through gift-giving[27] and re-selling, and where the lower bourgeoisie and servants also had access to them.[28] While the practice of emulation was a form of social control and ultimately a confirmation of the traditional hierarchy, the new fashions, by contrast, seemed to reflect subversion from above and that a crisis of aristocratic hegemony was already under way.

Taste as a means of social reform and the irreducible 'otherness' of Naples

While the old ostentatious elite enjoyed indulging in fashions which were inaccessible and incomprehensible to most of the population, the intellectual debate had long subjected it to harsh social criticism.[29] Enlightened thinkers condemned the traditional model of conspicuous consumption to the extent that it was associated with a parasitic feudal class which disdained the economic activity and squandered its revenue.[30] From the late-mercantilist point of view expressed by Carlantonio Broggia, luxury was an excess of wealth that was not based on virtue, where the latter is conceived as entrepreneurial activism and service to the nation.[31] Broggia did not actually deplore those goods that served to 'honestly and moderately delight' people,[32] but rather he foreshadowed the emergence of a virtuous economic elite who invested capital in agrarian improvements or the development of commerce. During the 1760s and the 1770s, however, luxury experienced a conceptual shift.[33] A new age of reform was beginning and the intellectuals, for instance, established themselves as a politically influential class.[34] During this time, treatise writing flourished, deconstructing the 'society of orders' and extolling certain merits and talents as a precondition for social primacy. Many of the intellectuals who participated in it came from the circle of Antonio Genovesi, who held in Naples the first Italian chair of 'mechanics and trade'.[35] Both Antonio Genovesi and Ferdinando Galiani endorsed the notion that luxury was a morally beneficial engine of desire and of economic and social development. Luxury, here, did not reflect the eye-catching excess of the old aristocracy, but rather 'the present luxury of Europe' which 'is nothing but kindness and gracious living'.[36] This concept complemented a new notion of virtue that was no longer tied to the barbarism of warfare, but to the refinements of living of an educated elite interested in playing a civic role.[37] In this sense, luxury became synonymous with civilization, for it was 'extremely beneficial not just to the greatness, power and wealth of a nation, but also to its humanity and virtue, at least for those [nations] which, like any wise nation, do not wish to be warriors'.[38]

In the second half of the century, the distinction between the old debased luxury of the aristocracy and the new luxury, i.e. 'the search for comfort and pleasure, which does not affect virtues and derives from the higher culture',[39] became a recurring topos even among moralists. The conviction about the centrality of 'good taste' as a rejection of Baroque aesthetics had gradually emerged in intellectual circles and the academies since the beginning of the century.[40] This attitude largely expressed the aristocratic search for new socially distinct languages as a response to the crisis of its traditional social hegemony, threatened by the mobility of nouveaux riches, as well as by the rise of the new absolutist state.[41] We know that this social striving sometimes assumed unmistakably subversive forms, such as the widespread engagement in Masonic sociability and the rejection of the traditional figure of the noble, who was characterized by militarism, excessive pomp, ignorance and superficiality.[42] At the end of the century, another enlightened intellectual welcomed the new-fashioned noblemen with these words: 'Employees in the court or in the army, we see them [viz. the barons] having acquired a politeness of manners so that they do not seem to be the grandchildren of some monsters that the older people still remember with horror.'[43]

It seems that the long-standing contrast – dating back at least to the Renaissance – between the two social archetypes of the educated, progressive and humanist noble on the one hand, and the ignorant, conservative and military noble on the other, was being exacerbated to the point of dissolving the very idea of a noble identity.[44] Rather than simply ushering in effective social change, the Enlightened discourses represented a political project of reform, which culminated in the strong anti-feudal meaning that the association of taste and virtue took on in the writing of Gaetano Filangieri, the author of the *Scienza della legislazione*.[45] The Enlightened reform project was inspired by the most advanced contexts of the trading nations. Indeed, it appeared to be evidence of the hegemony that central European powers were exerting on this cosmopolitan cultural elite.[46] Their fascination was not just with intellectual discourses on public happiness, but also, and more prosaically, with the materiality of everyday life. Antonio Genovesi deeply admired Paris, with its 'rich shops of all kinds of goods, pastry and sorbet shops, cellars filled with fresh, fragrant and overflowing old and new wines, apothecaries where all sorts of sweets and candies and sugary items are produced non-stop'.[47] In comparison, he deplored the imperfect development and the contradictions of Naples, which included the coexistence of wealth and poverty between 'the hovels of the populace and the rich houses of the elite'.[48] Upon returning from Paris in 1769, Ferdinando Galiani sombrely wrote to Madame d'Epinay that he felt as if he were in exile: Naples had none of the gallant and cultural pleasures that he had known in Paris.[49] In some respects, reformers' negative self-judgement resembled the often disdainful gaze of the educated Grand Tourists,[50] who were drawn to Naples by the classical antiquities in Herculaneum and Pompeii and by the natural beauty of the Gulf. Through the lens of their 'Orientalism', they invariably disparaged the 'bad taste' that supposedly dominated Neapolitan urban life. In their descriptions, the most conspicuous feature of Neapolitan society was the worship of appearances and the love for pompous forms of display. Naples appeared to be a city of extremes and contradictions, of splendour and misery, where it was easier 'to ruin one's own taste than to acquire it'.[51] The combination of coarseness and vanity were the hallmarks of a noble class that seemed very different from its European counterparts.[52] The ritual that took place in the Strada Nuova every Friday during the spring, a parade of carriages and horses – a kind of *potlatch* in which everyone made a display of his wealth – was often the subject of critical comment.[53] The Marquis de Sade was himself attracted and repelled by the public parades: golden chariots, sumptuously dressed servants, women covered with diamonds, and richly decorated churches provided the backdrop for a ritual which in his view seemed to keep the people close to the chains of ignorance: 'I don't pretend to say that luxury does not reign here, on the contrary, it is excess; but what luxury! [. . .] it is so clumsy and misunderstood! How far it is from that comfortable luxury that we know so well in France.'[54] Goethe was embarrassed by the liveried servants who bowed down in front of him in the residence of a rich Neapolitan noblewoman, feeling like 'the Sultan in Wieland's fairy tales'.[55] Like de Sade and many others, he also noted that so much wealth was relegated to public occasions.[56] In order to maintain this demonstration of wealth, the Neapolitan nobility was compelled to sacrifice its basic consumption.[57] The Naples that travellers describe is no doubt at least partly the result of the stereotypes that the circulation of travel literature produced not just on popular classes but also on the upper classes.[58] At the same time, the concept of taste that these travellers describe is redolent of the discourses of the reformers. It meant an elegant and not extroverted practice of distinction, which was not tied to the logic of blood nor to that of wealth; it was rather the expression of intrinsic qualities of aesthetic appreciation, a 'feeling' for beauty. The emulative idea of taste and politeness resulted in styles, objects and fashions that spread from the hegemonic centres of eighteenth-century Europe through travellers, diplomats, courts and intellectual circles. These subjects shaped a kind of global consumption field, in which one accumulated the necessary cultural capital to grasp what taste meant. While it was the new monarchy that initially accentuated these international entanglements, in the second half of the century these genuine global dynamics highlighted the growing weakness and contradictions of both the absolutist control of taste and of the cosmopolitan utopias of the reformers.

The failure of absolutism and the victory of (British) simplicity

The spread of French and foreign fashions clearly exerted a negative economic impact. In the dominant logic of active trade, the increasing dependence on imports of manufactured goods was self-defeating. While French luxuries initially represented an opportunity to refine tastes, they were increasingly seen as a mere variation of the old luxury, associated with the ostentation and the excess of spending, and with the role of feminine weakness in the spread of fashions.[59] In the Regency period (1759–1772), Bernardo Tanucci frequently deplored the taste of Neapolitan women for 'French feminine *bagatelle* and much more luxury',[60] and he tried to divert the taste-making role of the court towards the promotion of a national industry. In 1760, he proposed selecting the best silk-artisans of the Kingdom and to have them create the 'fashions and colours of every year' as in France.[61] In 1761, he wrote to the king in Madrid: 'On San Ferdinand's Day, His Majesty gave the Order of the Bath to Cav. Gray[62] with his usual spirit and good grace; on Sunday, wearing for the first time this summer Neapolitan clothes, he told everyone that the clothes were tailored in Naples with great taste. Somillier dressed the same. Maybe you are laughing about this trifle, but I consider it to be the most important news of the country, and welcome it, because I proposed and have promoted it as much as I could.'[63]

Indeed, the late mercantilism of the second half of the century introduced nationalist tones to the language of politics, civil economics and even culture.[64] Cosmopolitanism showed its intrinsic contradictions, for even among intellectuals there were some, such as Michele Torcia and Pietro Napoli Signorelli, who reacted against the stereotyped representations of Naples by proclaiming the progress of the culture in the Kingdom.[65] For political economic reasons, the distinction between the concept of passive and active luxury was directed, respectively, at the foreign manufacturers and the internal ones.[66] It was refined in the same discourses of the philosophes concerned with the *politesse*. Fashion, which Galiani condemned as a 'brain disease' that would not be justified other than as an imitation of the 'manners of the dominant nation', did not fall within the semantic field of the refinement of manners.[67] Further, in 1789, Galanti criticized the decline of national factories: 'a sovereign could perhaps get perfection from his factories, but only by using their products, and by showing distaste for those who dressed foreign draperies'.[68] He thus clearly expressed condemnation of the role that the sovereign had played in the spreading of xenophilia. Yet, the futility of mercantilist projects resided both in the difficulty of challenging international economic hegemonies,[69] and the diminished ability of the court and the king to effectively play a taste-making role. The growing importance of private markets for cultural and material goods fostered new dynamics of taste production: the public had its own preferences, which were autonomous from sovereign control.[70] In a twist of fate, the new dominant style in the European fine arts, which can be traced to the ancient Greek vases found in Neapolitan archaeological excavations, was finally a British invention by Sir William Hamilton, a supreme example of the late eighteenth-century *beau monde*.[71] As British Minister at the Court of Naples from 1764 to 1800, charged with reporting on the economic and trade conditions of the Kingdom, he ended up becoming a kind of Cicero of British Grand Tourists and a devotee of leisure and cultural activities. Thus, he set up a genuine marketing operation which promoted the simplicity and taste of ancient Greek vases as a model of the new neoclassical style which invaded the arts, handicrafts and, finally, the industrial production of English ceramics.[72] Through his association with Josiah Wedgwood, art entered into a new era of technical reproducibility.[73]

During the 1780s, the neoclassical style appeared in the new Capodimonte factory and rapidly replaced the widespread *chinoiserie* as the distinctive decorative style of furniture and domestic interiors, starting with the royal rooms.[74] Simplicity was definitely the material expression of taste and politeness, and British culture was its cradle. An increasingly attractive model for intellectuals and scholars of political economy, it affirmed as the very paradigm of civilization: '[A]lthough we have considerably improved in culture, we are far from the politeness that is common in England even in the taverns. The elegance of manners that is so cherished in the northern people derives from education and politeness.'[75] Already perceived in the first half of the century as a good commercial partner, Britain challenged the traditional patterns of urban consumption both in terms of style and in terms of the target market, as its products, from cottons to pottery, were aimed at a broader base of customers. [76] As opposed to the French elitist style, the British helped bring about the democratization of luxury. This was consistent with Newtonian culture and the inter-class sociability that merchants of the British Factory introduced, along with a widespread taste for the 'English' style in umbrellas, snuffboxes, watches and decorative items. Lord Hamilton, again, played an important role as a mediator between British merchants and diplomatic and courtly circles.[77] As in the aforementioned case of Marquis Piatti, Neapolitan inventories show a multiplicity of English or 'English style' materials and products: wood furniture, daily dishes, cups, trays, glasses, and even maps of the world.[78] Cultural hegemony came together with commercial hegemony after the Seven Years War, when Britain, also aided by the Austrian turn of Maria Carolina and Lord Acton, was best suited to exploit trade flows that had been traditionally controlled by the French.[79] Finally, despite (or perhaps because of) the rhetorical efforts of the sovereigns and the economists at the end of the century, the Neapolitan society was depicted as subdued by an empire of foreign taste: '[T]he foreigners have already managed to cast a spell in our country when it comes to their goods, so everything which does not come from the Seine, or is not scented with English brown coal, is considered to be quite unworthy of our taste and of our estimation.'[80]

Conclusions

During the eighteenth century, the international market was a powerful transformative force in the Italian 'Mezzogiorno'. The history of taste provides an interesting perspective on the complex encounter between market dynamics and political and cultural processes. In the eighteenth century, and in the heart of Europe, taste proved to be a powerful ideological and rhetorical means of founding a new practice of distinction in a society that no longer recognized corporate belonging as the basis of the social hierarchy. In the Kingdom of Naples, on the border of Europe, the aspiration to participate in this 'aesthetic civilization' was shared by both the political elite, if only on merely formal grounds, and by progressive groups and intellectuals. The forms and the objects of European taste were used politically as a tool both to legitimize sovereign power and to challenge the status quo. The former led the ruling elite to embrace foreign fashions, creating a collision of spheres of consumption and a growing distance between the court and the broader population. The latter created an intellectual elite, for whom taste implied moral values and civic virtue, and who moved closer to a more introverted practice of distinction. Both, however, experienced the contradictions between cosmopolitanism and the construction of national identity, which was also expressed through conflict between commercial dependence and the construction of a nation state. Taste, after all, resulted in this context in the pillar of an ideology of civilization that spread the social desirability of products exported by the European centres of civilization, that is, by the cores of commercial and industrial power.[81]

Notes

1 Archivio di Stato di Napoli (ASN), Processi civili, Pandetta corrente, f. 162, 1790.

2 Elio Catello, *Cineserie e turcherie nel '700 napoletano* (Naples: Sergio Civita Editore, 1992), 14.

3 Franco Venturi, 'Napoli capitale nel pensiero dei riformatori illuministi', in *Storia di Napoli*, vol. VIII (Naples: Società editrice Storia di Napoli, 1971), 38.

4 For example, with the enlightened intellectual Giuseppe Maria Galanti. On Galanti, see Maria Consiglia Napoli, *Giuseppe Maria Galanti: Letterato ed editore nel secolo dei lumi* (Milan: Franco Angeli, 2013), 60n; Barbara Naddeo, 'A cosmopolitan in the Provinces: G. M. Galanti, Geography, and Enlightenment Europe', *Modern Intellectual History* 10 (2013), 1–26.

5 Melissa Calaresu, 'Coffee, Culture and Consumption: Reconstructing the Public Sphere in Late Eighteenth-Century Naples', in *Filosofia, scienza, storia: Il dialogo fra Italia e Gran Bretagna*, eds Andrea Gatti and Paola Zanardi (Padova: Il Poligrafo, 2005), 135–73.

6 Adelaide Cirillo Mastrocinque, 'La moda e il costume', in *Storia di Napoli*, 789–857; Anna Maria Rao, 'Antiquaries and Politicians in Eighteenth-Century Naples', *Journal of the History of Collections* 2 (2007), 165–75; Anthony Del Donna, *Opera, Theatrical Culture and Society in Late Eighteenth-Century Naples* (Aldershot: Ashgate, 2012).

7 See Ilmakunnas and Stobart's chapter in this volume.

8 On the opposition between the old and new luxury, see Jan de Vries, 'Luxury in the Dutch Golden Age in Theory and Practice', in *Luxury in the Eighteenth Century: Debates, Desires and Delectable Goods*, eds Maxine Berg and Elizabeth Eger (Basingstoke: Palgrave Macmillan, 2003), 41–57; Rémy G. Saisselin, *The Enlightenment Against the Baroque: Economics and Aesthetics in the Eighteenth Century* (Berkeley: University of California Press, 1992); Leora Auslander, *Taste and Power: Furnishing Modern France* (Berkeley: University of California Press, 1996), 142; Cissie Fairchilds, 'Fashion and Freedom in the French Revolution', *Continuity and Change* 3 (2000), 419–33; Lawrence Klein, 'Politeness and the Interpretation of the British Eighteenth Century', *The Historical Journal* 4 (2002), 869–98; for a less dichotomous perspective, see the chapters by Pajur, Blonde and De Laet, Stobart and Steinrud in this volume.

9 For a general survey, see *Naples in the Eighteenth Century: The Birth and Death of a Nation State*, ed. Girolamo Imbruglia (Cambridge: Cambridge University Press, 2000); *New Approaches to Naples c. 1500–c. 1800: The Power of Place*, eds Melissa Calaresu and Hellen Hills (Aldershot: Ashgate, 2013).

10 Cesare De Seta, *Napoli* (Roma-Bari: Laterza, 1999), 189.

11 Giuseppe Galasso, *Intervista sulla storia di Napoli*, ed. Percy Allum (Roma-Bari: Laterza, 1978), 115; Gerard Labrot, *Baroni in città: residenze e comportamenti dell'aristocrazia napoletana (1530–1734)* (Naples: SEN, 1979), 140.

12 Alida Clemente, 'Innovation in the Capital City: Central Policies, Markets, and Migrant Skills in Neapolitan Ceramic Manufacturing in the Eighteenth Century', in *Cities and Innovation in Early Modern Europe*, eds Karel Davids and Bert De Munck (Aldershot: Ashgate, 2014), 315–35.

13 Alexander Echlin, 'Dynasty, Archaeology And Conservation', *Journal Of The History Of Collections* 26 (2014), 145–59; Carlo Knight, *Sulle orme del Grand Tour: Uomini, luoghi e società nel Regno di Napoli* (Naples: Electa, 1995).

14 On the role of the Spanish Bourbons in the spreading of French fashion, see the chapter by de Pinedo and Thépaut-Cabasset in this volume. On the spread of French fashion in the European periphery, see also Ilmakunnas's and North's chapters in this volume.

15 Sonia Scognamiglio, *Le istituzioni della moda: Dalle strutture corporative all'economia politica: Napoli e Francia (1500–1800)* (Bologna: Il Mulino, 2015), 391–418.

16 William H. Sewell Jr., 'The Empire of Fashion and the Rise of Capitalism in Eighteenth-Century France', *Past and Present* 206 (2010), 81–120.

17 Archivio di Stato di Napoli, Affari esteri, f. 4863, fs.1. Francesco Ventura: 'French trade is disadvantageous for our kingdom, because they export more things than they import [They can] sell them at exorbitant and excessive prices because our subjects, who are exceedingly vain, love foreign fashions . . .' See also Archives nationales de Paris, Affaires étrangers, B. III, 407.

18 The presence of French merchants in the early Neapolitan Latomism has been ascertained. Anna Maria Rao, 'La massoneria nel Regno di Napoli', in *Storia d'Italia: Annali 21. La massoneria*, ed. Gian Mario Cazzaniga (Torino: Einaudi, 2006), 516.

19 Roberto Zaugg, *Stranieri di antico regime: Consoli, giudici e mercanti nella Napoli del Settecento* (Rome: Viella, 2011), 169–201.

20 Patrick Chorley, *Oil, Silk and Enlightenment: Economic Problems in Eighteenth-Century Naples* (Naples: Istituto italiano per gli studi storici, 1965); Biagio Salvemini and Maria Antonietta Visceglia, 'Marsiglia e il Mezzogiorno d'Italia (1710–1846): Flussi commerciali e complementarietà economiche', *M.E.F.R.I.M* 103 (1991), 103–163; Biagio Salvemini, 'The Arrogance of the Market: The Economy of the Kingdom Between the Mediterranean and Europe', in *Naples in the Eighteenth Century*, ed. Girolamo Imbruglia, 44–69.

21 Rosalba Ragosta, *Napoli città della seta* (Rome: Donzelli, 2009); Daniela Ciccolella, *La seta nel Regno di Napoli nel XVIII secolo* (Naples: ESI, 2003).

22 'Dove si vidde mai/cosa si orrenda e brutta/che ogn'or la gente tutta/la fa maravigliar/per andare all'usanza/ed a foggia francese/si lascia del paese/la moda trasportar/[. . .]/queste signore dame/che sono all'ora uscite/voi bene mi capite/

senza farmi spiegar/di andare alla francese/anno buona raggione/altrimenti Frammassone/le sapria castigar . . .' Biblioteca della Società napoletana di storia patria (BSNSP), *Manoscritti* III. C. 5, Quaderno I, f.10.

23 BSNSP, *Manoscritti*. 'Who are those / that from their birth / want so lower themselves' ('Chi sono questi tali/che di loro natali/ vonno così abbassar').

24 BSNSP, *Manoscritti*. 'If this custom lasted / many people would die' (Che se quest'usanza durarebbe/ molta gente morirebbe).

25 Laura Barletta, *Il Carnevale del 1764 a Napoli: Protesta e integrazione in uno spazio urbano* (Naples: SEN, 1981), 60.

26 Barletta, *Il Carnevale*, 60.

27 It was not unusual for noblewomen to leave some of their objects, mainly textiles, to their servants. Alida Clemente, *Il lusso 'cattivo': Dinamiche del consumo nella Napoli del Settecento* (Rome: Carocci, 2011), 73.

28 The second-hand market shows clear signs of growth during the eighteenth century. One is the increasing number of the *giudecchieri*, i.e. the second-hand sellers of clothes. Alida Clemente, 'Gli spazi delle botteghe nella Napoli del Settecento: dinamiche di localizzazione, strategie commerciali e conflitti istituzionali nel secolo della "rivoluzione dei consumi"', in *Retail Trade: Supply and Demand in the Formal and Informal Economy from the 13th to the 18th Century*, ed. Giampiero Nigro (Firenze: Firenze University Press, 2015), 373. Another signal of the vitality of the second-hand market is the founding of magazines with private advertisements of second-hand objects. Clemente, *Il lusso 'cattivo'*, 160–1.

29 On the debate on luxury as a means of political reform, see Cecilia Carnino, 'From Luxury to Consumption in the Eighteenth-Century Europe: The Importance of Italian Thought in History and Historiography', *History of European Ideas* 2 (2014), 218–44; John Shovlin, *The Political Economy of Virtue: Luxury, Patriotism, and the Origins of the French Revolution* (Ithaca: Cornell University Press, 2007).

30 Clemente, *Il lusso 'cattivo'*, 60–7.

31 Koen Stapelbroek, '"The Proud Epithet of Enlightened": Ferdinando Galiani and the Neapolitan Debate on Colonies, Conquest and Commerce', in *Enlightened Reform in Southern Europe and its Atlantic Colonies, c. 1750–1830*, ed. Gabriel Paquette (Aldershot: Ashgate, 2013), 297–9.

32 Carlantonio Broggia, 'Del lusso', in *Il Banco ed il Monte de' Pegni: Del Lusso*, ed. Rosario Patalano (Naples: La città del sole, 2004), 143.

33 Carnino, 'From Luxury to Consumption', 218–44.

34 Anna Maria Rao, 'Fra amministrazione e politica: Gli ambienti intellettuali napoletani', in *Naples, Rome, Florence: Une histoire comparée des milieux intellectuels italiens (XVIIe–XVIIIe siècles)*, eds Jean Boutier et al. (Rome: École Française de Rome, 2005), 35–88.

35 Rao, 'Fra amministrazione e politica', 72.

36 'Il presente lusso d'Europa [. . .] non è che gentilezza e politezza di vivere'. Antonio Genovesi, *Lezioni di commercio o sia d'economia civile* (Bassano: Remondini, 1769), 146.

37 Ferdinando Galiani, *Della moneta: Libri cinque* (Naples: Giuseppe Raimondi, 1750), 190–91, 288. 'The old families came into existence in fierce times; their origin only comes from weapons, their wealth only from greed . . . The new ones have grown with the industry, within the peace, in the centuries of luxury [. . .]'. ('[. . .] le antiche famiglie essendo sorte in tempi feroci, non hanno altra origine che fra l'armi, nè altre ricchezze di quelle che la rapacità, le guerre e le discordie dettero loro. Le nuove coll'industria in seno alla pace ne' secoli di lusso si sono ingrandite')

38 '[. . .] di grandissimo giovamento non solo alla grandezza, potenza e ricchezza di una nazione, ma anche alla sua umanità e virtù, almeno di quelle che non amano essere guerriere e conquistatrici, come non dovrebbe esserlo nessuna che fosse savia'. Genovesi, *Lezioni*, 131.

39 'L'uso dei comodi e dei piaceri, che non pregiudica alle virtù, e deriva dalla cultura maggiore'. Domenico Ciaraldi, *Dissertazione morale politica sul problema se il lusso sia giovevole, o dannoso alle civili società* (Naples: Stamperia Simoniana, 1769), 12–13.

40 Lamindo Pritanio, *Riflessioni sopra il buon gusto intorno le scienze e le arti* (Venice: Per Luigi Pavino, 1708). See Pietro Napoli-Signorelli, *Vicende della coltura nelle due Sicilie dalla venuta delle colonie straniere sino a'nostri giorni*, t. VII (Naples: Orsini, 1811), 38.

41 *Signori, patrizi, cavalieri in Italia centro-meridionale nell'età moderna*, ed. Maria Antonietta Visceglia (Rome-Bari: Laterza, 1992), xxx–xxxi.

42 Maria Consiglia Napoli, 'Nobiltà e teatro: Dalle antiche accademie alla nuova società drammatica', in *Signori, patrizi, cavalieri*, ed. Maria Antonietta Visceglia, 351.

43 'Impiegati nelle cariche della corte e delle milizie, li veggiamo (*i baroni*) aver contratto una politezza di costume che non sembrano essere i nipoti di certi mostri, che i più vecchi rammentano ancora con orrore'. Giuseppe Maria Galanti, *Della descrizione geografica e politica delle Due Sicilie*, t. I (Naples: Presso i soci del Gabinetto letterario, 1793), 214.

44 Gaia Bruno, 'Cultura materiale aristocratica nel Settecento napoletano: l'esempio dei Carafa di Ielsi', *Studi storici* 4 (2014), 978.

45 Carnino, 'From Luxury to Consumption', 233.

46 Sophus A. Reinert, *Translating Empire: Emulation and the Origins of Political Economy* (Cambridge MA: Harvard University Press, 2011). The fascination of

Genovesi with Britain as an ideal model of commercial society started with his encounter of John Cary's *History of trade*, of which he published an annotated Italian translation in 1757.

47 '[. . .] ricche botteghe di ogni sorta di merci, le pasticcerie, le sorbetterie, le cantine ripiene di vecchi e nuovi vini freschissimi, odorosi e zampillanti, le spezierie ove ogni sorta di confetti e di canditi e zuccherini lavorasi senza intermissione'. Venturi, 'Napoli capitale,' 30.

48 'casematte della plebe e ricchi palazzi per gli grandi'. Venturi, 'Napoli capitale,' 30.

49 Elisa Novi Chavarria, *Sacro, pubblico e privato: Donne nei secoli XV–XVIII* (Naples: Guida, 2009), 121–22.

50 On travel literature on Naples, see Nelson Moe, *The View from Vesuvius: Italian Culture and the Southern Question* (Berkeley: University of California Press, 2002), 37–84.

51 C. L. de Montesquieu, *Voyage de Montesquieu*, s.e., cited in *Dadapolis: Caleidoscopio napoletano*, eds Fabrizia Ramondino and Andreas F. Muller (Torino: Einaudi, 1989), 255.

52 Giuseppe Galasso, 'Lo stereotipo del napoletano e le sue variazioni regionali', in *L'altra Europa: Per un'antropologia storia del Mezzogiorno d'Italia* (Milan: Mondadori 1982), 148.

53 Jerome Richard, *Description historique et critique de l'Italie, ou Nouveaux mémoires sur l'état actuel de son gouvernement, des sciences, des arts, du commerce, de la population & de l'histoire naturelle* (Paris: Delalaine, 1770), 235–6.

54 D.A.F. de Sade, *Voyage d'Italie*, cit. in Ramondino and Muller, *Dadapolis*, 295.

55 Johann Wolfgang Goethe, *Viaggio in Italia (1786–1788)* (Milan: Rizzoli, 2004), 206.

56 Richard, *Description*, 236. Abbé de Sainté-Non, *Voyage pittoresque de Naples et de Sicile* (Paris: Clousier, 1781), 225.

57 De Sade, *Voyage d'Italie*, 73, 295.

58 On stereotypes, see Melissa Calaresu, 'From the Street to Stereotype: Urban Space, Travel and the Picturesque in Late Eighteenth-Century Naples', *Italian Studies* 2 (2007), 189–203.

59 Cecilia Carnino, 'La femme vicieuse et l'homme vertueux: Le débat sur le luxe et la consommation au XVIIIe siècle en Italie', *Clio@themis* 3 (2010), 1–28; See also the chapter by Stobart in this volume.

60 *Lettere di Bernardo Tanucci a Carlo III di Borbone (1759–1776)*, ed. Rosaria Mincuzzi (Rome: Istituto per la storia del risorgimento italiano, 1969). Naples, 14 December 1762.

61 Mincuzzi, *Lettere*. Portici, 28 October 1760.

62 James Gray was the first British extraordinary envoy in Naples, from 1753 to 1764. Jeremy Black, *British Diplomats and Diplomacy: 1688–1800* (Exeter: University of Exeter Press, 2001), 20.

63 'Diede la M.S. nel suo giorno di S.Ferdinando l'ordine del Bagno al Cav. Gray, col solito suo spirito e buona grazia; e domenica, vestendo la prima volta da estate, di drappo fatto in Napoli, andava dicendo a tutti che era drappo di Napoli con sommo gusto. Il Somillier aveva un vestito uguale. Forse mi burlerete dello scrivervi di questa bagattella, ma io e la considero per una notizia delle più importanti del paese, e me ne rallegro, perché l'ho proposta e promossa quanto ho potuto.' 2 June 1761. Bernardo Tanucci, *Epistolario*, vol. IX, 1760–61, ed. Maria Grazia Maiorini (Rome: Edizioni di storia e letteratura, 1985).

64 See also the chapter by North in this volume.

65 Melissa Calaresu, 'Looking for Virgil's Tomb: The End of the Grand Tour and the Cosmopolitan Ideal in Europe', in *Voyages and Visions: Towards a cultural History of Travel*, eds Jas Elsner and Joan Pau Rubiés (London: Reaktion Books, 1999), 138–61.

66 Genovesi, *Lezioni*, 156.

67 Galiani, *Della Moneta*, 46.

68 Giuseppe Maria Galanti, *Nuova descrizione geografica e politica delle Sicilie*, tt. III–V (Napoli, 1789), 308.

69 Piero Bevilacqua, 'Il Mezzogiorno nel mercato internazionale (secoli XVIII–XX)', *Meridiana* 1 (1987), 19–45.

70 One example is found in theatre production. The royal monopoly of 'French' opera was supposed to give way to the public success of the comic opera and the growing autonomization of theatrical production. Mélanie Traversier, *Gouverner l'opéra: Une histoire politique de la musique à Naples, 1767–1815* (Rome: Ecole française de Rome, 2009), 187–9.

71 Carlo Knight, *Hamilton a Napoli: Cultura, svaghi, civiltà di una grande capitale europea* (Naples: Electa, 1990).

72 In 1772, Hamilton sold his collection of ancient vases to the British Museum for 8,000 guineas. Michael Vickers, 'Value and Simplicity: Eighteenth-century Taste and the Study of Greek Vases', *Past and Present* (1987), 98–137.

73 *Encyclopedia of Interior Design*, ed. Joanna Banham (London: Routledge, 2015), 1379.

74 Catello, *Cineserie e turcherie*, 25.

75 'Sebbene siasi molto avanzato in coltura, tuttavia siamo lontani dalla politezza che in Inghilterra è comunale fino alle taverne. Dall'educazione e dalla politezza deriva quell'eleganza di maniera che tanto piace ne' settentrionali'. Galanti, *Della descrizione*, 524.

76 Ettore Losardo, *Napoli e Londra nel XVIII secolo: Le relazioni economiche* (Naples: Jovene, 1991), 55.

77 Zaugg, *Stranieri*, 206.

78 Alida Clemente, 'Consumi di lusso ed economia mondo: Il Regno di Napoli nel XVIII Secolo', in *Luxes et internationalisation (XVIe–XIXe siècles)*, ed. Nadége Sougy (Neuchâtel: Editions Alphil – Presses Universitaires Suisses, 2013), 67–96; on the spreading of English fashion, see North and Ijäs in this volume.

79 The commercial balance was increasingly characterized by imports from England. Giovan Battista Maria Jannucci, *Economia del commercio del Regno di Napoli: 1767–69*, ed. Franca Assante (Naples: Giannini, 1981), 60; Giuseppe Maria Galanti, *Della descrizione geografica e politica delle Due Sicilie*, eds Franca Assante and Domenico Demarco (Naples: ESI, 1969), 563–4.

80 'I forestieri sono già riusciti d'introdurre nei nostri paesi un certo incantesimo per le loro merci, per cui tutto ciò che non vien dalla senna, o che non è profumato col carbone di terra inglese, da noi si reputa come affatto indegno del nostro gusto, e della nostra estimazione.' Giuseppe Spiriti, *Riflessioni politico-economiche d'un cittadino relative alle due province di Calabria* (Naples: Per Vincenzo Flauto, 1793), 154.

81 On the importance of cultural hegemony as a basis for commercial hegemony, see Philippe Norel, *L'Histoire économique globale* (Paris: Seuil, 2009), 122.

4

What About the Moorish Footman? Portrait of a Dutch Nabob as a Dedicated Follower of Fashion

Yme Kuiper*

In December 1762, the German scholar Johann Beckmann arrived in the city of Groningen after a visit to Amsterdam. Beckmann thought Groningen was a nice city, but it did not have the same allure and grandeur as Amsterdam – with one exception, the treasures of Mr Sichterman, who with black servants and a huge fortune had returned to the city of his birth from the East Indies. Seven years earlier, Beckmann's compatriot, the theologian Heinrich von der Hude, had also visited the treasures of this Jan Albert Sichterman (1692–1764). Sichterman had enjoyed a spectacular career in the Dutch East India Company (VOC), with his top positions being ten years as the Director of the VOC factory in Bengal, the Director in Chinsurah on the river Hooghly and briefly a member of the Council of the Indies (*Raad van Indië*) in Batavia. So what were these treasures? Von der Hude describes 'an unbelievable mixture of Japanese and Chinese porcelain, of gold and silver dinnerware, and a collection of the most expensive paintings, that decorates nearly every spot in the house [. . .] With one word, apart from the green pavilion in Dresden I have never seen a place with more luxury, more splendor and beauty.'[1]

These wonderful things stood and hung in the largest townhouse in Groningen. Even before he returned to the Dutch Republic, Sichterman had

* I would like to thank the editors of this book for their constructive comments and also my Dutch colleagues Christaan Jörg, Egge Knol, Wim Meulenkamp, Jan Holwerda, Gerda Huisman and Jort Hottinga for their bibliographical help.

Figure 4.1 *Chine de commande*: a dish of one of the ten table services (each more than 100 pieces) that Sichterman owned, with the Sichterman family arms (a crowned squirrel) and Chinese pagodas.

© Groninger Museum, Groningen.

built this mansion on a square just outside the city of Groningen. In 1743 he was making an architectural statement – in this urban palace, the 'king of Groningen' would shortly be coming to live.

As a young military officer in the Southern Netherlands, he originally had to flee east after fatally wounding his opponent in a duel over a woman. After a sea journey of over six months, Lieutenant Sichterman arrived in Batavia in October 1716. Within a year the Governor General and the councillors of the *Raad van Indië* sent him to Bengal with the rank of *onder-koopman*, junior factor. In the following years, he steadily rose through the ranks to the highest position, marrying a daughter of the VOC vice-director Sadelijn in Bengal in 1721.[2] It was obvious from his coach-and-six and his black footmen, which he used to travel around in the city of his birth, that Sichterman had done well in the East Indies. What was also noticeable was the extravagantly carved door of his imposing new mansion. The balcony above it was decorated with beautiful ironwork incorporating the monogram J. A. S. supported by two Moorish herms in sandstone. Because his mansion was not yet ready in 1745, Sichterman stayed for a while at his new country estate *Woellust* in Wildervank, about 20 miles from the city of Groningen. Surrounded by lanes with all kinds of trees, it had ornamental and kitchen gardens, a deer park, fishponds and even a pheasant preserve. Unusually for this part of the Republic, one of the formal gardens also had – as two of his biographers wrote – 'an artful Japanese play house'.

Sichterman appears to have been a dedicated follower of fashion with his enormous collection of oriental porcelain and furniture. As the owner of both a townhouse and a country estate, he imitated the lifestyle of other *nouveaux riches* in the Dutch Republic, the rich merchants of the Dutch cities, especially in the provinces of Holland and Zeeland (part of the Northern Netherlands). Here we find the families who had earned most of their fortunes in all kinds of trade in the East and West Indies, including slavery and plantations. In this chapter I will deal with three interrelated questions: first, how could Sichterman become a rich man in such a relatively short time; second, was he the Groningen example of a Dutch *nabob*; and last but not least, was his collecting on a grand scale, and his lifestyle in general, motivated by family-based status aspirations – was he at heart a new type of collector with a desire for luxury and the prestige of a *grand seigneur*, a lifestyle that he had already developed and cultivated in the Far East, or was he also a connoisseur, an expert in matters of taste and a trendsetter introducing luxury goods from the Far East?

The Bengal Sichterman: trade, social networks and luxury

From 1627 onwards, the Dutch East India Company had regular trade relations with Bengal. Since 1635 (and until 1795) Hooghly-Chinsurah, with Fort Gustavus (built in 1742), had been the most important Dutch factory in Bengal. The second VOC factory in order of importance was in Cassimbazar, where Sichterman also lived for some years. As we have already seen, Sichterman's marriage in 1721 to Sibylla, daughter of vice-director Jacob Sadelijn, was a big step in his Bengal career. In his rich study on the personnel of the VOC in Asia, the Dutch historian Frank Lequin has shown that the VOC elite in Bengal developed into a self-co-opting oligarchy in the first half of the eighteenth century, five interconnected families (Huysman, Van Dishoeck, Pelgrom, Sadelijn and Sichterman) holding the VOC directorship for about thirty-three years during the period 1700–1744.[3] Sichterman and his new wife had seven surviving children, most of them being sent back to the Dutch Republic at a very young age. His two oldest sons, Anthony Ewout (1722–1756) and Gerrit Jan (1725–1796), sailed home in 1725 and around 1730 respectively. During their early years they lived in Groningen, but later they moved with a Swiss tutor to The Hague, largely because French was more frequently and better spoken in the court circles there. His boys also needed a sound grounding in Latin and English, which in Sichterman's own estimation was 'beginning to become important across Europe', especially as the Prince of Orange had married an English princess in 1734. The Sichtermans had always been loyal to the House of Orange, he emphasized in a letter to the boys' tutor, written in precise French, underlining Sichterman as a politically calculating *pater familias*.[4] In autumn 1738, the boys moved back to Groningen. Their father in Chinsurah gave orders to buy them some good horses and appropriate equipage – Anthony and Gerrit did need to relax from time to time. Buying books was another instruction for the tutor, although a limit was set at 3,000 guilders because 'I have a quite voluminous library here with a lot of great series, which cost me a fortune [...] I wish to transport it to Groningen, for I cannot sell it here [in Hooghly] without a considerable loss'. He was fond of books and estimated once that he had invested about 30,000 guilders in his library in Chinsurah.

In the first years of his marriage, Sichterman faced hard times in the factory in Hooghly. He quarrelled constantly with the director Pieter Vuyst, who dismissed Sichterman and sent him and his young family back to Batavia at the end of 1723. There he stayed for some years as the guest of Anthony Huysman, a former director of Bengal, who lived in a suburban villa with a magnificent garden, just outside Batavia, and had a large staff of black servants.[5] Sichterman returned to Bengal in 1725 with a higher rank following Vuyst's removal and replacement by Sichterman's father-in-law Jacob Sadelijn. Sichterman himself had his finest Bengal hours during his own directorship in the years 1734–1744 during which time he became a very rich

Figure 4.2 The Hooghly factory of the Dutch East India Company in Chinsurah (Bengal) in the late seventeenth century. Sichterman was director of this trading post in the 1730s and 1740s. Painting by Hendrik van Schuylenburgh.

© Rijksmuseum, Amsterdam.

man, largely by owning textile factories in Chinsurah and by engaging in private trade. He particularly cherished his trade connections with other European merchants in Bengal. In the 1730s, his joint ventures in trade with Jean-François Dupleix, the French director in Chandernagore, seem to have been very lucrative and Sichterman was even a witness at Dupleix's wedding.[6] Another good business friend was the Flemish merchant François de Schonamille.[7] Via his bookkeeper and 'upper merchant' Anthony d'Arnaud, he made deals with another Flemish merchant, Andreas Jacobus Flanderin, who was also part of De Schonamille's network. Flanderin was the ideal contact for Sichterman to smuggle oriental treasures like Japanese toilet articles and oriental furniture to Groningen. Using misleading labels like tea or wood, these expensive objects were transported on a Swedish ship to Gothenburg in 1742 and afterwards on a Dutch vessel to Amsterdam. Here Sichterman's straw man Gerard Pauw, a wine merchant, stored these goods until his master and his family were back in the Dutch Republic.[8] These relationships were also cemented by the exchange of gifts, Sichterman often making presents of animals including rare birds of paradise, which underpinned the personal nature of trading relations.[9]

At the time that European trading companies came to Bengal, slavery was already a commonly accepted institution in the region.[10] Many slaves served in the houses of the VOC employees, most of them in the extended families of the upper merchants. The possession of slaves and a very large staff appear as forms of luxury and social superiority in this commercial elite. We do not know what Sichterman or his wife Sibylla thought about slavery, but they chose to bring two black male servants, probably slaves, back to Europe in 1745. In this they followed conventional practice; according to their rank, repatriating VOC personnel were allowed to bring with them a specific quantity of 'emancipated' serfs (i.e. slaves).[11] In his later Groningen years Sichterman had the reputation of a womanizer and stories went round that one of his sons was not his and Sibylla's child, but the result of a liaison with a slave. The truth of this is impossible to verify, but his black 'servants' were certainly a very public part of his status and identity.[12]

We know much more about Sichterman as the promoter of some major architectural projects in Chinsurah. In 1742 the VOC factory was fortified with impressive walls and Sichterman gave the new fortress the name Fort Gustavus, after Governor General Gustaaf Willem van Imhoff, his superior and friend, who he liked to address as 'cousin'. His other big project was building, at his own expense, a new 20 metre high bell tower, although his commitment to the Dutch Reformed Church was not absolute. Indeed, Sichterman's children were baptized by Anglican priests who came from Calcutta to Chinsurah especially for the occasion. In February 1739, the priest Gervasius Bellamy baptized young Christina Elisabeth Sichterman. It was a ceremony of pomp and circumstance with Governor Sichterman as the central person, accompanied by his wife Sybilla wearing a beautiful silk and cotton dress, following the latest English fashions.

The 'significant other' in Sichterman's life of luxury

The year 1744 was a decisive one in Sichterman's life: he received permission from his superiors to leave Bengal. In the transfer document for his successor,

Sichterman looked back proudly but sadly: the Bengal factory was still the best in Asia, but not as flourishing as it had been in earlier days.[13] On arrival in Batavia in July 1744, Sichterman heard that he had been appointed to the Council of the Indies. Only a few months earlier, he had read in a letter from a close relative that his oldest son Anthony Ewout, the up-and-coming star of the family, had married the daughter of a Groningen nobleman. This was both good and bad news. The twenty-year-old student Anthony had married an eighteen-year-old rich girl with a splendid family name, but he had eloped with his sweetheart and her family was not amused. By the time Sichterman received his letter in Chinsurah, the marriage was already a year old. In no time the young couple had three sons and a daughter. After studying law for some time at the University of Groningen, Anthony joined the Republic's army in 1745 and served in it as a captain until 1753, when he sold out. A man of independent means, he died suddenly in The Hague only three years later. His two brothers also had military careers, with the youngest dying on the battlefield in 1750. Eventually, all the Sichterman children would marry partners from patrician or noble families – two daughters married Van Iddekinge brothers, scions of a very influential patrician family in the province and town of Groningen – a clear sign of the family's rise in status.[14]

Sichterman did not stay long in Batavia. He was granted a very honourable mission, a present from his cousin, Governor General Van Imhoff: admiral of the 1744 return fleet to the Dutch Republic, commanding fifteen heavily loaded VOC ships transporting pepper, cloves, cinnamon, saltpetre, oriental wood, indigo, coffee, tea, cotton, chintz, three Japanese lacquered 'comptoirs' and 195 boxes and 125 bundles of porcelain.[15] On 2 September 1745 Sichterman sailed into the harbour of Rammekens, near Flushing in the province of Zeeland, after a journey of 13,500 miles, which took him nearly ten months. He went immediately to Middelburg to inform his superiors in the VOC Zeeland Chamber about his successful return journey. Here he heard the news that his former patron Ewout Van Dishoeck had died the previous year. Undoubtedly, he visited Van Dishoeck's widow, who still lived in a beautiful mansion in Middelburg with a rich collection of paintings by the most famous Dutch and Flemish painters, including Brueghel and Rubens.

Van Dishoeck himself had commanded a return fleet of twenty-three ships, which had arrived in the Dutch Republic exactly twenty years earlier. Like

Sichterman, he had made a great fortune in Bengal, and immediately after his return to his province of birth he bought the country mansion *Zeerust* (Sea Rest) near Middelburg, followed in 1732 by the acquisition of the lordship of Domburg (for 19,500 guilders) and the accompanying stately home *Hof te Domburg* (Court of Domburg). One year later he was given a permanent seat on the VOC Zeeland Chamber in Middelburg. He had asked an Antwerp architect to renovate the house and gardens, but only some of his plans could be realized before his death in 1744. Van Dishoeck's art and natural objects collection in his Middelburg mansion was quite famous.[16] He was also a man who liked luxurious clothing. On his marriage to his cousin, Adriana Van Dishoeck, in Chinsurah in 1708, he wore a blue and scarlet robe with golden buttons, a waistcoat and breeches with golden flowers, and carried a massive golden sword at his side.[17] At that time Van Dishoeck was no more than head of the administration of the VOC factory. The story is a nice illustration of Boxer's observation of 'the excessive preoccupation of the senior employees with official rank and social status. [. . .] In the overseas possessions of the two Dutch India Companies in general, and at Batavia in particular, class distinctions and social gradations were carried to grotesque lengths.'[18] Indeed, Van Dishoek's only son, Anthony Pieter, born in Chinsurah, lived in the most beautiful patrician house in Flushing, which his father had ordered to be built in the early 1730s. Sichterman could not have missed it in the late summer of 1745.

The reason that we are paying attention here to the biography of Ewout Van Dishoeck is that he was the 'significant other' in the life of Jan Albert Sichterman. He had been his superior in Bengal at a crucial moment in Sichterman's life – his marriage to Sibylla – which gave him opportunities to participate in the networks of the director families in Bengal. Van Dishoeck was probably also present at their wedding and at the baptism of their first son, Anthony. In a 1740 letter to the tutor Burnand, Sichterman instructed him to make a summer tour with his two sons along the most important towns of the Dutch Republic. Then Sichterman immediately wrote: 'My sons must also see Zeeland and visit Mr Dishoeck; my eldest son has his surname and the same is true for Mr Huysman, who is a cousin of mine.'[19] Giving his first son the names of his superiors was also an act of imitation on Sichterman's part. Ewout Van Dishoeck had also given his son, Anthony Pieter, the names of his superiors Anthony Huysman and Pieter Van Dishoeck.[20] During his stay in Bengal, Sichterman wrote many letters to relatives, friends and clients in the Dutch Republic and the Southern Netherlands. It is obvious that he knew that his former superior could still pull strings in the VOC upper echelons at home and what his lifestyle was like in town and countryside: collecting art and other valuable

Figure 4.3 Portrait of Jan Albert Sichterman and two of his sons; painting by Philip van Dijk (1683–1754), 1745. Van Dijk was for some time court painter and art dealer of the landgraves of Hesse-Cassel; Sichterman made use of his advice to build up his own collection of paintings.

© Groninger Museum, Groningen.

objects, hunting in the right seasons, visiting friends at their country estates or welcoming them to his own, and, of course, telling exciting stories about life in Bengal.

Grand seigneur in Groningen: a 'town palace' and a country estate

When their parents finally arrived in Groningen, late in September 1745, all the Sichterman brothers and sisters were gathered in the brand-new mansion on the Ossenmarkt. The entire clan was reunited in Groningen – the town of birth of only the *pater familias* himself. Was Sichterman moved when he saw his mansion in Groningen for the first time? It had already been the talk of the town for some years. The house had three storeys, thirty rooms, a magnificent double staircase leading from the *bel étage* to the second floor, and behind it a coach house, the stables and the servant's quarters. Also behind the house was a fashionable garden and a summer pavilion, to which sixty-six paintings were later moved because the house had not enough walls to hang the still growing collection of paintings by famous masters. Sichterman was back and every citizen of Groningen knew it. His coach, drawn by six horses with black servants as coachman and footman, were amazing and so too was the interior of his 'palace' with its floors, gilt leather wallpaper and stucco-ceilings – quite the equal of its impressive late Louis XIV-façade.

Others have written extensively about the interior, especially the rich collection of oriental porcelain, furniture, statues, boxes, mirrors and other rare objects.[21] Special attention has been paid to his *Chine de commande*. Here, my perspective will not be that of a specialist of ceramic history but of a historical anthropologist interested in the social and cultural processes of imitation, the symbolic aspects of social superiority and the development of personal and collective taste. Sichterman liked to show his collections to his visitors, who came from his own province, elsewhere in the Republic and from abroad. Inventory lists drawn up after his death in 1764 make it possible to reconstruct a route through the house. All the principal rooms on the *bel étage* were connected by wide French doors, giving visitors the impression of one great space. Behind the mansion an octagonal room had been added to show many cabinets full of oriental and European porcelain. Organizing dinners and eating with many guests off his own Chinese porcelain service with his coat of arms must have been one of Sichterman's greatest pleasures. Perhaps these events also triggered memories of dinners and parties that he had organized or been invited to in Bengal or in Batavia.

Of course, Sichterman was not the only nabob who had returned as a rich man to the northern provinces of the Republic. Most of them also bought country estates, had porcelain collections and spent the summer in the countryside. However, in comparison to many Frisian nabobs, Sichterman's collection of about 4,000 pieces of porcelain (including 43 tea and coffee services of 36 pieces each and 10 dinner services of 150–180 pieces) and 400 paintings was hugely impressive, both in size and quality.[22] Sichterman was one of the top collectors of armorial porcelain in the Dutch Republic, a practice which peaked in the 1730s and 1740s.[23] He ordered great quantities of *Chine de commande* between 1740 and 1744, the period right before his departure from the Indies. Even in the hall of his country house visitors were struck by beautiful Chinese blue-and-white porcelain with the oriental-looking Sichterman squirrel sitting on it. This country house, called *Woellust,* was built in the years 1745–1746 and lay on a peninsula, virtually surrounded by water. It was part of an estate that was long and thin, like many estates with relatively newly built country houses in this region. Relatives and friends of Sichterman also had their country houses nearby. His brother, Gerrit Sichterman, for example, had bought the neighbouring house of *Woelwijk* in 1722, but died in 1730. Now Gerrit's granddaughter owned the house and it was regularly a centre of entertainment with poetry and literature. In such a cultural climate, Sichterman was again ready to impress his guests with oriental porcelain and art or paintings by Dutch masters, although the bulk of his collection of paintings hung in Groningen. In the 1764 catalogue, we find three Rembrandts, and also works by Frans Hals, Jan Steen, Peter Paulus Rubens, Salomon Ruysdael, and so on. How did he build up such a rich collection in such a short time? Sichterman probably made use of the European-wide network of the painter Philip van Dijk, who painted many portraits of couples and children in the Sichterman clan. As a court painter in Germany (in Hesse-Kassel) and a popular portraitist in the Dutch Republic, especially in Zeeland (he also painted a portrait of Ewout Van Dishoek and his wife), Philip Van Dijk was

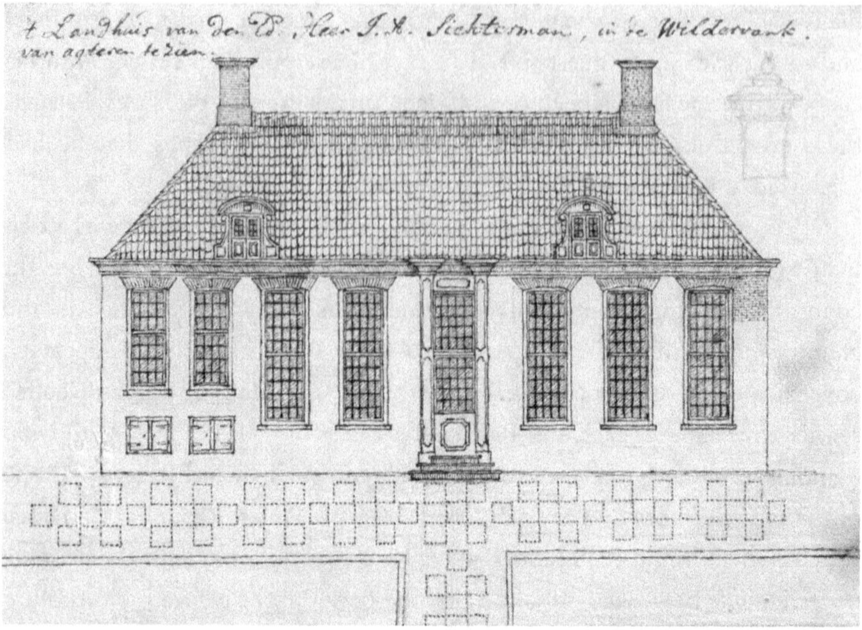

Figure 4.4 Rear view of Sichterman's country house *Woellust*, about 20 miles from the city of Groningen. Its gardens were even more impressive than the house itself. Drawing in ink, by Theodorus Beckeringh, *c.* 1760.

© Groninger Museum, Groningen.

Sichterman's ideal art dealer and broker for fashions in high society, such as collecting Chinese, Japanese, French and Saxon porcelain or silver objects.

One of the greatest attractions of Sichterman's country house was the surrounding formal gardens with their very special Japanese garden house, where Sichterman had his own billiards room; perhaps the construction of this remarkable building harked back to the Far East. Without doubt, the fashion to build Chinese or Japanese pagodas and pavilions in European gardens started somewhere around 1750 and reached its peak in the last quarter of the eighteenth century. Apart from the late 1750s Chinese creations of William Chambers in England, who in the 1740s made three journeys to Bengal and China in the service of the Swedish East Indian Company, very early Chinese garden houses were built at Wilhelmsthal, near Kassel in Germany, and at Drottningholm in Sweden.[24] So where does Sichterman's Japanese garden house fit in? It looks as if he was not a follower of fashion in this respect, but more of a trendsetter, at least in the Dutch Republic. As far as we know, there are very few other Dutch country houses that had wooden Japanese or Chinese pavilions or pagodas in their formal gardens,[25] although this fashion would become much more popular after the introduction – all over Europe – of the English landscape garden with its typical follies. In addition to this undoubted novelty, Sichterman's country house was surrounded by orchards and kitchen gardens. Another striking feature of the estate were the charming bridges across small canals, and in the great canal lay a covered yacht 'with two rooms' for recreational boating. As in Bengal, Sichterman enjoyed hunting on his Wildervank estate and in the surrounding countryside. He kept many kinds of animals on his estate, including West Indian pigs, greyhounds and army dogs.

In the summer of 1761 Sichterman and his wife Sibylla drew up their last will and testament. They left all of their belongings to the surviving spouse. In a 1762 codicil, written in their country house (in February), they added legacies for their coachman, two maids and their black servants Klaasje, Simon, Laurens and Jacob (Uytvlugt).[26] Shortly thereafter one of them travelled back to the Far East. Sichterman suddenly fell ill in December 1763; his 'notary', the lawyer Theodorus Beckeringh, was called and instructed to arrange the inheritance.[27] On 15 January 1764 Sichterman died in his mansion in Groningen. He was buried in the family grave in the oldest church in Groningen, the Martinikerk.[28] Less than three weeks after Sichterman's death an inventory of the contents of his house (room by room) and other possessions in the town of Groningen and of the country house and other farms and fields in the countryside was already available. Even a house in Bengal was registered in this inventory. In May and August 1764 auctions were held to sell all the treasures that he had collected: books, prints, natural specimens, paintings, oriental lacquer work and ornaments, Japanese and Chinese porcelain, crystal and furniture. Sybilla died in 1781, and her six heirs each inherited 62,000 guilders in stocks and cash. The big townhouse and the country house had been sold in 1770 and 1764 respectively. Only the armorial porcelain with the crowned and seated squirrel was kept in the family.

Conclusions

Only one in four employees in the service of the VOC in Bengal returned to Europe in the eighteenth century; their average length of service was fourteen years. Jan Albert Sichterman lived for over twenty-five years in Bengal. It was not his VOC salary that made him a rich man, but his private trade and entrepreneurial investments, using his high VOC position to develop networks and his own interests. Sichterman's family background was a solid one of ministers and military officers, but his splendid career in the Indies and his profitable marriage in Bengal made it possible for his children to marry patrician and even noble partners, even in his own town and province of birth. Sichterman himself was a social climber who succeeded in joining the networks of superiors who were indeed of patrician birth. It was an unlucky incident that took Sichterman to the Indies, but he always intended to return to Europe one day. However, he was very lucky to find the 'right connections' in Bengal. And life in Bengal was viewed in Dutch and British eyes as 'the fat pasture' or 'shaking the pagoda tree' respectively.[29]

As a white, wealthy and senior employee of a successful company in the Indies, Sichterman lived on a scale of conspicuous consumption that he could not have afforded in his home country. Cheap labour and many servants, living in slavery or not, were crucial for such a lifestyle. The Dutch historian and anthropologist, Van Leur, once argued that 'eighteenth-century colonial society in the Indies' was a Dutch society only to a limited extent 'because its elite had developed the opulent lifestyle of the upper classes in the Indies, with their country seats, their pomp and ceremony, their retinues of slaves and serfs.' In short, it imitated the lifestyle of the native nobilities. The English historian, Boxer, has strong doubts about Van Leur's argument. Not only the architecture and gardening stayed European, the pomp and splendour of the Europeans was also very different from, among others, the complex culture of the Javanese *kratons* or the court culture of the Bengal nawabs. 'Most of the VOC's officials cared very little about the oriental cultures with which they came into contact', Boxer argued; the overwhelming majority of them remained stubbornly Eurocentric.[30] In contrast, and around the same time, Edward Said argued that 'the Orient [including the Far East] is an integral part of European *material* civilization and culture.'[31]

What can we say about our Sichterman in this context of contrasting views? Since the 1970s, a great deal has been written about *chinoiserie*, *Chine de commande*, 'Japan China', European-China hybrids, 'India' goods or, more broadly, about Eastern exoticism or, a more tricky term, 'imperial objects' in the eighteenth century.[32] It is clear now that not only the traditional elites in Europe, such as royal and princely families, higher and lower nobility or the landed gentry, were involved in collecting oriental treasures; so too were rich merchants, manufacturers and senior officials, including English and Dutch nabobs (but see the chapters in this volume by Clemente and Stobart). Collecting porcelain, furniture, lacquer, ivory objects, statues, folding screens, and the like from the Far East became popular and widespread in Europe during the eighteenth century. This was also, as many authors have rightly argued, the age of a rise in the consumption of luxury goods among broader segments of society. As the works of Georg Simmel, Norbert Elias, Pierre Bourdieu and Jean-Pascal Daloz amply show, there is a strong connection between specific styles of consumption and patterns of social distinction.[33] In particular, residences, interiors, country houses, parks and gardens, libraries, cabinets and collections of art, archaeological and natural objects or scientific instruments functioned as codes and styles of distinction within and between elites in the eighteenth century. Only case studies can reveal how the various aspects of the cultural consumption of these elites, such as luxury, taste and fashion, were interrelated – and not only from the perspective of the whole group but also from a more individual, biographical point of view. Collectively, eighteenth-century nabobs are usually associated with conspicuous consumption and portrayed as typical *nouveaux riches*; they lacked the specific form of distinction that Bourdieu has discovered: the seemingly natural, embodied superiority in social intercourse. They tended to compensate for this by demonstrating material luxury. However, in the eighteenth-century intellectual debates about luxury, good taste and refinement became popular and were no longer only framed by moral standards, as we can see in the writings on luxury by Hume, Voltaire and Montesquieu. They connected the notion of luxury to civilization, refinement, happiness and economic benefits.[34] Only against this background can we try to understand the longing for luxury and the development of taste as dispositions embedded in the lifestyle of our Sichterman.

On the one hand, Sichterman was a typical senior VOC employee, used to an opulent lifestyle which he tried to continue in his home country. Living in Bengal, he remained deeply involved with what was happening at home, both in Groningen and in the Dutch Republic. We do not know how many black servants or slaves Sichterman had in Bengal, but the fact that the entrance to his Groningen house was decorated with two Moorish herms is surely significant. On the other hand, he seems to have been a man of letters, who built up a rich library in the large director's house at Chinsurah and probably read his books in the tea house that stood apart in the beautiful gardens of the VOC factory. We can guess that his first superior in Bengal, Ewout Van Dishoeck, had a great influence on the aspirations and the lifestyle of the Bengal Sichterman. In the province of Zeeland, and especially in its capital city Middelburg, Sichterman recognized later a mentality and a lifestyle among its commercial-intellectual elite that matched his own worldview and ethos. This Zeeland political and commercial elite was strongly connected with the Dutch slave trade in the first half of the eighteenth century, but also – via mercantile contacts and using the expertise of Flemish architects and artists – with elite lifestyle in the Southern Netherlands.[35] And here we encounter one of the most ambivalent and paradoxical aspects of the history of slavery, aptly demonstrated by Sichterman's personal life: the treatment of his own black servants, who were probably once his slaves. We know so little of Klaasje, Laurens, Simon and Jan. However, when Heinrich von der Hude and a friend visited Sichterman's town palace in 1755, the first made a very remarkable observation in his travel diary: 'we were everywhere accompanied by a black man who had the keys to all rooms and cabinets, even to the very considerable collection of coins'.[36] Sichterman had the reputation of being an Enlightened and religious person. In his Groningen library he had books by René Descartes, Pierre Bayle, Christian Wolff, Anthony van Leeuwenhoek and Isaac Newton.[37] Did he feel obliged to educate his black servants? The only thing that we can guess here is that their relationship with their patron was deeply influenced by paternalism, one of the basic ingredients of the mental structure of the *Ancien Régime* and of colonial society.[38] This is one way in which the typical nouveau riche Sichterman exemplifies a confrontation between Old and New Luxury: on the one hand, the multitude of servants, part of Sichterman's Eastern lifestyle; on the other, the fashionable and urbane consumption, but also stimulating innovation and a work ethic among entrepreneurs.[39]

There is still the riddle of Sichterman as an *individual* collector. He had become a rich man – and he knew it. But had he also developed an aesthetic taste and did he enjoy his treasures as objects of beauty? Certainly, his aspirations as a collector were immensely broad, as we have already seen. In many respects, he collected in the same way as the *mercator sapiens* had done in the seventeenth century. He probably saw his own collection of shells, minerals, gems, stuffed birds and other animals as part of God's Book of Nature. However, above all, buying porcelain, furniture, silver, paintings and books, and being constantly busy with arranging, exhibiting and moving his treasures, seems to have given him much pleasure. Jan Albert Sichterman's late lifestyle of conspicuous consumption and being a man of the world (his Grand Tour had been his life in the East) appear to have been perfectly matched. Why would you leave behind after your death 127 tablecloths and 1,330 napkins? And why would you order only golden frames for your family portraits and for nearly all of your 400 other paintings? Perhaps such details will help us to come as close as we can to the individual peculiarities of the collector Sichterman. After all, was it not the splendour of his life in Bengal that made him at the end of it 'the king of luxury' in Groningen?

Notes

1 Johan Adriaan Feith, 'De Bengaalsche Sichterman', *Groningsche Volksalmanak voor het jaar 1914* (1913), 31–2. The original citation: 'In eine unglaubliche Menge von Japanischen und Chinesischem Porzellan, von Gold- und Silbergeschirr, und den kostbarsten Gemälden, dass fast ein jedweder Fleck im Hause damit gezieret ist. [. . .] Mit einem Wort ich habe ausser dem grünen Gewölbe in Dresden keinen Ort gesehen, wo mehr Kostbarkeiten, mehr Pracht und Schönheit an zu treffen.'

2 Frank Lequin, 'Het personeel van de Verenigde Oost-Indische Compagnie in Azië in de achttiende eeuw, meer in het bijzonder in de vesting Bengalen' (Unpublished dissertation, University of Leiden, 1982), 185.

3 There is an ongoing debate among Dutch and British historians about just how closed the VOC top in Asia actually was in the eighteenth century. See Femme S. Gaastra, *De geschiedenis van de VOC* (Zutphen: Walburg Pers, 2002), 97. Compare Jacob Cornelis van Leur, 'On the Eighteenth Century as a Category in Indonesian History', in Jacob Cornelis van Leur, *Indonesian Trade and Society. Essays in Asian Social and Economic History* (Dordrecht: Foris Publications, 1983; orig. 1955), 268–90; Charles Boxer, 'On the Eighteenth Century as a Category in Indonesian History: A Reconsideration of J.C. van Leur', *Documentatieblad Werkgroep 18de eeuw* 41/42 (1979), 4–16.

4 Notwithstanding his mercantile career and military background the social climber Sichterman, striving for acceptance in fashionable, 'civilized' society, preferred to use French in his correspondence. See also Johanna Ilmakunnas's chapter in this book about the influence of French culture on the lifestyle of elites in eighteenth-century Sweden.

5 Boxer, 'On the Eighteenth Century', 552–3.

6 See Holden Furber, *Rival Empires of Trade in the Orient 1600–1800* (Minneapolis: University of Minnesota Press, 1981), 140; Lequin, 'Het personeel', 105.

7 Jan Parmentier, *De holle compagnie: Smokkel en legale handel onder Zuidnederlandse vlag in Bengalen, ca. 1720–1744* (Hilversum: Verloren, 1992), 28, 49–50.

8 Parmentier, *De holle compagnie*, 75–6; Lequin, 'Het personeel', 544; Sichterman also used the Swedish route to transport his armorial porcelain, ordered in Canton.

9 Wiet Kühne-van Diggelen, *Jan Albert Sichterman: VOC-dienaar en 'koning' van Groningen* (Groningen: Regio Projekt, 1995), 46. In the following sections I draw on her fine biography and also Christiaan Jörg, 'Jan Albert Sichterman: A Groninger Nabob and Art-Collector', in *All of One Company: The VOC in Biographical Perspective* (Utrecht: HES Uitgevers, 1986), 178–95 and the revised and extended version in *Jan Albert Sichterman, 1692–1764: Een imponerende Groninger liefhebber van kunst*, eds Egge Knol Christiaan and Denise A. Campbell (Groningen: Groninger Museum, 2014), 9–25.

10 Zakiuddin Ahmad, 'Slavery in Eighteenth-Century Bengal (1757–1785)', *Journal of the Asiatic Society of Pakistan* XI (1966), 73.

11 Ahmad, 'Slavery in Eighteenth-Century Bengal', 179.

12 The Fifth Earl of Kintore (Anton Adriaan Lord Falconer of Haulkerton; his mother was the daughter of a Groningen patrician) married Sichterman's youngest daughter Christina Elisabeth in 1766; *Jan Albert Sichterman, 1692–1764*, 34–5; Kühne-van Diggelen, *Jan Albert Sichterman*, 73.

13 Kühne-van Diggelen, *Jan Albert Sichterman*, 51–2.

14 Most of the information in this paragraph comes from Kühne-van Diggelen, *Jan Albert Sichterman*, 62–5, 70–1.

15 Kühne-van Diggelen, *Jan Albert Sichterman*, 77. The cargo list of the return fleet was printed in the *European Mercurius* of July 1745, the last three items on the list probably belonging to Sichterman.

16 See Martin van den Broeke, *Jan Arends: Buitenplaatsen op Walcheren* (Alphen aan den Rijn: Canaletto, 2001), 74–6.

17 Martin van den Broeke, *Jan Arends*, 75.

18 Charles Boxer, *The Dutch Seaborne Empire 1600–1800* (London: Penguin, 1965), 210.

19 'Mes fils pourroient aller aussy voit la Zélande, et donner une visite à Monsieur Dishoeck dont mon ainé porte le nom, ainsy qu'à Monsieur Huysman, mon cousin', Kühne-van Diggelen, *Jan Albert Sichterman*, 61.

20 Lequin, 'Het personeel', 58.

21 Compare Feith, 'De Bengaalsche Sichterman', *passim*; Jörg, 'Jan Albert Sichterman', *passim*; *Jan Albert Sichterman, 1692–1764*, 21–5; Daniel Lunsingh Scheurleer, *Chinese Export Porcelain: Chine de Commande* (London: Faber and Faber, 1974), 100–25 (especially Plates 101, 102).

22 See Femme S. Gaastra and Wilma Seybel, 'Een Kollumer koopman in de Oost: Eyso de Wendt (1718–1780)', *De Vrije Fries* 74 (1994) 85–102.

23 Jochem Kroes, *Chinese Armorial Porcelain for the Dutch Market* (Zwolle: Waanders BV, 2007), 94, 96–7.

24 Osvald Sirén, *China and Gardens of Europe of the Eighteenth Century* (New York: The Ronald Press Company, 1950), 62–3, 171–2.

25 See Wim Meulenkamp, *Theekoepels en tuinhuizen in de Vechtstreek* (Weesp: Uitgeverij Heureka, 1995). Until now most authors have viewed *chinoiserie* in eighteenth-century Dutch gardens (from the 1760s) as an aspect of French Rococo influence, in the so-called '*les jardins Anglo-Chinois*'; see Martin van den Broeke, *Jan Arends*, 31, 40, 112–13. However, it might be fruitful to look at global connections between the lifestyles of Western elites in the East and garden architecture in Europe.

26 Groninger Archives, Family archive Sichterman, inv.nr. 289. 'Black servant' Klaasje would have the biggest legacy (300 guilders); if one of the family could offer him a job than he or she 'will profit from this legacy'.

27 Beckeringh also made drawings of Sichterman's country house and a plan of his estate. These are kept in the Groninger Archives and the Groninger Museum, respectively.

28 Kühne-van Diggelen, *Jan Albert Sichterman*, 105–6.

29 Compare Peter Marshall, *East Indian Fortunes: The British in Bengal in the Eighteenth Century* (Oxford: Oxford University Press, 1976).

30 Boxer, 'On the Eighteenth Century', 7.

31 Edward W. Said, *Orientalism* (New York: Vintage Books, 1994; orig. 1978), 2. As founder of the early English Orientalists in India, Said mentions the legal scholar William Jones, who wrote – among other things – about the 'Best Mode of Governing Bengal'; Said, *Orientalism*, 77–8.

32 See, for example, the highly stimulating essays by Emile de Bruijn, Kate Smith, Patricia F. Ferguson and Helen Clifford on 'Eastern connections, adaptations and

imitations' in *The Country house: Material Culture and Consumption*, eds Jon Stobart and Andrew Hann (Swindon: Historic England, 2016), 95–133.

33 Georg Simmel, 'Fashion', *The American Journal of Sociology* 62 (1957; orig. 1904), 541–58; Norbert Elias, *The Court Society* (Oxford: Blackwell, 1983; orig. 1933); Pierre Bourdieu, *Distinction: A Social Critique of the Judgement of Taste* (Oxford: Blackwell, 1984; orig. 1979); Jean-Pascal Daloz, *The Sociology of Elite Distinction. From Theoretical to Comparative Perspectives* (Basingstoke: Palgrave Macmillan, 2010); for luxury in Paris around 1750, see (including Voltaire's ideas on taste for luxury from exotic regions) Charissa Bremer-David, 'Introduction: In Defense of Luxury', in *Paris: Life & Luxury in the Eighteenth Century*, ed. Charissa Bremer-David (Los Angeles: J. Paul Getty Museum) 1–11.

34 Daloz, *Elite Distinction*, 12.

35 During the eighteenth century, the barriers between the lifestyles of the more 'bourgeois' elite of rich merchants and the more 'noble' or 'aristocratic' elites in the Northern Netherlands were blurring; old and new forms of luxury intermingled into a more European, 'Grand Tour-inspired' lifestyle – see also the chapter on the Southern Netherlands by Blondé and De Laet. In the first half of the eighteenth century the Dutch Republic was also strongly involved in military campaigns and battles in the Southern Netherlands; many officers and diplomats (including our young Sichterman and his elder brother) in Dutch service could experience elite lifestyle and ethos in many towns in the Southern Netherlands.

36 Feith, 'De Bengaalsche Sichterman', 49; see for the original source *Joh. Bernouilli's Sammlung kurzer Reisebeschreibungen*, Bänder XIII and XIV (Berlin 1784); see also Gerda C. Huisman, '*Bibliothecae instructissimae:* Geleerd boekenbezit in Groningen in de 17e en 18e eeuw', in *Onderwijs en onderzoek: Studie en wetenschap aan de academie van Groningen in de 17e en 18e eeuw*, ed. A. H. Huussen Jr. (Hilversum: Verloren, 2003) 299–328. During the late Ming dynasty (1368–1644), Chinese connoisseurs of ancient porcelain, acting as arbiters of taste, wrote treatises about what should be owned and what avoided in civilized society. These books were popular among nouveaux riches in China. Europeans knew nothing of this status and taste game. In the eyes of Chinese gentlemen, the Chinese porcelain (especially carrack porcelain) that the Dutch exported to Europe was of inferior quality. Moreover, Chinese consumers did not appreciate the export ware made for the European market. Cf. Timothy Brook, *Vermeer's hat: The Seventeenth Century and the Dawn of the Global World* (London: Profile Books, 2009) 70–6.

37 *Catalogus van (. . .) Nederduitsche, Fransche en Latijnsche boeken* (Groningen: Hajo Spandow, 1764); University Library Groningen.

38 On this kind of paternalism: Dienke Hondius, *Blackness in Western Europe: Racial Patterns of Paternalism and Exclusion* (New Brunswick and London: Transaction Publishers, 2014); for Groningen: Lieuwe Jongsma, *Slavery Dynasty: Networks of Kinship around Transatlantic Slavery and Slave Trade in the Province of Groningen 1622–1863* (Groningen: Research Master's Thesis, 2015); for Britain: *Slavery and the British Country House*, eds Madge Dresser and Andrew Hann (Swindon: English Heritage, 2013).

39 Jan de Vries, *The Industrious Revolution: Consumer Behavior and the Household Economy, 1650 to the Present* (Cambridge: Cambridge University Press, 2008) 65–6. See also Jon Stobart and Mark Rothery, *Consumption and the Country House* (Oxford: Oxford University Press, 2016), esp. 7–15, 51–2.

5

Fashion and Luxury in Eighteenth-Century Germany

Michael North

This chapter will elucidate the fashion and luxury debate in eighteenth-century Germany, focusing on the role of the *Journal des Luxus und der Moden* (Journal of Luxury and Fashion). Although the German states were some distance from the European centres of cultural exchange, such as Paris and London, German periodicals like the *Journal des Luxus und der Moden* made art and books as well as fashion trends, theatre performances and concerts accessible to a growing number of cultural consumers – whether materially or virtually. French and English fashions competed with each other in the luxury journals for influence over the homes and gardens of German burghers and aristocratic elites. Already Daniel Purdy has made it clear that the luxury journals are constructions of luxury and fashion, since their rhetoric was often received by the readers as fact.[1] On this basis, I will argue that the luxury debate and the 'luxury reality' examined by historians are often mere constructions. Furthermore, I will examine how the *Journal des Luxus und der Moden* constructed the role of cultural consumer, providing, for example, systematic product information and overviews of the market and advertisements, and even addressing its clientele directly as 'ladies of taste'. References to the local production of luxury goods also created a regional location and identity for consumption and taste. Finally, I will peep into the wardrobes of certain consumers to examine whether the discourse of the journals had any impact on the 'real' fashion world.

Definitions of fashion (*Mode*) and luxury

Around the middle of the seventeenth century the word *Mode* (fashion) entered the German language, taken from the French phrase *à la mode*. The word evolved from its original use for clothing fashions to a more general reference to lifestyles and all they entailed. In this way, a body of writing emerged around the notion of à la mode, which was often quite critical of France.

In the eighteenth century we find a number of definitions of fashion or *Mode*. For example, Zedler's *Universal Lexicon* noted that fashion encompassed '[. . .] more generally, and in its broadest meaning, the manner, mode, usage, custom, genre, form, shape or pattern, but more particularly the common or usual mode of dress, furnishings, coaches and rooms, buildings, manufactures, manners of speaking and writing, compliments, ceremonies and other pomp, feasts and other modes of living'.[2] Although other authors, such as Adelung in his 1798 Dictionary, supported this view and understood fashion as 'the established manner of deportment in social life, customs, habits and in the narrower sense, the changeable mode of dress',[3] in general usage the word came to be used above all to refer to clothing styles. Friedrich Justin Bertuch, editor of what was probably the most influential lifestyle magazine of the era, the *Journal des Luxus und der Moden*, also fought against this restriction of meaning. This effort is evident in a particularly drastic example of 1794 in which he published an article 'On the Invention and Antiquity of the Guillotine', justifying its inclusion as follows:

> After all, we are not writing a Ladies' Journal or a work for the dressing-table, in which one seeks nought but nectar and ambrosia, and wishes to breathe only the sweet scents of Elysium. We leave that to others. Nay, we are writing the chronicle of the Spirit of our Age, to the degree that it is ruled, guided and shaped by Fashion; and from this standpoint one will easily see that our field of observations is very wide, and the manifestations therein highly diverse and rich in contrasts.[4]

Friedrich Justin Bertuch was a cultural entrepreneur who worked as treasurer for Duke Carl August of Saxony-Weimar, built up a large publishing house based on periodicals and established the Landes-Industrie-Comptoir, a trading business for luxury goods. That is why he had the idea to publish a luxury journal with monthly reports:

> on each new fashion and invention as it appears in France, England, Germany and Italy, in whatever branch of luxury it may be [. . .]. The subjects of interest to us are, thus 1) female and male dress; 2) millinery; 3) jewellery; 4) knickknacks; 5) furniture; 6) all manner of tableware and drinking vessels, for example silver, porcelain, glasses, etc; 7) equipage, both wagons and horse trappings and liveries; 8) house and room furnishings and decorations; 9) gardens and country houses.[5]

The journal also published accounts 'from social life' as well as on art and literature, which later came to be known as *feuilletons*. Bertuch combined fashion with luxury, the definition of which also expanded in the eighteenth century so that it no longer had the solely negative connotations of excess, ostentation or display; various scholarly disciplines also treated luxury from different perspectives.[6] No one expressed this ambiguity better than Friedrich Justin Bertuch himself in the introduction to his *Journal*:

> According to followers of the physiocratic system, Luxury is the Scourge of the State! It squanders the rich revenues on fruitless expenditures, prevents reproduction, enervates the physiocratic forces of the Nation, dissolves all sense of Morality and Honour, ruins the well-being of families and supplies the State with hordes of beggars!
>
> Luxury, says the financier and the technologist, is the richest source for the State; the almighty motive force of Industry, and the strongest mechanism of Circulation. It erases all traces of Barbarism in Manners, creates Arts, Sciences, Commerce and Trades, increases the Population and Forces of the State, and leads to Delight and Joy of Living! – Who of the two is wrong? – Both, we believe, when they make absolute claims about this important matter. The entire dispute rests upon an incorrect, or at least an insufficiently pure definition of Luxury.[7]

This discourse on fashion, which brought forth its own media, was not new for the eighteenth century; as so often, the phenomenon originated in France. Bertuch was familiar with, and inspired by, a long tradition of fashion books and journals in France and England, such as Rétif de la Bretonne's *Monuments du costume*, which went through fifteen editions between 1774 and 1793[8] or the *Calendrier des Dames* of 1750. Direct forerunners of Bertuch's *Journal* were the *Journal des Dames* and the *Lady's Magazine*. All of these periodicals placed fashion and taste in the broader context of taste formation by linking art and fashion, thus reaffirming the cultural conditionality of fashion. New English magazines such as the *Fashionable Court Guide* and the *Gallery of Fashion* propagated English dress on the Continent and elevated London to the capital of fashion. This did not create a new trend, but merely bowed to a movement in taste that had been gaining momentum for some time.

The material realities of London and Paris arrived in Germany mainly as literary constructs. Particularly outside the large urban centres such as Hamburg or Frankfurt, it was magazines, novels and letters that helped to constitute Western European consumer culture. As in other cultural fields, the German territories lagged behind Western Europe in the area of fashion.[9] The magazines accordingly illustrated the new fashions in word and image, which also made it possible to produce cheaper imitations. Coloured engravings brought the clothes alive and formed the basis for their artisanal and technical reproduction. Germans were torn between the new English trends and old French influences. While the (North German) educated middle classes developed a yearning for the English way of life, Paris continued to be the model for aristocratic elegance. Even the new 'English style' spread and was marketed to the Continent by way of Paris. The cultural chasm could run through families, often along gender lines, the *Journal des Luxus und der Moden* noting that:

> The inhabitants of Mecklenburg are like other Germans; they imitate both the English and the French, though with one important difference. The men arrange their clothes, their households, their carriages and gardens in the English style, while elegant ladies still follow the lead of Parisian fashion dealers, who send their outdated goods to the North.[10]

In this way gender roles were constructed and then cleverly supplemented with national stereotypes, such as the Anglo-French dualism, in order to keep readers interested. 'And yet it is not France alone whose magic wand we must fear. England and the perfected craft of her factories will and must necessarily become just as dangerous to us.'[11] It was, after all, the new English culture of commodities or consumption that was also becoming increasingly attractive on the Continent:

> The tasteful simplicity and solidity that England succeeded in bestowing upon all of her manufactured goods so recommends itself to and attracts us Germans that at present the word English [or] English goods already has

> such an irresistibly magical allure for us, and has become nearly synonymous with perfection and beauty in works of craft.[12]

Bertuch accordingly reported monthly not just on new fashions and inventions from abroad, but also on social life as well as art and literature. As time went on, these reviews of plays, concerts and books, which Bertuch had not originally planned, took up more and more space in the magazine, so that he eventually changed the title of his publication to reflect the new content. From 1813 it was known as *Journal für Luxus, Mode und Gegenstände der Kunst* (Luxury, Fashion and Art Objects) and from 1815 as *Journal für Literatur, Kunst, Luxus und Mode* (Literature, Art, Luxury and Fashion).

The *Journal* was accompanied by the so-called intelligence gazette (*Intelligenzblatt*) as an independent advertising supplement in which publishers, manufacturers and merchants could promote their wares. These ranged from English tea-urns and cucumber slicers to editions of prints from Rost Art Dealers in Leipzig, new sheet music, wallpapers, musical clocks and 'balloon stoves'. The range of luxury goods was quite comparable with that available in England. The luxury trades in the areas of silver, ceramics, glass, clocks and furniture maintained a leading position until technical innovations made it possible in the eighteenth century to put cheaper, mass-produced imitations on the market – including tea tins of silver-leaf or brass instead of solid silver and Wedgwood stoneware instead of porcelain – which soon asserted themselves in the fashion cycle.[13] The same can be said of Bertuch's offer of 'beautiful Wedgwood so-called Cameo Buttons, finished in the Stile of antique Gems'[14] as well as cheaper imitations made in Saxony-Weimar. These luxury products could be purchased from Bertuch's trading business, the Landes-Industrie-Comptoir, which maintained a putting-out system with sample fairs. By perusing the *Journal* and ordering from Bertuch, the reader-consumer participated in the European world of commodities and consumer culture.

Reading was a decisive factor in the formation of consumer desires and the literary discourse about them included particular aesthetic objects in personal lifestyles.[15] The *Journal* accordingly became an important voice in the cultural life of the emergent bourgeoisie, influencing both the traditionally Francophile aristocracy and above all the functional elites with their as yet uneducated tastes – making it an extraordinary source for historians.[16] For readers, the

Figure 5.1 Subscribers to the *Journal des Luxus und der Moden*, 1791.

yearly subscription price of 4 talers for twelve issues was also affordable. That the magazine was also an economic success is evident not just from the subscription figures (1,488 in 1788 and 1,765 in 1799, with reading societies and other forms of communal reading raising the number of readers to perhaps ten times these figures), but also the longevity of this periodical, which appeared monthly for no fewer than forty-one years. An examination of the subscribers shows a spread of the *Journal* in the Holy Roman Empire and in the neighbouring countries as well, for example in Copenhagen or Riga (see Figure 5.1).

National styles and the propagation of a national taste

What did the *Journal des Luxus und der Moden* convey to German readers? The very first volume of the magazine featured colour plates showing the latest English fashions for men and women. The English ladies' costume was described as follows:

> It is extremely flattering to a well-proportioned figure, shows a beautiful waist in all its grace thanks to the bodice, which is tight below and wide and somewhat loose above, and in general possesses the noble and unostentatious appearance of tasteful simplicity and decorum that so enhances the charms of the fair sex.[17]

All this notwithstanding, the *Journal* reported more frequently on French or Parisian fashion, although the editors' sympathies lay with English style and culture more generally. This circumstance is clear, for example, from Bertuch's plea for comfortable and suitable dress for children, the success of which the *Journal* noted in 1798. In the spirit of the Enlightenment, the *Journal* presented new clothing for children, for 'in his or her dress, too, a child should look like a child, and not a grown man or a little lady'.[18] English models were influential here, but so too were new ideals of child-rearing. Accordingly, Bertuch also offered advice on raising children, suggestions of appropriate games and later a series of children's literature.[19]

Despite his sympathies for the British Isles, Bertuch was well aware of the competition raging between English functionality and French elegance, and thus of a cultural division that split Germany in two:

> The goods sold at the Frankfurt and Leipzig fairs have now been distributed to the storehouses of fashion everywhere, and provide an overview of new inventions and arrivals in this field. France offers us its left hand across the Rhine and the Main. The chief emporium of elegant sales is Frankfurt, Mainz etc. Leipzig, in contrast, and other northern cities such as Hamburg and Bremen enrich central Germany with English products. For that reason, one can surely wager that the former part of Germany will be supplied with more tasteful, elegant, frivolous and graceful articles of fashion, and the latter with finer, daintier, more solid but not seldom also stiffer and more affected ones.[20]

In promoting English fashions the *Journal*'s attitude towards Vienna was correspondingly critical, since the city was allegedly still wholly in French hands. And yet, however critical they were of France, writers were compelled to note that the success of English fashion also hindered the development of an independent German tradition:

> It is striking how England now sets the tone far more than France in all fancy goods, and fills the German market with them. I have good reason to doubt that Germany gains thereby, for English fancy goods, as fancy goods, are just as subject to the frivolous changes in fashion, but too solid and too dear. Germany can thus easily end up twice as indebted to England as it was to France.[21]

At the same time, efforts were also under way to distance Germans from the dictates of French taste. These efforts were nothing new: in the very first volume of the *Journal*, Bertuch had called for a promotion of native trade and industry and thus also for increasing consumption among local German elites, particularly the functional elites. Thus, in this first volume in 1786 Bertuch launched the test balloon of national dress and posed the question, 'Would it be useful and possible to introduce a German national costume?' In so doing, he took up old stereotypes and mercantilist ideas, according to which the slavish emulation of the French was deleterious to morals, finances and the balance of trade, and deemed certain characteristics of national dress to be necessary. He wrote:

> Thus, only two points are essential here:
>
> 1) the choice of clothing, and
> 2) the manner in which it would be agreed upon and introduced.
>
> As to the first point, I believe we can accept the following principles. The clothing must be
>
> a) cheap
> b) of colours that do not easily show dirt, durable, easy to wash and neither invented by nor dependent upon the whims of fashion;
> c) appropriate for all ages
> d) easily acquired by the distinguished and the common, by rich and poor alike
> e) adapted to our climate
> f) not phantastical
> g) not deforming to the body
> h) bearing the mark of Germanness
> i) wearable in all seasons [. . .].
>
> There are, alas, some people who ridicule all things; there are others who see something dangerous or perfidious everywhere; finally, there are still others

> who find no good in anything unless it was discovered or proposed by themselves or some party to which they belong. That is sad, and from such as they I must surely expect no justice from any quarter for my recommendations, but this does not bother me. I am conscious of making these suggestions out of good, honest and patriotic German intent. I belong to no party, have devised these ideas on my own, and would be mightily pleased if the matter were to succeed, without any honour or even mention of my name.[22]

When a woman reader announced a 'female rebellion', the idea was swiftly dropped,[23] although, Bertuch found himself in good company in his efforts on behalf of German national costume. Justus Möser had already called for the introduction of a national dress code, graduated by rank, which was intended to counteract the efforts of contemporaries to represent status through clothing and thus to combat sartorial ostentation.

Ultimately, this idea only bore fruit outside of Germany: in 1791 the Danish Academy of Sciences offered a prize for the best proposal concerning the introduction of national dress.[24] The entrants referred to the Swedish reform of 1778 as well as the sumptuary codes in St Petersburg and Russia's Baltic provinces.[25] Nevertheless, German fashions were propagated both overtly and covertly, which even had some effect in the area of male attire. Thus, for example, in the first volume of the *Journal*, a picture of a French horseman in the *Cabinet des Modes* is juxtaposed with the ideal of a German horseman, although the influence of English style on the latter is unmistakeable. In this, the *Journal* picked up seamlessly where a previous fashion, namely the Werther costume, had left off. The cult of *The Sorrows of Young Werther* changed the manners, leisure activities, reading behaviour and clothing of the younger generation of the educated middle class. Werther fashion (a blue frock coat, yellow waistcoat and knee breeches) was thus the first trend in eighteenth-century German culture to be inspired by a literary discourse and not a court, although Carl August of Saxony-Weimar made the costume (known as the 'Werther-Anzug') popular at his own court. Thus began – and this was central for all magazines – a culture of fashion in which literary fiction could easily set in motion trends in material culture. With the Werther costume, young men adopted an identity of their own, so that appearing in public in it was comparable to wearing jeans at a festive occasion nowadays. The success of the Werther outfit was not simply a product of reading, however; positive associations with the English gentry and the Prussian military also played a role.

The propagation of national taste was a characteristic shared by many European fashion magazines, which often employed clichéd references to other European countries, especially England and France. By tracking down new trends and influencing taste, the magazines sought to fill the gap in the market between vendors, producers and traders.[26] By reading the *Journal des Luxus und der Moden*, for example, readers throughout the German territories participated in the new world of European commodities.

Wardrobe realities

As we have seen, the *Journal des Luxus und der Moden* affords interesting insights into the fashion discourse of the late eighteenth and early nineteenth century. To what extent was this discourse reflected in material reality? First, we need to ask how widely read the magazines were and whether they succeeded in realizing the new trends in the European centres in a fashion cycle of five to seven months. We know that the *Journal* had several hundred subscribers in each of the large cities and was disseminated in smaller towns at least through reading societies, so it was widely read across modern Germany. How this translated into the choices made by individual consumers is less easily traced. The material reality that we find, for example using estate inventories, forms only a partial reflection of the tastes and fashions advocated in the magazines; but this may be a result of the unfortunately rather sparse inventories that have come down to us for the decisive period in the modernization of dress, between 1770 and 1790.

Some inventories certainly appear to confirm the developments familiar to us from the fashion periodicals. Thus in 1772, the Hamburg shopkeeper's widow Anna Plaehn left two *contuches* (a kind of overdress) of cotton in addition to two of silk, reflecting English fashion.[27] The English clothes mentioned in Münster inventories of the late eighteenth century indicate even more clearly the gradual adaptation to such taste; the preference for cotton material or cotton dresses (perhaps even chemise gowns) is also in keeping with this orientation towards English fashion.[28] A willingness to make qualitative changes becomes evident along with the increase and differentiation in the clothing, gloves, hats, cloaks and other accessories mentioned by the inventories, which increasingly appeared in a wide variety of colours and fabrics.[29]

We also have evidence of new men's fashions, at least in the estate inventory of the Jewish merchant Friedrich Maximilian Beer of Frankfurt, who died in 1795. He left a wide assortment of clothing, which included not just a cotton dressing gown, a silk dressing gown embroidered with yellow flowers (lined in taffeta, with a matching waistcoat), fourteen pairs of underpants, thirty-seven shirts and countless pairs of cotton and silk stockings, but also green woollen riding breeches, black jersey trousers, black cashmere trousers, black silk trousers, salt-and-pepper cloth trousers, grey cashmere trousers and striped 'Nanking' trousers of brown and yellow cotton after a Chinese model. Among his coats, a grey English cloth coat, a salt-and-pepper frock coat, a striped woollen frock coat and a blue coat with yellow buttons (in the Werther style) particularly stand out. His collection of thirty-six different waistcoats ranged from white muslin to white silk with a coloured border, and also included versions in red cashmere, yellow stripes, black stripes, green checks or half-silk flowered embroidery.[30] With these outfits he could easily approximate the ideal of a 'London buck' presented in the 1791 *Journal*, as well as the Werther fashion. Moreover, Beer's collection contradicts the prejudice fomented by the magazines that only women succumbed to fashion mania. To what extent he was exceptional in this respect, or whether such sumptuous male wardrobes were common, is a question for further research, especially using estate inventories of the early nineteenth century.

From these examples, it is clear that Bertuch's assertion that 'fashion is indeed a cosmopolitan, who does not permit herself to be enclosed in a single country, and according to her innate penchant for contradiction prefers to rig herself out with contraband',[31] is not without justification. Thus, on the one hand, a German fashion magazine like the *Journal des Luxus und der Moden* addressed its readers as members of a nation purportedly backward in relation to fashion, and on the other it measured German fashion trends against a Western European (fashion) identity, thereby paying homage to German progress. English and French developments were compared with trends in Hamburg, Mecklenburg, Berlin and Vienna, offering various potential identities to aristocratic elites and members of the educated middle classes. In this way, the *Journal des Luxus und der Moden*, like other periodicals, created a virtual marketplace for boundless cultural consumption.

Only against the background of the Napoleonic occupation, and above all in the political journalism of the Wars of Liberation, were high-necked dark dresses stylized as a 'German national costume', and were also promoted in the pages of the *Journal* in 1814 in a mood of patriotic euphoria. A direct line was drawn here between the invasion of French customs along with French dress and the demise of the Holy Roman Empire, since the former had allegedly undermined German customs and with them 'the foundations of the throne and constitutions'.[32] For that reason, in 1814 a Munich woman suggested clothing reform, with the aim of 'the greatest possible simplification of garments' and the introduction of a 'formal dress code for all classes'. She recommended that the uniform of Bavaria's *Landwehr* or reserve army, which was already considered as a national costume there, be adopted as national dress for all German men.[33] Bavarian dress – which has survived into the twenty-first century with loden jackets and dirndls – appears, however, to have had as little lasting influence as any of the other excessively patriotic fashion tips of the period around 1815.[34]

Conclusion

The role of the consumer was constructed in various ways in the journals and intelligence gazettes. The *Journal des Luxus und der Moden* created the role of cultural consumer through systematic product information, overviews of the market and advertisements; it even addressed this clientele directly as 'ladies of taste' or 'connoisseurs of fine and beneficent luxury'.[35] The articles, illustrations and advertisements demonstrated to readers the latest fashions in clothing and showed them which home furnishings were indispensable for an elegant way of life. References to the local production of luxury goods created a further regional location and identity for consumption and taste. This also applied to the print editions sold by art dealers or the newest sheet music, which – although published in different parts of Germany – could be purchased through periodicals with local roots. The periodicals instructed their readers in matters of taste while confirming – as the journal *Charis* did in 1805 for the 'cultivated' ladies of Leipzig – their vast superiority 'in the culture of taste and manners' to the 'female world' of other cities.[36] In this way they located (cultural) consumers, regardless of their regional or national roots, in a European culture of taste. Regional and national identities thus entered into dialogue with the 'entire cultivated world'.[37]

Notes

1 Daniel L. Purdy, *The Tyranny of Elegance: Consumer Cosmopolitanism in the Era of Goethe* (Baltimore: Johns Hopkins University Press, 1998).

2 '[. . .] überhaupt und nach seinem weitläufftigsten Verstande die Art, Weise, Gebrauch, Gewohnheit, Gattung, Gestalt, Manier, Façon oder Muster, besonders aber die gewöhnliche oder gebräuchliche Tracht und Manier in Kleidungen, Meublen, Kutschen und Zimmern, Gebäuden, Manufacturen, Schreib- und Red-Arten, Complimenten, Ceremonien und anderm Gepränge, Gastereyen und übrigen Lebens=Arten.' Johann Heinrich Zedler, *Großes Vollständiges Universal-Lexikon* (Leipzig and Halle, 1739; reprint, Graz: Akademische Drucks-und Verlagsanstalt, 1995), vol. 21 'Mi-Mt', 700–1.

3 Christoph Adelung, *Grammatisch-kritisches Wörterbuch der Hochdeutschen Mundart, mit beständiger Vergleichung der übrigen Mundarten, besonders aber der Oberdeutschen*, 2nd edn, vol. 3 (Leipzig: Breitkopf, 1798), cols 253–4, quoted according to Doris Kuhles, 'Das "Journal des Luxus und der Moden" (1786–1827). Zur Entstehung seines inhaltlichen Profils und seiner journalistischen Struktur', in *Friedrich Justin Bertuch (1747–1822). Verleger, Schriftsteller und Unternehmer im klassischen Weimar*, eds Gerhard R. Kaiser and Siegfried Seifert (Tübingen: Niemeyer, 2000), 489–99, quote on 494, and *Journal des Luxus und der Moden 1786–1827. Analytische Bibliographie mit sämtlichen 517 schwarzweißen und 976 farbigen Abbildungen der Originalzeitschrift* (Munich: K. G. Saur, 2003). Still important is Ruth Wies, 'Das Journal des Luxus und der Moden (1786–1827), ein Spiegel kultureller Strömungen der Goethezeit' (unpublished PhD thesis, University of Munich, 1953). For the aspect of fashion, see Gisela Jaacks, 'Modechronik, Modekritik oder Modediktat? Zu Funktion, Thematik und Berichtstil früher deutscher Modejournale am Beispiel des "Journal des Luxus und der Moden"', *Waffen- und Kostümkunde* 24 (1982), 58–61.

4 'Wir schreiben ja kein Damen-Journal oder ein Toilettenwerk, worinn man nichts als Nektar und Ambroisa sucht, und nur Wohlgerüche aus Elysium athmen will.

Dieß sey Andern überlaßen. Nein, wir schreiben die Chronik des Geistes unser Zeit, in so fern er von der Mode beherrscht, geleitet und geformt wird; und aus diesem Standpuncte sieht man leicht, daß unser Feld der Beobachtungen sehr groß, und die Erscheinungen darauf höchst verschieden und abstechend sind.' *Journal des Luxus und der Moden* (April 1794), 193.

5 '[. . .] von jeder neuen Mode und Erfindung, so wie sie in Frankreich, England, Teutschland und Italien erscheint, in welchem Zweige von Luxus es auch sey, [. . .]. Unsere Gegenstände darinnen sind also 1) weibliche und männliche Kleidung; 2) Putz; 3) Schmuck; 4) Nippes; 5) Ammeublement, 6) alle Arten von Tisch- und Trinckgeschirre, als Silber, Porcellain, Gläser usw.; 7) Equipage, sowohl Wagen als Pferdezeug, und Livreen; 8) Häuser- und Zimmereinrichtung und Verzierung, 9) Gärten und Landhäuser'. *Journal des Luxus und der Moden* (reprint, Leipzig: Edition Leipzig, 1967), 29–30.

6 See *Consumers and Luxury: Consumer Culture in Europe 1650–1850*, eds Maxine Berg and Helen Clifford (Manchester: Manchester University Press, 1999), and *Luxury in the Eighteenth Century: Debates, Desires and Delectable Goods*, eds Maxine Berg and Elizabeth Eger (London: Palgrave Macmillan, 2003).

7 'Luxus sagt der Anhänger des physiokratischen Systems, ist die Pest der Staaten! Er verschwendet den reichen Ertrag zu unfruchtbaren Ausgaben; hindert die Reproduction; entnervt die physiokratischen Kräfte der Nation; lößt alles Gefühl für Moralität und Ehre auf; zerrüttet den Wohlstand der Familien, und liefert dem Staate Schaaren Bettler! Luxus, sagt der Finanzier und der Technolog, ist die reichste Quelle für den Staat; der allmächtige Hebel der Industrie, und das kräftigste Triebwerk der Circulation. Er verwischt alle Spuren der Barbarey in den Sitten; schafft Künste, Wissenschaften, Handel und Gewerbe; vermehrt die Population und die Kräfte des Staates, und bewürkt Genuß und Glück des Lebens! – Wer von Beyden hat Unrecht? – Beyde, däucht uns, wenn sie unbedingt über diese wichtige Materie deklamieren. Der ganze Streit ruht auf einem unrichtigen oder wenigstens nicht rein genug bestimmten Begriffe vom Luxus'. *Journal des Luxus und der Moden*, introduction to vol. 1, no. 1 (January 1786), 4–5.

8 Daniel Roche, *The Culture of Clothing: Dress and Fashion in the Ancien Regime* (Cambridge: Cambridge University Press, 1994), 13–15.

9 For the following see Michael North, *Material Delight and the Joy of Living: Cultural Consumption in the Age of Enlightenment in Germany* (Aldershot: Ashgate, 2008), 45–60.

10 'Die Meklenborger sind, den übrigen Teutschen gleich, Nachahmer der Engländer und Franzosen; doch mit dem Unterschiede, daß die Männer ihre Tracht, ihren Hausrath, ihre Equipagen und Gärten nach englischem Geschmack anordnen, hingegen die geputzte Dame sich noch nach dem Eigensinn einer Pariser

Modehändlerin richtet, die ihre verlegene Waare nach Norden schickt.' *Journal des Luxus und der Moden* (September 1787): 301. English translation in Purdy, *Tyranny of Elegance,* 176.

11 'Jedoch Frankreich ist es nicht allein, dessen Zauberstab wir zu fürchten haben. England und der vervollkommnete Kunstfleiß seiner Fabriken wird und muß uns nothwendig ebenso gefährlich werden.' *Journal des Luxus und der Moden* (August 1793), 410. Justus Möser also expressed similar ideas, recommending the introduction of a German fashion journal to reduce the expense of acquiring information from France. Furthermore, this fashion journal would enable domestic industries to compete with France; see Wolfgang Cilleßen, 'Modezeitschriften', in *Von Almanach bis Zeitung. Ein Handbuch der Medien in Deutschland 1700–1800,* eds Ernst Fischer, Wilhelm Haefs and York-Gothart Mix (Munich: Beck, 1999), 207–24, quote: 219–20.

12 'Die geschmackvolle Simplicität und Solidität, welche England allen seinen Fabrikwaaren zu geben gewußt hat, ist für uns Teutsche so ausserordentlich empfehlend und anlockend, daß das Wort Englisch, englische Waare, schon dermalen einen unwiderstehlichen Zauberreiz für uns hat, und beynahe ein Synonym der Vollkommenheit und Schönheit bey Werken des Kunstfleißes worden ist.' *Journal des Luxus und der Moden* (August 1793), 410.

13 Maxine Berg, 'French Fancy and Cool Britannia: The Fashion Markets of Early Modern Europe', in *Fiere e mercati nella integrazione delle economie Europe secc. XIII-XVIII*, ed. S. Cavaciocchi (Prato: Le Monnier, 2001), 540–46, and Maxine Berg, *Luxury & Pleasure in Eighteenth-Century Britain* (Oxford: Oxford University Press, 2005), 85–110.

14 *Journal des Luxus und der Moden* (August 1786): 295–6.

15 Astrid Ackermann, *Paris, London und die europäische Provinz: Die frühen europäischen Modejournale (1770–1830)* (Frankfurt: Lang, 2005), 107–8.

16 See also Purdy, *Tyranny of Elegance,* 1–21.

17 'Sie ist einem wohlgewachsenen Körper überaus vortheilhaft, zeigt eine schöne Taille, durch das unten enge und oben weite und etwas lockere Corset, in ihrer ganzen Grazie und hat überhaupt das edle prunklose Ansehen einer geschmackvollen Simplicität, und Wohlanständigkeit, welches die Reize des schönen Geschlechts so sehr erhöhet.' *Journal des Luxus und der Moden* (April 1786), 141.

18 *Journal des Luxus und der Moden* (February 1787): 17ff.

19 Ulfhardt Stoewer, 'Der "Kulturunternehmer" Friedrich Justin Bertuch im Spiegel seines "Journals des Luxus und der Moden"' (Unpublished dissertation as part of the state secondary school teachers' examination, University of Greifswald, 2001).

20 'Die Frankfurter und Leipziger Meßwaren sind jetzt wieder allenthalben in den Magazinen der Mode vertheilt, und gewähren eine Uebersicht des neu Erfundenen und Angekommenen in diesem Gebiete. Frankreich reicht uns die Linke über den Rhein und Main. Sein Stapelplatz des eleganten Absatzes ist Frankfurt, Mainz u.s.w. Leipzig hingegen und andere nördliche Städte, wie Hamburg und Bremen, bereichern Mittel-Teutschland mit den englischen Produkten. Daher man auch sicher darauf rechnen kann, daß jener Theil Teutschlands geschmackvoller, eleganter, frivoler und anmutiger, dieser hingegen feiner, zierlicher, solider, aber auch nicht selten steifer und gezierter in seinen Modeartikeln besorgt ist'. *Journal des Luxus und der Moden* (June 1802), 353, quoted in *Frankfurter Modespiegel,* exhibition catalogue, Historical Museum of Frankfurt am Main (Frankfurt, 1962), with an introduction by Bernward Deneke.

21 'Es ist auffallend wie anjezt England weit mehr als Frankreich in allen Mode-Waaren den Ton angiebt, und in Teutschland den Markt damit füllt. Daß Teutschland dabey gewinnt, zweifle ich mit Recht; denn die Englischen Mode-Waaren, sind als Mode-Waaren, eben so dem frivolen Wechsel der Mode unterworfen, dafür aber zu solid und zu theuer. Teutschland kann also leicht an England doppelt so zinßbar werden, als es an Frankreich war', *Journal des Luxus und der Moden* (December 1791), 687.

22 'Es käme also nur auf zwey Puncte an: 1) Auf die Wahl der Kleidung, und 2) auf die Art, über dieselbe einig zu werden und sie einzuführen. Was den ersten Punct betrift, so glaube ich folgende Grundsätze annehmen zu dürfen: Die Kleidung muß seyn: a) wohlfeil; b) von Farben, die nicht leicht Schmutz annehmen, dauerhaft, leicht zu waschen, und von dem Eigensinne der Mode, weder erfunden, noch von demselben abhängig sind; c) für jedes Alter passend; d) vom Vornehmen wie vom Geringern, vom Reichen wie vom Armen, leicht anzuschaffen zu tragen; e) unserm Klima angemessen; f) nicht phantastisch; g) unseren Körper nicht entstellend; h) das Gepräge von Teutschheit tragend; i) in allen Jahreszeiten brauchbar [. . .]. Es giebt leider! Leute, welche alle Dinge in das Lächerliche ziehen; es giebt Andre, die in allem etwas Gefährliches oder Hinterlistiges sehen; Es giebt endlich noch Andre, welche nicht gut finden, als was sie, oder irgend eine von den Partheyen, zu welchen sie gehören, gefunden oder vorgeschlagen haben – Das ist traurig, und von Diesen muß ich freylich erwarten, daß sie meinem Vorschlage, von irgend einer Seite, keine Gerechtigkeit werden wiederfahren lassen; Allein das beunruhigt mich nicht. Ich bin mir bewußt, aus guter, ehrlicher, patriotischteutscher Absicht, diesen Vorschlag zu thun; Ich gehöre zu keiner Parthey, habe mir das Ding selbst so ausgedacht, und würde mich herzlich freuen, ohne weiter Ehre davon zu haben, auch je meinem Namen

nennen zu wollen, wenn die Sache gelingen sollte. . .', *Journal des Luxus und der Moden* (February 1786), 72.

23 *Journal des Luxus und der Moden* (February 1786), 79.

24 Enrico Wagner, 'Die Nationaltrachtdebatte im 18. und 19. Jahrhundert: Motivation und Durchsetzung einer nationalen Kleidertracht in Schweden, Deutschland und Dänemark 254–86' (Unpublished dissertation, University of Greifswald 2013).

25 Purdy, *Tyranny of Elegance*, 180–5.

26 For a nicely observed study of the phenomenon, see A. Ackermann, 'Eine nationale Aufgabe – Mode und Kommerz', in *Identitäten: Erfahrungen und Fiktionen um 1800,* eds Andreas Klinger and Gonthier-Louis Fink (Frankfurt: Peter Lang, 2003).

27 Staatsarchiv Hamburg, Erbschaftsamt (Inheritance Registry) D 71.

28 Uwe Meiners, 'Stufen des Wandels. Aspekte der Periodisierung der bürgerlichen und bäuerlichen Kultur im Münsterland (1500–1800)', in *Wandel der Alltagskultur seit dem Mittelalter. Phasen – Epochen – Zäsuren,* ed. Günter Wiegelmann (Münster: Coppenrath, 1987), 300–1.

29 Meiners, 'Stufen des Wandels', 302.

30 Institut für Stadtgeschichte, Frankfurt am Main, records of the Imperial Chamber Court, file 802: 'Auszug Inventariums über entseelten Bürgers und Handelsmannes Friederich Maximilian Beer, Nachlaß vom 4. und 6. May 1795' (Extract from the inventory of the late citizen and merchant Maximilian Beer, estate of 4 and 6 May 1795).

31 'Die Mode wäre durchaus eine Weltbürgerin, [die] sich in kein Vaterland einschließen lasse und der ihr eingeborenen Neigung zum Widerspruch zu Folge, sich am liebsten mit Kontrebanden ausstaffire', *Journal des Luxus und der Moden* (March 1802), 162.

32 *Journal des Luxus und der Moden* (June 1814), 388.

33 *Journal des Luxus und der Moden* (June 1814), 387 and Table 16. See also Wies, 'Journal', 153–4.

34 Wagner, Nationaltrachtdebatte, 213–49.

35 *Journal des Luxus und der Moden* (January 1786), 16.

36 *Charis* (1805): 341–2. Quoted in Ackermann, *Paris, London und die europäische Provinz*, 110.

37 Friedrich Schiller to the Inspector of the Gallery of Antiquities in Dresden Wilhelm Gottlieb Becker, 10 October 1802, in *Schillers Werke: Nationalausgabe*, ed. S. Ormanns, vol. 31 (Weimar: Böhlau, 1985), 164–5.

Part Two

Making and Acquiring Taste

6

Taste Inequalities in the Art Consumption of Prince Nicolaus I Esterházy 'the Magnificent'

Kristóf Fatsar

The appreciation of the flamboyant entertainments and tasteful luxury of Prince Nicolaus I Esterházy (1714–1790),[1] who rightly earned the epithet 'the Magnificent' from later generations (see Figure 6.1), changed dramatically in certain regards during his own lifetime but also in the light of more recent scholarship. This change has many aspects. On the one hand, they highlight his background interests that, for example, resulted in shifting but informed enthusiasm for different musical genres, yet adapted slowly to changing fashions in landscape design. More significantly, they reveal the revolutionary transformation of ideas about the social responsibility of the higher classes that characterized late eighteenth-century Europe. Luxury was still politically necessary for the monarchical state in the years when Nicolaus became prince – Montesquieu even expected the rich to be lavish in support of the poor.[2] Subsequently, there was a growing expectation that the rich would invest rather than waste, but this was only coupled to the long-standing recognition of the moral dangers of luxury for the individual towards the end of the century. Whilst grandeur as an expression of luxurious spending might previously have been thought tasteful, Enlightenment thinkers taught society to distinguish between luxury and taste.[3] As we shall see, Prince Nicolaus became increasingly exposed to such enlightened views during his lifetime.

Prince Nicolaus rose to the princely title only in his late forties and held it for almost three decades. One can wonder if it was reasonable to expect him to adjust his taste to the latest fashions during his ageing years, let alone

Figure 6.1 Prince Nicolaus I Esterházy in 1770, engraved by Karl Pechwell after the painting of Lorenz Guttenbrunn.

© Historical Gallery of the Hungarian National Museum.

to modify his attitude towards modes of spending. According to Jan de Vries's definitions, he was mainly a man of Old Luxury, bent on pursuing his pleasures;[4] so it is not surprising that his character has been the subject of praise but also disapproval, both in his lifetime and by modern historians. In reality, it is near impossible to do justice to his taste, partly because even the more straightforward aspects of his biography have still to be written.[5] Nevertheless, pointing out his sensitive approach to certain things and reluctance to engage with others helps to explain his character as a patron of the arts, while the changing tone of the descriptions of his attitude and his creations reflects the age in which he lived. As both his connoisseurship and its perception are dynamic in nature and not necessarily connected, their confrontation offers a fascinating insight into the self-expression of one of the wealthiest magnates of the period.

His contemporaries all agreed that Prince Nicolaus was a captivating character, a friendly and straightforward person with excellent social skills, and an excellent host.[6] The Hungarian equivalent of his epithet could be translated to English as 'the Shining' and the German as 'the Splendour-lover'; both of which say much about his lifestyle. One might think that he was extravagant in his spending, but this was not the case. Even though he built up enormous debts during his lifetime, this was not at all unusual among his peers; in fact, Prince Nicolaus's financial deficit seems to have stayed manageable. On the things he liked, he was very lavish in his spending; in others, he was content with local masters and petty artistic solutions. The present essay approaches his personality through some of his artistic ideas, particularly his landscaping programmes, set in the context of both contemporary descriptions and more recent scholarship. The rationale behind this is that landscape design can perhaps be seen as the litmus test for progressiveness during the period; after all, this is the time when the truly radical change from the formal styles to a more natural-looking (commonly called English) landscaping came into fashion. Prince Nicolaus's unwillingness to follow suit in this matter can be traced back to a number of possible motives, as this chapter will demonstrate. In contrast, his obsession with music and theatrical performances offers a most favourable view of his connoisseurship, never questioned in his lifetime or since; it is thus used here to highlight the uneven nature of his art consumption and his taste.

The origins of the Esterházy princes' wealth and the unlikely succession of 'the Magnificent' Nicolaus into its possession

The Esterházy family were of modest means until the seventeenth century when a few exceptionally talented figures, backed by excellent marriages and a return to Catholicism, made them by some distance the wealthiest and most prominent family in the Kingdom of Hungary. Indeed, by the eighteenth century, the Esterházy princes enjoyed an income several times greater than any other magnate in the country; they were so wealthy that their spending habits are almost incomparable to the rest of the Hungarian nobility. The first member of the family elevated to the peerage was the Palatine of Hungary, Miklós Esterházy (1583–1645) who was created baron in 1613 and count in 1626. His brothers were also created barons in 1619 and although all members of the Esterházy family eventually became counts or countesses (Hungarian peerage is usually extended to all descendants of both sexes) in the late seventeenth or early eighteenth centuries, only one line of the family rose to the rank of Princes of the Holy Roman Empire. The first Prince Esterházy was a son of Palatine Miklós and himself a Palatine of Hungary, Pál Esterházy (1635–1713).[7] Until the tenure of Nicolaus 'the Magnificent', only the oldest surviving male member of this line of the family had ascended to the princely title, but Nicolaus obtained the privilege to extend it to all his descendants of both sexes.

Nicolaus was the fifth Prince Esterházy, but an unlikely holder of the title. His grandfather, the Palatine Prince Pál had well over twenty children, but his oldest son who survived him, and thus became the second Prince, only had daughters. The next in line was a younger brother, the Palatine's fifteenth child, but the only other surviving son, Prince József (1688–1721), who held the title for only a few months before he followed his brother to the grave. Besides a daughter, he also left two sons, the older becoming the fourth Prince, Paul Anton (1711–1762), and the younger, Nicolaus, later to become 'the Magnificent' but a long time merely a count.

The young Nicolaus was only seven when his father died. His mother, Maria Octavia, née Baroness von Gilleis (1688–1762), together with two Hungarian noblemen formed a Council of Surrogates that took good care of the young boys. They had Nicolaus's country house at Süttör finished and equipped with

Figure 6.2 Süttör Manor, the country seat of Count Nicolaus, around 1761, photograph taken in 1928 of a painting lost during the Second World War.
© Esterházy Kastélymúzeum, Fertöd.

the necessary outbuildings and furnishings, designed and built by the Viennese and later imperial court architect (*Baumeister*), Anton Erhard Martinelli (1684–1747).[8] Originally the construction was destined for the young boys' father, Count József Esterházy, but it was completed for Count Nicolaus (see Figure 6.2). The Surrogates also made sure that Nicolaus received just as good an education as his princely elder brother, both attending the University of Leiden in Holland and also studying in Vienna. Finally, just before Nicolaus took full control of his estates in 1738, they had a fashionable garden created at Süttör, designed by no less a person than the imperial landscape architect (*Garteningenieur*) Anton Zinner (*c.* 1676–1751).

Hungarian tradition did not exclude younger brothers from the inheritance; in many cases family estates were equally divided between the surviving sons, and even daughters were given a share. In the case of the Princes Esterházy, the vast majority of the family estates were held by the 'reigning' prince as a trust fund (*fideicomissum*), but the second-born son also possessed enough to maintain a comfortable lifestyle. The estates of Count Nicolaus included Süttör, where his country house stood and which he decades later transformed into the truly magnificent château of Eszterháza, dubbed by contemporaries as the Hungarian Versailles. Count Nicolaus married a German countess, Maria Elisabeth Ungnad von Weissenwolff (1718–1790), in 1737 and with her secured the persistence of the princely line by means of sons. His older brother, on the other hand, failed to produce an heir and thus all the Prince Esterházy estates fell into the hands of Nicolaus in 1762, when he was already forty-eight years old.

When succeeding to the title, he decided not to move to Kismarton (modern Eisenstadt in Austria), the traditional seat of the Princes Esterházy, but to create his own princely court in Süttör where he already had great, and partly implemented, plans to subdue the entire landscape. His choice of that remote village was probably determined by the opportunities of the wider landscape – he could surround his château with a large game park and abundant open land to create great gardens and outbuildings. In contrast, his castle in the royal free town of Eisenstadt, which had plenty of privileges that secured it against his authority,[9] did not offer the same opportunities. This practical choice was probably seconded by an emotional desire to stay at the place that he called home for so long.

The art consumption of Prince Nicolaus during the early days of his tenure

Prince Nicolaus started to extend his château as early as 1762, which suggests that he already had ideas about what he wanted to achieve there. The next year construction accelerated and continued for almost a decade. Around the early days of 1766 he boldly renamed his château Eszterháza (see Figure 6.3), impertinently suggesting that this was the place from whence the entire family originated.[10] The famed large-scale festivities of Eszterháza started in 1768 and reached their social peak in 1773 when Nicolaus was bestowed the honour of receiving Empress Maria Theresa, Queen of Hungary.[11] However, work did not stop then: Prince Nicolaus altered the château and the grounds several times before the mid-1780s when he stopped construction work, probably due to his advancing years, and lived a quieter life in his remaining days, dying in Vienna at the age of seventy-six.

The elevation of his status had consequences other than just offering the opportunity to fulfil his visions for his château. Besides obvious distinctions like becoming Lord Lieutenant of Sopron County, which was an hereditary

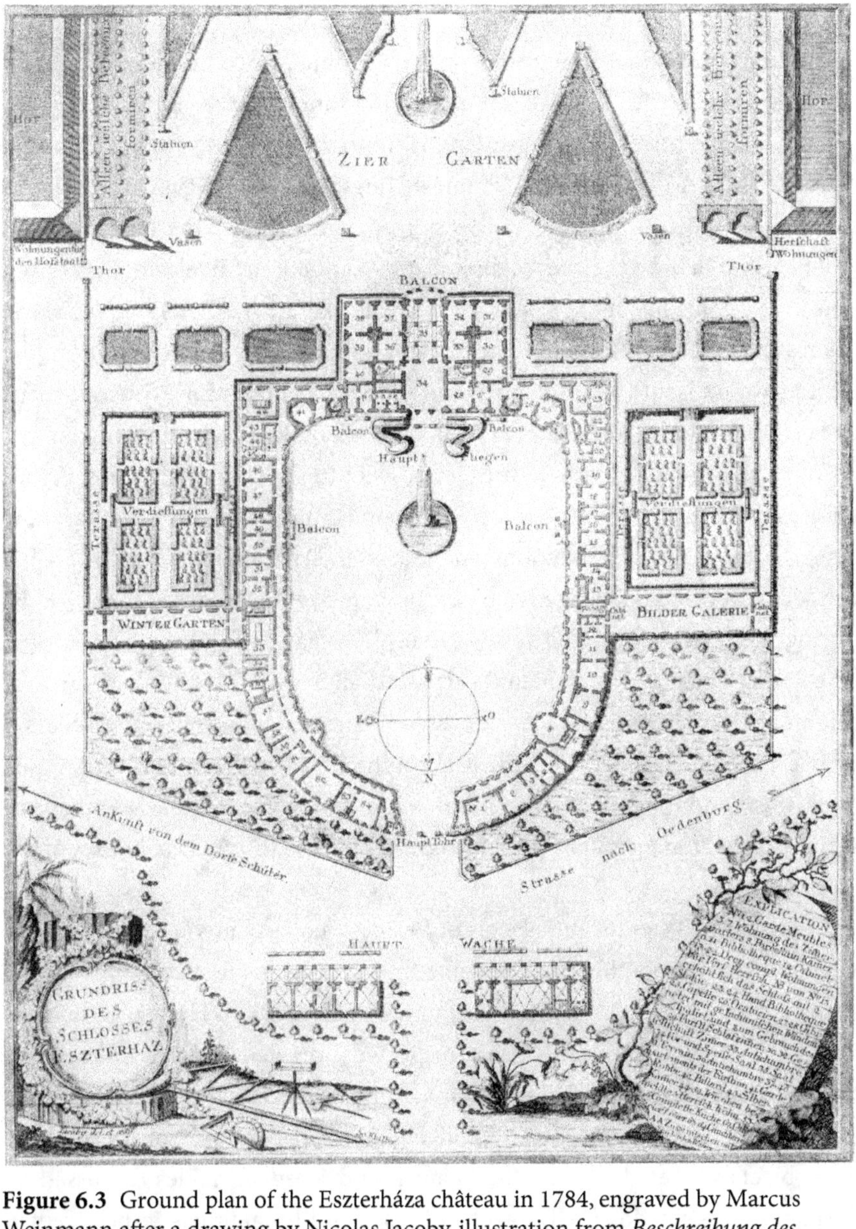

Figure 6.3 Ground plan of the Eszterháza château in 1784, engraved by Marcus Weinmann after a drawing by Nicolas Jacoby, illustration from *Beschreibung des Hochfürstlichen Schlosses Esterháß im Königreiche Ungern* (Preßburg: Anton Löwe, 1784).

© Esterházy Privatstivtung, Schloss Eisenstadt – Bibliothek.

role of the Princes Esterházy, or being ordained a Knight of the Golden Fleece, becoming a traditional conferment on the reigning prince, he was soon to step onto the world stage as one of the most important magnates of the Habsburg Empire, being entrusted to represent his monarch. In 1764, Archduke Joseph of Austria was to be elected as the new King of the Holy Roman Empire to succeed his father, Emperor Francis I of Lorraine, should the latter decease. After careful behind the scenes diplomatic negotiations, all electors agreed to vote for Joseph. One of the electors was the new king's mother, Empress Maria Theresa, as Queen of Bohemia. She was not present at the election (most of the electors were absent), but sent envoys on her behalf, appointing Prince Nicolaus as her first ambassador and proxy for Bohemia.[12] This was a prestigious but costly duty as representatives of this rank had to cover all their costs. Prince Nicolaus was probably flattered by the opportunity and did not spare any expense: the balls, illuminations and other entertainments that he lavishly produced were acknowledged to be the best among those offered to the public during the celebrations. The young Johann Wolfgang von Goethe found that 'Prince Esterházy's arrangements surpassed all the rest' at the final show of illuminations, 'by which each ambassador strove to outshine the others'.[13] Prince Nicolaus stepped on a stage where none of his ancestors had stood. With this action, he placed the family on a par with the Schwarzenberg or Liechtenstein: the Esterházy princes became equal to the greatest houses of the German lands.[14]

There are two significant aspects of Prince Nicolaus's mission to Frankfurt, which throw light on his taste. For one thing, it was his first real opportunity abroad to buy luxury items for his country home, back in Hungary. Nicolaus was to develop a substantial and respected porcelain collection over the following decades and he purchased many choice pieces while in Frankfurt for the election, in effect founding his collection.[15] His preference for French taste and objects was evident: like the Spanish and Swedish nobles discussed by Fernández-de-Pinedo and Thépaut-Cabasset, and Ilmakunnas respectively in this volume, he not only transported cooks but ordered furniture, clocks, firedogs and many other household objects from Paris. Interestingly, his first known pieces of Meissen porcelain were also bought from there and, although there is no record of purchases of French porcelain, he bought a giant set, many statuettes and other objects from the Frankenthal factory whose products show the influence of Sèvres.[16] Most importantly, however, he showed his lifelong dedication to French architecture and design: the temporary installations and illuminations at Frankfurt were based on Parisian designs,[17] an act that proved to be decisive in his vision to develop Eszterháza.

The other significant aspect of his Frankfurt stay is that his huge expenditure met with public approval. He spent well over 50 per cent more on his entertainments than the chief representative of the Viennese court at the elections, Prince Liechtenstein, and this does not even include his Parisian purchases.[18] The joy of profusion was very much characteristic of the era and that really suited the prince; but his enthusiasm for ostentatious display had consequences later. It might be questioned whether Prince Nicolaus's smooth alignment with public opinion and taste is a proof of his personal preferences or whether he watched what others of his rank surrounded themselves with and then did the same: buying objects that he felt would enhance his status. This seems unlikely because, despite his occasional purchases of conventional art objects, all his previous and later actions – and particularly his building programme and evolving preferences for various stage performances – indicate that he had a genuinely individual set of ideas about taste and that his opinion on artists and art objects was hardly influenced by others.

It is not without precedent that a person has excellent taste in certain things and less admired gusto in others. Doubts have never been raised concerning the worth and exquisite taste of the Eszterháza collection of china or clocks, for example; but his taste in portraiture has lately been described as 'modest' and the portraits he commissioned both 'conservative' (that is, old fashioned) and of 'middling' quality.[19] Just a few years after the death of Nicolaus, foreign visitors also reported that the paintings at Eszterháza were mediocre (*mittelmäßig*) or even 'unusually bad'.[20]

However difficult it might be to capture the discrepancies in Nicolaus's taste, it is worth noting some tendencies that explain the varying quality of his art consumption. At first sight, analysing expenditure on different pursuits appears to be a good approach as it is likely that more money would be spent on favourite interests. But interest and taste are not identical, and it is difficult to make such comparisons when the required resources are very different, as they would be with architecture or in sculpture, for example. There is another basis for comparison: the esteem in which the artists employed were held by wider society. The careers of the artists, their stations or projects in previous or successive years, tell much about their appreciation.

Prince Nicolaus employed superstars in his orchestra and for his stage at Eszterháza. It is enough to mention his Kapellmeister who grew into international fame, Joseph Haydn (1732–1809), one of the greatest composers in musical history. Haydn was originally employed in 1761 as Vice-Kapellmeister by Nicolaus's predecessor, Prince Paul Anton. When Nicolaus succeeded to the title in 1762, he immediately gave a 50 per cent pay rise to Haydn and to other personnel, though not to the semi-retired Kapellmeister Gregor Joseph Werner, nominal head of the princely musicians until his death in 1766.[21] One of the beneficiaries of this generosity was Nicolas Jacoby (1733–1784), a Lotharingian engineer who was given 400 gulden (a year's wages) in less than a month after Nicolaus became prince. If nothing else, it was a strong sign of the desire to keep him in service; but he had likely done something more to deserve such early attention from his master. As Jacoby is now widely accepted as having been responsible for most of the planning and design in the subsequent evolution of Eszterháza including interiors and landscapes (see Figure 6.4),[22] he might have provided designs to put Nicolaus's visions on paper during the early days of the new prince's tenure. Certainly, Jacoby was already in charge of upgrading the interiors of Nicolaus's Frankfurt residence in 1764.[23]

It is intriguing that, if the prince was so careful in choosing the best art objects in Frankfurt or hiring cooks and architectural designers from Paris, he did not employ great masters of landscape design or architecture for his country residence. One of the explanations is that he was a faithful and loyal man, not only to his monarch but also to his employees. If he had no particular reason to distrust his men, he kept them in his service. It should not be overlooked that Haydn was a young deputy Kapellmeister for several years, but Nicolaus trusted him and his faith was rewarded as Haydn's later career demonstrated. Was Jacoby just as gifted despite the reluctance to recognize his greatness? Possible, but unlikely. Great architects and landscape designers provided drawings for many houses and grounds and they usually had the liberty to deliver their plans to patrons other than their employer. At the nearby country house of Count Antal Széchényi in Nagycenk, for example, two professionals supplied plans for the pleasure grounds around 1760, one of

Figure 6.4 Map of Eszterháza in 1784, engraved by Marcus Weinmann after a drawing by Nicolas Jacoby, illustration from *Beschreibung des Hochfürstlichen Schlosses Esterháß im Königreiche Ungern* (Preßburg: Anton Löwe, 1784).

© Esterházy Privatstivtung, Schloss Eisenstadt – Bibliothek.

them being the gardener of the Prince Primate of Hungary, the other an engineer of the Hungarian Chamber, also a respected garden designer.[24] Haydn's example also shows that Prince Nicolaus was not jealous of his services: Haydn composed music for other patrons and the prince did not even require royalties. There is nothing to suggest that his architect or landscape designer could not do the same, and yet neither Jacoby nor the princely gardeners appear to have been commissioned by any other landholder – or, if they did, they refused the offer, which seems improbable. Their sole achievement is Eszterháza and, despite its grandeur, it stands alone among country houses and gardens of the wider region, making it difficult to see its influence and real significance, apart from its splendour.

Change and constancy in Prince Nicolaus's taste

Changes in taste on the individual and public level do not necessarily go hand in hand. This could be best demonstrated by Nicolaus's shifts in preference for musical and theatrical genres while perhaps too slowly adapting to new fashions in landscape gardening. Prince Nicolaus's musical taste changed quite significantly over the years, even if Haydn remained responsible for pleasing princely desires during this evolution. Haydn's main duty during the early years in Nicolaus's service was to compose symphonies, concertos, divertimentos and vocal pieces for special occasions. Later, for a decade or so until the mid-1770s, he continued to compose symphonies, but he also served his master's own musical performances with writing baryton trios, as Prince Nicolaus was himself a baryton player. He also started to feed Nicolaus's obsession with operas during this period, first abandoning baryton trios and, by the early 1780s, symphonies as well. During this time operas became Haydn's most important output in the service of the prince.

One can argue that these different genres belong to the same oeuvre, namely Haydn's, but this assumption suggests that the composer never disappointed his master, which was not the case. In truth, Nicolaus was nearly always satisfied with the music Haydn offered and knew very well how much the services of his Kapellmeister were worth. The few exceptions of Haydn's failure to please his master, that Haydn himself also realized and recorded, can probably be traced back to Prince Nicolaus's developing depression. However, very occasionally Nicolaus did not like a particular performance or at least did not want to see it more than once, despite the huge cost attached to each opera production. Yet these nuances had no effect on Nicolaus's appreciation of Haydn. On the contrary, recent musicology has speculated that Haydn's innovative power is directly connected to his frequent seclusion from urban life and to his secure position at the Eszterháza court, something that the composer himself acknowledged in a later interview. Haydn was not isolated from other musical developments, but he did not have to rely on satisfying popular taste, which many of his contemporaries were forced to do. Rather he had to gratify his sole audience and thus had to be resourceful in ideas in order to offer something new, yet pleasing. Haydn's composing skills and Nicolaus's musical refinement both benefited from this arrangement. In effect, by the later stages of his career, Haydn became the most influential composer in defining European musical taste.[25]

In sharp contrast to the musical life of Eszterháza, the gardens around the château have always lagged behind the times, although the landscaping programme at the first manor of Süttör had started favourably. The Council of Surrogates commissioned a garden for Süttör from the imperial garden designer Anton Zinner.[26] Zinner had already redesigned the gardens of Nicolaus's princely brother at Eisenstadt a few years earlier, between 1728 and 1731, and then it was Count Nicolaus's turn to have fashionable gardens at his residence. In Süttör there was no garden to transform, thus Zinner had a free hand to create the pleasure grounds as he liked, albeit within financial limitations. He produced a well-proportioned garden, square in shape with an exedra at its far end and divided into intricate parterres of flowerbeds. It was probably finished in 1738, the year when Nicolaus came of age and exercised full ownership over his estates.

Despite Zinner's mature design, Nicolaus decided to alter the layout less than ten years after its completion. He added one oblique avenue on each side of the main axis of the entire ensemble to create a *patte d'oie* ('goosefoot'),[27] a powerful tool to organize space with the help of radiating alleyways leading to one focal point. This focal point was the centre of his manor, of course, and the *patte d'oie* undoubtedly gave a majestic appearance to his seat, raising its importance in the surrounding landscape. However, the oblique lines led to the corners of Zinner's original garden and, although the shape of the parterre was successfully altered to deal with this disadvantageous solution, the new avenues very noticeably and disagreeably cut through parterres on both sides and arrived at the corner points of the most delicate internal parterre. The French canon of baroque garden design had solutions to overcome this situation, but none of those were used at Süttör. Instead, this awkward design existed for about three decades, even during the time of Maria Theresa's visit, when Nicolaus concentrated his efforts on embellishing the groves behind the pleasure grounds. Finally, in the middle of the 1770s, the entire parterre was transformed and the oblique lines of the *patte d'oie* were at last allowed to reach the façade of the château and meet with the main axis. The new garden doubtlessly had a more elegant layout, with large grass areas that might refer to the fashionable English style of design (see Figure 6.5). However, its structure went back to the *Parterre du Nord* in the gardens of Versailles created more than a hundred years earlier. To put this into a broader context, Lancelot 'Capability' Brown had already been a professional landscape designer for a

Figure 6.5 Eszterháza from the gardens, engraved by Ferdinand Landerer after a painting by Bartolomeo Gaetano Pesci, illustration from *Beschreibung des Hochfürstlichen Schlosses Esterháß im Königreiche Ungern* (Preßburg: Anton Löwe, 1784).

© Esterházy Privatstivtung, Schloss Eisenstadt – Bibliothek.

quarter of a century by this time, and the English landscape garden movement was in full swing.

Admittedly, even before this transformation, the garden was admired – and not only by the untrained and uneducated eye. Vicomte de Laval (later Comte de Montmorency, 1748–1809) fell in love with the gardens when he visited in 1773, declaring that they were the most beautiful outside France.[28] His travelling companion, the Scottish physician and writer John Moore (1729–1802), did not offer an opinion on the gardens; being British and used to more naturalistic creations he perhaps looked away rather than expressing his disapproval. His true impressions can be judged by the description he gave of another landscape in Hungary, in which he preferred the parkland further away from the house because it was less artificial. Similarly, Moore very much admired the groves and game park of Eszterháza, which he found charming. This difference of opinion reveals the rivalry between gardening styles during this period. Moore was slightly teasing Laval when he asked whether the Eszterháza gardens could be compared to those of Versailles. Laval was outraged by the suggestion and declared that no gardens could be compared to Versailles, although this was perhaps more a political statement than an expression of taste or the aesthetic supremacy of French baroque gardening. In Eszterháza, Vicomte de Laval could admire a garden design tradition that was about to be outmoded even in France, but was found here in its old form.

Nicolaus was clearly not oblivious to changed taste in garden design and attempted to create some less formal parts in his garden. Some of these were already present from much earlier: from the 1760s, many paths twined through the large woodland to facilitate hunting and these were probably reinvented as the curving English walks that were mentioned by visitors in the 1780s. From 1779, when the first of Hirschfeld's highly influential five-volume *Theory of Garden Art* appeared, properly introducing the English style of gardening to the German-speaking realm, there was an increasing pressure on patrons to change the layout of the landscape around their country seats.[29] Making the revolutionary leap from the formal to the informal style must have been difficult for many, both for financial and emotional reasons.[30] Certainly, Prince Nicolaus was not ready to give up his very formal garden layout, particularly because it was based on his own ideas, if contemporary records – that he himself commissioned – can be trusted.[31] He was no doubt emotionally attached to a landscape where he spent most of his life while improving and developing it. Despite having a small 'English garden' hidden somewhere within the wooded area of the groves,[32] and an informally arranged winter garden as well,[33] it would have been a financially daring move to transform the parterre just five or ten years after its creation. In this respect, the prince's readiness to 'waste' opera productions after just one performance should not be confusing: theatrical or musical productions involved very different resources to those required in reconfiguring the landscape.

Perhaps more surprisingly, the prince went on to extend the formal design of the pleasure grounds: developing previously unexecuted designs for two symmetrically arranged viewing terraces at the end of the parterre in 1784. By this time, four of the five volumes of Hirschfeld's work were already out, the fourth one having been published in 1782, providing plenty of references to the latest fashion of landscape design. One year after finishing the viewing terraces at Eszterháza, Hirschfeld's fifth volume came out; it included a scathing assessment of Hungary's country houses and gardens and, mentioning only Eszterháza by name, claimed that they were executed with great pomp but with little taste.[34] His words suggest that formal layouts were no longer acceptable. Moreover, the view that the prince's landscaping project followed the latest French fashion, and was therefore *comme-il-faut*,[35] disregards Jean-Jaqcues Rousseau's argument, made in *Julie ou la nouvelle Héloïse* (published in 1761), that geometric gardens were forms of artificial luxury and thus to be rejected.[36] Nicolaus, it seems, was not even conforming with current French taste.

Eszterháza and the prince's taste falling victim to the tide of social concerns

Among the critics who wrote about the gardens of Eszterháza in the first half of the 1780s, Prince Charles-Joseph Lamoral, seventh Prince de Ligne (1735–1814), deserves special attention because he was an expert author on gardens and his critical essay on European gardens circulated widely on the continent.[37] His uncomplimentary remarks aligned with those by other garden-lovers educated in the latest fashion, but he introduced a new and more devastating line of attack on the prince: he hints that Nicolaus could have done better with the enormous amount of money he spent on Eszterháza. Although de Ligne would have preferred to see improvements in the landscape – more in the English style, of course – Prince Nicolaus was also criticised by others in terms of what the money spent on gardens could have done to raise the condition of the poor.[38] Landscape fashions and spending habits: these were the fields where the prince was deemed to have lost touch with the times, or perhaps simply did not want to adapt to them.

Another sort of social responsibility was expected from him when his Hungarian compatriots wanted him to take part in the patriotic awakening of the nation. Instead of compassion with the poor, they demanded partisanship in promoting the national language both in administrative and cultural life.[39] In the year of his death he was even called on to commission Hungarian plays, instead of the Italian operas that dominated the stage at Eszterháza.[40] Prince Nicolaus, being an entirely Germanized and loyal courtier, could not please his countrymen with patriotic behaviour; but he had advocates to defend his excessive expenditure. As early as 1772 the Hungarian poet and noble guard to the queen, György Bessenyei (*c.* 1746–1811), whose commander as Captain of the Hungarian Noble Guard in Vienna was Prince Nicolaus, claimed that the large expense associated with the construction of and the festivities at Eszterháza did great service to the nation as the prince demonstrated to the world what artistic heights Hungary was able to reach.[41]. Other sympathizers pointed out that the building work gave employment to many local people and the dam that the prince built across the nearby marshlands facilitated transport and reclaimed land for cultivation.[42] Moreover, opera performances and the park were open to all and free of charge, whilst the Esterházy princes, at least from Nicolaus's tenure, maintained a rather generous pension system for their former employees.

Despite instances of disapproval, Prince Nicolaus mostly remained a respected figure whose dreamland Eszterháza was generally viewed as a proof of his good taste. The prince's charming character did not begin to fade with his advancing years: a visitor described him as an agile and vivid person at the age of seventy-four, just two years before his death.[43] Nonetheless, the very fact that the achievements of Hungary's richest and most distinguished magnate were questioned by his peers and by members of lower social ranks show that his public image was not flawless. This must have been an unprecedented and even unimaginable experience for a Prince Esterházy.

Conclusion

When Nicolaus inherited the princely title, he not only became the owner of the largest landed estate in Hungary, but also a master of many artists among his workforce, originally employed by his older brother. Some of them, like Haydn, were excellent choices; but his choice of architect and designer is perhaps more questionable. Entertaining himself and his guests seems to have been Nicolaus's favourite occupation. Eszterháza was the stage set for these entertainments and, although it was important, the performances were much more so. This might be the reason behind his indulgent way of extending and developing his country seat; he had strong ideas of what he wanted to achieve and he was content with his own personnel in implementing them. Yet this led to problems: when the garden statues were sold in 1800, most of them were found to be virtually worthless.[44] On the other hand, his good taste in the performing arts prompted him to invite world-class artists to Eszterháza. In other words, he spent money as he thought fit and he was probably convinced that the architectural setting did the job perfectly well. The grandiosity of Eszterháza impressed its visitors, but just a few years after the prince's death, when the meticulous maintenance was given up, the imperfections of its architecture and landscapes became immediately apparent, as a contemporary travel writer observed: 'Rather splendour reigns here than taste.'[45]

Despite his somewhat 'do-it-yourself' approach in the evolution of his palace, including its interior and its setting, we rightly remember him as a man of exquisite taste in most things and the generous employer of Haydn. During the prince's lifetime, the widespread praise of Haydn's performances (both in Vienna and Eszterháza) and the ever-increasing international success of his scores have continuously reassured Nicolaus's sense of luck in having him, and the musical life of Eszterháza has survived the strongest scrutiny ever since. The prince's ideas about how to display his wealth and rank through his luxurious spending were less successful elsewhere, showing that the taste of a strong-minded individual can very easily go astray. He took this risk in his design decisions by following both his artistic and spending preferences, yet Prince Nicolaus's amiable character still shines through the fading splendour of Eszterháza.

Notes

1 His given name is Miklós in Hungarian, but outside Hungary he is better known by the German form of his name and, since he himself also used it that way, this chapter adheres to it, too. This rule applies to his similarly Germanized brother (Paul Anton) and grandson (Nicolaus II), but not to his predecessors who will appear under their Hungarian names. This is justified by the fact that earlier - and in fact, later - family members used Hungarian as their first language of communication, but from the 1720s until the second half of the nineteenth century the Esterházy princes were brought up principally in German.

2 Rémy G. Saisselin, *The Enlightenment against the Baroque: Economics and Aesthetics in the Eighteenth Century* (Berkeley: University of California Press, 1992), 34–7.

3 Saisselin, *The Enlightenment against the Baroque*, 105–9.

4 Jan de Vries, 'Luxury and Calvinism / Luxury of Capitalism: Supply and Demand for Luxury Goods in the Seventeenth-Century Dutch Republic', *The Journal of the Walters Art Gallery* 57 (1999), 73–85.

5 Most of the short references to his life are actually from biographies of Joseph Haydn, although more recent research has revealed many inaccuracies in earlier publications. However, a good introduction to his life in English is Rebecca Gates-Coon, *The Landed Estates of the Esterházy Princes: Hungary during the Reforms of Maria Theresia and Joseph II* (Baltimore and London: Johns Hopkins University Press, 1994), esp. 9–10.

6 Edit Szentesi, 'Eszterháza 18. századi leírásai', in *Kő kövön: Dávid Ferenc 73. születésnapjára*, eds Edit Szentesi, Klára Mentényi and Anna Simon (Budapest: Vince, 2013), vol. II, 165–229, collected all eighteenth-century accounts of Eszterháza including many references to the prince's personality.

7 Horányi's brief introduction to the origins of the family's wealth is still valid - see Mátyás Horányi, *The Magnificence of Eszterháza*, trans. by András Deák (London: Barrie and Rockliff, 1962), 14–16; Gates-Coon's summary on the same subject adds a few more details - see Gates-Coon, *The Landed Estates*, xv–xvii.

8 Kristóf Fatsar, 'Anton Erhard Martinelli 1720: évi tevékenysége Süttörön', *Ars Hungarica* 23 (2000), 191–6.

9 On the tensions between town and the princely family see Gates-Coon, *The Landed Estates*, 4.

10 Esterházy (or Eszterházy as other lines of the family spelled their name) means 'of Eszterháza'. The territorial designation of all lines of the family is in fact 'of Galántha'. There is no doubt about Nicolaus's intentions because he first renamed his seat Új-Galántha (New Galántha) around the 1730s, see Mátyás Bél, *Sopron vármegye leírása II: Descriptio Comitatvs Semproniensis II*, ed. Katalin Mária Kincses, trans. by Gergely Tóth (Sopron: Győr–Moson–Sopron Megye Soproni Levéltára, 2006), 130–1.

11 Ferenc Dávid and Kristóf Fatsar, 'Esterházy "Fényes" Miklós herceg itineráriuma és az általa rendezett ünnepségek hercegi rangra emelkedésétől haláláig (1762–1790)', *Levéltári Közlemények* 75 (2004), 83–103, list the festivities at Eszterháza and the itinerary of the prince; on the visit of Maria Theresa to Eszterháza, see Kálmán Varga, *Mária Terézia Eszterházán* ([Budapest:] Műemlékek Állami Gondnoksága, 2001), including an English translation.

12 A recent study, focusing on the art consumption of Prince Nicolaus while on his mission, is Stefan Körner, '"Evviva il nostro prence, che il mondo fa stupir!": Esterházy I. Miklós követsége II. József 1764. évi frankfurti koronázásán: szertartásrend, ünnepségek, műtárgyvásárlások,' in *Kő kövön: Dávid Ferenc 73. születésnapjára*, eds Edit Szentesi, Klára Mentényi and Anna Simon (Budapest: Vince, 2013), vol. II, 25–52.

13 Johann Wolfgang von Goethe, *The Autobiography of Goethe: Truth and Poetry: from my own life*, trans. by John Oxenford (London: Henry G. Bohn, 1848), 173. Prince Nicolaus was clearly able to fill the role of his absent monarch as was expected of an ambassador; although writing about an earlier period, Helen Jacobsen's words are still valid for the middle of the eighteenth century: 'Luxury consumption was indelibly associated with royal courts, and the visual display of wealth associated with embassies and diplomats was intended to convey a message or set of messages which formed part of diplomatic communication just as much as any formal negotiations or written memorials.' Helen Jacobsen, *Luxury and Power: The Material World of the Stuart Diplomat, 1660–1714* (Oxford: Oxford University Press, 2012), 1.

14 Körner, 'Evviva il nostro prence', 46–7.

15 Körner, 'Evviva il nostro prence', 36–7.

16 On the collection of Meissen procelain and also its context as the subject of art consumption, see *Triumph of the Blue Swords: Meissen Porcelain for Aristocracy and Bourgeoisie, 1710–1815*, eds Ulrich Pietsch and Claudia Banz (Leipzig: E. A. Seemann, 2010).

17 Körner, 'Evviva il nostro prence', 45–6.

18 Körner, 'Evviva il nostro prence', 47.

19 Enikő Buzási, 'A herceg Esterházyak 18. századi ikonográfiájáról Johann Georg Bauer, Johann Georg Weickert és Ignaz Unterberger műveinek meghatározásával', in *Kő kövön: Dávid Ferenc 73. születésnapjára*, eds Edit Szentesi, Klára Mentényi and Anna Simon (Budapest: Vince, 2013), vol. II, 11. The author contrasts Nicholaus's taste in portraiture as an exception to his otherwise careful search for exceptional quality, but this chapter argues that things were more nuanced than this allows.

20 Alphonse de Fortia de Piles, *Reisen und merkwürdige Nachrichten zweier Neufranken durch Deutschland, Rußland, Polen und die Oestreichischen Staaten während des jezigen wichtigen Krieges* (Leipzig: Weigand, 1797), II: 302; Robert Townson, *Travels in Hungary, with a short account of Vienna in the year 1793* (London: G. G. and J. Robinson, 1797), 39. This harsh critique probably applies to the canvases only; some of the most important ceiling frescos were painted by the celebrated Mildorfer – see Elisabeth Leube-Payer, *Josef Ignaz Mildorfer 1719–1775: Akademieprofessor und Savoyisch-Liechtensteinischer Hofmaler* (Vienna: Böhlau, 2011).

21 For a concise history of Haydn's life in the service of the Princes Esterházy see László Somfai, 'Haydn at the Esterházy Court', in *The Classical Era: From the 1740s to the end of the 18th century*, ed. Neal Zaslaw (Houndmills/Basingstoke: Macmillan, 1989), 268–92; Howard Chandler Robbins Landon's exhaustive five-volume Haydn biography contains numerous sources in translation and is a mine of information in many respects. However, his architectural, and – in a broader sense – Hungarian, historiography is less reliable; see H. C. Robbins Landon, *Haydn: Chronicle and Works* (London: Thames and Hudson, vol. I, 1980): *Haydn: the early years*; and vol. II (1978): *Haydn at Eszterháza, 1766–1790.*

22 Mihály Mőcsényi, *Eszterháza fehéren-feketén* ([Budapest]: Mőcsényi, 1998) was the principal promoter of this notion; For Jacoby's large extra-salary payment in 1762, see Mőcsényi, *Eszterháza fehéren-feketén*, notes a169 and a170. The architectural and landscape history of Eszterháza has mostly been written in compendious forms as the enormous wealth of archival materials hitherto proved to be too difficult to elaborate. The last fifteen years have seen a rather substantial revision of the history of Eszterháza based on previously unknown sources still held by the Esterházy trust fund in their Castle Forchtenstein in Austria. The architectural history of Eszterháza has been recently studied by Ferenc Dávid: on the role of the principal designer see Ferenc Dávid, 'Nicolaus Jacoby(?): Eszterháza, Erweiterungsplan des Schlosses Eszterháza, 1774', in *In Arte Venustas: Studies on Drawings in Honour of Teréz Gerszi*, ed. Andrea Czére (Budapest: Museum of Fine Arts, 2007), 215–18. Crucial parts of Eszterháza's eighteenth-century garden history has been revised by the author of this chapter in several short publications in

recent years, some of which will appear in the notes below; however, the latest summary is Géza Galavics, 'Eszterháza 18. századi kertje,' in *Kő kövön: Dávid Ferenc 73. születésnapjára*, eds Edit Szentesi, Klára Mentényi and Anna Simon (Budapest: Vince, 2013), vol. II, 63–84.

23 Körner, 'Evviva il nostro prence', 31–2.

24 Kristóf Fatsar, *Magyarországi barokk kertművészet* (Budapest: Helikon, 2008), 161.

25 László Somfai, 'Joseph Haydn és közönsége', in *Kő kövön: Dávid Ferenc 73. születésnapjára*, eds Edit Szentesi, Klára Mentényi and Anna Simon (Budapest: Vince, 2013), vol. II, 151.

26 Kristof Fatsar, 'Anton Zinner im Dienste der Esterházys', *Die Gartenkunst* 19 (2007), 285–94. The date of the creation of the Süttör gardens and some details and circumstances of Zinner's work were amended by Kristóf Fatsar, 'Átváltozások: Eszterháza nagy parterjének vázlatos története', in *MM XC: Tanulmányok és esszék a 90 éves Mőcsényi Mihály tiszteletére*, ed. Kristóf Fatsar (Budapest: BCE Tájépítészeti Kar, 2009), 77–90.

27 Kristóf Fatsar, 'Az eszterházai lúdlábsétány kialakulásának története', *4D Tájépítészeti és Kertművészeti Folyóirat* 3 (2006), 10–17.

28 John Moore, *A View of Society and Manners in France, Switzerland and Germany* (London: Strahan - Cadell, 1779), II, 308. Moore's impressions were analysed by Szentesi, 'Eszterháza 18. századi leírásai', 172, 190.

29 Christian Cay Lorenz Hirschfeld, *Theorie der Gartenkunst* I–V (Leipzig: Weidmann, 1779–1785).

30 On the psychological, social and other difficulties of transforming 'old-style' geometric gardens in Hungary during this period, see Kristóf Fatsar, 'European Travelers and the Transformation of Garden Art in Hungary at the Turn of the 19th Century', *Studies in the History of Gardens and Designed Landscapes* 36 (2016), 166–84.

31 Most notably the official tour guide of Eszterháza: *Beschreibung des Hochfürstliches Schlosses Esterháß im Königreiche Ungern* (Preßburg: Anton Löwe, 1784), 42.

32 Gottfried von Rotenstein, *Lust-Reisen durch Bayern, Würtemberg, Pfalz, Sachsen, Brandenburg, Oesterreich, Mähren, Böhmen und Ungarn, in den Jahren 1784 bis 1791* (Leipzig: Friedrich Schneidern, 1793), III, 177.

33 Gábor Alföldy, 'Eszterháza kamarakertjei: Adatok és megfigyelések,' in *Kő kövön: Dávid Ferenc 73. születésnapjára*, eds Edit Szentesi, Klára Mentényi and Anna Simon (Budapest: Vince, 2013), vol. II, 85–106, here 87–8.

34 Hirschfeld, *Theorie der Gartenkunst*, vol. V, 314. Hirschfeld did not see Hungarian country house gardens himself but he relied on a favourable description of them written by a Hungarian nobleman around the year 1780, and published in 1783, see Szentesi, 'Eszterháza 18. századi leírásai', 177–9.

35 Géza Galavics, *Magyarországi angolkertek* (Budapest: Balassi: 1999), 10.

36 Saisselin, *The Enlightenment against the Baroque*, 102.

37 Charles-Joseph de Ligne, *Coup d'œil sur Belœil* (Belœil: Charles de Ligne, 1781), 71–3. This work reached three French editions and was also published in German in 1799.

38 *Mindenes Gyüjtemény* 4, no. 15 (1790), 236. Passages from this journal regarding the prince were quoted in Szentesi, 'Eszterháza 18. századi leírásai', 196.

39 *Mindenes Gyüjtemény* 4, no. 15 (1790), 236.

40 *Mindenes Gyüjtemény* 4, no. 3 (1790), 46.

41 György Bessenyei, *Az eszter-házi vígasságok* ([Vienna: Esterházy,] 1772), 3–4. Prince Nicolaus himself sponsored the publication of this opinion, but in any case, it shows that his expenditure was under attack quite early.

42 Szentesi, 'Eszterháza 18. századi leírásai', 174–5, 187.

43 Rotenstein, *Lust-Reisen* III, 180–1.

44 Fatsar, 'Átváltozások', 89–90.

45 [Carl Gottlob Küttner,] *Wanderungen durch die Niederlande, Deutschland, die Schweiz und Italien in den Jahren 1793 und 1794* (Leipzig: Voß, 1796), II, 466, quoted by Szentesi, 'Eszterháza 18. századi leírásai', 201.

7

Making an English Country House: Taste and Luxury in the Furnishing of Stoneleigh Abbey, 1763–1765

Jon Stobart

In a 1774 inventory of Stoneleigh Abbey, the ancestral home of the Leigh family, a bed chamber named for its distinctive wrought work drapery included, amongst a wide array of furnishings: six mahogany back stools, two French elbow chairs, 'a fine old Japan Cabinet', a Wilton carpet, a steel stove grate and a 'large pier Glass in a Rich Carved and Gilt frame'.[1] In many ways, this room represents the eclecticism of the English country house, combining influences and objects from Britain, Europe and the wider world in a blend of materials, cultures and styles.[2] The English elite had long drawn inspiration from contemporary and historical cultures in mainland Europe, most notably Italy, the Netherlands and France. Classical Rome and Renaissance Italy had a huge impact on architectural styles, most notably in the rise of Palladianism in the early eighteenth century. French influences were more important in terms of the layout of English country houses in the early decades of the eighteenth century, and French taste had a big impact on furnishings styles following the Restoration and again from the 1770s.[3] As the chapters by Clemente, North and Ilmakunnas make clear, the English elite was part of a broader alignment of European elite taste with French modes and fashions; but they also shared in an episodic critique of French luxury as emblematic of decadence, ostentation and excess.[4] Nonetheless, continental Europe was an important source of ideas and material objects, including paintings, sculptures, books, furniture and clothing. These were often collected whilst on the Grand Tour, on specific shopping trips or via auctions of the collections of deceased or dispossessed noblemen – an increasingly common feature of post-Revolutionary France. Equally, there were a growing number of British dealers who could supply their well-heeled customers with luxury goods, especially from France which was increasingly constructed as the locus and arbiter of refined taste.[5]

Overlain onto these European influences and goods were an ever-larger range of products and tastes coming into Britain from the wider world, especially India and China. These sparked the enduring fashion for *chinoiserie*, both in the form of genuine Indian cottons, Chinese wallpapers and Chinese and Japanese porcelain, and the European copies that proliferated through the seventeenth and eighteenth centuries.[6] Whether seen as 'physical representations of empire' or a reflection of a taste for the exotic, goods and commodities from the East and West Indian trade were increasingly common in English houses, not least in the shape of mahogany – a material that became central to English furniture making.[7] In some instances, there was a blending of European and oriental styles, both in terms of broad designs – most famously, perhaps, Thomas Chippendale's *chinoiserie* – and in the fabric of individual pieces, as seen for example in the painted mirrors in the Ante Room at Shugborough.[8] This kind of cosmopolitanism is often seen as a core characteristic of the European elite. It was a means of defining and defending their status, in part by marking their 'reach' as consumers – that is, their ability both to afford such luxuries and forge the right connections through which they might be obtained – and in part because it signalled their taste and discernment; they knew which goods to select and how to integrate them into their material culture.[9]

It is easy to find examples of these cosmopolitan cultures of consumption amongst English country houses. They are perhaps most obvious in those with close connections to empire, often because the owners wished either to celebrate or hide the source of their new-found wealth, and amongst those where the owner had political or social ambitions, marked by a desire to move on a European stage.[10] However, there has been little attempt to question the extent to which this cosmopolitanism characterized the English landed elite more generally, beyond a proliferation of mahogany furniture and desire to dine *à la Francaise*. In this chapter, I explore the processes and priorities involved in furnishing a country house, Stoneleigh Abbey, in the mid-1760s, and stress the importance of English suppliers and the construction of a largely

English material culture, albeit one that drew materials and decorative cues from overseas. In taking a case study approach, it is clearly impossible to state which modes of behaviour were more typical of the English elite as a whole; but it offers the opportunity to explore in detail the networks of craftsmen and retailers which supplied one particular house and the ways in which they related to each other and to the owner of the house in making and implementing a particular form of elite English taste.

Stoneleigh Abbey in Warwickshire was formerly a Cistercian Abbey which was purchased by Thomas Leigh, a London merchant, in 1571. A Baronetcy and later a Barony were conferred during the seventeenth century and, through purchase and marriage, the estate grew in size so that, by the time that Edward, fifth Lord Leigh, came of age in 1763, it produced an income of around £10,000 per annum. It was at this time that Edward began to refurnish a house that had been left incomplete by his grandfather and had lain empty during Edward's minority following the death of his father in 1749. The Leigh archive includes an extensive set of bills which reveal much about the decoration and furnishing of the house, as do a number of memoranda drawn up following Edward's coming of age. Unfortunately, there is only a small amount of personal correspondence, in part because most of Edward's letters were burned following his death. It is therefore easier to trace the processes of consumption than uncover underlying motivations.

The network of supply

The bills indicate that furniture was acquired in a piecemeal fashion through the first half of the eighteenth century. Walnut chairs came in a variety of styles, John Taylor's bill from 1736 listing twelve matted, six carved and eighteen compass chairs. There was also a range of parcel-gilt furniture: John Pardoe of Temple Bar supplied, amongst other things, a 'neat carved' gold chimney glass, and there are sets of parcel-gilt walnut chairs with matching pier tables provided for the Great Apartment.[11] In addition, Edward, third Lord Leigh commissioned a set of seven walnut veneered and gilt-gesso chairs with painted coats of arms and embroidered covers depicting scenes from Ovid's *Metamorphoses*, possibly from Pardoe or from Thomas How of Westminster.[12]

By the 1740s, Thomas, fourth Lord Leigh, had moved on stylistically and was buying mahogany furniture, particularly tables. Five were supplied by H. Hands; they cost between £2 2s. 6d. and £3 apiece, suggesting that they were either modest in size or quite plain.

The overall impression gained from these bills is that the Leighs had fairly conservative taste, following the trends rather than leading them. Some of the gilt walnut pieces were quite grand, and they created a suitable display of wealth and status when assembled in the Great Apartment,[13] but this was not a family indulging in the luxurious splendour of baroque or rococo in the French style, as seen at Wilton House, for example. Moreover, the quantities and costs involved were modest, certainly in relation to the surge of spending that took place in preparation for Edward, the fifth Lord Leigh's occupation of the house. In just two years, much of Stoneleigh Abbey was substantially refurbished, some rooms in the west range being properly finished for the first time since their construction nearly forty years earlier. There were major purchases of silver tableware, including a chased epergne costing £139 14s., from Thomas Gilpin of Serle Street, Lincoln Inn Fields and a wide variety of napkins and tablecloths in damask, dimity and diaper, plus hundreds of yards of Irish linen for sheets, supplied by Jordan Biggar, whose shop was on Leadenhall Street.[14] Both were items that might be found in any respectable household, but the quantity and quality marked this out as the consumption of a wealthy landowner, whilst the engraving of crests and coats of arms on the silverware was a constant reminder of Edward's rank and dignity.[15]

Spending on silverware and household linen ran to a total of £1,116 10s. 7d. between 1763 and 1765, but these were not the key items or suppliers in this programme of refurbishment. Three men dominated Edward's outgoings and did much to shape the subsequent character of Stoneleigh Abbey, at least beyond the Great Apartment laid out by his grandfather in the late 1720s and 1730s. They were the furniture maker, William Gomm; the wallpaper merchant, Thomas Bromwich, and the upholsterer, Thomas Burnett, who together supplied goods to the value of £4,659 15s. 5d.[16] William Gomm had opened his workshops and showroom in Clerkenwell Close in 1736 and enjoyed a good reputation amongst contemporaries, although he is little known today.[17] He appears to have been influenced by Chippendale, subscribing to his *Director* in 1754. Designs believed to be in Gomm's hand resemble Chippendale's

Anglicized rococo, but he also sketched others in gothic and Chinese style, indicating versatility and an ability to respond to the tastes of individual clients.[18] Thomas Bromwich had a reputation as one of the leading wallpaper merchants of the mid-eighteenth century, supplying many wealthy customers, including Horace Walpole.[19] His showroom on Ludgate Hill was an important venue for selecting wallpapers, Walpole's friend, the poet John Gray, describing in detail the range of gothic, flock and stucco papers available, whilst Mrs Lybbe Powys noted with approval his work at Fawley Court in Buckinghamshire. Here, the papers were Chinese in style and 'adorn'd with very good prints, the border cut out and the ornaments put on with great taste'.[20] Both Gomm and Bromwich were clearly able to meet a taste for English, European and exotic designs. Far less is known about Thomas Burnett. Like Gomm, he was not of the top rank, yet was clearly well-established by the 1760s and is named as a Fellow of the Society for the Promotion of Arts, Manufactures and Commerce between 1761 and 1768. Together with his partner, Gilbert Burnett, he had premises on the Strand, from which they ran a substantial business, capable of supplying elite customers with large quantities of drapery and soft furnishings, as well as items of furniture and a range of upholstery services.[21] Significantly, they were identified in directories as upholstery, cabinet and carpet warehousemen, undertakers and appraisers; in short, they do not appear to have made furniture themselves, but rather specialized in the supply of pieces made by other tradesmen – a role by no means unusual for upholsterers at this time.

Looking to metropolitan suppliers was quite normal when making such important purchases especially in the second half of the eighteenth century when Chippendale, Mayhew and Ince, and later Hepplewhite, Sheraton and many others, began to issue sample books which allowed provincial customers to choose from a range of possible designs in the comfort of their own homes.[22] What is perhaps more surprising is that the Leighs never appear to have looked beyond London in the manner seen at Boughton House or Swallowfield Park, where goods were acquired direct from French dealers or on shopping trips to Paris, and at Englefield House and Sichtermannn's Groningen mansion with their arrays of exotic goods acquired via the English and Dutch East India Companies (see Kuiper's chapter).[23] Yet this dependence on English and especially London craftsmen was also seen at Audley End, Arbury Hall and many other country houses, including Nostell Priory (see

Bristol's chapter). Does this reflect a taste for English furniture, the emergence in the mid-eighteenth century of what John Cornforth calls 'an age of English craftsmanship and decoration',[24] or merely the convenience of buying from suppliers whose workshops and showrooms were relatively accessible and whose reputation was familiar? Were the goods supplied by these men also English?

Supplying luxury and taste

Gomm's furniture was mahogany and mostly for bedchambers and dressing rooms. The 183 chairs he supplied were intended for upholstery, most being described as 'stuff back and seat' or 'nail seats with neat carved backs' and were finished with Chinese trunk, ogee or plain feet.[25] There were chests of drawers, Pembroke tables, clothes presses and chests, sometimes with fretwork cornices, and serpentine commodes, perhaps resembling that in one of his designs. Gomm was thus supplying suites of furniture very much in line with restrained English taste, although the 'French elbow chairs' were probably rococo and perhaps built to the pattern shown in his manuscript designs.[26] The upholstery work undertaken by Burnett mostly involved covering Gomm's chairs, either with silk, mixed or worsted damask or more often morine – a watered and stamped woollen fabric widely used in domestic furnishings.[27] Some pieces of furniture were also supplied, either in mahogany or, in the case of beds, in wainscot with mahogany legs and posts. However, the bulk of his bill comprised bedding (including mattresses, bolsters and quilts) and drapery, generally in the same fabric and colour used for the chairs. The result was a series of bedchambers and dressing rooms which were colour-coded and graded according to the quality of the drapery: Yellow Damask, Blue Morine, Crimson Worsted Damask, and so on. These colour schemes were continued through the wallpapers supplied by Bromwich. In the Blue Morine room, for instance, he hung 'fine saxon blue and white mock embossed' paper, whilst 'crimson ground stucco paper' was put up in the Crimson Worsted Damask room.[28] Most rooms had papers described as mock embossed, stucco, ground stucco, sprig or embossed – the kind of 'neat and not too showey' papers desired by the wallpaper buyers discussed by Amanda Vickery.[29]

Viewed as a whole, then, this huge outlay on furniture, drapery and wallpaper appears to be an exercise in large-scale refurbishment in a restrained manner. The overall spending was massive, but so too was the quantity and range of goods being acquired. Importantly, however, the bedchambers were not all treated the same in terms of outlay and décor, the differences between them revealing much about Edward's ideas of taste and luxury.

A series of bedchambers and dressing rooms, numbered 2 to 8 on the bills presented by all three tradesmen, were furnished in a broadly comparable manner. They all had stucco or mock embossed wallpapers, costing between 3d. and 6d. per yard, and were furnished with morine drapery costing 2s. 4d. per yard. The furniture supplied for each room was fairly uniform: Gomm's bill itemises a night table, chest of drawers, dressing table, basin stand or Pembroke table, and usually a set of chairs for each; the cost varied according to whether there was a dressing room en suite, rather than reflecting differences in the quality of the pieces (Table 7.1). The beds installed by Burnett were of a standard type: 5 foot 3 inches by 6 foot 6 inches, made from wainscot and uncarved mahogany, and costing £4 17s. The overall cost for each room was the equivalent of three to six year's wages for a senior servant, and in this sense they were luxurious reflections of Lord Leigh's wealth and standing.[30] However, they were by no means magnificent. Typical of ordinary guest rooms in an English country house, they were situated on the second floor and were comfortable and practical, rather than splendid.

Table 7.1 Cost of furnishing standard guest bedchambers at Stoneleigh Abbey, 1763–1765 (£ s. d.)

Room	Burnett	Bromwich	Gomm	Total
2. Blue morine (bed)	40-0-2	4-0-1	19-13-0	63-13-3
3. Yellow morine (bed)	42-14-5	2-19-3	19-13-0	65-6-8
4. Crimson morine (bed/dressing)	73-1-5	7-16-5	36-8-0	117-5-10
5. Green morine (bed/dressing)	68-3-4	8-9-2	36-8-0	113-0-6
6. Green morine (bed)	46-13-9	5-16-4	36-8-0	88-18-1
7. Blue morine (bed/dressing)	68-3-5	8-4-8	46-8-0	122-14-1
8. Crimson morine (bed/dressing)	54-19-1	7-7-9	39-18-0	102-6-10
Average	56-5-1	6-7-8	33-10-10	96-3-7

Source: SCLA, DR18/3/47/52/15, bill from Thomas Burnett, 1765; DR18/5/4402, bill from Thomas Bromwich, 1765; DR18/5/4408, bill from William Gomm, 1765.

A different standard of furnishing characterized the rooms on the first floor (Table 7.2). A conventional approach to luxury can be seen in No.14 and No.15, although this is less apparent in either the furniture supplied by Gomm or the wallpaper than in the richness of Burnett's drapery and upholstery work and the quality of the bedding. The bedsteads were wider, longer and taller, with 'gothic feet posts, neatly carv'd' and a 'set of rich carv'd Cornishes & carv'd testers'. In all, they cost £18 16s. – four times those found in the standard rooms. In No. 14, the 'mixt Damask' hangings, with their lustring linings and lace trimmings, together with a fringed silk valance came to just short of £100. The bed itself was stuffed with the 'best sweet Goose feathers', further comfort and luxury being added by the 'superfine' white calico quilt (costing £6 10s.) and Wilton carpet (£4 14s. 6d.). The window curtains were again of blue mixt damask and the chairs supplied by Gomm were covered in the same fabric and trimmed with silk. Next door, No.15 was fitted out in a very similar fashion, the pair offering a vivid picture of refined luxury: rich carving, costly fabrics, and a fine feather bed. In this context, luxury was something sensual and pleasurable, but also splendid and costly; it defined Lord Leigh as a man with a taste for the finer things in life and a purse that allowed him to indulge these tastes. Importantly, these were rooms for guests and so offered the opportunity for displaying luxury and taste, but they exhibited little sign of the exotic or the cosmopolitan; these were conventional signs of rank and status in an English house. Much the same was true of the Dining Parlour and Chapel, which were similarly luxurious in their use of drapery. For the former, Burnett supplied

Table 7.2 Cost of furnishing 'special' bedchambers at Stoneleigh Abbey, 1763–1765 (£ s. d.)

Room	Burnett	Bromwich	Gomm	Total
14. Blue Damask	235-10-2	6-6-1	25-7-0	267-3-3
15. Yellow Damask	241-9-1	11-0-5	21-1-0	273-10-6
17. Crimson Damask	71-9-11	24-14-3	30-10-0	126-14-2
18. Crimson Damask	71-9-11	27-7-6	30-10-0	129-7-5
20. Miss Leigh's	296-13-6	35-1-0	59-2-0	390-16-6
21. Lord Leigh's	209-12-8	21-1-11	27-12-0	258-6-7
Average	187-14-2	20-18-6	32-7-0	240-19-9

Source: SCLA, DR18/3/47/52/15, bill from Thomas Burnett, 1765; DR18/5/4402, bill from Thomas Bromwich, 1765; DR18/5/4408, bill from William Gomm, 1765.

200 yards of 'rich green silk and worsted damask' for curtains, with further quantities for cushions made for the window seats and for covering a set of twenty-four chairs, again supplied by Gomm. The total cost of £211 18s. 8½d. was easily overshadowed by the £473 0s. 10¼d. laid out on the chapel, in which in a 'rich crimson Genoan velvet', edged with gold fringe, was used for hangings, seat covers and cushions. This opulence was given a rococo twist in the form of a communion table made by Gomm to designs by Timothy Lightoler, Lord Leigh's architect at Stoneleigh. This is described in the bill as 'An Exceeding handsome Mahogy Communion Table the feet very neatly carved with Flowers & foliage, the Frame very richly Carv'd, on the Front a Cherubins Head, Foliage & Flowers'. At £31 10s., it was easily the most costly piece supplied by Gomm and the only one that suggests anything like a significant departure from plain English furniture.[31]

It would be a mistake, however, to think that this was the only taste exhibited by Lord Leigh. As with any aristocratic house, different rooms served different functions and carried different meanings. A contrast is often drawn between rooms of state and those for the family, or between dining and drawing rooms, and I have discussed elsewhere the distinction between Stoneleigh Abbey's Great Apartment, as a symbol of rank and heritance, and the Dining Parlour and Breakfast Room, which were more fashionable and sociable spaces.[32] We can also see engagement with diverse systems of taste being played out in different bedchambers. For No.17 and No.18, Gomm and Burnett supplied conventional furniture and drapery, the cost of which was in line with that for other bedchambers; but Bromwich hung Chinese wallpaper, giving the rooms a completely different character. In the former, he hung fourteen sheets of 'Indian Taffaty paper' at 30s. per sheet and a papier-mâché border; in the latter, he charged for twenty-seven sheets of 'Indian Birds and flowers' at 12s. per sheet, a papier-mâché border and Indian Colours. From the price, and the fact that the paper came in sheets rather than by the yard, it is likely that these were Chinese not English papers;[33] either way, they demonstrated a rather different side of Lord Leigh's sensibility and taste. By this date, Chinese wallpapers were starting to be viewed simply as another decorative option rather than a direct reference to the Orient, but they reveal an exoticism rarely glimpsed at Stoneleigh Abbey.[34] Moreover, their deployment alongside English style furniture and drapery suggests the kind of eclectic cosmopolitanism highlighted by Barczewski, Berg and others, and encapsulated in the silver epergne supplied by Gilpin. Whether viewed as *chinoiserie* or exuberant rococo, the pineapple which tops it is a link to the exotic and the luxury of these fruit.[35]

This eclecticism was still more apparent in Lord Leigh's own bedchamber and that for his sister, Mary. Her rooms were furnished with particularly high quality pieces, including a clothes press costing £12 12s., a serpentine commode dressing table at £15 15s. and a bed 'richly carv'd with Reeds and Ribbons' and hung with green mixed damask. There were curtains to match and a very fashionable 'fine pea green paper' costing 12d. per yard. This display of conventional luxury is reflected in the large totals for the bills from Gomm and Burnett (see Table 7.2); Mary's rooms were clearly intended to reflect her status. More remarkable, perhaps, is the presence alongside these of a total of seventeen 'Indian Pictures in Party gold frames' for which Bromwich charged £17 11s., plus another £9 9s. for a matching papier-mâché border. These Chinese landscapes were hung as pictures in a manner that was peculiarly English, and were set alongside gilded mirrors and family pictures; the room thus combined old and new luxuries and an emphasis on family. Yet eclecticism could involve more than a blending of East and West. In Lord Leigh's rooms, Bromwich supplied '147 yards of painted paper to match a Chintz' that was being used for the bed hangings. The latter appears to have been present already as there is no account of it in Burnett's bills, which is perhaps unsurprising as its use was formally prohibited at this time, and it must have given Lord Leigh's room a flavour of orient. At the same time, however, Burnett charged £3 16s. for leather and work to renovate the gilt leather hangings that remained in the room from an earlier decorative scheme. Old and new, tradition and fashion, heritance and exoticism again coincided within this a single room.

Making taste and making compromises

Developing and implementing this decorative scheme was a long and drawn out process, with changes and compromises inevitably being made along the way.[36] Determining who was responsible for its overall conception is difficult in the absence of Lord Leigh's correspondence, but it appears that the architect played a limited role. Lightoler designed various fireplaces and the communion table built by William Gomm, but he lacked the strong hand that Robert Adam wielded at Osterley, Harewood and elsewhere in producing his fashionable but ultra-expensive neo-classical interiors. Indeed, there are several unexecuted room designs, mostly in a 'frilly rococo', the absence of which is notable from the walls and ceilings of Stoneleigh.[37] There is nothing to indicate that he influenced the overall plans for furnishing. The earliest indication of planning this is a memorandum written by Samuel Butler, the steward, on 2 October 1762. It mostly notes the need for painting in various rooms, but decisions about furniture must have been made around this date as a letter to Burnett, dated 27 April 1763, gives directions about which rooms are ready to take furniture.[38] He was certainly involved at an early stage as he drew up his own 'Memorandum about furniture for the Rooms' which is sketchy in detail and clearly records a developing situation in which many decisions about the final appearance of various rooms were still to be made.[39] This was entirely in keeping with the practices of upholsterers, at least in the first half of the eighteenth century,[40] but it does not mean that he was responsible for drawing up as well as executing the designs. Indeed, it seems certain that Lord Leigh himself had a hand in developing the decorative schemes. Such involvement was common amongst his contemporaries and there is a surviving note in Edward's own hand that records his intentions for furnishing the chapel, plus some thoughts on a number of other rooms.[41] In this he probably benefited from the help of William Craven, his former guardian and maternal uncle. Craven was certainly present at Stoneleigh Abbey for considerable periods of time during the early 1760s, Burnett's early schedule of work identifying 'Mr Cravens Room' in the south-west corner of the attic storey of the west range. With no wife and little prospect of getting one, the young Edward Leigh appears to have leant heavily on his kinsman for support and advice, many bills being sent to Craven even when Edward had officially reached his majority.[42]

There were, then, several individuals offering advice and input as the plans for decorating and furnishing Stoneleigh Abbey developed: architect, upholsterer and uncle. It was probably one of these men that persuaded Lord Leigh to adopt crimson for the drapery in the chapel, rather than the blue suggested in his note, and there were undoubtedly other modifications along the way. However, it is apparent that, once the overall scheme for each room was determined, he left much of the detail to the respective craftsmen – men who could be trusted to execute the plans to a high standard of taste and quality. Indeed, the scale of the refurbishment meant that this kind of delegation was inevitable. In this light, Bromwich especially was an obvious choice: a dealer with an established and strong reputation for serving the gentry, and one with kudos and the capacity to provide a range of fashionable papers. Burnett and Gomm are less famous, but clearly had similar qualities.

This is not to say that the refurnishing process always went smoothly. Through 1763 the house was in a state of chaos, with carpenters, plasterers and carvers completing work on the Hall and some of the bedrooms; gilt leather hangings being moved from one room to another, and painters everywhere. In response to a letter from Burnett, which informed him that the 'shades' (i.e. window blinds) for most rooms were ready for delivery, Butler replied in February 1764 that 'our house is now in greater confusion than ever [. . .] as we are making great alterations in the middle part of the house'.[43] Rooms were furnished as and when they were ready, with many of the attic rooms being the first to be completed. Yet there were inevitable delays: Bromwich charged £8 8s. for '24 Days, 2 Men stud still for want of the Rooms being ready'.[44]

This was a minor grievance; more serious was a dispute that arose between Samuel Butler and Mr Greenhouse, Burnett's foreman who was responsible for overseeing the various workmen engaged in assembling and fitting the furniture, and undertaking a wide range of upholstery work. The circumstances were described in detail in a letter from Butler to Burnett, dated 13 October 1763. A consignment of goods was unpacked was found to be sub-standard. It was:

> universally complained of, the Wood appearing to be (as it really is) very green, & the workmanship very [poor]; this prov'd the topic of discourse the next day at Dinner when every person present (without exception to any) agreed in the above relation and Mr Greenhouse particularly mentioned that he supposed that they were such as Mr Gomm usually exported.[45]

Gomm was duly written to, but clearly replied to deny all knowledge of the consignment, which meant that the shoddy furniture must have come from Burnett. Lord Leigh then directed that the goods be returned to Burnett at the upholsterer's expense, but Butler reports that, upon hearing this, Greenhouse:

> Seemed not inclineable to comply, but desireous of retaining some of the best of them. I do not blame him for endeavouring to serve his Master as far as he decently may, but S^r when I have his Lordship's orders how I am to act, I shall not submit to have them countermanded by any workman about the House [. . .] I assure you Sir, I have so good an opinion of you as to believe that you would not endeavour to impose any goods upon his Lordship, but what were deserving of reception, & I conclude these were sent before you had inspected them. It is true they are intended chiefly for Servants Rooms, & therefore only to be plain, but yet ought to be neat & good in their kind [. . .].

Here, we see Butler expressing the irritation felt at the poor quality of the goods, but more particularly at Greenhouse's attempts to defend the shoddy furniture, and emphasizing the need to meet certain standards of workmanship in order that the furniture would comply with Lord Leigh's requirements. In the end, the matter was resolved amicably enough: Craven agreed on Lord Leigh's behalf that the faulty furniture could remain, at a reduced price, and Butler wrote again to Burnett saying that 'the affair between Mr Greenhouse & myself is ended, as you desire, for indeed wee never had any dispute before or since the time I wrote to you about it – we are now, as I hope we ever shall remain, good friends'.[46]

I have dwelt on this episode at length because it shows that questions of quality and taste were contingent, not absolute. Standards were established and judgements were made, even about furniture for servants; but pragmatism played an important part. Even the wealthiest might choose to accept goods that are not the best because it was simpler and cheaper to do so. What is also striking is the speed at which this dispute escalated and subsequently subsided. The initial letter to Gomm was written on 27 September and the matter was rounded off with Butler's letter to Burnett barely a fortnight later.

Conclusion: taste and identity

What, then, did taste and luxury mean for Lord Leigh and how does this inform our broader understanding of the country house and elite taste and identity? Perhaps the most notable feature is its mix of conservatism and fashion, old and new, Englishness and exoticism. Luxury is seen in the costly drapery and high quality furniture that characterized much of the work undertaken at Stoneleigh Abbey in the early 1760s. There were important nuances, however: different grades of luxury made certain bedchambers stand out in terms of the richness of their furnishings, whilst different types of luxury were seen in the *chinoiserie* and the retention of older decorative features in other rooms. One striking omission is the absence of overt references to European and especially French taste. The latter was increasingly questioned in broader society as unpatriotic and unmanly, and formed part of a wider critique mounted against the aristocracy by an increasingly vocal middling sort. Aristocratic excess and decadence contrasted with the solid virtues of the middling sort in a manner that parallels the conflicts in taste described in Clemente's chapter on Naples. Yet, despite the costs involved, Stoneleigh Abbey has much in common with these sentiments: over and again in the bills presented by Burnett, Gomm and Bromwich, we see richness being qualified neatness and elegance – ideals that, as Vickery argues, encapsulate provincial gentility.[47] The emphasis was on the solid virtues of mahogany and upholstery, rather than gilding and rococo flamboyance. We might even see this as representing in material terms the English (or British) self-identity as solid, manly and virtuous – although this was far from being the kind of patriotic consumption seen in attempts to create national styles of dress (see North's chapter).

This is not to say that Stoneleigh Abbey lacked gilded magnificence or the splendour of silver tableware epitomized in the epergne but also seen in an array of candlesticks, tureens, tea urns and cutlery. Indeed, the blending of these two genres was an important part of country house culture. Families like the Leighs occupied an important borderland between the national aristocracy and local gentry; a position which can, in some ways, be seen in the material culture of their houses. It is significant, however, that these two worlds were represented by different parts of the house: the state rooms of the Great Apartment paraded aristocratic credentials in crimson drapery and gilded furniture; the Breakfast Room, Dining Room and bedchambers formed the stage on which the Leighs showed themselves to be tasteful, social and English. Yet this Englishness did not preclude an eclecticism that happily blended mahogany, *chinoiserie*, rococo and Gothicism with neatness and elegance. The cosmopolitanism that this implied was matched by pragmatism, both in the design of tasteful interiors and the process of furnishing the house. Bedchambers were equipped, first and foremost, to be comfortable and convenient; choices about styles, colours and textures were contingent and negotiated, with craftsmen playing a key role in shaping the detail of the resulting decorative schemes, and decisions and standards were always susceptible to the vagaries of everyday life – quality might be compromised for convenience. Above all, what emerges from this study is the huge time and effort required of the owner, architect, craftsmen and senior servants to produce a tasteful expression of luxury.

Notes

1 Shakespeare Centre Library and Archive (SCLA), DR18/4/43, 1774 inventory with 1806 amendments.

2 See Stephanie Barczewski, *Country Houses and the British Empire, 1700–1930* (Manchester: Manchester University Press, 2014), 180–88.

3 Mark Girouard, *Life in the English Country House: A Social and Architectural History* (New Haven: Yale University Press, 1978); Geoffrey Beard, *Upholsterers and Interior Furnishings in England, 1530–1840* (New Haven: Yale University Press, 1997), 81–6; Dena Goodman, 'Furnishing Discourses: Readings of a Writing Desk in Eighteenth-Century France', in *Luxury in the Eighteenth Century*, eds Maxine Berg and Elizabeth Eger (Basingstoke: Palgrave Macmillan, 2003), 71–88.

4 William H. Sewell, 'The Empire of Fashion and the Rise of Capitalism in Eighteenth-Century France', *Past and Present* 206 (2010), 81–120.

5 See Francis Haskell, 'The British as collectors', in *The Treasure Houses of Britain*, ed. Gervase Jackson-Stops (Washington: National Gallery of Art, 1985), 50–59; Jennifer Jones, 'Repackaging Rousseau: Femininity and Fashion in Old Regime France', *French Historical Studies* 18 (1994).

6 Emile De Bruijn, 'Consuming East Asia: continuity and change in the development of Chinoiserie', in *The Country House: Material Culture and Consumption*, eds Jon Stobart and Andrew Hann (Swindon: Historic England, 2016); John Cornforth, *Early Georgian Interiors* (New Haven: Yale University Press, 2004), 253–63; Anne Gerritsen and Stephen McDowall, 'Material Culture and the Other: European Encounters with Chinese porcelain, ca. 1650–1800', *Journal of World History* 23:1 (2012), 87–113; Maxine Berg, *Luxury and Pleasure in Eighteenth-Century Britain* (Oxford: Oxford University Press, 2005), 77–84, 105–10.

7 Barczewski, *Country Houses*, 137. See also *Encounters: The Meeting of Asia and Europe, 1500–1800*, eds Anna Jackson and Amin Jaffer (London: V&A Publications, 2004).

8 Stephen McDowall, 'Shugborough: Seat of the Earl of Lichfield', *East India Company at Home* (August 2014), http://blogs.ucl.ac.uk/eicah/shugborough-hall-staffordshire/

9 For more on these aspects of luxury consumption, see: Arjun Appadurai, *The Social Life of Things: Commodities in Cultural Perspective* (Cambridge: Cambridge University Press, 1986), 3–63; Berg, *Luxury and Pleasure*, 28–31.

10 For example, the various case studies published as part of the project *East India Company at Home* (http://blogs.ucl.ac.uk/eicah/case-studies-2/); several of the chapters in *Country House*, eds Stobart and Hann; Barczewski, *Country Houses*, 136–96.

11 SCLA, DR18/5/2047, DR18/5/2218; J. Cornforth, 'Stoneleigh Abbey', *Country Life*, 14 March 2002.

12 Jackson-Stops, *Treasure Houses*, 202–3.

13 According to the 1738 inventory, the furniture in the Great Apartment had a combined value of £834 5s. 6d. – SCLA, DR18/4/9.

14 For example, SCLA, DR18/5/4251, 4028, 4193, 4343–5.

15 On middling consumption of linen, see Woodruff Smith, *Consumption and the Making of Respectability, 1600–1800* (London: Routledge, 2002), 130–8. For its use in elite households, see D. M. Mitchell, 'Fine table linen in England 1450–1750: Ownership and Use of a Luxury Commodity' (Unpublished PhD thesis, University of London, 1999).

16 SCLA, DR18/5/4408, DR18/5/4402, DR18/5/4571, DR18/3/47/52/15.

17 Lindsay Boynton, 'William and Richard Gomm', *The Burlington Magazine* 122 (1980), 395–6.

18 The designs are held at the Henry Francis du Pont Winterhur Museum in Delaware, USA. See Boynton, 'William and Richard Gomm', 396.

19 E. A. Entwistle, 'Eighteenth-Century London Paperstainers, Thomas Bromwich at the Golden Lyon on Ludgate Hill', *Connoisseur* (October 1952), 106–10.

20 Alan Sugden and John Edmundson, *A History of English Wallpaper, 1509–1914* (London: Batsford, 1926), 79; Caroline Powys, *Passages from the Diaries of Mrs Philip Lybbe Powys of Hardwick House, Oxon: AD 1756–1808* (London: Longmans, Green & Co., 1899), 146.

21 Geoffrey Beard and Christopher Gilbert, *Dictionary of English Furniture Makers, 1660–1840* (London: Maney & Son, 1986), 131–2.

22 See Amanda Vickery, 'Women and the World of Goods: A Lancashire Consumer and her Possessions, 1751–81', in John Brewer and Roy Porter, *Consumption and*

the World of Goods (London: Routledge, 1993), 281; Clive Edwards, *Turning Houses into Homes: A History of the Retailing and Consumption of Domestic Furnishings* (Aldershot: Ashgate, 2005), 66–71; Beard, *Upholsterers*, 161–3, 223–5, 257–8.

23 Margot Finn, 'Swallowfield Park, Berkshire', *East India Company at Home* (February 2013), http://blogs.ucl.ac.uk/eicah/case-studies-2/swallowfield-park-berkshire/; Kate Smith, 'Imperial Objects? Country House Interiors in Eighteenth-Century Britain', in *The Country House: Material Culture and Consumption*, eds Jon Stobart and Andrew Hann (Swindon: Historic England, 2016). Furniture made by English craftsmen was sometimes upholstered with French tapestries; for example, several sets of chairs supplied by Chippendale being finished with specially commissioned tapestries from the Gobelins factory. See Jackson-Stops, *Treasure Houses*, 333.

24 Cornforth, *Early Georgian Interiors*, 191–203.

25 SCLA, DR18/5/4408.

26 Henry Francis du Pont Winterhur Museum in Delaware, USA.

27 SCLA, DR18/5/3/47/52/15. On morine or moreen, see Clive Edwards, *Encyclopaedia of Furnishing Textiles, Floorcoverings and Home Furnishing Practices 1200–1950* (Aldershot: Ashgate, 2007), 142–3.

28 SCLA, DR18/5/4402. The rooms are named in this way on both Bromwich's and Burnett's bills.

29 Amanda Vickery, *Behind Closed Doors: At Home in Georgian England* (New Haven: Yale University Press, 2009), 166–83, quote from 177; see also Sugden and Edmundson, *English Wallpapers*.

30 Jon Stobart and Mark Rothery, *Consumption and the Country House* (Oxford: Oxford University Press, 2016), chapter 1.

31 SCLA, DR18/5/4408.

32 See Cornforth, *Early Georgian Interiors*, 275; Jon Stobart and Mark Rothery, 'Fashion, Heritance and Family: New and Old in the Georgian Country House', *Cultural and Social History* 11 (2014), 385–406; For a similar analysis of Audley End, see Hannah Chavasse, 'Fashion and "Affectionate Recollection": Material Culture at Audley End, 1762–1773', in *The Country House: Material Culture and Consumption*, eds Jon Stobart and Andrew Hann (Swindon: Historic England, 2016), 67–77.

33 See Ellen Kennedy Johnson, 'The Taste for Bringing the Outside in: Nationalism, Gender and Landscape Wallpaper (1700–1825)', in *Women and Material Culture, 1660–1830*, eds Jennie Batchelor and Cora Kaplan (Basingstoke: Palgrave Macmillan, 2007), 121–3; Emile de Bruijn, Andrew Bush and Helen Clifford, *Chinese Wallpaper in National Trust Houses* (Swindon: National Trust, 2014). It is

also telling that Bromwich charged for a total of 26 days labour for hanging paper and borders in the two rooms.

34 Cornforth, *Early English Interiors*, 253–64; Jackson-Stops, *Treasure Houses*, 432–95.

35 Barczewski, *Country Houses*, 136–96; Berg, *Luxury and Pleasure*, 77–84, 105–10.

36 Richard Wilson and Alan Mackley, *The Building of the English Country House, 1660–1880: Creating Paradise* (London: Hambledon Continuum, 2000).

37 SCLA, DR18/5/4203; DR671/33. Gomme, 'Abbey into palace', 97.

38 SCLA, DR18/3/47/52/6.

39 SCLA, DR18/3/47/52/14 – no date.

40 Cornforth argues that cabinet makers were increasingly taking on many of these responsibilities in the second half of the century: Cornforth, *Early Georgian Interiors*, 212–14.

41 SCLA, DR18/3/47/52/12, Memorandum from Edward, fifth Lord Leigh, concerning the chapel, no date. See also Edwards, *Turning Houses into Homes*, 44–52, 66–71; Hannah Greig, *The Beau Monde: Fashionable Society in Georgian London* (Oxford: Oxford University Press, 2013), 32–62; Geoffrey Tyack, *Warwickshire Country Houses* (Chichester: Phillimore, 1994), 12–15.

42 For example, SCLA, DR18/5/4028, DR18/5/4069. On the influence of wives, see Vickery, *Behind Closed Doors*, 83–8.

43 SCLA, DR18/17/27/96 – 1 February 1764.

44 SCLA, DR18/5/4402.

45 SCLA, DR18/17/27/84 – 13 October 1763.

46 SCLA, 18/14/27/85 – 27 October 1763.

47 Jon Stobart, 'Luxury and Country House Sales in England, c. 1760–1830', in *The Afterlife of Used Things: Recycling in the Long Eighteenth Century*, eds Ariane Fennetaux, Amelie Junqua and Sophie Vasset (London: Routledge, 2015); Amanda Vickery, *The Gentleman's Daughter: Women's Lives in Georgian England* (New Haven: Yale University Press, 1998), 161.

8

Between the Exotic and the Everyday: Sabine Winn at Home 1765–1798

Kerry Bristol

Architectural historians of the long eighteenth century in Britain have seemingly been reluctant to give up a male-centred methodology that has privileged exteriors over interiors and architects at the expense of patrons. Since the publication of Mark Girouard's *Life in the English Country House* (1978), privileging form to the exclusion of function may no longer be tenable but, as an academic discipline, eighteenth-century architectural history has not been gender friendly because it relies on the traditional tools of drawings, bills, receipts and financial accounts. Men owned the estates on which country houses were built, men signed the contracts and, by implication, men made the stylistic choices that displayed their classical learning and the taste they had developed on the Grand Tour. The subject of women is often relegated to a separate chapter or part thereof that typically centres on interior decoration (as distinct from interior design) and 'craft' rather than 'art'. Thus, while aristocratic women had a taste for luxury goods such as mahogany furniture, silver and ormoluware, *ipso facto*, it was on a smaller scale than that of their husbands. However, a radical rethink in recent years of the ways in which we approach the country house as a social and cultural entity has sent us scuttling back to the archives in search of female agency.[1] Frances Harris's masterful exploration of Sarah, Duchess of Marlborough, as an architectural patron (and her attempts to control her family by using her properties as tools of manipulation) and Rosemary Baird's *Mistress of the House*, in which the author investigated the relationships elite women had with their homes – from custodian of family history to enthusiastic builder – are two of the more successful attempts to redress the balance, but one must still question how typical a Duchess of Marlborough or an Elizabeth Montagu were within the wider female experience of country house culture.[2]

By comparison, social and economic historians questioning notions of gender, consumption and the world of luxury goods in eighteenth-century Britain have placed elite women front and centre, as active agents in a retail world that bears more than a passing resemblance to our own. Women shopped, and did so for goods ranging from exotic hand-painted Chinese wallpapers to fashionably lightweight cottons from the mills of Yorkshire and Lancashire, books and journals from London and regional printers, and household provisions from supply networks extending from the capital into local towns and villages. In conjunction with this, Amanda Vickery, Claire Walsh, Hannah Greig and others have demonstrated that shopping was seldom a solitary activity relying on an encounter between shopper and merchant or tradesman/woman, while Jon Stobart and Mark Rothery have cautioned against seeing gender through simple binary opposites such as 'husband' and 'wife'.[3]

With some notable exceptions, we have a paucity of women in one discipline and an embarrassment of riches in the other. Between these two extremes, where then might 'reality' lie? How might an elite woman assume her role as mistress of an English house, with all the gender-prescribed responsibilities that entailed, while constructing a personal identity, a sense of *self*, through the purchase of luxury goods that demonstrated her own tastes and interests? Might problems arise when that woman was foreign? These questions cannot be answered definitively, of course, but the experiences of Sir Rowland Winn, fifth baronet, and his Swiss-born wife Sabine d'Herwart may present a useful middle ground for they were exceptional in some choices and more than mundane in others.

The Winns were descended from London-based textile merchants who had made their fortune under Elizabeth I and invested that wealth in estates in north Lincolnshire in the 1620s and the Nostell estate in West Yorkshire in 1654.[4] The old monastic buildings at Nostell became the main family residence and remained so until Sir Rowland Winn, fourth baronet, began to build a new house in the 1730s. At his death in 1765, the main house was structurally complete but not all of the wings had been constructed and many rooms were still unfinished, lacking plasterwork, chimneypieces and furniture. The fifth baronet dismissed James Paine, his father's architect, and employed Robert Adam to finish the interiors and add new wings, although all work stopped after Sir Rowland's death in 1785 and the house remained incomplete until the early nineteenth century.

The eighteenth-century Winns are not particularly illustrious. The fourth baronet was a Rockingham Whig but eschewed any genuine political activity and the fifth baronet's failure to win a parliamentary seat, despite numerous attempts between 1768 and 1784,[5] meant that neither man was a public figure of note outside the county. Indeed, the family would attract little attention now were it not for the beauty of Nostell and the richness of its archive for, in claiming their place among Yorkshire's elite, the Winns turned to firms in York, Leeds, Hull, Pontefract, Wakefield, Doncaster and London. They saved letters from haberdashers and milliners replete with fabric samples, while trade cards and bills indicate purchases of fashionable hot drinks such as coffee and tea, and an obsession with dental hygiene and sweet-smelling hair.

Such records exist because the Winns were reluctant to throw anything away but also because of the way they shopped – by correspondence and by proxy. As discussed by Claire Walsh and Ellen Hartigan-O'Connor, and by Steinrud in this volume,[6] neither form of shopping is unusual for the era but, as I will argue, the unique circumstances of the fifth baronet's marriage made instances of these types of shopping particularly well documented. In 1756, at the age of seventeen, Rowland Winn was sent to Lausanne to complete his education. A Grand Tour of Italy was discussed, but his tutor Isaac Dulon thought his young charge too susceptible to the dissipations of the British abroad and instead recommended a course of experimental physics at the Academy of Geneva.[7] Instead, Rowland fell in love with Sabine, reluctant wife of Colonel Gabriel May and sole heiress of Jacques-Philippe d'Herwart, Baron de Saint-Légier, Governor of the district of Vevey.[8] Although the d'Herwarts had links with Britain in the form of English cousins, a foreign match was not what either family desired.[9] After Sabine was widowed in 1759, however, no one could stop the couple marrying. By this date (1761) Rowland was a headstrong twenty-two and Sabine a flighty 27-year-old still unable to speak English. This cannot have eased her transition into life at Nostell or the marital home at Badsworth, which she described as 'one of the more desolate and ill-fated corners of the universe'.[10] Against the odds, the couple had a happy marriage, albeit one that excluded his family because they quarrelled with almost all of Rowland's sisters and alienated his aunts. At the root of their disagreements was the money his unmarried sisters needed to support themselves and the dowry that his brother-in-law claimed was his (not Rowland's) to control. The fifth baronet preferred to spend the same money buying a London townhouse in fashionable St James's Square, updating Nostell, and filling both houses with furniture, pictures and other luxury goods, large and small.

Degrees of luxury: creating tasteful interiors at Nostell

Although the Winns enjoyed the London season and spent much time in the capital in the early years of their marriage, neither Rowland nor Sabine made much of a mark on the interiors of their London townhouse. The same cannot be said for Nostell, where the Adam interiors and furniture by Thomas Chippendale are even better documented than at Adam and Chippendale's other great Yorkshire commission, Harewood House. Yet there are differences between the two houses that reveal more avant-garde architectural taste on the part of the Winns than that expressed by Edwin Lascelles at Harewood.

Eileen Harris has suggested that the presence of John Carr as executant architect at Harewood constrained Adam's ability to do what he did best – design rooms of different shapes derived from Roman bath planning.[11] In spite of enormous wealth derived from West Indian sugar plantations, Edwin Lascelles was ever mindful of his purse, informing Adam that he 'woud not exceed the limits of expence that I always propose to myself. Let us do every thing properly & well, mais pas trop'.[12] The result remains undeniably beautiful but the interiors at Harewood are more like glorified boxes with the occasional coved ceiling than characteristic of Adam's signature 'movement'. Their Neo-Classical ornament is only skin deep. A decade earlier they could have been rococo. One is always conscious that Harewood could have been so much more interesting had Lascelles thrown financial caution to the wind and given Adam his head.

Conversely, while the Winns' income never matched that of the Lascelles family, 'mais pas trop' never entered the conversation at Nostell. Although financial constraints rather than client disapproval meant that not everything Adam proposed for Nostell was executed, the plan and ornament of the Upper Hall is the architect at his very best. The transformation of what had been a dressing room in the south-east corner of the house into a Breakfast Room – a dedicated space unheard of earlier in the century – suggests that the Winns were also far more sensitive to new fashions than was Lascelles.

How much of this reflects Lady Winn's own tastes is frustratingly unknowable. Disappointingly for a woman described as so loving 'variety ... [she] may truly be Cald Lady Restles',[13] the only room where documentary evidence survives of her involvement is the Drawing Room. Today it is known as the Tapestry Room and only the Adam ceiling with its inset paintings by Antonio Zucchi survives. Chippendale sent samples of silk damask for the walls in 1767, but by 1781 Sabine had still not made her choice and the room was unfinished at her death in 1798.[14] We also have indirect evidence of her interest in Adam's proposals in the form of a drawing for the saloon ceiling where the colours are identified in French, not English.[15] There would be no other reason why the annotations are in French unless it was to assist Sabine.

The other difference between Harewood and Nostell is made manifest in Chippendale's furniture, where the roles of stylistic leader are reversed. At Harewood, the accounts 'refer almost exclusively to state furniture,'[16] and the collection is rightly renowned for such pieces as the recently restored state bed and the magnificently Neo-Classical Diana and Minerva commode, which cost £250 and £86 respectively when they were delivered in 1773.[17] At Nostell the furniture is much more conservative in nature and the accounts run the gamut from a mahogany library table at £72 10s. to a 'Green silk scarf for a Tambour' at eight shillings.[18] The former was for Sir Rowland, the latter for his wife. Like all women of her age and class, Lady Winn did needlework although no mention of this is made in her correspondence, nor does anything by her hand exist in the house today.

Few other items in Chippendale's accounts for Nostell are readily identifiable as belonging to Lady Winn, although the ten 'Mahogany french arm Chairs stuffd and coverd with blue Morine & brass naild', for which he charged £32 10s were certainly supplied for her blue dressing room (now the Little

Dining Room), which was densely hung with paintings, most in matching Chippendale frames.[19]

Lady Winn's shopping practices I: supplying the household

Building and furnishing aside, there is little doubt that Sabine Winn struggled to adjust to her new circumstances. Her command of English was still remarkably skeletal long after she had left Switzerland and the Winns corresponded with each other in French throughout their married life. One presumes that they spoke the same language at home. Even when preparing medicines and cosmetics in her still room at Nostell, the texts on which Sabine relied were French; she must have been relieved to discover that she could order these from London after John Murray responded to her request for the best books on what she called 'officinal Botany' with a list of three: 'Lewes's hist. of Materia Medica 4to', '____ New Dispensatory 8vo' and 'Pomets hist. of Drugs 4to'.[20] This no doubt explains the handwritten notice in French of a new edition of Pomet's *Histoire Generale des Drogues Simples et Composees* in the archive.[21]

Correspondence buying and proxy shopping

Early in her marriage, Sabine's relations with her sisters-in-law were as cordial as they could be when neither party spoke the other's language with ease, but two years after her arrival in the United Kingdom she still did not know them well enough to guess what they might like as gifts from London when her husband visited the capital. The best she could do was request that he buy them 'some trifles' at a guinea apiece.[22] What is more significant here is that as early as 1763 she was shopping by proxy, meaning that two or more people were involved, with one person acting for the other.

This was a harbinger of things to come for Lady Winn withdrew into self-imposed exile at Nostell after the birth of her son in 1775 and thereafter refused to travel. Sir Rowland, on the other hand, was perpetually on the move, to London to see to legal or financial matters, to oversee his Lincolnshire estates, to Switzerland to settle his mother-in-law's affairs, and twice to Bath to seek relief from gout and other ailments.[23] Deprived of the opportunity to shop on her own behalf, and unable to use her in-laws as proxy shoppers, Lady Winn combed the newspapers for advertisements and then relied on her husband, servants or trusted purveyors to purchase goods for her.[24] She also began to correspondence buy from her favourite London businesses, often requesting that the porter employed at the couple's townhouse collect and dispatch the goods north.[25] As we shall see below, the paradox is that Lady Winn's isolation at Nostell invariably rendered her dependent upon the opinions and choices of others – and most of those 'others' were English.

As the presence of the Breakfast Room at Nostell demonstrates, the Winns were fashionable eaters. Rowland's disapproving cousin Catharine Harrison noted that they kept 'very late, irregular hours, breakfasting at twelve or one, and dining at seven or eight',[26] but what she deemed eccentric behaviour in fact only anticipated the times when many aristocratic families were eating by the end of the century.[27]

Much of the food consumed by the family came from their various estates, but Lady Winn's desire for the best quality imported foodstuffs could only be satisfied by London purveyors and she seldom shopped locally for such goods. Her favourite London purveyors included Clarke and Pickering; Joseph Baker; Henry Pressey, a grocer of Nos 3 and 4 Henrietta Street, Covent Garden, who sold everything from coffee to candles, starch and mustard; and Joshua Long, grocer and tea dealer of No. 73 Cheapside, who supplied candied ginger and almonds in 1776 and white wine vinegar and 'Syrup de Capalain' in 1785.[28] A fragment of a bill from Bartholomew Valle and Brother, No. 21 St James's Hay-Market, records expenditure on macaroni, vermicelli and cheese.[29]

Economies on luxury goods were occasionally made, but the evidence suggests that it was Sir Rowland's fortuitous presence on his north Lincolnshire estates – and thus his proximity to Hull – that prompted a request in 1775 that he purchase the least expensive spermaceti candles that he could find.[30] This is the exception that proves the rule as the surviving memoranda and letters dealing with the acquisition of luxury goods otherwise relate to his journeys to London.

Goods for the servants were another matter, although the manner in which they were acquired was similar. Linens feature in several letters between Sabine and Rowland when the latter was visiting his Lincolnshire estates in 1775 and thus in close proximity to Hull, which may have offered a wider choice than Wakefield or Doncaster. As Sabine was well aware, sourcing linens was not normally a man's responsibility but she never visited the Thornton Curtis or Appleby estates and, in any case, her pregnancy prevented her from travelling that year.

A request for new linens was made in June 1775, and discussed again in October, when Sabine described the types of fabric she needed to make sheets for the servants, informed him of what he should expect to pay (14d. or 15d. per yard for the upper servants and 10d. per yard for the lower servants), and enclosed a sample of what she wanted.[31] Receiving a rapid response, her next letter thanked him for 'wanting to speak about linen' and reminded her husband 'not to buy linen with roughness in it'.[32] By 11 November, she was able to reply: 'Your linen is good and low-priced and as we are greatly in need of sheets, I will take a fair quantity of it. You will find on each pattern which I am sending you the number of pieces we want'.[33]

Lady Winn's shopping practices II: presenting the self

The state of the Winns' finances at the time of the fifth baronet's sudden death in 1785 precluded any further opportunity for Lady Winn to stamp her own taste on Nostell beyond the usual household items, but she continued to spend on personal items such as clothing and toiletries as if there had been no change to her circumstances. Here, we see several intertwined practices: a search for genuine French goods, correspondence buying from London and shopping local to buy global.

Although Hugh Douglas Hamilton's celebrated double portrait of the fifth baronet and his wife does little justice to either sitter, Sabine was a beautiful woman who took pride in her appearance,[34] relying on a combination of London purveyors and Yorkshire businesses. For example, in 1764 she spent £7 2s. 6d. on lace, a tucker, tippets, lappets, and more specialized needlework such as a stomacher and sleeve knots from Mary Reynoldson of York,[35] but over the years the number of London purveyors increased until towards the end of her life when she again turned to Yorkshire tradesmen.

It is in the middle years of her life that Lady Winn's predilection for French luxury goods is most discernible. Her status as wife of the fifth baronet and mother of the sixth would always have necessitated an elite appearance, but she was not subject to strong concerns about foreign luxuries and social class such as those experienced in Tallinn as considered by Astrid Pajur nor the sumptuary laws and heavily regulated economy of Sweden explored by Sofia Murhem and Göran Ulväng.[36] Likewise, her acquisition of French fabrics and accoutrements was not influenced by contemporary court culture (see the chapters on Spain by Fernández-de-Pinedo and Thépaut-Cabasset and Sweden by Ilmakunnas) nor was it merely an expedient means of indicating membership of an international elite similar to that discussed by Clemente (Naples) or North (the German states). Instead, Lady Winn's insistence on French-made markers of female membership of polite society – so strikingly at odds with the quintessentially English interiors of Nostell – must surely be seen as her way of preserving her own cultural contexts, of asserting her own personality in the face of almost overwhelming familial pressure to become 'English'. It must also be placed in the context of her legal worries after 1785 as her in-laws pursued her through the courts in an attempt to remove her young son from her care. Preserving dignity may never have been among her strong points, but it was vital in this instance.

Shopping *à la Française*

The presence of a trade card or advertisement is not necessarily evidence of a purchase, of course, but a remarkable number of such ephemera in the Winn archive are related to French goods; evidently Lady Winn had no qualms about buying French imports during or immediately after the Seven Years' War.[37] Instead, her choices are direct evidence of something more than the generic taste for French-style luxury goods typical of Britain's elite, as they were the very means by which she presented herself to the world. In 1764 and 1765 she placed orders for ribbons, a pink hat, handkerchiefs and other sundries with Anne Blanchet; in 1770, L. D. Bourgeois provided goods such as toothbrushes, garters, and eau de cologne; and in 1785 Gaillard and Toussaint supplied gloves, bonbonieres, and French chalk.[38] An account for toilet waters, toothbrushes, horse brasses, a pair of dividers, and a little dog from a Monsieur Martinnant dated 25 March 1785 is written in a curious mix of French and English that goes well beyond the occasional insertion of a foreign word.[39] Lady Winn also kept undated advertisements from 'Thevenot, Ladies Hairdresser' who could provide the latest fashions direct from 'Mr LEvecque, who is one of the greatest Milliner[s] in Paris', from 'De Romand french Hatter from Paris', and from 'Sommar Ladies Shoemaker No.7 by Southmolton Street . . . [who] begs leave to acquaint the Ladies in general, that though his residence in this Kingdom has been Short he has already Served Several of the Nobility &c'.[40]

Of the London purveyors of French goods, the best documented is the milliner Ann Charlton.[41] Mrs Charlton was obviously the sort of shopkeeper to cultivate because she dealt in contraband or black market goods; French gloves are described as 'to[o] dangerous a thing to deal in'[42] (which must be why she offered Sabine twenty pairs) and 'in regard to the gause it is a French one & the Common wedth of french ones the reason we cut the selvage of[f] is that we may run no risk in keeping it in the house'.[43]

Her letters are more valuable than the unveiling of illegal practices, however, as they were accompanied by samples of gauzes and ribbons. Mrs Charlton 'exploited tactile engagement with goods to the full, playing with excitement and anticipation by revealing goods in elaborate sequences and encouraging . . . handling' before any order was made.[44] Aware that Lady Winn liked to give ribbon and lace to her friends and protégés, she also sent small gifts in the form of unwanted stock.[45]

The correspondence begins in March 1783, when Mrs Charlton wrote to inform Lady Winn that 'I have a great many new things from Paris . . . I was there my self last summer we have some very pretty new Caps . . . & most Elegant handkercheifs & french ribbands[,] shoes, watch chains' and so on.[46] Soon dispatched on the coach north was a parcel containing gauzes and ribbons as well as an unsolicited three watch chains and a French chemise and sash 'much newer & prettier then any other dress . . . [sashes] are quite the fashion & no Ladys go without. . .'.[47] The dress, which had cost Mrs Charlton the equivalent of nine guineas in France, was offered for four guineas and could be returned if undesired.

A mere eight days later, we learn that Lady Winn had accepted the chemise, thought her shoe bows were a little tarnished but been offered a discount, had enquired about the appearance of a 'Rutland hat' and a 'Westmoreland handkerchief', and wanted peach roses for her slippers.[48]

In July 1783 a box containing the Westmoreland handkerchief, samples of velvet edging, bows 'made of the new Marlbrough strip-d ribband nothing else is now worne in town it is . . . quite the fashion', and some unsolicited samples of black ribbon was on its way to Nostell, along with the teaser: 'I expect very soon a large asortment of blond edging from Paris & will as soon as I have got them send your ladyship all the patterns . . . I sent your Ladyship before all the pattrens of french gauses they are not worne much in England'.[49] As this statement suggests, Lady Winn's tastes were still more continental than English in spite of the twenty-two years she had lived in Britain.

Mrs Charlton was not the only London merchant to send samples to Nostell. A 1797 letter from Daniel Ecoffay and one of 1798 from H. Faulding both contain swatches of chintz.[50] Ecoffay appears several times in the archive. In 1791 he supplied stockings, a handkerchief, a porcelain 'boite de Toilette', various chains, and 'une Superbe Jupe des Indes peint', and his account for 1793–1796 reveals that he also acquired goods from other merchants on Lady Winn's behalf.[51]

Correspondence buying and proxy shopping for English goods

Personal grooming is an area in which the archive is rich in material although, in contrast to Sabine Winn's expression of *self* through wearing French apparel, almost all of the purveyors and the goods themselves were English. Invariably these were small items intended for everyday use, but the Winns always bought high-end goods and they often turned to the newspapers and made notes on various products to try.[52] A bill from Charles Sharp reveals that Lady Winn purchased a brush, comb, garters and a tongue scraper in 1779 and, related to this order, is an undated note giving orders for shopping in London that was clearly intended for one of the servants to fulfil.[53] In 1781, W. Vickery supplied lavender and Hungary waters.[54] She also purchased rosewater, jasmine pomade, soap and other items from Peter Grellier in 1785.[55] Bayley became a favoured purveyor in the 1790s. Sabine bought sundry trinkets in 1795; was in receipt of a parcel containing toiletries, seals, and bonbon boxes in 1797, and in 1798 she returned a parcel of goods and was soon to receive more in exchange although 'this being the season when the Town is quite full we take the liberty to request the articles your Ladyship does not Keep, may be return'd by the first opportunity'.[56]

Shopping local to buy global

Of more local haberdashery businesses patronized by Sabine Winn, Shillito of Wakefield supplied: ribbons; handkerchiefs; caps, hats and bonnets; mittens and gloves; muslins, lawn, and cambric; thread, pins, and tea.[57] John Teale and Son of Leeds supplied fine white hose in 1789, and William Radford provided hair chains, watch chains, bracelets, rings and the like in 1797, and in 1798 sent for inspection knee buckles, pocket knives, and pins or brooches.[58] George Spurr, a Doncaster linen and woollen draper, supplied fabrics, muslin handkerchiefs, chintz gowns, ribbons, striped silk hose, buttons, thread, and knee bands in 1789, and the Doncaster mercers, Wrightson and Firth, were suppliers for a number of years in the 1790s.[59]

Lady Winn was particularly faithful to the Wakefield haberdasher Thomas Yeamans, who supplied items such as: jewellery; a muslin cloak trimmed with lace; handkerchiefs; ribbons; gowns of Indian chintz, calico or muslin; 'A Bosom Friend' and '1 Gown long live the King', amounting to an outstanding sum of over £116 by October 1789.[60] In an undated letter, Yeamans also informed his client that he had sent her a parcel of 'French Cambricks . . . [and] a Peice of the Newest Chintz'.[61]

As Hannah Greig has suggested, newness in clothing and accessories was a key contributor to the public persona of the elite, especially for anyone who attended court or had aspirations in that direction.[62] Royal birthdays were celebrated with costly new garments and, in the case of the celebrations marking George III's recovery from madness in 1789, with a sartorial display that included headdresses emblazoned with 'God save the King'. It is in this context that we must see the 'long live the King' gown.

With Lady Winn's refusal to leave Nostell and her husband's failure to receive a much-desired elevation to the peerage[63] and subsequent death, any opportunity to attend court had long since passed but, even in the isolation of the West Riding, she deemed it necessary that the king's return to health be marked by a display of loyalty to the crown. Sabine was not a political animal – she came from a country where women had few opportunities to participate in politics in the ways that British women did[64] – and her in-laws had been right to fear that she would be of little use in furthering Sir Rowland's political career, yet, at a time when contemporaries were casting an uneasy eye on events unfolding across the Channel, she must have been acutely aware that her French fashions, her library of French books, and the language which she spoke, made her loyalties suspect, even if (or perhaps because) she had been born in republican Switzerland. In a distant echo of the ways in which the dress of the women of early modern Tallinn had been regulated to reflect the place of birth and social position of their husbands or fathers, now was the time and place for Sabine Winn to be as 'English' as possible. Whether anyone outside Nostell saw the dress is a moot point; it is highly unlikely that she was alone in ordering such a garment from Yeamans, who would naturally have discussed this dress with his other clients.

Conclusion

What conclusions might we draw about the Winns' tenure at Nostell between 1765, when Rowland inherited, and the death of his widow in 1798? The first is that they were an aspirational couple who employed a renowned architect and one of the best cabinetmakers in London to update a house that they could not afford. Their taste in architecture was definitely more *avant-garde* than their taste in furniture and, had they possessed wealth akin to that of the Lascelles family, Nostell might be a very different house from the one National Trust members visit today. The correspondence between Sir Rowland, Adam and Chippendale is characteristically male-centric, but the evidence that Sabine played some role in determining the appearance of her home cannot be denied.

A second conclusion is that, like most elite women of her era, Sabine Winn shopped locally and nationally for a wide array of household goods, using a variety of means. She repeatedly turned to London purveyors to provide the most expensive high-end toiletries and foodstuffs – many of which were British in origin – but occasionally economized by shopping more locally when the opportunity presented itself. This typically happened when her husband was visiting his Lincolnshire estates and was thus near enough to take advantage of the emporia of Hull. Because the fifth baronet travelled so frequently, his wife and children were able to access a much wider range of luxury goods than Sabine's self-imposed isolation at Nostell would otherwise have allowed.

A final conclusion is that, in the one area where Lady Winn had the most freedom to express herself, this cuckoo in the nest was unafraid to express overtly Francophile tastes that went well beyond the norm. Apart from the exceptional 'long live the King' gown, Sabine's clothing was genuinely French in origin rather than generically 'French' in style and this was as true in 1798 as it had been at the time of her marriage in 1761.

Notes

1 See, for example, Dana Arnold, *The Georgian Country House: Architecture, Landscape and Society* (Stroud: Sutton Publishing, 1998), 79–99 and *Reading Architectural History* (London and New York: Routledge, 2002), 199–204.

2 Frances Harris, *A Passion for Government: The Life of Sarah, Duchess of Marlborough* (Oxford: Clarendon Press, 1991); Rosemary Baird, *Mistress of the House: Great Ladies and Grand Houses, 1670–1830* (London: Phoenix, 2004).

3 *Gender, Taste, and Material Culture in Britain and North America 1700–1830*, eds John Styles and Amanda Vickery (New Haven and London: Yale University Press for the Paul Mellon Centre for Studies in British Art, 2006); Hannah Greig, *The Beau Monde: Fashionable Society in Georgian London* (Oxford: Oxford University Press, 2013); Jon Stobart and Mark Rothery, 'Men, Women and the Supply of Luxury Goods in Eighteenth-Century England: The Purchasing Patterns of Edward and Mary Leigh', in *Luxury and Gender in European Towns, 1700–1914*, eds Deborah Simonton, Marjo Kaartinen and Anne Montenach (New York and London: Routledge, 2015), 97–115.

4 Sophie Raikes and Tim Knox, *Nostell Priory and Parkland*, 6th edn (2008; repr., Swindon: National Trust, 2009), 50–1.

5 Christopher Todd, 'A Swiss Milady in Yorkshire: Sabine Winn of Nostell Priory', *Yorkshire Archaeological Journal* 77 (2005): 213–14.

6 Claire Walsh, 'Shops, Shopping, and the Art of Decision Making in Eighteenth-Century England', in *Gender, Taste, and Material Culture in Britain and North America 1700–1830*, eds John Styles and Amanda Vickery (New Haven and

London: Yale University Press for the Paul Mellon Centre for Studies in British Art, 2006), 170; Ellen Hartigan-O'Connor, 'Collaborative Consumption and the Politics of Choice in Early American Port Cities', in *Gender, Taste, and Material Culture in Britain and North America 1700–1830*, 125–6.

7 Isaac Dulon to Sir Rowland Winn, fourth baronet, August 1757, Nostell Papers, WYW1352/1/1/4/27, West Yorkshire Archive Service (Wakefield). Hereafter, the Nostell papers at WYAS (Wakefield) will be cited as NP.

8 For Sabine Winn's family, see Christopher Todd, 'A Swiss Milady in Yorkshire: Sabine Winn of Nostell Priory', *Yorkshire Archaeological Journal* 77 (2005): 205–24.

9 Todd, 'A Swiss Milady in Yorkshire', 209.

10 Sabine Winn to Rowland Winn, undated, NP, WYW1352/1/4/29/17.

11 Eileen Harris, *The Genius of Robert Adam: His Interiors* (New Haven and London: Yale University Press for The Paul Mellon Centre for Studies in British Art, 2001), 132–55.

12 Edwin Lascelles to Robert Adam, 19 November 1766, quoted in Harris, *The Genius of Robert Adam*, 138.

13 Ann Elizabeth Winn to Sir Rowland Winn, fourth baronet, 9 December 1763, NP, WYW1352/1/4/11/8.

14 Raikes and Knox, *Nostell Priory*, 27; Harris, *The Genius of Robert Adam*, 203; Christopher Gilbert, 'New Light on the Furnishing of Nostell Priory', *Furniture History* XXVI (1990): 60–1.

15 Harris, *The Genius of Robert Adam*, 205.

16 Lindsay Boynton and Nicholas Goodison, 'The Furniture of Thomas Chippendale at Nostell Priory-I', *The Burlington Magazine* 111, No.794 (May 1969): 282.

17 Caroline Storey, 'Harewood House 1767–1797: Chippendale's Most Magnificent Commission', in *The Art of Thomas Chippendale Master Furniture Maker*, ed. Jane Sellars (Leeds: Harewood House Trust, 2000), 29, 31.

18 Sir Rowland Winn, fifth baronet, correspondence and accounts with Thomas Chippendale, 1767–1785, NP, WYW1352/3/3/1/5/3/47.

19 Sir Rowland Winn, fifth baronet, correspondence and accounts with Thomas Chippendale, 1767–1785, NP, WYW1352/3/3/1/5/3/45. See also Thomas Chippendale to Sir Rowland Winn, *ca.*1771, NP, WYW1352/3/3/1/5/3/31 and Raikes and Knox, *Nostell Priory*, 34.

20 Several sheets of paper containing details of various products to be bought from different tradespeople in London, undated, NP, WYW1352/1/4/32/17.

21 Several sheets of paper containing details of various products to be bought from different tradespeople in London, undated, NP, WYW1352/1/4/32/17.

22 Sabine Winn at Nostell to Rowland Winn, 19 March 1763, NP, WYW1352/1/1/5/9/2.

23 For Sir Rowland's illnesses, see Todd, 'A Swiss Milady in Yorkshire', 216.

24 There are many lists of shops for Sir Rowland to visit and items to purchase in the Winn archive. See, for example, Memoranda of Commissions for Lady Winn, NP, WYW1352/1/4/91/3. For servants and friends, see Lydia Hudson to Sabine Winn and to Mrs Lambelet (Esther Winn's French governess), 1779, NP, WYW1352/1/1/6/6; Samuel Thompson to Mrs Fleming, 12 December 1779 and E. Nicholson to Sabine Winn, 12 October [1782], NP, WYW1352/1/1/6/5. The Winns' use of advertisements is akin to the German consumers of periodicals devoted to fashion and taste discussed by Michael North in Chapter 5 of this volume.

25 Documents relating to Samuel Thompson, the Winns' porter at St James's Square in the 1770s and early 1780s, reveal that this was a frequent occurrence. See receipt from Robert Jackson, 5 August 1777; Samuel Thompson to [Sir Rowland Winn?], 18 November 1775; Samuel Thompson to [Mr Taylor?], 10 July 1781; bill and receipt from Nicholas Sanders, chocolate maker of Greek Street, Soho, 3 August 1778, NP, WYW1352/3/4/3/1.

26 *Memoirs of the Life of the Late Mrs. Catharine Cappe, written by herself*, ed. Mary Cappe (London, 1822), 98.

27 Sara Paston-Williams, *The Art of Dining: A History of Cooking and Eating* (London: The National Trust, 1999), 241–5.

28 Bill of sale from Clarke and Pickering, 30 April 1776, NP, WYW1352/3/4/3/1; Bill of sale from Joseph Baker, 22 December 1779, NP, WYW1352/3/4/3/1; Bill of sale from George Pressey, 3 October 1780, NP, WYW1352/3/4/3/2; Bill and receipt from Joshua Long, 13 May 1776 and receipt from Joshua Long, 18 July 1785, NP, WYW1352/3/4/3/2.

29 Receipt from Bartholomew Valle and Brother, 4 January 1785, NP, WYW1352/3/4/3/2.

30 Sabine Winn to Sir Rowland Winn, 9 October 1775, NP, WYW1352/1/4/29/6. See also WYW1352/1/4/29/9, WYW1352/1/4/29/2, WYW1352/1/4/29/14 and WYW1352/1/1/5/9. Spermaceti is an oily substance found in the heads of sperm whales that was much desired in the production of clean-burning and odourless candles. The expense of making these candles rendered them luxury goods. Servants would have used tallow candles.

31 Sabine Winn to Sir Rowland Winn, 14 October 1775, NP, WYW1352/1/4/29/8.

32 Sabine Winn to Sir Rowland Winn, 19 October 1775, NP, WYW1352/1/4/29/9.

33 Sabine Winn to Sir Rowland Winn, 11 November 1775, NP, WYW1352/1/4/29/11.

34 Cappe, *Memoirs*, 85–6.

35 Bill from Mary Reynoldson, 21 August 1764, NP, WYW1352/3/4/3/1.

36 Interestingly, some members of the Swiss confederacy maintained sumptuary laws throughout the eighteenth century – when they were much approved of by visiting

Englishmen and women – but these laws were not in effect in Vevey when Lady Winn was a child nor, had they been, would such a high-ranking member of the town's elite been affected.

37 See the note in French recording toiletries received from Mr de Boffe as well as a list of French medical books ordered from him, Medical prescriptions and culinary recipes collected by Sabine Winn, *ca.*1765–1785, NP, WYW1352/3/4/7/8. Contemporary concerns about the purchase of French goods are discussed in Maxine Berg and Elizabeth Eger, 'The Rise and Fall of the Luxury Debates', in *Luxury in the Eighteenth Century: Debates, Desires and Delectable Goods*, eds Maxine Berg and Elizabeth Eger (Basingstoke and New York: Palgrave Macmillan, 2003), 14.

38 Bill of sale from Anne Blanchet, 10 June 1765, NP, WYW1352/3/4/3/1 (the bill is signed in French, not English); Account of Lady Winn with L. D. Bourgeois, 1775, NP, WYW1352/1/4/113/11 (Bourgeois is also mentioned in an undated letter to Sabine Winn, NP, WYW1352/3/4/3/1); Bill and receipt from Gaillard and Toussaint, 18 April 1785, NP, WYW1352/3/4/3/2.

39 Account from Mr Martinnant, 25 March 1785, NP, WYW1352/3/4/3/2. Martinnant appears in a number of rather confusing documents, making it difficult to determine his identity. See NP, WYW1352/1/1/5/9 and WYW1352/3/4/3/2.

40 Handwritten advertisement for Thevenot, ladies' hairdresser, undated, NP, WYW1352/1/4/54/6; Several sheets of paper containing details of various products to be bought from different tradespeople in London, undated, NP, WYW1352/1/4/32/17.

41 List of Tradespeople in London, *ca.*1770s, NP, WYW1352/1/4/30/22.

42 Ann Charlton to Sabine Winn, 30 May 1783, NP, WYW1352/3/4/6/8.

43 Ann Charlton to Sabine Winn, 20 August 1783, NP, WYW1352/3/4/6/8.

44 Walsh, 'Shops, Shopping, and the Art of Decision Making in Eighteenth-Century England', 169–70.

45 Ann Charlton to Sabine Winn, undated, NP, WYW1352/3/4/6/8. The memoirs of Catharine Cappe also reveal that Sabine made gifts of ribbons and other adornments to her friends and acquaintances, although her rationale for doing so was perhaps not always to her credit. Cappe, *Memoirs*, 99–100.

46 Ann Charlton to Sabine Winn, 31 March 1783, NP, WYW1352/3/4/6/8.

47 Ann Charlton to Sabine Winn, 22 May 1783, NP, WYW1352/3/4/6/8.

48 Ann Charlton to Sabine Winn, 30 May 1783, NP, WYW1352/3/4/6/8.

49 Ann Charlton to Sabine Winn, 23 July 1783, NP, WYW1352/3/4/6/8.

50 Daniel Ecoffay to Sabine Winn, June 1797 and H. Faulding to Sabine Winn, 17 January 1798, NP, WYW1352/3/4/6/9. For Faulding, see also Serena Dyer, 'Shopping, Spectacle & the Senses', *History Today* 65 (March 2015), 36.

51 Bill from Daniel Ecoffay, 29 December 1791, NP, WYW1352/3/4/3/2; Account of Sabine Winn with Daniel Ecoffay, 1793–1796, NP, WYW1352/3/4/3/2.

52 Several sheets of paper containing details of various products to be bought from different tradespeople in London, undated, NP, WYW1352/1/4/32/17.

53 Bill of sale from Charles Sharp, 19 August 1779, NP, WYW1352/3/4/3/1; Unsigned letter giving orders for London shopping, NP, WYW1352/3/4/3/1.

54 Bill of sale from W. Vickery, 10 July 1781, NP, WYW1352/3/4/3/1.

55 Bill of sale from Peter Grellier, NP, WYW1352/3/4/3/2.

56 Receipt from Bayley and Clarkson, 3 June 1795, NP, WYW1352/3/4/3/2; Letter from Bayley Son and Blew to Sabine Winn, 2 December 1797, NP, WYW1352/3/4/3/2; Letter and bill from Bayley Son and Blew to Sabine Winn, 1 February 1798, NP, WYW1352/3/4/3/2.

57 Receipt from Mary Shillito, 17 March 1789, NP, WYW1352/1/4/103/13 and Bill from N. Shillito, 1785–1786, NP, WYW1352/3/4/3/2.

58 Bill from John Teale and Son, 29 September 1789, NP, WYW1352/3/4/3/2; Bill and receipt from William Radford, 5 June 1797, NP, WYW1352/3/4/3/2; Bill from William Radford, 29 June 1789, NP, WYW1352/3/4/3/1.

59 Bill of sale and receipt from George Spurr, 1789, NP, WYW1352/3/4/3/2; Accounts of Wrightson and Firth, 1790–1791, NP, WYW1352/3/4/3/2; Bill and letter from Joshua Firth to Sabine Winn, 29 November 1795, NP, WYW1352/3/4/3/2; Bill from Joshua Firth, 27 January 1796, NP, WYW1352/3/4/3/2; Bill and letter from Joshua Firth to Sabine Winn, 30 March 1798, NP, WYW1352/3/4/3/2; and Bill from Joshua Firth, 21 April 1798, NP, WYW1352/3/4/3/2.

60 Yeamans accounts are all NP, WYW1352/3/4/3/2.

61 Thomas Yeamans to Sabine Winn, undated, NP, WYW1352/3/4/6/9.

62 Greig, *The Beau Monde*, 99–130, especially 126–8.

63 Sir Rowland Winn to Sabine Winn, 17 April 1777, NP, WYW1352/1/1/6/3.

64 Clive H. Church and Randolph C. Head, *A Concise History of Switzerland* (Cambridge: Cambridge University Press, 2013), 77.

9

Books, Wine and Fine China: Consumption Patterns of a *Brukspatron* in Early Nineteenth-Century Sweden

Marie Steinrud

It has been said that no private title in Sweden has, before or after the eighteenth and nineteenth centuries, had such reputation and prestige as a *brukspatron*. The Swedish title refers to the owner and manager of large-scale ironworks, a distinct elite group of a special kind of iron producers – also called ironmasters – mostly living on estates close to their ironworks, attending to the business and life on site.[1] In this chapter, I will discuss the consumption patterns of one of them, the wealthy and powerful nobleman and *brukspatron* Per Reinhold Tersmeden (1751–1842). He lived in the parish of Ramnäs, some 150 kilometres northwest of Stockholm, where at the start of the nineteenth century he had built himself a mansion.[2] Per Reinhold Tersmeden was a nobleman; an active part of society, both on a local and a national level, and a prominent member of the emerging group of Swedish ironmasters. He serves as a case study to illustrate the ironmasters as a group and how they acquired and communicated luxury as well as taste. His main interest was his business and he reinvested the profits, thus expanding the business over the years. He never married and had no children. Although he regularly took part in the political life in Stockholm, he preferred to stay at his estate, avoiding the hustle of the big city. His eclectic background and life made him a typical *brukspatron*.[3] The ironmasters were, during this period, engaged in forming themselves as a group with common interests, which was manifest in the foundation of Jernkontoret, the Swedish steel producers' association, in the mid-eighteenth century, as well as the creation of a special uniform to be worn by the ironmasters.[4]

Figure 9.1 Per Reinhold Tersmeden wearing the ironmasters uniform with the chemical symbol for iron on his collar. He is also wearing the Royal Order of the Sword. Together they were important and distinct symbols of his identity as a nobleman, a military man and a *brukspatron*.

Lithograph after a painting by Per Krafft from 1823.

Figure 9.2 View over Per Reinhold Tersmeden's estate in the parish of Ramnäs around the mid-eighteenth century.

© Thora Thersner, Jernkontoret.

This chapter focuses on the interaction between this nobleman-ironmaster and the people around him, with whom he discussed all sorts of goods, including flowers, furniture, porcelain, clothes and trinkets, and who provided him with the goods as well as information about what to buy, when and where. Communication with private commissioners constituted a great deal of Per Reinhold Tersmeden's correspondence and makes it possible to study what kind of goods he desired and how he knew what to buy, even though he lived far from shops, boutiques and markets.[5] Do his letters show the consumption of a nobleman or did he affiliate himself with the up-and-coming group of iron producers in this district? More generally, how does the *brukspatron* Per Reinhold Tersmeden and his sense of luxury and taste connect with broader debates about luxury and flamboyance?

What can be found out about consumer behaviour on an everyday personal level during this time is naturally governed by the available source material. Personal correspondence is well suited here, since it allows access to an individual's own thoughts and ideas about their life. In drawing on the correspondence of Per Reinhold Tersmeden, I will focus on the informal connections between the one who wants to make a purchase and the one doing the actual purchase, the commissioner. As with all historical sources, letters suffer from limitations: their form or style as well as the fact that they were not understood as the personal affair it is today influenced what was written, and how.[6] Nevertheless, correspondence gives an invaluable insight into the ideas of consumption and the act of acquiring goods. Per Reinhold Tersmeden was, like most of his peers during this time, a frequent letter writer. After he moved in to his new estate during the first years of the 1800s, he wrote on average four letters each day.[7] About three hundred letters can be found in various archives in Sweden.[8] In the available letters, the commissioners engaged by Per Reinhold Tersmeden formed a network that provided him not only with goods and personal items, but also with vital information regarding everything from who was marrying whom to the price range of pig iron. The letters reveal an outspoken man with many thoughts about politics, the iron industry and his everyday life at the estate. He was forthright about his finances and money in general, but he seldom wrote about his own shopping or goods he purchased while travelling or during his visits to Stockholm. His letters allow us to follow discussions between Per Reinhold Tersmeden and his commissioners about what to spend money on and what was considered wasteful, as well as ideas about their consumption and often that of others. These discussions reveal consumption patterns within a group in the process of forming itself as an elite in society, possessing monetary, as well as political, power during the early modern period.

Necessary spending

The strive for power, status and luxury is by no means a new one. Luxury and what is considered splendour and extravagance must be understood in its historical and cultural context.[9] The consumption patterns of Per Reinhold Tersmeden, the discussions he was engaged in as to what could be obtained and what was *à la mode* is part of what has been called a consumption revolution in the eighteenth and nineteenth century: a time when the consumption of different, and often luxury, goods increased remarkably.[10] This so-called consumer revolution had a great impact on everyday life, which is the focus of this chapter. The correspondence of Per Reinhold Tersmeden reveals his many wants and needs regarding a vast amount of goods and it is evident that objects played an important role in the life of the ironmaster; not least as props when displaying social status. During the eighteenth century, the grand houses in Sweden were gradually filled with art and a growing range of consumption goods – a process which relied on the availability of new products, but also the development of new supply systems, themselves built on improved and more affordable logistics and transportation.[11] Private channels and networks were an important part of this supply system and of the consumption revolution. A recurrent feature in the private correspondence during this time are commissions, dealing with the mediation and procurement of goods, the writers asking the recipient to order or to buy different goods on the writer's behalf.[12]

It was Thorstein Veblen who, in his classical work *The Theory of the Leisure Class*, used the term 'conspicuous consumption' for the kind of apparent and manifest consumption that was especially appropriate to maintain social status. Veblen alluded to the nouveaux riches of his own time; a group he saw as preoccupied with consuming expensive luxury goods. Through social emulation, which describes the idea that we consume like our social superiors, and social distinction, where we consume in a way that marks difference from other generally lower social groups, consumption itself creates and maintains cultural meaning and is a central part of the construction of our identity. The recurrent question evolves around who we want to associate ourselves with – and dissociate ourselves from.[13] Peter Burke has drawn on Veblen's theories to elucidate elite consumption and points out that, to fully understand the behaviour behind the consumption, the consumption itself must be seen as rational, logical and necessary; necessary in the sense that it allows an aspiration upwards, but also identification with the group of people one aspired to belong to.[14] What one consumes is a way to present oneself, thus making consumption a vital part of the interaction with others.[15]

But consumer patterns and the consumption of goods – luxury or not – must be contextualized to be understood. Different groups in society would be expected to consume in different ways. Financial conditions were, naturally, of great importance, as was knowledge about what kinds of goods to consume. The nobility was all about consumption; the big question for them was rather what to spend money on, not whether to spend it. But Per Reinhold Tersmeden was not just a nobleman, his role as an ironmaster was vital in forming his identity. Maxine Berg shows in her research the clashes between what Jan de Vries calls old luxury and new luxury. Old luxury is usually connected with the established nobility while new luxury is linked with the up-and-coming middle class and the nouveau riche, individuals that had earned their fortune rather than inherited it. Berg points out that the different groups consumed luxury in different ways. New luxury was all about commerce, utility, taste and comfort while the language of the old luxury evolved around wealth, status and power.[16] Even though Per Reinhold Tersmeden was born a nobleman, his family was recently ennobled and their wealth was strongly connected to iron production. It is possible to say that he grew up and lived with one leg in the nobility and the other in the emerging group of genteel business-owners. It is also important to note that Per Reinhold Tersmeden lived in a time were old and new luxury existed side by side, challenging each other; an antagonism that can be traced in his correspondence.

The commissioners

In 1825, Per Reinhold Tersmeden asked his nephew, living in Stockholm, to send him some hyacinth bulbs for the front garden – not too expensive though – so that the scent of the flowers later on would bring delight to the noses of his elderly aunts, living with him at the mansion. The nephew promptly answered his uncle and soon the hyacinth bulbs – along with a number of other goods – were on their way to brighten the lives of Per Reinhold Tersmeden and his relatives.[17] The nephew was Knut von Troil (1791–1853), working as a civil servant within the government. From the time he set up his own household in Stockholm as a young man, von Troil was one of Per Reinhold Tersmeden's most frequently engaged commissioners. The letters between them are filled with Per Reinhold Tersmeden's directions about what to buy, when and where; sometimes detailed and long-winded, sometimes surprisingly meagre and brief. Besides Knut von Troil, Wilhelm Fredrik Tersmeden (1802–1879), the only son of Per Reinhold Tersmeden's favourite brother, was engaged almost as much as his cousin. Wilhelm Fredrik Tersmeden was also his uncle's designated successor and spent a lot of time with his uncle. Both of the nephews lived as adults in Stockholm and could easily access the shops and stores of their uncle's choosing.[18] He regularly referred to them as his 'most trusted commissioners' and, although he also consulted his siblings, this was less frequent and only when they already had revealed plans to visit a special shopkeeper or a town, rarely being asked to take a detour on behalf of Per Reinhold Tersmeden.[19]

The source material does not reveal whether Per Reinhold Tersmeden bought goods on his own travels to Stockholm. On a personal level, he seemed tired and distressed every time he visited the city. In a letter to his nephew he revealed his displeasure with both Stockholm and his business there, and he complained about the discussions at the House of the Nobility which, according to him, dealt with nothing.[20] He flatly stated that he had no desire or urge to stay in the city any longer than was necessary and that he would rather leave purchases to his favourite commissioner as 'you know best what I need'.[21]

The network of commissioners surrounding Per Reinhold Tersmeden consisted mostly of relatives, and for the most part close relatives, but it was by no means an all-male network. His sisters as well as his nieces all at some point acted as commissioners on his behalf, although he seemed to rely on these women to purchase certain kinds of goods or at least give advice to the men on what to buy. This was particularly true of smaller items used in the household, such as needles, cutlery, buttons, thread, flowers and curtains.[22] The commissions themselves were numerous. On average, Per Reinhold Tersmeden wrote his nephew Knut von Troil one letter every week and every third letter contained at least one commission. The commissions were of course very varied, and could stretch from small requests like the delivery of a letter or a parcel to a friend to larger undertakings like purchases of wine or furniture. Nonetheless, all the commissions must have taken up a great deal of time and as a rule the commissioners did not get paid for their work. On the other hand, Per Reinhold Tersmeden acted as a father figure to many of his younger relatives, providing them with a home and sometimes an education. For example, he helped Knut von Troil financially when he got married and furnished his home in Stockholm. Moreover, like his cousins, Knut von Troil could take part in and, in time, be a member of the network surrounding his uncle, a network that in turn provided him with both commissioners and vital information.

Following the consumption network of Per Reinhold Tersmeden during the first half of the nineteenth century, it is possible to see changes over time. Since there is no information about his consumption patterns before he left the army and settled as an ironmaster, we can only speculate how it may have looked. Most likely, his habits changed when he realized he was to be the next ironmaster in Ramnäs, which is not surprising.[23] One obvious change in the network is the fact that, in the beginning of the period, he turned to his brothers and sisters, and some of his cousins and other relatives. His brother Fredrik Tersmeden had a house in Stockholm and spent most of his time there, together with his family. In these letters, Per Reinhold Tersmeden discusses his consumption mostly with his brothers; they gave each other advice that could be both frank and outspoken. In a letter to his brother, Fredrik, Tersmeden tells him directly that he should not give way to the temptation to provide someone with too expensive a gift, since it only will give him displeasure in the future, trying to keep up with the same level.[24] When the nephews set up households of their own, Per Reinhold Tersmeden gradually turned to them for commission, as we have already seen. In the correspondence, it is clear that

Per Reinhold Tersmeden had strong ideas about his own consumption, as well as that of others, but discussions with his commissioners also shows that this was a complex situation. It is not always clear who was driving the processes behind consumption choices; rather some of the purchases seem to be more like a mutual decision between the people involved.

Objects of attraction

Per Reinhold Tersmeden was inspired by others as regards to what to spend money on. Letters between him and his relatives, in Stockholm but also in other parts of Sweden, show that he used them as his foremost source of inspiration, together with newspapers, in which he regularly indulged. He rarely asked his commissioners to provide him with the mundane goods of everyday life, such as potatoes, flour and fresh fish. Most likely, these goods came from towns and villages in the surrounding area, and he seemed to lack personal commissioners for these kinds of things. Judging from the letters, he relied on more formal connections with shopkeepers and tradesmen to acquire such provisions.[25] Instead his personal commissioners worked with the never-ending task of providing him with clothes and shoes, books and newspapers, jewellery and trinkets, china, glassware, curtains, furniture, wine, and fine tea and coffee. He most frequently asked for books, usually in the field of science in general, and the iron and mining industries in particular, but he also enjoyed wine, and in some instances he also asked for china and lacquer, revealing an interest in products from the Far East, although this did not stretch as far as that of the nabob studied by Kuiper elsewhere in this volume.[26]

In a letter to one of his nephews he depicts a visit to his neighbour, Knut Lindorm Posse (1802–1840). In spite of the considerable difference in age, Knut Posse and Per Reinhold were close friends.[27] They had a lot in common; both were old army men, spending long hours hunting and discussing different ways of improving the iron industry.[28] Posse also spent considerable time in in Stockholm, from where he brought home news of different commodities as well as the goods themselves. Per Reinhold Tersmeden noticed and remembered. He trusted Posse to know what was in fashion and where to buy different kinds of goods.[29] At one of Per Reinhold Tersmeden's frequent visits he observed new pieces of china among Posse's possessions. The new fine bowls and cups and saucers, all from the same place and with the same theme and colours, interested Per Reinhold Tersmeden. He was now keen on bringing his own sets of cups and saucers up to date and he wanted his nephew's help in this, writing that: 'You know best what to buy, but it needs to fit the colours in the small parlour'.[30]

Knut Lindorm Posse was not the only one of Per Reinhold Tersmeden's neighbours who inspired him to consume. About five kilometres north of Ramnäs, the ironworks at Seglingsberg was owned by Johan Schön (1753–1805).[31] His daughter Gustava Schön (1779–1857) spent most of her summers in Seglingsberg with her children while her husband was occupied with business in Stockholm. Per Reinhold Tersmeden and Gustava Schön became friends during the years they spent living close by and, when her sister married one of his younger brothers, the friendship deepened. One of Gustava Schön's interests was gardening and she and Per Reinhold Tersmeden soon found this a common subject of conversation. They both had a practical attitude towards the garden – it should combine business and pleasure – but with one big difference: where Gustava Schön personally dug and planted, groomed and pruned, her neighbour preferred to hire someone to do the work. Gustava Schön and her garden was one of the sources of inspiration when Per Reinhold Tersmeden improved his own garden.[32]

Living with Per Reinhold Tersmeden were his sisters' orphaned daughters, who helped him to manage the big household. With regard to the goods needed to fulfil the mansion's purpose of being both a home for their uncle (and themselves) and a representative house for the nobleman and ironmaster, they regularly presented their uncle with requests. More often than not, the goods were things for the garden, such as hyacinth bulbs, a rosebush, an ornament for the footpath or something for the kitchen, like lemons or spices. It seems that their uncle was prompt to fulfil their wishes.[33]

To consume as a *brukspatron*

To revert to Veblen's concepts, Per Reinhold Tersmeden was concerned in his consumption with emulating his peers, the group he desired to belong to: the iron producers. At the same time, he wanted to distinguish himself from the 'wasteful nobility'. His letters show that he used relatives, neighbours and friends living close by as inspiration for what to buy. Those who had closer connections to Stockholm, and spent more time there, served as models for him and he paid more attention to their consumption. When Posse returned from one of his longer visits to the capital, Per Reinhold Tersmeden was keen to visit him and see what kind of novelties and innovations he could report.[34] On the other hand, it is possible to detect Per Reinhold Tersmeden's own taste and understanding of what was appropriate and what was not. First and foremost, he turned against those who spent, according to him, too much money, especially when there was no longer any prospect of being able to pay the bills and balance the accounts.[35] He described his own taste as 'cautious and prudent',[36] and spent money on what he considered 'stable values' (jewellery, fine china and improving his buildings) rather than clothes and consumer goods. In his own estimation, he had 'traditional' tastes, but did not preclude a strong vein of cosmopolitanism as the influences from abroad were many.[37]

For Per Reinhold Tersmeden, being 'traditional' meant that he had no desire for things that had no meaning for him, by which he meant his conviction that things should be both beautiful and useful.[38] On the other hand he swiftly adapted to new-fangled ideas and was fascinated by new techniques and achievements in the field of science. He installed – among other things – a water fountain and he had water pipes installed in the mansion at the beginning of the nineteenth century.[39] In this, it is possible to see a will to constitute an identity – to in every aspect become a *brukspatron*, an ironmaster. On some occasions, Per Reinhold Tersmeden even dissociated himself from some of the members of the nobility and their ways, particularly when he considered these to be wasteful and thoughtless. He himself preached modesty, circumspection and temperance to the younger generation. It was a fine line between overspending and consuming as their peers. The letters to his dedicated successor, Wilhelm Fredrik Tersmeden, are full of exhortations: he was to pay attention to his financial conditions, and not to overspend. Ending up in debt was something Per Reinhold Tersmeden dreaded and over and over again he pointed that out to his nephews.[40] The message was clear: do not compromise the business. As we have seen, in a practical way, he also taught them how to think about consumption by making them a part of his consumption network.

A question of trust

Notwithstanding the fact that it was Per Reinhold Tersmeden himself who decided what to buy, his commissioners often came with suggestions. Knut von Troil had once visited a mutual friend and gave a detailed account of what the tableware looked like and how the coffee was served. He ended his letter with a subtle enquiry into whether his uncle needed anything for the serving of food.[41] This suggests that Knut von Troil was familiar with what his uncle owned and that he also knew what he needed and liked.

It is hard to say whether his marital status affected Per Reinhold Tersmeden's consumption. Not much is known of the consumption patterns of single men and women from the gentry.[42] Marriage was the normal marital status and the adult life was often divided into the time before marrying and after, concentrating on the family as a consumption unit. This should not be understood as single women and men being an exception, rather they constituted a large minority in society – about 30 per cent of Swedish aristocratic men never married.[43] Did his unmarried status make Per Reinhold Tersmeden more extravagant and wasteful, since he did not have any children to whom he could leave his large fortune, or did he hold back, finding it meaningless to accrue goods to improve his legacy? It is clear that he did spend his money on luxury items and sometimes he thought he indulged himself; but for the most part he showed a great deal of moderation, at least regarding what he asked his commissioners to buy on his behalf. Moderation and temperance seem to have been his guiding-stars and he often commented when instructing his commissioners on what to buy: 'not too expensive' or 'you know my spending limits'. Considering his large fortune, this was self-chosen moderation, with a purpose of strengthening his identity as an ironmaster.

Trust was also an essential ingredient in the delicate question of what, precisely, to buy. Per Reinhold Tersmeden usually laid down general outlines regarding appearance and function, but seldom gave detailed instructions. The idea of trust between the commissioners and Per Reinhold can also be seen as a way of sharing the same ideals – they were part of a common culture. Per Reinhold Tersmeden trusted his commissioners (for the most part) to make the right decisions about what to buy. They seem seldom to have had any kind of disagreement about the goods arriving at the mansion in Ramnäs. Did this depend on Per Reinhold Tersmeden not caring too much about candlesticks, mirrors, fine china and shirts? Or were his trusted commissioners so familiar with his wants and needs?

To be able to answer this, it is important to also examine those occasions when disagreements did arise. Once, one of his nephews had bought his uncle a silver pen, which was to be a gift for a close relative. When Per Reinhold Tersmeden received knowledge of the purchase, he disapproved, not of the idea of buying such an item as a gift or to the idea of gift-giving in general, but rather to the cost of the silver piece. He considered it inappropriate as a gift, since it was too costly. One should not buy such expensive items for such an occasion, he wrote to his nephew, and gave him the instruction to return the item and get a cheaper one.[44] Per Reinhold Tersmeden gave himself the right to educate his nephew on what was appropriate and not. In this case, it is clear that the relationship between Per Reinhold Tersmeden and his nephew Wilhelm Fredrik Tersmeden is not an equal one, but rather a relationship between a parent and a child.[45] The same kind of relationship status can be seen in the connections between Per Reinhold Tersmeden and Knut von Troil. Even if he was the commissioner most often used, he occasionally made the wrong kinds of purchases. At one time, he had – without asking his uncle – bought him some fine china. Upon its arrival at the mansion, Per Reinhold Tersmeden disapproved, though again not to the items themselves, their appearance or their function. In a long and roundabout letter, he explained in many words that he preferred in the future that his nephew asked him before making such a decision. Once more, it was the price of the objects that had upset him.[46] However, the china pieces seem to have stayed in Ramnäs, but there are no more letters revealing Knut von Troil doing such a thing again.

Not all of Per Reinhold Tersmeden's commissions were delegated so lightly and casually. The purchase of wine was precisely and exactly monitored. For this, he rarely turned to anyone except his nephew Knut von Troil, giving him detailed instructions in letter after letter: where to make the purchase, what kind of bottles to acquire, from whom, how to draw off the wine in the barrels into bottles, at what time of day and – perhaps more important than anything else – how to pack the bottles for the long voyage from Stockholm to his estate in Ramnäs. For every step of the way, Per Reinhold Tersmeden also gave long-winded and almost ceremonious explanations to why things should be done in the way he requested.[47] When the bottles finally reached their final destination, both he and his nephew could breathe more easily.[48] He rarely asked for other colonial goods or edible goods such as dried fruit, rice and chocolate, which leads to the suspicion that his housekeeper managed this part of the consumption.

With a reliance on commissioners came the unavoidable question of funding. Per Reinhold Tersmeden solved this in two different ways. Knut von Troil, his other nephews and his brothers all kept an account, meticulously counting every expense they had for their relative. This account was then settled a couple of times every year. This, of course, demanded that funding was available from the commissioners or that they could run into debt with the ones selling the goods.[49] Another way was to give his commissioners an amount of money he thought he would spend during a fixed amount of time, usually six months at a time. This procedure he usually adopted when it came to his unmarried nieces and female relatives. The source material does not reveal whether this was a question of gender, or that the commissioner did not have enough money to spend.[50] Whichever was the case, and in both forms of funding, trust was again central to the commissioner networks drawn on by Per Reinhold Tersmeden.[51]

Conclusion

In this chapter, I have examined the consumption of the nobleman and *brukspatron* Per Reinhold Tersmeden. Living far from shops and boutiques, he relied on others – commissioners – to provide him with the goods he considered necessary and desirable. His network of commissioners was first and foremost a personal one, consisting of close friends and relatives. Items as varied as lemons, fine china, laces and books regularly arrived at the estate, mainly from Stockholm and sometimes from abroad. Neighbours, friends and peers as well as relatives were sources of inspiration to consume. His consumption can thus be seen as a way to distinguish himself and his family as ironmasters. Per Reinhold Tersmeden usually delegated the details of the commissions; he trusted his commissioners to make the right choices about what to buy, although the correspondence also shows that decisions were based on an on-going dialogue and sometimes on teamwork. There was a shared culture, a common view on what was appropriate and suitable for the ironmaster of Ramnäs, and a common view of the future. Per Reinhold Tersmeden had no children, but he kept improving and refurbishing his houses into his late eighties and he often asked his younger relatives – his heirs – what was *à la mode* and what they liked.

Per Reinhold Tersmeden seldom called his purchases 'luxuries' or revealed in any way that he considered himself wasteful – on the contrary. Nevertheless, he indulged in books and newspapers and as far as novelties, money was not an issue, especially when he was improving the buildings or decorating his house. These were things he needed, things that would brighten his life, or those of his relatives, or others living with or working for him. He wanted to provide those depending on him with delight and an easy everyday life. Exploring the commissioners and their work for the ironmasters is not only a study of luxury and material goods, but also a study of how cultural phenomena are mediated and spread. The commissioners' work also shows that there were no clear boundaries between relatives, friends and business partners, rather the roles were mixed and intertwined – which also made them stronger. The study of the consumption patterns of Per Reinhold Tersmeden reveals not only the importance of material goods, of course the right kinds of goods, but it also shows the complicated and complex relationships behind the consumption itself.

Notes

1 Tom Söderberg, *Bergsmän och brukspatroner i svenskt samhällsliv* (Stockholm: Gidlund, 1948); Sten Carlsson, *Ståndssamhälle och ståndspersoner 1700–1865: Studier rörande det svenska ståndssamhällets upplösning* (Lund: Gleerup, 1949), 245–7, 306–16.

2 Marie Steinrud, 'Per Reinhold Tersmedens Ramnäs: Bruksherrgården som scen för statuskonsumtion och manifestation i början av 1800-talet', *Historisk Tidskrift för Finland* 98 (2013).

3 Gösta Selling, 'Bruken som kulturmiljö', *Blad för bergshanteringens vänner* 33, no. 2 (1959).

4 Karl-Gustaf Hildebrand, *Fagerstabrukens historia,* part 1, Sexton- och sjuttonhundratalen (Uppsala: Almqvist and Wiksell, 1957), 165–70. See also Bertil

Boëthius and Åke Kromnow, *Jernkontorets historia*, part 1, Grundläggningstiden (Stockholm: P. A. Nordstedts and söner, 1947), 192–220 and Carl Sahlin, 'Brukspatronsuniformen och bergsmansdräkten', *Med hammare och fackla* 1 (1928).

5 This was in fact a common way to obtain goods, see Anna Maria Åström 'Kolonialvaror och vardagsting i den europeiska marginalen: Konsumtionsvägar, levnadssätt och varor på en herrgård i östa Finland under slutet av 1700-talet och början av 1800-talet', *Finskt museum* 117 (2010/2011), Jon Stobart 'The Language of Luxury Goods: Consumption and the English Country House, c. 1760–1830', *Virtus. Yearbook of the History of the Nobility* 18 (2011) and Ylva Hasselberg, *Den sociala ekonomin: Familjen Clason och Furudals bruk 1804–1856* (Uppsala: Acta Universitatis Upsaliensis, Uppsala University, 1998), 132–7. See also the chapters by Stobart and Bristol in this volume.

6 Marie Steinrud, *Den dolda offentligheten: Kvinnlighetens sfärer i 1800-talets högreståndskultur* (Stockholm: Carlsson, 2008), 36–43; see also Dauphin, Cécile, 'Letter-Writing Manuals in the Nineteenth Century', in *Correspondence: Models of Letter-Writing from the Middle Ages to the Nineteenth Century*, eds Iain Boureau, Roger Chartier and Cécile Dauphin (Oxford: Polity Press, 1997).

7 Marie Steinrud, 'Hemmet som scen: Brukspatron Per Reinhold Tersmeden och tingens teater', *Bergslagsarkiv: Årsbok för historia och kulturhistoria för Bergslagen* 25 (2013).

8 The letters here used can be found at the Uppsala University Library in Uppsala (Uppsala universitetsbibliotek, UUB) and in the Tersmeden family archive at the National Archives (Riksarkivet, RA).

9 Consumption during the consumer revolution has been studied in several aspects; see for example Gudrun Anderson, *Stadens dignitärer: Den lokala elitens status- och maktmanifestation i Arboga 1650–1770* (Stockholm: Atlantis, 2009), 107–11 who has studied the elites and their ostentatious consumption in a Swedish town, and Maxine Berg, in her study of the consumer revolution, the consumers and the goods makes comparisons with the rest of Europe, *Luxury and Pleasure in Eighteenth-Century England* (Oxford: Oxford University Press, 2005).

10 Berg, *Luxury and Pleasure*, 21–45. See also the chapters by Ilmakunnas, Ijäs and Stobart in this volume.

11 Carolina Brown, 'Portraits *en savoyarde* and the Shepherdess of the Alps: Portraits, Prints, Literature and Fashion in Eighteenth-century Sweden', *Konsthistorisk tidskrift* 82, no. 3 (2013).

12 This was a very common way of obtaining goods; see for example Johanna Ilmakunnas, *Ett ståndsmässigt liv: Familjen von Fersens livsstil på 1700-talet*

(Helsingfors and Stockholm: Svenska litteratursällskapet i Finland and Atlantis, 2012), 203–17.

13 Thorstein Veblen, *The Theory of the Leisure Class: An Economic Study in the Evolution of Institutions* (New York, 1899); Peter Dellgran and Niklas Karlsson, 'Konsumtionsmönster och välfärd under 1990-talet', in *Välfärdens finansiering och fördelning: SOU 2001:57*, eds Johan Fritzell and Joakim Palme (Stockholm: Fritzes, 2001); cf. Johanna Ilmakunnas, 'Ståndsmässig konsumtion: Högadelns penningbruk och konsumtionsvanor i Sverige under senare delen av 1700-talet', *Historisk Tidskrift för Finland* 86 (2001).

14 Veblen, *The Theory of the Leisure Class*; Peter Burke, 'Res et verba: Conspicuous consumption in the early modern world', in *Consumption and the World of Goods*, eds John Brewer and Roy Porter (New York: Routledge, 1993); cf. Peter Burke, *The Historical Anthropology of Early Modern Italy* (Cambridge: Cambridge University Press, 1987), 132–49; see also Amanda Vickery, who in her article shows how women gained knowledge on what to buy, 'Women and the World of Goods: A Lancashire Consumer and her Possessions, 1751–81', in *Consumption and the World of Goods*, eds John Brewer and Roy Porter (New York: Routledge, 1993).

15 Stobart, 'The Language of Luxury Goods', 98.

16 Berg, *Luxury and pleasure*; Jan de Vries, *The Industrious Revolution: Consumer behaviour and the Household Economy, 1650 to the present* (Cambridge: Cambridge University Press, 2008), 44–5, 70.

17 Per Reinhold Tersmeden to Knut von Troil, 4 February 1825, Knut von Troil to Per Reinhold Tersmeden, 15 February 1825, UUB.

18 Steinrud, 'Per Reinhold Tersmedens Ramnäs'; Steinrud, 'Hemmet som scen'.

19 There is a clear contrast with Sabine Winn's limited range of proxy shoppers – see Bristol's chapter in this volume.

20 Per Reinhold Tersmeden to Knut von Troil, 21 June 1834, UUB.

21 Per Reinhold Tersmeden to Knut von Troil, 3 July 1834, UUB.

22 See Vickery, 'Women and the world of goods', 280; Per Reinhold Tersmeden to Adolfina Ulrika Tersmeden, 5 June 1833, UUB, to Marie Charlotte Tersmeden, 2 July 1826, RA and to Jacquette Elisabeth Tersmeden, 3 November 1835, UUB. Per Reinhold Tersmeden also wrote to his brother and asked him to please get his wife's assistance in the purchase of corks for his wine bottles. See Per Reinhold Tersmeden to Herman Adolf Tersmeden, 22 September 1829.

23 Mary Leigh acted in a similar way when she inherited Stoneleigh Abbey – see Stobart, 'The Language of Luxury Goods'.

24 Fredrik Tersmeden to Per Reinhold Tersmeden, 6 May 1803, UUB.

25 Even if there are no letters revealing this kind of purchase, traces of it can be found in letters to his siblings and his nephews.

26 Leos Müller, 'Kolonialprodukter i Sveriges handel och konsumtionskultur, 1700–1800', *Historisk tidskrift* 124 (2004).
27 Per Reinhold Tersmeden to Knut von Troil, n.d. (March?) 1823, to Fredrik Tersmeden, n.d., UUB; see also chapter by Murhem and Ulväng in this volume.
28 Per Reinhold Tersmeden to Herman Adolf Tersmeden, midsummer 1832, RA. See also to Fredrik Tersmeden, n.d. (August?), RA.
29 Per Reinhold Tersmeden to Knut von Troil, n.d. (1820s) and to Herman Adolf Tersmeden, 19 August (n.d., probably around 1800).
30 Per Reinhold Tersmeden to Knut von Troil, n.d. (probably around 1830), UUB.
31 Carl Forsstrand, *Köpmanshus i gamla Stockholm. Nya bidrag till skeppsbroadelns historia* (Stockholm: Geber, 1917).
32 Steinrud, 'Per Reinhold Tersmedens Ramnäs'; See also Gustava Schön to Hans Niklas Schwan, 26 August 1805, RA.
33 For ex. Per Reinhold Tersmeden to Herman Adolf Tersmeden, 19 May 1820, 3 September 1827, to Wilhelm Fredrik Tersmeden, 12 June 1832, to Knut von Troil 9 January 1826, UUB.
34 Per Reinhold Tersmeden to Fredrik Tersmeden, n.d., UUB.
35 Steinrud, 'Per Reinhold Tersmedens Ramnäs'; see also Per Reinhold Tersmeden to Knut von Troil, 15 March 1830, UUB.
36 Per Reinhold Tersmeden to Knut von Troil, n.d. (1832?), UUB.
37 Brown, 'Portraits *en savoyarde* and the Shepherdess of the Alps', 240–2.
38 Steinrud, 'En överste i brukspatronfrack', 208–25; see also Per Reinhold Tersmeden to Marie Charlotte Tersmeden, 31 March, 10 November 1825, RA.
39 Steinrud, 'Per Reinhold Tersmedens Ramnäs', 243–5.
40 Per Reinhold Tersmeden to Wilhelm Fredrik Tersmeden, [n.d. probably September] 1829, 1 January 1830, 3 May and 15 April 1832, UUB.
41 Knut von Troil to Per Reinhold Tersmeden, 12 September 1823, RA.
42 Some interesting exceptions are Stobart's articles about Mary Leigh, see, for example 'Status, Gender and Life Cycle in the Consumption Practices of the English Elite: The Case of Mary Leigh, 1736–1806', *Social History* 40 (2015) and Margot Finn 'Men's Things: Masculine Possessions in the Consumer Revolution', *Social History* 25 (2000).
43 Brita Planck, *Kärlekens språk: Adel, kärlek och äktenskap 1750–1900* (Gothenburg: Institutionen för historiska studier, University of Gothenburg, 2014), 35 – this refers to aristocratic men born between 1700 and 1859. See also Ingvar Elmroth, *För kung och fosterland: Studier i den svenska adelns demografi och offentliga funktioner 1600–1900.* (Lund: LiberLäromedel/Gleerup, 1981), 49. Cf. Amanda Vickery, *Behind Closed Doors: At Home in Georgian England* (New Haven: Yale University Press, 2009), 208, who shows almost the same numbers for England.

44 Per Reinhold Tersmeden to Wilhelm Fredrik Tersmeden, 27 August 1831, UUB.

45 Marie Steinrud, '"Lätt mina råd och förmaningar altid vara hos dig": Manlighetsideal i det tidiga 1800-talets högreståndskultur', in *Med börd, svärd och pengar: Eliters manifestation, maktutövning och reproduktion 1650–1900*, eds Gudrun Andersson, Esbjörn Larsson and Patrik Winton (Uppsala: Opuscula historica Upsaliensis, Uppsala University, 2003).

46 Per Reinhold Tersmeden to Knut von Troil, 11 May 1834, UUB.

47 Per Reinhold Tersmeden to Knut von Troil, 29 October 1831, UUB.

48 Per Reinhold Tersmeden to Knut von Troil, 13 November 1831, from Knut von Troil to Per Reinhold Tersmeden, 1 November 1831.

49 Overall, the upper classes and the credit market is an interesting and complicated affair, see for example Ilmakunnas, *Ett ståndsmässigt liv*, 369–71, 377; cf. Steinrud, *Den dolda offentligheten*, 167.

50 Per Reinhold Tersmeden to Knut von Troil, 3 April 1827, UUB, to Wilhelm Fredrik Tersmeden, 15 September 1832 and to Adolfina Ulrika Tersmeden, 18 July 1831, RA; cf. Ilmakunnas, 'Ståndsmässig konsumtion', 198.

51 Klas Nyberg, '"Jag existerar endast genom att äga kredit": Tillit, kreditvärdighet och finansiella nätverk i 1700-talets och det tidiga 1800-talets Stockholm', in *Sakta vi gå genom stan: Stadshistoriska studier tillägnade Lars Nilsson*, ed. Mats Berglund (Stockholm: Stockholmia förlag, 2005); Leos Müller, *The Merchant Houses of Stockholm, c. 1640–1800: A Comparative Study of Early-Modern Entrepreneurial Behaviour* (Uppsala: Acta Universitatis Upsaliensis, Uppsala University, 1998), 36.

10

To Buy a Plate: Retail and Shopping for Porcelain and Faience in Stockholm during the Eighteenth Century

Sofia Murhem and Göran Ulväng

What is good taste? What objects are tasteful? Clearly, the answers to such questions vary over time and are to a large extent historically and geographically determined. During the long eighteenth century, consumption, both actual and perceived, increased in Sweden; but at the same time, the Swedish economy was heavily regulated. The guilds had an enormous impact, restricting the number of shops, shopkeeping and advertisements. In addition, there were a high number of sumptuary laws and high tariffs and import duties.

The eighteenth century, especially in the Anglo-American literature, has been seen as the century for retail and shopping. In cities, shops at fixed addresses became common, streets dedicated to shopping emerged and shopping became a pleasure in itself. The demand for novel goods increased in all strata of society.[1] But what happened in a city with a heavily regulated economy, such as Stockholm? We aim in this chapter to explore how a taste for luxury and novel goods was created and shaped in interaction with the regulations, and how that taste was satisfied by consumption in a regulated economy with few shops and hardly any shop windows or advertisements. China is the focus for our study, here defined broadly to include real porcelain, faience and flint-ware. The reason for choosing china is twofold. First, novel goods did not have a natural place in the ordered system of sellers and thus potentially were sold, bought and marketed in a different way to ordinary restricted goods. Second, even if lower social groups started to buy Chinese porcelain in the eighteenth century, it was still considered a luxury and spread more slowly than other kinds of exotic goods, such as coffee.

How retail and shopping in Stockholm evolved in the eighteenth century remains largely unknown. Previous research has primarily focused on the textile trade and has mainly been interested in the merchants themselves; how corporate interest groups such as guilds acted in order to protect their territory and consequently how those territories were challenged.[2] Klas Nyberg has characterized the regulations on the textile trade in Stockholm as being unusually comprehensive. Martin Wottle has discussed how clothes brokers were sued by guilds on the grounds that they had attempted to sell new objects and thus interfered with guild territory. The guilds had the right to make searches for infringements on their area of monopoly.[3] Monopolies sometimes collided, such as when the drapers argued that tailors often stocked fabrics and, by selling them to their customers, infringed on the drapers' monopoly. The tailors in turn tried to get a permit for selling ready-made clothes, which the drapers opposed.[4] Marshall Lagerquist, in his discussion of the furniture trade, revealed how dealers also competed within the guilds.[5] Sofia Murhem, Göran Ulväng and Kristina Lilja have argued that restrictions on manufacturing led to the increased importance of auctions as means of distribution.[6] A few studies have focused on the consumption of noble families and the attitudes towards consumption. Johanna Ilmakunnas, in her study on the lifestyle of the noble family von Fersen, has argued that the family used their consumption as a means for distinguishing themselves, and Leif Runefeldt showed that novel goods were often perceived as threats, as they broke the rules of the ordered society.[7]

Stockholm: a regulated city yearning for exotic goods

Like most countries in Europe, Sweden became involved in global trade during the eighteenth century, which, together with an agrarian revolution and nascent industrialization, led to increased wealth and a growing demand for goods.[8] The mercantilist policy of the time supported the founding of the Swedish East-Indian Company (*Svenska Ost-Indiska Compagniet*), based in Gothenburg on the west coast.[9] Manufactories were encouraged and, in some cases, grew into large businesses. The most important were textile manufactories. In 1750 there were 100 textile manufactories, but only two making china.[10]

Stockholm was by far the largest city in Sweden. It was the administrative capital of the country, with king, government, parliament and guilds, and one of the most important merchant cities, both for domestic and international trade. The city had more than 60,000 inhabitants in the 1750s, increasing to 75,000 in 1780. Artisans and tradesmen were the largest group among the working population, with grocers and drapers the most numerous trades. In order to become an artisan or a tradesman, one needed burghership (*burskap*), to be a master if one were a craftsman or have sufficient training to become a tradesman, and the guilds protected their positions by limiting the number of members. Other ways of decreasing competition between members and thereby increasing profits were rules limiting the number of shops a guild member could have, restricting opening hours, limiting the number of apprentices allowed, forbidding advertising of prices and in general condemning advertising as unfair competition. As in England, annual fairs began to lose their importance in relation to fixed shops during the eighteenth century, a development encouraged by the authorities.[11] But in Stockholm, the so-called Free Fair (*frimarknaden*), consisting of stalls and temporary shops, which began in September and continued for two weeks, was still important during the entire eighteenth century. There was an annual Christmas Fair (*julmarknaden*) as well. All year round, vegetables, meat and groceries were available from markets, each foodstuff being sold in a certain square.[12]

Most shops were located within a limited area in the oldest part of Stockholm, the so-called City between the Bridges (*Staden mellan broarna*) or Old Town. As in many old cities at the time, shopping was localized to the traditional centres or thoroughfares and displayed a high degree of continuity.[13] With its medieval layout and narrow streets, the Old Town was not only the political, economic and administrative centre of the city, but also its cultural and social heart. The hub of activity was *Riddarhustorget* (The House of the Nobility Square), which housed The House of the Nobility, the city administration and the peasants' representatives to the Diet, as well as political clubs, billiard saloons, coffeehouses, taverns and alehouses. The street *Storkyrkobrinken*, which began at the royal castle and ended in *Riddarhustorget* and through which royal processions always passed, was the main shopping street for luxury items. Most furniture shops and porcelain sellers were located here. The Old Town was not only a centre for the old aristocracy. On the east side of the island is *Skeppsbron*, home to the rich merchants, the so-called Skeppsbro Nobility (*Skeppsbroadeln*), their palaces and their warehouses. The fairs were held in *Skeppsbron* (the Free Fair) and in *Stortorget* (the Christmas Fair), only a few streets from there.

The number of tradesmen, merchants not included, grew from 451 in 1722 to 473 in 1800, but population increase meant that the number of tradesmen per citizen decreased from 1 retailer per 100 inhabitants at the beginning of the eighteenth century, to 1 retailer per 160 inhabitants at the end of the century.[14] By comparison, Antwerp had about 1 retailer per 50 inhabitants in the middle of the sixteenth century and in 1773 about 1 retailer per 16 inhabitants: ten times the ratio in Stockholm.[15]

The creation of taste in a regulated economy

Swedish society had a complicated relationship with shopping and the consumption of novel goods in the eighteenth century – a characteristic shared with many other states in Europe, as the chapters in this volume by North and Clemente attest. There was great demand, but the prevailing mercantilist ideals caused the government to restrict imports and consumption and to attempt replacing them with domestic products instead. Many people of rank felt defenceless against what they perceived as a rapidly changing world in which novel goods and consumption played the leading part and they urged a return to the good old days. The idea of over-consumption, especially in relation to one's position in life, but also within one's own social group, was considered threatening. The mercantilist notion of the damage that could be done to a country overspending on foreign goods, and where the lower classes did not know their place but tried to imitate their betters, was the origin of the many sumptuary laws that characterized Swedish society at this time. That the lower classes did not, in reality, consume many foreign and exotic goods mattered little: sumptuary laws (*överflödsförordningar*), of which there were fifty-eight in all during the eighteenth century, tried to control unnecessary consumption, mostly of foreign or exotic goods. The most severe one in 1766 more or less forbade all imports of china, even East-Indian, but was never really imposed. A new regulation, less severe, went into effect in 1770, but instead china imports, except for East-Indian porcelain, were restricted by high tariffs.[16]

The fear of over-consumption and the social stigma of being too fashionable, refined or ostentatious, led to an ideal of moderation in relation to one's social standing being defined as tasteful (see also Ijäs's chapter in this volume). To act one's part and be aware of who one was were the signs of good taste. In a 1753 drama, we find the Baron Alfvarsam (Baron Straight-face), who was rich enough to live in the manner required of him as a nobleman, but not too fashionable. He changed his clothes according to last year's fashion, not this year's, and never wore plumes.[17] While being new was at the heart of fashion, taste was to some extent opposed to novelty.[18] It was important to be just right when it came to fashion or furnishings: not too modern, but not too old-fashioned; not too ostentatious, but not too dull or cheap. The notable diarist Märta Helena Reenstierna described her dinner party as including a 'decent but not superfluous amount of dishes'.[19]

For the nobility, luxury consumption was part of who they were; ergo, the consumption of luxuries was necessary and refinement in taste was expected. As in most states in Western Europe, French culture and style dominated in the higher strata.[20] Sweden had particular close relations with France for more than 180 years, until the Napoleonic Wars, despite differences in religion and the fact that Sweden went from being a great military power in the Northern sphere to becoming a state on the periphery. Apart from the huge subsidies, which in some years made up 25 per cent of the Swedish national budget, these close connections had a great influence on Swedish politics, economy, cultural life and social mobility.[21]

Taste can be seen as being created and acquired through the purchasing process. The retailer gains a reputation for having tasteful goods because he is known to sell to people of good taste. But it works both ways: his customers gain a reputation for good taste because they buy their goods from someone known for selling tasteful goods. One way of becoming known as a seller of distinguished goods was to supply the royal court. Adolph Ludvig Levin was one of the most distinguished in this respect. Early in his career, he began to help the royal family by lending them money and in 1757 he gained his burghership as a furniture dealer. Already in his first year, he supplied the Crown Prince, the future King Gustav III, and in 1766 he was appointed Fiscal Administrator to the royal court. In 1772 he let the furniture business to his assistant, while he himself devoted his time to the estates and ironworks he had bought.[22] By retiring from business, Levin was transformed from a purveyor of luxury goods to a consumer of them. Another furniture dealer who gained many commissions from the court was Nils Palin. He became a burgher in 1762 and was especially requested to take on the furnishing of the Duchess Hedvig Elisabeth Charlotta's apartment at the castle in 1774. Obviously performing well, he was given the highly sought-after commission to furnish the apartment of the future crown prince in 1778. The two other important furniture dealers, Diedrich Tellerstedt and Carl Henrik Grevesmühl, also supplied the court.[23] However, being closely associated with the royal court, and especially with King Gustav III, was not without risks. After his peaceful coup d'état in 1772, the king had strengthened his grip on power at the expense of the Diet. Gradually during the absolute monarchy, parts of the aristocracy became more and more hostile towards the king, a hostility ending with his murder in March 1792.

To be associated with the right people was important for both sellers and customers. Visits to other people's homes provided an opportunity to see what items were fashionable in that particular circle. Social life in high society consisted to a great extent of visits of various kinds. When entertaining, people could display their homes and their taste; when visiting, they could see and judge others. The importance of keeping up appearances during the long eighteenth century can be illustrated by the ironworks-owning family Clason. The most expensive objects they owned were those used for sociability, the amount being more or less constant over time. Hard times meant that personal consumption had to stand back. In 1810, the son, Gustaf, had inadequate winter clothes, while social consumption was maintained at the usual level.[24]

Tellerstedt, the furniture dealer, used an innovative way of associating his goods with the right people; in 1762, he decorated magnificent apartments in his new house at *Storkyrkobrinken*, letting these out or using them as showrooms to attract potential customers. The suite of rooms were let to people such as Prince Heinrich of Prussia in 1770, for the considerable sum of

4,000 Rd (*Riksdaler specie*) – an amount equivalent to about 20 per cent of the total value of Tellerstedt's stock in 1765.[25] When the apartments were let, Tellerstedt made money and the apartments and their impressive furniture served as advertisements and perhaps, in addition, gained some of the splendour of the guests. When not leased, they could be used for display. Viewings before auctions worked in much the same way: to communicate taste and to show what certain people owned. In the case of house auctions, there was also the extra benefit that one could see the home of the person in question. Cynthia Wall has compared the house viewing to a stage, with spectators as both the public and co-creators. The house auction could work both as a source of identification with the seller and his or her home, and as a source of destruction of that person and home. The social and material life of the seller was available to view and to take home in parts. In buying parts of someone else's life, which thus was fragmented, buyers could recreate their own.[26] Visiting house auction viewings, one could gain access to circles one did not usually move in. Not only could one see how others had furnished their homes and what goods they had on display, one could also buy that very particular object one desired.

The possibilities of spreading news of modern taste and fashion through advertisements in newspapers or by fashion journals – important in Britain and the more developed states on the continent – was limited in Sweden due to guild regulations. Only to a limited extent were goods advertised in the newspapers.[27] Generally, these were quite rudimentary, listing the objects for sale, but rarely describing them in detail. In contrast, all Gothenburg auctions of cargoes of the Swedish East-India ships were advertised in the national press. While most other advertisements were only a few lines, these extended over several pages, indicating the richness and splendour of the cargo, and always started on the front page of the newspaper. Such advertisements, while admittedly functioning as information for potential auction buyers, could be viewed as a way of creating demand for novel goods. Line after line telling the reader about all the various goods had an enchanting power. So even if the advertisements were pure information in Stigler's terms, they could serve a higher purpose. Those for the large estate auctions from deceased rich and powerful people worked in the same way. First of course, they informed potential buyers, but as they declared all the goods available they provided a picture to the public of what kind of goods the rich and powerful owned. This in turn signalled what could be bought at the auction, but also in the shops, now or in the future.[28] Similar in function was the advertisement by Grevesmühl, announcing the new location of his shop. Here, Grevesmühl listed his splendid stock, among it East-Indian and Saxon porcelain, in a long list of all possible objects that could be manufactured from china.[29] Cox and Dannehl use the term 'goods virtually supplied',[30] and these lengthy lists certainly created a vast universe of supply, widening the receiver's knowledge of the world of commerce.

Finally, let us not forget the importance of private correspondence, which enabled the spread of news about fashion and information on where to purchase objects, and carried commissions to buy goods for friends and relatives – as the chapters by Steinrud and Ijäs in this volume make clear.[31] Letters could also contain discussions of what was good taste, giving a more explicit opinion on what was seen as suitable or not.[32] There is reason to believe that correspondence was of greater importance to the inhabitants of Sweden than was the case in other countries: population was sparse, the distance to towns was vast and many of the roads were often in a bad shape, making travel difficult.

The satisfaction of taste in a regulated economy

The supply of china and faience in eighteenth-century Sweden stemmed mainly from two sources: principally the large imports by the Swedish East-India Company and secondly the largest Swedish manufactories, Rörstrand and Marieberg, located in Stockholm. These were government supported works, founded in 1726 and 1758 respectively, and their production consisted to a large extent of faience. Marieberg was the only manufactory to produce genuine porcelain, but only in small batches.[33] Imports, apart from the privileged Swedish East-India Company, were restricted. Since tariffs and import duties were so high, the amount of china from Germany, England and France was limited. In fact, the tariffs and taxes were so high that, when the Dowager Queen Lovisa Ulrika visited her brother, King Frederick the Great of Prussia, her son King Gustav III wrote to her and asked her to buy Berlin porcelain for him, but to declare it as a gift from King Frederick in order to avoid paying duties.[34] Only the largest furniture dealers sold German, French and British china, and then at very high prices. We rarely find European china, except for Swedish products, advertised in the newspapers, whereas advertisements for East-Indian china were quite common.

The fact that shops were comparatively few and specialized meant that the nobility, who consumed a great deal, spent much time visiting shops to buy or order goods, as well as writing to request particular objects. Since 1717, Swedish manufactories were entitled to have their own shops in Stockholm to sell their products.[35] The Marieberg manufactory sold its wares from the factory until 1762, when it advertised that its products could only be bought in its shop at *Storkyrkobrinken*.[36] In 1770, an additional shop was opened in *Skeppsbron*. The Rörstrand manufactory advertised their porcelain factory shop in the Old Town in 1771, but one could still buy directly from the factory.[37] It seems that, after Rörstrand bought Marieberg in 1758, both Marieberg's shops were used for Rörstrand's production as well.[38] In 1793 Märta Helena Reenstierna wrote that she bought two punch bowls and two sauce boats in Nordenstolpe's Porcellain Magasin.[39] Nordenstolpe was the owner of Rörstrand and a personal friend of Reenstierna and her husband. In 1796 Reenstierna went to visit 'Mrs Nordenstolpe in Rörstrand, where I was received with all possible tokens of friendship and courtesy and spent a quite amusing couple of hours there'.[40] But even if she remained a loyal customer of Rörstrand – buying items from them as late as 1822 – she also owned other kinds of china. On Christmas Eve 1796, she served a turkey on an East-Indian platter and she had a dinner service with her own coat of arms, made in China.[41]

We find little evidence of the sociability of shops found in much of the literature: as places where one could socialize, drink coffee and talk to one's friends.[42] In Stockholm, most shops did not have a direct entrance from the streets; one had to enter the hallway of the building in question and from there a door led to the shop. Windows were small, with limited possibilities to display goods. Indeed, many shops in Stockholm were located upstairs, without windows opening to the street. In general, shops were small and comparatively sparsely furnished.[43] It seems that shopping was more straightforward and that socializing activities instead took place in private homes or in public restaurants. Most likely, the lack of competition meant that strategies to draw in customers by making one's shop more attractive by furnishing social areas were simply not necessary.

There were a few shops, such as the Sugar- and Porcelain-store (*Socker- och Porcellainsboden*), which specialized in selling porcelain. Interestingly, the only advertisements found from them have to do with their trying to sell almost anything other than porcelain (for example, textiles could be left there for further preparation in 1797), whilst Rörstrand's porcelain shop advertised writing paper on several occasions in 1771 and in 1788 had British hams and other foodstuffs for sale.[44] There are several advertisements stating one could inquire within regarding anything from leasing a country estate to lost property.[45] Clearly, shops were used as information centres. Conversely, household and furniture shops sold porcelain. The first to gain a burghership as a furniture dealer was Tellerstedt in 1750 and, as noted earlier, there were only three other furniture dealers of any importance – Levin, Palin and Grevesmühl – plus a few other minor dealers. An inventory of Tellerstedt's shop made in 1765 included eight potpourri urns, two large Chinese china figurines and two smaller ones, among other china objects, mostly figurines. However, china only accounted for just over 1 per cent of the total value of his stock. In Grevesmühl's inventory from 1781, china accounted for about 10 per cent of the total value of the stock. Here, a multitude of objects were found: nine groups of Saxon porcelain, twenty-two punch bowls, 200 pairs of 'fine teacups' and four English dinner services, among other things.[46] Considering the rarity and cost of English and German china in Sweden, this was truly a remarkable stock.

Since East-Indian china was not regulated by guilds, it was possible for sellers of other kinds of wares to include it among their stock. Manufactories often used their shops to sell items other than those produced by the manufactory. For example, a silk stocking manufacturer advertised that he sold among other things tea, nankins, rhubarb, tobacco and East-Indian porcelain.[47] Spice dealers seemed to have taken advantage of the fact that they already dealt in exotic goods and increased their stock with the occasional East-Indian tea set. The spice dealer Nordman advertised East-Indian china on a regular basis along with teas, spices and nankins. More unusually, he also advertised flint-ware. There were others who seem to have acquired East-Indian china, including the hat maker Svanhjelm, who advertised several tea sets, whilst the Swedish East-India Company Stockholm office announced in 1771 that the commissionaire Gullstierna had tea and East-Indian tea sets for sale.[48]

The fact that opportunities for window shopping were rare probably increased the attractiveness of both fairs and auction viewings. Reenstierna recalled visiting the Christmas Fair on Christmas Eve 1795 to buy a golden watchband for her husband, observing that 'we shouldered dreadfully among a mass of wandering spectators, who hardly bought anything'.[49] She seems to have been very fond of the Free Fair, visiting it every year to view the items for sale and to shop, buying china plates and flint-ware bowls on 30 September 1794;[50] but the fairs were a far cry from the polite pedestrian shopping streets evolving in other parts of Europe.[51]

The lack of retailers meant that second-hand markets were important channels for consumption. In addition, the shortage of goods caused by import restrictions and by the guilds restricting production often meant long periods of waiting for purchases. One possible way of getting goods immediately was to buy second-hand. A considerable number of auctions were held in Stockholm, either on the premises of the auction house or in the seller's own home. During the eighteenth century, auctions were held three to four times a week. In 1781 almost 33,000 lots were auctioned, each lot on average containing three objects, meaning that around 100,000 objects were sold every year, both new and second-hand. The new goods came mostly from merchants who used the auctions as a means of selling directly to the customers since it was so difficult to open a shop, but there were other non-professional sellers who had bought a small batch of new goods, often at the cargo auctions of the Swedish East-India Company, and sold them on in the hope of making a profit. On average, there were between 50 and 100 buyers present at each auction. Many of them were regulars, but there were 7,000 unique buyers per year. In 1781, of all Stockholm citizens, including children, about one-tenth bought objects at the Stockholm auction house, a figure which equates with over one in three households. The number of objects equalled more than one object per citizen and about five per household.[52]

There were two different types of auctions in Stockholm where porcelain was sold. The first was professional merchants or accountants selling a large stock of (Chinese) porcelain, most likely bought in Gothenburg at auctions held by the Swedish East-Indian Company. The second comprised estates of wealthy deceased people, such as that of the late Queen Lovisa Ulrika (d. 1782), in which porcelain did not form the most important part, but accounted for a large number of items and had a considerable value nevertheless. We will here focus mainly on the estate auction, where luxury items were found.

Of all kinds of porcelain at the auctions, Chinese porcelain dominated, followed by Swedish and, to a small extent and only in estate auctions from very wealthy households, English, German and French porcelain. It seems that the Chinese porcelain in Stockholm auctions was both used and unused, while in the countryside virtually all objects sold were second-hand. Swedish faience, and porcelain and faience from other European countries, tended to be used. The auctions served an important function for distributing second-hand objects and for city merchants to sell unused objects, sometimes to other retailers. However, most auction objects were sold by private individuals, professional merchants selling just three or four times a year on average. But when it comes to porcelain, the proportion of professional traders selling new goods was considerably higher than average.

The goods available at estate sales varied by seller. Those of burgher estates included only a very few Swedish faience objects and hardly any Chinese porcelain, but this was more common amongst sales of estates from the nobility and especially the magnificent royal sale of Queen Lovisa Ulrika's household. In general, teacups, plates and serving plates made up the majority of objects, the furnisher Johan Lundberg, for example, selling hundreds of Chinese teacups in 1785. The estate auctions were, for obvious reasons, more varied than those of professionals, with more figurines and pots. Consider the estate of the nobleman Johan von Cahman, where among many other items, a pair of Chinese frog figurines were sold to Baron Cederström. The average value increased in the case of the nobility, and of course the queen, compared to auctions held by merchants. On average, the value per item for the merchants' auctions was 0.37 Rd, while for the noble estate auctions the average was 0.56 Rd and for Lovisa Ulrika's it was a remarkable 3.71 Rd. To put this into perspective, a day labourer in Stockholm would have had to work about one-third of a day to be able to afford the average item sold at merchant auctions, two-thirds of a day to afford the average item at the noble estate sales, and more than four days to buy the average object at Lovisa Ulrika's sale.[53]

The new goods sold by merchants were clearly aimed more at a mass market. This is still more apparent when looking at the buyers. At a general auction in 1781 at Stockholm's Auktionsverk, 6 per cent of buyers belonged to the nobility, 52 per cent were burgers, 12 per cent civil servants and 30 per cent landless. However, porcelain was predominantly bought by the wealthier: 31 per cent of buyers were nobility, 55 per cent were burghers and civil servants and only 15 per cent were landless. Looking at the above-mentioned lots sold by Johan Lundberg, we find among the buyers Baron Stevel and Madam Krus. The differences become clearer still when we look at the estate sales. At the sale of the nobility's estates, 43 per cent of the buyers belonged to the same class, and the rest were burghers and civil servants. The percentage of nobility was slightly higher, 45 per cent, at the royal sale. When the Dutch ambassador to Sweden, Baron von Lünden, died in 1781, his splendid estate, including many porcelain objects, was sold. Among the buyers are found both professionals, such as the furnisher Grevesmühl, and persons of noble birth, such as the Hon. Miss Hägerskiöld and Count Gyllenborg.[54]

The queen's sale is a special chapter. Her auction included much Chinese porcelain, but also a few pieces described as Japanese, the only objects of that kind we have found so far. Clearly, Japanese porcelain was so rare on the Swedish market that it was only owned by royalty or perhaps the very richest nobility. The auctioned objects were not only more valuable; among the buyers were some of the wealthiest and highest-ranking people, including Baron De Geer, owner of several ironworks in Sweden. But we also find professionals, men such as the merchant Jacob Hahr of the East-India Company and the textile merchant Johan Samuel Ekstein. Many of the queen's minor employees, such as her pastry cook Anton Aubert, also bought several objects, in his case butter boxes among other things. Some buyers were more frequent than others, the furnisher Grevesmühl acquiring several lots, many of them probably destined to be sold in his shop.[55] Most likely, the provenance would add some extra value to the objects.

Conclusions

The formation and satisfaction of taste in Stockholm was apparently affected by restrictions and regulations. Mercantilist ideas about consumption, in combination with the deeply felt threat from a changing society, called for moderation in taste. Luxury was a duty for the nobility, but it should be a moderated luxury. Taste was created and communicated in interaction with others and the lack of polite shopping streets with shop windows meant that the formation of taste through viewing objects was articulated at fairs and auction viewings instead of visits to upstairs shops. The viewings held before the auctions, especially if they were house auctions of important people, could also work as shapers of taste. In addition, one could bring a part of that taste home. In comparison to other countries, such as England, where shops were used for sociable meetings and to mould taste, the limitations of competition, which put a limit on the number of shops, provided little incentive for shop keepers to try to make their shops more attractive. If one worked too hard, the guild may strike, with accusations of unfair competition. Hence, Swedish shops were often small and generally situated on the first floor. Shop window displays were not important – customers would find their way to the shop anyway because very often they had few other places to go – and it was safer not to appear too competitive. That is not to say that shopkeepers did not contribute to the formation of taste, but they did so in a less obvious manner and they sometimes had to come up with innovate ways of doing so, such as the furniture dealer Tellerstedt with his furnished apartments ready for noble customers.

The fact that advertisements were rather crude should not be interpreted as them being unimportant in the construction of taste. We argue that the fact that advertisements merely listed goods did not prevent them from creating demand for the goods. Taken together, the long lists – whether of the cargo of a Swedish East-India Company ship, the contents of a count's auction sale or the stock of a furniture dealer – helped to create a picture of what was available, and an alluring picture at that.

The limitations put on the number of retailers made tradesmen find ways to circumvent the restrictions. Manufacturers took advantage of their right to have a shop in Stockholm both to sell their own wares and a range of other goods, whilst many spice dealers, who already dealt with exotic goods and probably bought them at Gothenburg auctions, distributed the odd tea set or other china objects. We also have a hat maker who sold porcelain, but, according to Wottle, the hat makers seemed to sell anything, except perhaps hats. Limits on the number of shops, in combination with limits on opening hours, made shopping a time-consuming business. To obtain the goods sought after, the shopper had to visit a number of shops and often order objects rather than take them home. One channel for selling both new and second-hand goods, unregulated by the guilds and societies, were the auctions. Those in Stockholm were an important way of distributing and buying porcelain; at the estate auctions, objects were mainly bought by private individuals and moved sideways or downwards in society. Private buyers could obtain goods otherwise difficult or too expensive to get their hands on, not the least in the case of the royal sale of Queen Lovisa Ulrika's household. Auction goods, at least if from very noble estates, could have had the added benefit of not being too fashionable and thus keeping on the right side of good taste; they could also retain some of the attributes of the former owner. Perhaps most importantly, all these auctions formed ways of acquiring knowledge about taste and luxury as well as luxurious and tasteful objects.

Notes

1 Jan Hein Furnée and Clé Lesger, 'Shopping Streets and Cultures from a Long-term and Transnational Perspective', in *The Landscape of Consumption: Shopping Streets and Cultures in Western Europe, 1600–1900*, ed. Jan Hein Furnée and Clé Lesger (Basingstoke:Palgrave Macmillan, 2014).

2 Cf. Martin Wottle, *Det lilla ägandet: Korporativ formering och sociala relationer inom Stockholms minuthandel 1720–1810* (Stockholms universitet, 2000); *Till salu: Stockholms textila handel och manufaktur 1722–1846*, ed. Klas Nyberg (Stockholm: Stads- och kommunhistoriska institutet, 2010); *Borgerskap och grosshandelssocietet i Stockholm. D. 1, Storköpmän som samhällskraft: 1736–1850*, eds Klas Nyberg and Håkan Jakobsson (Stockholm: Informationsförlaget, 2012).

3 Martin Wottle, 'What's New? Legal Discourse on Second-Hand Goods in Early Nineteenth-Century Stockholm', in *Modernity and the Second-Hand Trade: European Consumption Cultures and Practices, 1700–1900*, eds Jon Stobart and Ilja Van Damme. (Basingstoke: Palgrave Macmillan, 2010).

4 Martin Wottle, 'Detaljhandeln med kläder och tyger, 1734–1834', in *Till salu: Stockholms textila handel och manufaktur 1722–1846*, ed. Klas Nyberg (Stockholm: Stads- och kommunhistoriska institutet, 2010).

5 Marshall Lagerquist, *Den yrkesmässiga möbelhandeln i Sverige intill år 1780: Studier i rokokotidens möbelhantverk och möbeldistribution* (Stockholm: Nordiska Museet, 1981).

6 Sofia Murhem, Göran Ulväng and Kristina Lilja, 'Tables and Chairs Under the Hammer: Second-Hand Consumption of Furniture in the Eighteenth and Nineteenth Centuries in Sweden', in *Modernity and the Second-Hand Trade: European Consumption Cultures and Practices, 1700–1900*, eds Jon Stobart and Ilja Van Damme (Basingstoke: Palgrave Macmillan, 2010).

7 Johanna Ilmakunnas, *Ett ståndsmässigt liv: Familjen von Fersens livsstil på 1700-talet* (Helsingfors and Stockholm: Svenska litteratursällskapet i Finland and Atlantis, 2012); Leif Runefeldt, *Att hasta mot undergången: Anspråk, flyktighet, förställning i debatten om konsumtion i Sverige 1730–1830* (Stockholm: Nordic Academic Press, 2015).

8 Christer Ahlberger, *Konsumtionsrevolutionen: Om det moderna konsumtionssamhällets framväxt 1750–1900* (Gothenburg: Gothenburg University, 1996).

9 *Global historia från periferin: Norden 1650–1800*, eds Leos Müller, Göran Rydén and Holger Weiss (Lund: Studentlitteratur, 2009).

10 Eva Eggeby and Klas Nyberg, 'Stad i stagnation 1720–1850', in *Staden på vattnet: Del 1, 1252–1850*, eds Göran Dahlbäck and Lars Nilsson (Stockholm: Stockholmia, 2002).

11 Claire Walsh, 'Stalls, Bulks, Shops and Long-Term Change in Seventeenth- and Eighteenth-Century England', in *The Landscape of Consumption: Shopping Streets and Cultures in Western Europe, 1600–1900*, eds Jan Hein Furnée and Clé Lesger (Basingstoke: Palgrave Macmillan, 2014), 49.

12 Marshall Lagerquist, *Den yrkesmässiga möbelhandeln i Sverige*, 98–100; Christine Bladh, *Månglerskor: Att sälja från korg och bod i Stockholm 1819–1846* (Gothenburg: Gothenburg University, 1991) 47; Eva Eggeby and Klas Nyberg, 'Stad i stagnation', 197–201.

13 Jan Hein Furnée and Clé Lesger, 'Shopping Streets and Cultures', 4; Natacha Coquery, 'Shopping Streets in Eighteenth-Century Paris: A Landscape Shaped by Historical, Economic and Social Forces,' in *The Landscape of Consumption: Shopping Streets and Cultures in Western Europe, 1600–1900*, eds Jan Hein Furnée and Clé Lesger (Basingstoke: Palgrave Macmillan, 2014), 62.

14 Wottle, *Det lilla ägandet.*

15 Bruno Blondé and Ilja Van Damme, 'Retail Growth and Consumer Changes in a Declining Urban Economy', *Economic History Review* 63 (2010): 638–63.

16 There were probably two reasons why East-Indian china was allowed on the Swedish market. The first was that the company was considered a pride of

the nation and was highly profitable, and porcelain functioned as ballast for the tea which generated most of the profits. The second was the lack of Swedish high quality china. See Leos Müller, 'The Swedish East India Trade and International Markets: Re-exports of Teas, 1731–1813', *Scandinavian Economic History Review* 51 (2003), 28–44 and Carl Hernmarck, *Marieberg: En lysande representant för svenskt sjuttonhundratal* (Stockholm: Wahlström and Widstrand, 1946), 43.

17 Leif Runefelt, *Att hasta mot undergången: Anspråk, flyktighet, förställning i debatten om konsumtion i Sverige 1730–1830* (Lund: Nordic Academic Press, 2015), 202–3.

18 For a discussion on the concept of the new being central to fashion, see Maxine Berg, *Luxury and Pleasure in Eighteenth-Century Britain* (Oxford: Oxford University Press, 2003), 250–1.

19 Märta Helena Reenstierna, *Årstadagboken: Journaler från åren 1793–1839. Del 1, 1793–1812* (Stockholm: Esselte kartor, 1966), 164.

20 See, for example, the chapters by Ilmakunnas (on Sweden), North (Germany) and Clemente (Naples) in this volume.

21 See, for example, 'Subsidies and the French-Swedish relations', an ongoing research project by Professor Svante Norrby, Lund University.

22 As Sheila Ogilvie has remarked, the guild system made it possible for some to become very rich at the expense of the wider economy. Sheila Ogilvie, *Institutions and European Trade: Merchant Guilds 1000–1800* (Cambridge: Cambridge University Press, 2011); Marshall Lagerquist, *Den yrkesmässiga möbelhandeln i Sverige*, 111–15.

23 Marshall Lagerquist, *Den yrkesmässiga möbelhandeln i Sverige*, 110–29.

24 Ylva Hasselberg, *Den sociala ekonomin: Familjen Clason och Furudals bruk 1804–1856* (Uppsala: Uppsala universitet, 1998), 178–9.

25 Marshall Lagerquist, *Den yrkesmässiga möbelhandeln i Sverige*, 104–6.

26 Cynthia Wall, 'The English Auction: Narratives of Dismantlings', *Eighteenth-Century Studies* 31 (1997), 8–10.

27 The newspapers studied here are the weekly national papers *Posttidningar* and *Inrikes Tidningar*, and the local *Stockholms Weckoblad* and *Dagligt Allehanda*.

28 For a similar remark, cf. Ilja Van Damme with Laura Van Aert, 'Antwerp Goes Shopping! Continuity and Change in Retail Space and Shopping Interactions from the Sixteenth to the Nineteenth Century', in *The Landscape of Consumption: Shopping Streets and Cultures in Western Europe, 1600–1900*, eds Jan Hein Furnée and Clé Lesger (Basingstoke: Palgrave Macmillan, 2014), 96.

29 *Inrikes Tidningar*, 6 April 1772.

30 Nancy Cox and Karin Dannehl, *Perceptions of Retailing in Early Modern England* (Aldershot: Ashgate, 2007), 69.

31 See, for example, Ylva Hasselberg, *Den sociala ekonomin*, 90–1, 177; Marie Steinrud, *Den dolda offentligheten: Kvinnlighetens sfärer i 1800-talets svenska högreståndskultur* (Stockholm: Carlssons bokförlag, 2008), 152; Ilmakunnas, *Ett ståndsmässigt liv*, 205–17.

32 In a letter dated 1789, written by Countess Ulrika Eleonora Spens after a visit to the wealthy Baroness Falcker at Svartå Manor, she complains over the amount of carpets, curtains and cushions, which in her opinion would be more suitable in a city house, but not so in the countryside. The letter is summarized in Göran Ulväng, *Herrgårdarnas historia: Liv, arbete och bebyggelse på Uppländska herrgårdar* (Uppsala: Hallgren and Björklund, 2008), 194–6.

33 Hernmarck, *Marieberg*, 108–16.

34 Hernmarck, *Marieberg*, 20.

35 Per Nyström, *Stadsindustriens arbetare före 1800-talet* (Lund: Lunds universitet, 1955).

36 *Stockholms Weckoblad*, 13 November 1762.

37 *Inrikes tidningar*, 31 January 1771, 4 May 1772.

38 *Inrikes tidningar*, 23 November 1782.

39 Reenstierna, *Årstadagboken*, 41.

40 Reenstierna, *Årstadagboken*, 123.

41 Reenstierna, *Årstadagboken*, 132.

42 Jon Stobart, *Sugar and Spice: Grocers and Groceries in Provincial England, 1650–1830* (Oxford: Oxford University Press, 2013), 135.

43 Lagerquist, *Den yrkesmässiga möbelhandeln i Sverige*, 97–8.

44 *Inrikes Tidningar*, 31 January 1771, 25 April 1771, 29 April 1771, 19 June 1788, 7 April 1797.

45 *Inrikes Tidningar*, 23 November 1782, 5 July 1773, 14 March 1778, 2 November 1780, 14 July 1783, 21 May 1792, 28 July 1796.

46 Lagerquist, *Den yrkesmässiga möbelhandeln i Sverige*, 276–86.

47 *Inrikes Tidningar*, 14 October 1771.

48 *Stockholms Weckobladh*, 1 December 1770, 15 December 1770.

49 Reenstierna, *Årstadagboken*, 103.

50 Reenstierna, *Årstadagboken*, 78.

51 Ian Mitchell, *Tradition and Innovation in English Retailing, 1700–1850* (Ashgate: Farnham, 2014), 98–112.

52 Göran Ulväng, Sofia Murhem and Kristina Lilja, *Den glömda konsumtionen: Auktionshandel i Sverige under 1700- och 1800-talen* (Möklinta: Gidlund, 2013), 65.

53 Stockholms stadsarkiv, Stockholms Auktionsverks protokoll 1 February 1781, 22 April 1781, 18–26 February 1783; Lennart Jörberg, *A History of Prices in Sweden 1732–1914, vol 1* (Lund: Gleerup, 1972), 592.

54 Stockholms stadsarkiv, Stockholms Auktionsverks protokoll 22 April 1781, 28–29 May 1781.

55 Stockholms stadsarkiv, Stockholms Auktionsverks protokoll 18–26 February 1783.

Part Three

Crossing Boundaries of Taste and Luxury

11

A Taste for French Style in Bourbon Spain: Food, Drink and Clothing in 1740s Madrid

Nadia Fernández-de-Pinedo and Corinne Thépaut-Cabasset*

The eighteenth century saw the culmination of a process of consolidation for commercial networks between continents and cultures, East and West being connected in Europe by semi-luxurious and luxury goods.[1] However, we must remember that each country and region had complex socio-economic and cultural networks that were interconnected yet distinctive. As Ina Baghdiantz McCabe noted, 'each society, even every city, has its own history'.[2] The patterns of consumption in Madrid were therefore not necessarily the same as those found in the rest of Spain. Nevertheless, cities were nodes of encounter, the best places to show off – to see and be seen – and they represent an ideal scene to study the consequences of the circulation of goods and people. In the eighteenth century, Madrid was a major capital marked by enormous differences between social groups that competed for political power and position, not only in the city but also in the colonies, where dress and appearance were important cultural codes. These characteristics made the city a place of eager exchange of new products and fashions. In this sense, it was open to the world and modern in its consumption patterns. It should not be forgotten that Madrid was an imperial capital and, as with other such capitals, consuming while producing very little meant that it played a limited role in terms of redistribution.[3]

* Authors acknowledge financial support under grants HAR 2012-35965 Consumption, Living standards and Inequality in Spain 1400–1870. Corinne Thépaut-Cabasset, Marie Curie Research Project hosted at CTR/SAXO Institute, University of Copenhagen 2015–2017: *Dressing the New World: The Trade and the Culture of Clothing in the Spanish Colonies 1600–1800.*

This chapter attempts to offer a picture of how taste and luxury channelled urban consumption in Madrid in the 1740s, focusing on a segment of society with high average income that lived in the capital and was in contact with the court and with new trends. Taste was shaped by individual choices, availability and popularity. This particular case study reveals the importance of demand for French products with regard to their exclusivity and quality – France had, of course, attained an international renown with an image linked to elegance, luxury and style that all Europe wanted to imitate (see also the chapters by Clemente, North and Ilmakunnas).[4] It also offers a window on the ways in which taste for French products and fashionable goods interfered in luxury networks throughout eighteenth-century Spain.

Although French products always had a significant presence in the Castilian market,[5] war and the arrival of Philip V, Duc d'Anjou, and the grandson of Louis XIV – who first married Marie Louise of Savoy (1701–1714) and then Elizabeth Farnese (1714–1746) – had an important influence on material culture and social practices in Madrid.[6] Influenced by his grandfather, Philip changed the relationship between the court and the state, as the French Bourbons did, to ensure greater influence of the administration of the state.[7] A new elite emerged that was linked more to the administration of the state than to the traditional relations of the old aristocracy. This new wealthy group was associated with establishing a peerage for services, especially during the War of the Spanish Succession (1701–1714), and with the sale of noble titles related to the financial needs of the monarchy.[8] These political adjustments, which provoked widespread opposition among the long-established elite, were accompanied by changes in ceremony and were an attempt to reform the court with a significant impact on taste and luxury.[9] Courtesy and etiquette, viewed as a socio-economic and political system, began to change in the eighteenth century.[10] On a European scale, kings popularized and even mandated major fashion trends among the elite.[11] Cantillón alludes to this trickle-down effect when he noted that the prince 'who is copied by his court, normally determines the inspiration and tastes of the other landlords in general'.[12] With a French king in Spain, French goods were associated with luxury and status, and determined the style of the court, as Clemente demonstrates for Naples in this volume. If we consider goods to be an information system, gifts (e.g., paintings and sculptures, bibelots, ceramics from Sèvres, Gobelins tapestries, and jewellery) fuelled an incessant trade in information between France and Spain; they were ruled by the same dynasty and linked by new commodities in the market.[13] French commodities acquired a 'court status', linked to good taste which makes attempts to distinguish between taste and luxury a challenging task, especially when Louis XIV's court *à la mode* reached its peak.

Taxes, imports and luxury

The document used as a source for this chapter is a tax called the *décima* (the tenth) which was levied to finance the War of Jenkins' Ear against England and would disappear once the specified amount was fully collected.[14] In theory, the *décima* had to be collected as a direct tax on the income of every subject of the Crown except for persons with special immunity such as clergy (but not nobility) and according to their assets. In reality, it was collected in different ways, according to the characteristics and agreements reached in each place. In some towns, the collection was based on direct taxes, but, probably because of the incapacity of the administration or the resistance of privileged groups, it was often levied as an indirect tax and collected by a top-down quota system in various different ways.[15]

In Madrid, the collection of this tax was assigned to the Big Five Guilds of the city because they were the ones that advanced the King the amount estimated to be collected in the town. In exchange, the Big Five Guilds charged town customs duties to everyone who brought goods for their own consumption through the city's gates.[16] The advantage of this when using the tax records as a source lies in the fact that it reflects a specific levy that was applied solely and exclusively to a series of products for personal consumption. The tax did not affect basic goods such as bread, but others of a wider scope. Some of the products were 'everyday goods' (olive oil, wine, pork fat, etc.), others might be characterized as 'luxuries' or even 'positional goods' (textiles, jewellery, exotic tapestry) and, in between, 'semi-luxury goods', a category that would include products such as sugar or cocoa since they might have transformed from luxury to common goods during these years, particularly in urban environments. We therefore have a snapshot of the shopping basket of durable and semi-durable goods, colonial products and groceries consumed by the wealthy classes. What makes this tax particularly interesting is the fact that it effectively shows the intention to tax the upper or middle classes, which were previously free of other indirect taxes. Moreover, it has an advantage over probate inventories in that it records a wider range of goods and gives us a dynamic rather than a static picture.

We present here analysis of the tax records for the period 1741–1743. With the aim of analysing the structure of demand, we have first classified the 450 products listed into eight major groups, which in turn are divided into subgroups.[17] The items recorded most frequently were *clothes and articles for personal use* (50.7 per cent), followed by *luxury food* (37.3 per cent) and *household goods* (9.6 per cent); other categories being of minor importance. When it was possible to standardize measures, such as with spices or certain textiles, we were able to establish per capita consumption by gender and social class. We have assigned 3,819 people into seven categories or social classes based on the information provided in the document: Crown, Ecclesiastic, Charitable Foundation, Ambassador, Nobility (7 per cent), Upper Middle Class (73.7 per cent), and Lower Middle Class (17.8 per cent).[18]

When looking at gender, we see that men managed both income and purchases (90.4 per cent of goods were introduced by men) and that they bought articles for both men and women. However, women introduced products that were focused more on personal and domestic use, such as fabrics, bedclothes, table and kitchen linens, underwear, footwear, dresses and decorative articles, as well as certain domestic objects such as braziers and spices. Women appear to demonstrate a certain preference for this type of shopping because they are the ones who spend more time at home and are, therefore, the ones who are responsible for domestic spaces.[19]

French commodities in Madrid: clothing textiles

At the beginning of the eighteenth century, Madrid, as an imperial capital, was a distinctive consumer of new goods coming from the East and West.[20] With a French king at the Spanish court luxury was inevitably represented by 'French taste, food and design' as it was already happening amongst elite circles of all Europe.[21]

In our source, we know the origin of 20 per cent (1,440 of 7,477) of all the goods, of which almost 13 per cent came from France. This percentage is certainly higher because many products, especially fabrics, cloth, gloves, gold and silver lace, silk and thread, were made in France. However, we have considered only those entries where the origin was specified (75.8 per cent Spain, 13 per cent France, 4.7 per cent China, 2.4 per cent Holland and 1.9 per cent for Cuba, Germany, Venezuela, Indies, Italy, Portugal and Flanders combined). French products came primarily via three routes: the north, particularly through the port of Bilbao that served as a warehouse for all of Castile up to Madrid; the south, through Cadiz; and the east, through the ports of Barcelona, Alicante and Malaga.[22] In the Mediterranean, merchants from Marseille sent cloth from Carcassonne, Toulouse, Lyon to Cadiz and Cartagena and Languedoc, in addition to American and Asian products.[23] Where did most of the demand for French items come from? Only 4 per cent of French products were introduced by women; per capita the nobility purchased the most items, followed by the middle upper class and lower middle class (see Table 11.1).

Moral and ethical values had always been associated with appearance and the consumption of luxury, especially after the religious Reformation in the seventeenth century, so clothing was important in signalling status and character.[24] Sempere and Guarinos related laziness and relaxed attitudes to a certain type of clothing, and sumptuary laws sought to regulate it.[25] Trade, religion, culture and economic politics influenced taste and determined the

Table 11.1 Table of demand for French products by social class, 1741–1743

Type of Product	Mid-Lower Class	Mid-Upper Class	Ambassador	Nobility
Colonial Stimulants		1		
Confectionary		5		1
Sugar		6		2
Bedclothes		8		1
Table and Kitchen linen	3	10		3
Underclothes	1	6		
Fabrics	20	106	1	11
Leather and Fur	1	1		

Source: AGS, Tribunal Mayor de Cuentas, leg. 1862.

gradual adoption or abandonment of certain habits or styles. In this sense, Madrid combined two facets that were decisive for fashion-makers: it was both a metropolis and home to a royal court.[26] The court emphasized the setting of 'Paris fashion' in Europe;[27] indeed, Charles II ordered the court to wear 'a la francesa',[28] but this only took place with a clear passive resistance on behalf of the Spanish population, which favoured the 'traje de golilla',[29] black suit, 'jubón', breeches and petticoat and 'brial' in the case of women. In an apparently less domineering way, Philip V sought to standardize French fashion, and in 1707, French dress was common: frock coat, waistcoat and breeches, wigs, high-heeled shoes and big buttons.[30]

It is important to note that, throughout the eighteenth century, many products played a central role as social markers, especially in urban populations. To adopt or not the new fashion was connected to the dichotomy of Spanish-tradition-plain/French-novelty-colourful.[31] It addresses two relevant matters. On the one hand, clothing expressed political aspirations and can be seen as a weapon and as a symbol of transgression, exemplified by the words of Roche 'in the battle of appearance'.[32] Until the eighteenth century, the power of clothing as a code had been allowed to distinguish social classes, but also to demonstrate good taste to others.[33] For example, wearing a military uniform was a way to follow a style that Louis XIV brought into fashion.[34] Furthermore, emulation by wearing luxurious clothes could disguise and disturb social origin since one of the large issues in the *ancien régime* was appearance and status.[35] The need to be distinguished by social class was one of the reasons behind the Pragmatics of 1723, which specified the dress code for each trade.[36]

On the other hand, critics of the French trend focused on the amount of fabric that this fashion entailed, as this inevitably meant greater expense in textiles taking into account that more than a dozen suits were desirable in order to maintain a public impression of prosperity and well-being.[37] French dress, as a dress uniform, was denoted by fabric type and colour.[38] French taste could be seen as conspicuous consumption since a showy and not easily affordable mode had significant economic connotations. Considering that an appreciable amount of expensive fabrics were imports, there were also implications for the balance of trade. Add to this the extra costs faced by individual consumers and one can readily appreciate both the criticism of this type of dress and the project to introduce a national dress. As the chapters by Clemente, North and Stobart make clear, the criticism of 'Frenchism' can also be seen elsewhere in Europe, especially England.[39] In the rise of social and economic British patriotism, French dress proved to be valuable cultural propaganda.

Textiles seem to have been closely connected to demand factors (Figure 11.1), such as income availability (collection of wine and grain income) or even religious holidays (Christmas and Easter). As Giorgio Riello has pointed out, textiles 'can assume as wide a range of meaning as the uses for which they are employed'.[40] It is difficult to estimate the percentage of textiles used for clothing or furnishing in the 'fabric' section of our source. What is recorded is the amount of the fabrics introduced, not its final use. But we do know the nature of the textiles. The majority of those from France (measured in metres) were linens, with market seasonality in two months: March and especially October, coinciding with the collection of land rents and change of season. Savary noted that there was a very specific market in the capital because all woollens and linens that were sent through Bilbao to Madrid should be 25 per cent 'coarser and better' than those sent to Cadiz, Andalusia and the Indies, not only because the court was located in Madrid but also because the continental climate meant cold winters and thicker clothes. French ships were sent to Bilbao in August–September to distribute goods to the interior of Castile for the autumn

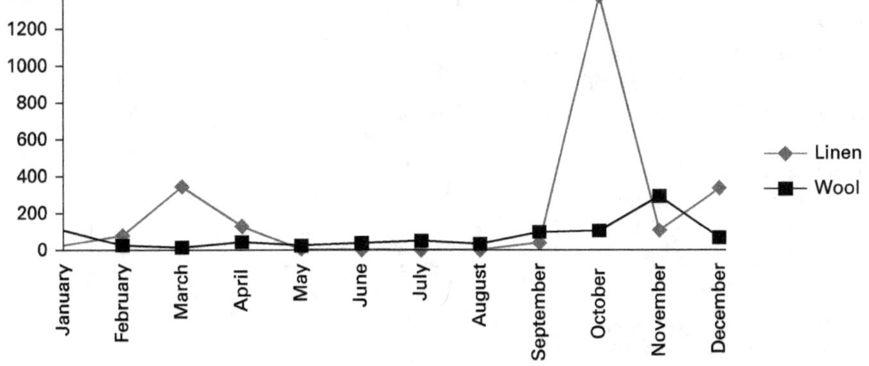

Figure 11.1 French fabrics, linen and wool, introduced in Madrid (1741–1743) in metres by months.

AGS, Tribunal Mayor de Cuentas, leg. 1862.

and winter.[41] However, it is important to note that linen is a product that had constant demand because items such as bedclothes, underwear and tableware were made from it and were usually bought and used throughout the year. The common view was that linen was associated with cleanliness, making linen ideal for domestic use.[42] Among the 2,646.47 metres of French linen fabrics, those that stand out come from Morlaix, Rouen and Troyes, the last being renowned for the variety and quantity of its linen and mixed hemp-linen products. When analysing by social class, half of all linen (1,376 metres) was bought by the nobility, who especially favoured linen from Rouen, reputed for its fine cloths. The upper middle class and lower middle class focused less on one type of linen, and introduced a great variety of fabrics and a fuller range of prices and qualities (see Table 11.2).

Woollen fabrics where the prices are noted reflect two trends: the purchase of cheap fabrics such as sempiternal, serge, calamanco and druggets, and the expensive and high-quality woollen cloth from Elbeuf and Abbeville that

Table 11.2 Purchase of linen French fabrics, by type and metres and social strata

Linen Fabric	Middle Upper Class	Lower Middle Class	Nobility
bretaña/Brittany	49		
crea		35	
cambray/Cambric	26.9		
estopilla/long lawn	48.72		
lienzo cambray/Cambric linen	60.48		
lienzo casero/home-made linen	26.04		
lienzo de Bretaña/brittany linen	16.1		
lienzo de Francia/French linen	61.6		
lienzo fino de Francia/French thin linen	23.1		
lienzo estopilla de cambray/ Cambric long lawn linen	8.4		
lienzo morlés/Linen Morlais	469.28		14.38
lienzo Trué/Troyes linen	307.44		
lienzo ruán/Rouen linen	101.64		1375.92
londrina encarnada de Francia/ Scarlet woolen cloth weaved in London	1.47		
terliz/drill or ticking	21		

Source: AGS, Tribunal Mayor de Cuentas, leg. 1862.

relied on merino wool (see Table 11.3). It is noteworthy that the top French superfine cloth from Louviers does not appear in the tax records. Colour was one of the most significant issues when classifying and choosing fabrics, and three stand out in the records: blue, black and scarlet. From the 1720s onwards, there were constant complaints from Castilian manufacturers regarding the Spanish inability to achieve the quality and vividness of foreign ones, especially in mixing and grana.[43] Gerónimo de Uztáriz wrote that 'the quality of fabrics will do little if it is not accompanied by the nuances and colorful' and gave the example of Lyon silk fabrics.[44] Both Lyon and Sedan provided fine cloth, especially in colours that the Spanish were unable to reproduce.[45] There was high demand for bright colours and fine fabrics among the middle and upper classes. The French textile industries of Bretagne, Picardie, Languedoc-Roussillon and Haute-Normandie found a good opportunity in the Castilian market.[46] The impression one gets is that very few Castilian woollen cloths reached the prices of Abbeville and that most of the woollen cloths introduced in Madrid, from Alcoy, Béjar and Segovia, were of average quality.

Higher prices for wool ranged from 75–90 reales for woollen grana cloth, the most valuable of all the fabrics, down to 48–50 reales for Elbeuf second. Among the costliest were cochineal, scarlet, France écarlate or blue or black Sedan, indicating that the colour of the cloth was an important element of value. This is also seen in cheaper fabrics such as rateen, where the price for scarlet ranged between 22–30 reales. Clothes with scarlet colour were associated with 'wealth and royalty'.[47] Imports of cochineal into Europe greatly encouraged the manufacture of bright scarlet and crimson fabrics. France imported part of its supply of cochineal from Saint Domingo and, from the seventeenth century, Spain imported from Mexico to Seville and Cadiz.[48] Improvements in dyeing were the hallmark of French fabrics, the attraction of which has several interpretations. As is apparent from Table 11.3, coloured fabrics were higher priced than plain fabrics of the same quality, giving them an added attraction to consumers of all social categories. On the other hand, the high price reinforced the exclusivity that converted them into luxury goods and markers of status. According to Savary, this regular demand favoured the abuses committed by some French traders, despite the strong regulations established by Colbert in the second half of the seventeenth century.[49] There were incidents of fabrics covered with trademarks of lead that were not standard-issue according to the regulations.

Table 11.3 Table of type and value of woollen French fabrics purchase in Madrid by social strata, 1741–1743, in reales and metres

Fabric	Value in reales		Metres by social class			
	Price min.	Price max.	Upper Middle Class	Lower Middle Class	Nobility	Ambassador
Bay/bayeta/flanelle	18	18	6.72	2.52		
Calamanco/calamaco/calmande	7	10	49.56			
Drugget/droguete/droguet	7	10	43.68	32.97	12.6	
Flowery droguet/droguetillo/droguet fin	8	11	25.2			
Serge-like woollen stuff/estameña/ étamine/	5	11	73.08			
Red Serge-like woollen stuff/estameña encarnada/étamine écarlate/	8		5.04			
Cochineal/grana/écarlate	75	90	12.6		8.61	
Abbeville woollen cloth/paño de Abbeville/drap d'Abbeville	56	64	38.22		5.04	
Carcassonne woollen cloth/paño de Carcasona/drap de Carcassonne	40	50	5.04	6.93		
France woollen cloth/paño de Francia/ drap de France	40	45	29.19			
France blue woollen cloth/paño azul de Francia/drap bleu de France	50	50	10.08			
France woollen cloth fine-thin/paño fino de Francia/drap fin de France	48	60	25.62		6.72	
France woollen cloth poor-quality/paño ordinario de Francia/drap commun de France	22	25	5.88	5.46		

Sedan black woollen cloth/paño negro de Sedan/drap noir de Sedan	50	50			5.04	
Elbeuf woollen cloth/paño ElBeuf/drap d'Elbeuf	46	50	61.5972	12.39		
Elbeuf common woollen cloth/paño común ElBeuf/drap commun d'Elbeuf	40	50	26.46		23.1	
Elbeuf fine woollen cloth/paño ElBeuf fino/drap fin d'ElBeuf	55	64	34.86		5.04	5.04
Elbeuf second woollen cloth/paño ElBeuf segundo/drap second d'Elbeuf	48	50	7.14			
Red floss/pelusa encarnada de Francia/ peluse incarnate de France	20	20	4.2			
France principela/principela de Francia (used for cloak, cape and dresses)	8	9	26.04	14.28		
Red-scarlet wide Rateen/ratina ancha encarnada/ratine large incarnate	30	40	6.93			
Wide Rateen/ratina ancha/ratine large	40		1.26			
Tight Rateen/ratina angosta/ratine étroite	14	30	51.492	5.88		
Red-scarlet tight rateen/ratina angosta encarnada/ratine étroite encarnée	22	30	79.8	3.36	9.24	
Sateen-woollen printed or flowery cloth/saetin/	8	9	15.12	13.44	0	
Woollen serge/sarga/serge	4.5	8	61.32			
Light serge/sargueta/serge legère	5		11.76			
Sempiternal/sempiterna/sempiterne	8	9	2.52	22.68		

Source: AGS, Tribunal Mayor de Cuentas, leg. 1862.

In 1740, the supervisor general ordered manufacturers to refrain from sending defective fabrics to Spain, in an attempt to take advantage of the war and gain the confidence of Spanish traders in the face of English competition.[50]

To differentiate fashion, taste and luxury is a complex matter. It is well-known that France had no rival from the seventeenth century in terms of elegance and luxury, but it is hard to ascertain whether demand for French products in Madrid was due to the desire for luxury or a reflection of the taste for French style. It is clear, however, that there were significant differences in the quality of French woollens bought by different social groups. The nobility bought only 8 per cent of the French woollen cloth registered in our source, but nearly three-quarters of this comprised expensive fabrics (upwards of 40 reales per metre) and including the 'grana sencilla color escarlata' (at 90 reales) introduced by the Marquis of Escalona, and also cloth from Abbeville, Sedan and Elbeuf. It seems that the nobility selected only certain fabrics; not in vain, French dress was associated to sartorial refinement. The cheaper cloth bought by the nobility (especially drugget) was probably for servants' liveries or lining.[51] The upper middle class bought the bulk of French woollen fabrics, of which only one-third were fabrics costing around 40 reales per metre. Because this class formed the majority of our sample, they were also the ones bringing the greatest variety of fabrics into the city, from the cheapest to the most expensive. Expensive woollen cloth from Carcassonne and Elbeuf, and middle quality tight scarlet rateen can also be found, but never fabrics of 50 reales per metre and above (see Table 11.3). On the other hand, the middle lower class introduced 13 per cent of the cheapest drugget, sempiternal, sateen-woollen printed or French principela, which they used for cloaks, capes and dresses. Amongst these, colour remained important.

The war would have hindered or prevented the importation of cheap English fabrics and favoured French sempiternals and bays: fabrics that competed with British ones were now excluded because of embargos.[52] Sempiternals and baizes were medium-priced fabrics commonly used by various social groups; perpetuanas were a sturdy and tightly woven fabric, often worn by poor people, and bays were fabrics made with thin and loose wool favoured by the clergy and used for blankets among other uses. In fact, even before the war, France was concerned about British competition and tried to get around it by imitating English fabrics. In the correspondence between the 'contrôleur general des finances' and inspector of manufactory of Beauvais in 1708, the former pointed to the rivalry between French and English sempiternals and bays.

French commodities in Madrid: household demand

In a city where keeping up appearances mattered, following fashion not only involved textiles for dress but also affected household demand. As Braudel himself asked 'after all, where is luxury more conspicuous than in the home, furniture and dress?'[53] Eating was more than food itself; how and where one ate were also important. The manner of dining with napkins, crockery or tablecloths was part of the material life and luxury. According to Benito J. de Feijóo, visiting and writing letters were two common practices of sociability.[54] Homes were a place for showing off just as much as traditional spaces of sociability – such as the court, balls, ceremonies and gardens – or new ones linked to cultural aspects of the city, such as theatres and the opera.

The bedroom was central in domestic life and in the use of all types of textiles, from covers to curtains, and linens and pillows from Morlaix, Rouen or Laval could be seen in Madrid.[55] Some French manufacturing centres specialized in export fabrics; Laval, for example, produced mainly low-quality woollens to make skirts for the poor and exported to the Indies or to Southern Spain and Madrid.[56] The demand for French ready-to-use products was based on shirts and handkerchiefs that were highly popular from the middle and upper social class who wanted to be bearers of French fashion.[57]

New refinement and social manners stimulated the renewal of household furniture and utensils and for napkins and particularly tablecloths (see Table 11.4). A new code and behaviour associated with cleanliness and elegance was settled even if some foods were still being eating with the hands. In Spain, the royal Maestranza of table linen in Coruña supplied the royal family and upper classes. This manufacturer had a great reputation both within and outside Spain. Despite this, 746 metres of French tablecloths and table napkins (8.5 per cent of the tablecloth entries) were brought into Madrid from Normandy and Picardie, especially by the upper middle class.

Table 11.4 Household demand of French fabrics, 1741–1743

Fabric	Unit
Pillow (Morlaix)	12
Sheet (Laval, Morlaix, Rouen, domestic)	28
Decorative cloth table (France)	4
Shirt (Brittany, Morlaix)	30
Handkerchief (Cambray)	7

Source: AGS, Tribunal Mayor de Cuentas, leg. 1862.

This hierarchy of consumption, especially with regard to the consumption of some household items such as tablecloths, suggests what Veblen called vicarious consumption. Nonetheless, it is necessary to emphasize the problem of transport costs versus product prices. Considering that most of the products consumed in Madrid were textiles, one of the explanatory elements is the weight:price ratio. An expensive fabric weighs more or less the same as a cheap one, so the transport cost will be roughly the same (except for the risk of theft and insurance) and will thus affect a cheap fabric more than an expensive one. In line with this fact, recent scholarship has noted changes in consumer habits in some Mediterranean regions, including Spain, arising from intense contact with French merchants acting as agents.[58]

French style had also involved the ascent of some professionals, such as hairdressers, 'couturières', interior decorators and chefs.[59] At the beginning of the eighteenth century, the popularity of Spanish cuisine was superseded by French – as Braudel noted: 'fashion governs cooking like clothing'.[60] Spices that were basic to medieval cuisine were relegated to a minor role with respect to new ingredients such as wild mushrooms, capers or sugar, and diets thus began to be diversified and enriched. During the seventeenth century, sweet dishes began to be served at the end of the meal, thereby separating salty and sweet food and consolidating the long-established dessert with a new type of confectionery made with sugar.[61] The Comtesse of Aulnoy gave an account of the crystallized fruit (*glacé dans le sucre*), a fashion imported from Italy, which she ate at a meal served in the court.[62] In the *Tableau de Paris*, Mercier noted that the new rages of fashion led Elizabeth Farnese to accept a hairdresser and a cook from France.[63] More recently, Aileen Ribeiro has pointed out 'the devotion to French tastes in the fashionable world made French tailors, valets, maids, dancing masters and cooks esteemed commodities',[64] and, in her chapter in this volume, Johanna Imakunnas notes that Swedish aristocrats frequently employed cooks trained in Paris. Similarly, from 1709 to 1745, two French cooks were in charge of the daily diet of the royal family in Madrid: Pedro Benoist and Pedro Chatelain.[65] According to our source, both brought into the city 120 kg of 'conserva de dulce' (preserved sweet). Other foreigner residents also demanded French sweets, including Monsieur Arsan, Monsieur Duboucher or Monsier Spinetti, as well as the Earl of Jeves and the Countess of Belalcanzar. So too did many of the Spanish nobility.

More generally, what can be seen through this source is that Madrid's citizens introduced an enormous quantity of sweet foodstuffs, especially around Christmas, with 45 per cent of imports of this nature coming into the city in November and especially December. In the case of French sweets, demand seems to be particularly concentrated: December registered 94.9 kg of sweets, 11.4 kg occurred in January, and April had 81.4 kg – most likely coinciding with Easter. Sweets also accompanied cups of hot chocolate in afternoon social gatherings. Colonial drinks were 'aspects of elite sociability' and ultimately the manifestation of the rivalry between nations.[66] Each empire had its networks, which consumption reflected. In Spain, unsurprisingly, chocolate was the leading stimulant in the eighteenth century and the inhabitants of Madrid took it thick and spiced with cinnamon.[67] This is one of the reasons why sugar was in great demand; it was used as a condiment in the kitchen, in confectionery and distilleries, but it was especially used to sweeten chocolate. Palacio Atard stated that in 1789, the consumption of chocolate and cacao per capita in the capital reached 3.4 kg per year.[68] The high degree of social contact between the Spanish peninsula and the Spanish colonies favoured the transmission of new products, and it is significant that only the upper middle class introduced sugar from France, mainly in October (1,637.4 kg), with only 3.5 kg of sugar in May and 71.7 kg in July. The only entry (79 kg) of French cocoa was accounted in the name of Don Antonio Spinetti, who also introduced 48.31 kg of sugar.

The assimilation of semi-luxury colonial products into daily life in Madrid followed a different rhythm from the exotic to the ordinary. Sugar and chocolate in the first half of the century were still closer to the upper middle upper class and the nobility than they were to common people. As part of a global process,

Spanish cooking integrated commodities as well as new household furniture that became more accessible in the long run. French cooking and cooks were part of this process.

Conclusions

What was happening in the 1740s in Spain regarding the consumption of luxury and semi-luxury goods? Determining living standards in the mid-eighteenth century helps in understanding the circulation of goods and the assimilation of new trends and fashions.[69] Demand depended on prices, but the ability to afford luxuries also played a role in discussions of consumption, especially in the case of expensive commodities. Nonetheless, we must not forget that the emulation effect could be as important as incomes in the case of certain desirable and *à la mode* goods. However, these changes were unique in each city and the wealthier classes were largely the forerunners when it came to the ability to access such products.

The constant circulation of goods and customs refashioned and altered the patterns of consumption among the population, particularly in urban areas and mainly in Madrid. What emerges from our research is that there were different grades of luxury that channelled identity. During the eighteenth century, Spanish society witnessed a refinement of manners from neighbouring France which especially affected the upper classes and the emerging bourgeoisie. French fashion helped to shape taste, a preference that seemed to trickle down from the court. It held particular significance because appearance and identity were very close. Emulating the upper classes was a way of attempting to move up the social ladder which is why a large proportion of Madrid society showed a preference for French commodities, especially fabrics. The heterogeneous upper middle class seemed to be especially influenced by French modes, by its coloured (blue and scarlet) high-priced fabrics, but also by food and household goods, such as table linen. Good taste was attached to French fashion, hence the purchase of high-priced and high-quality French fabrics, reputable by their colour and quality,[70] which reinforced the idea that these fabrics were regarded as luxury products which could underpin status and life style. The nobility focused their consumption of

French cloth onto the more expensive linen fabrics from Rouen and woollen cloths from Elbeuf, Sedan and Abbeville, including the most expensive woollen écarlate and the scarlet rateen. Their preferences seem to be well defined, especially by quality. In this sense taste, seen as refined preference, and luxury went hand in hand; but luxury was above all determined by price and was not therefore synonymous with taste.[71] Not everyone was able to afford the consumption of such commodities; much depended on the level of income of each family or social group. Moreover, the preference for colourful fabrics can be seen as a choice linked with the aesthetic and quality, but also with political connotations and power. This relationship between preferences, taste and politics has also been underscored by Aline Clemence in her study of Naples in this volume. Material culture is a dynamic process shaped by incomes, novelty, religion, political economy, imperialism, taste and, in the words of Braudel, also by social behaviour.

Notes

1 Rafael Dobado-González, Alfredo García-Hiernaux and David Guerrero-Burbano, 'West versus East: Early Globalization and the Great Divergence', *Cliometrica* 9 (2015), 235–64; Maxine Berg, 'In pursuit of Luxury: Global History and British Consumer Goods in the Eighteenth-Century', *Past and Present* 182 (2004), 85–142.

2 Ina Baghdiantz McCabe, *A History of Global Consumption: 1500–1800* (London and New York: Routledge, 2015), 3.

3 Louis-Sébastien Mercier, *Tableau de Paris* (1781), vol. 2, 302.

4 Joan DeJean, *The Essence of Style: How the French Invented High Fashion, Fine Food, Chic Cafes, Style, Sophistication, and Glamour* (New York: Free Press, 2005), 3.

5 Manuel Pérez-García, *'Vicarious Consumers': Trans-National Meetings between the West and East in the Mediterranean World (1730–1808)* (London: Ashgate, 2013).

6 Biblioteca Nacional de España, Mss/10680 (241–5). Marie-Louise of Parme kept track of every French mode. Before that, Marie-Louise d'Orléans brought French fashion and taste to Madrid. Corinne Thépaut-Cabasset, 'Marie-Louise d'Orléans Queen of Spain,' in *Spanish Fashion at the Courts of Early Modern Europe*, eds J. L. Colomer and Amalia Descalzo Lorenzo (Madrid: CHEE, 2014), 267–92.

7 Pablo Vázquez Gestal, *Una Nueva Majestad: Felipe V, Isabel de Farnesio y la Identidad de la Monarquía (1700–1729)* (Madrid: Fundación de Municipios Pablo de Olavide-Marcial Pons, 2013), 325.

8 In total 322 titles were created during his reign. María del Mar Felices de la Fuente, *Condes, Marqueses y Duqueses: Biografías de Nobles Titulados durante el Reinado de Felipe V* (Aranjuez: Doce Calles, 2013), 12.
9 Gómez-Centurión, 'Etiqueta y Ceremonial Palatino durante el Reinado de Felipe', *Hispania: Revista española de historia*, 56 (1996), 965–1005.
10 Jesus Cruz, *The Rise of Middle-Class Culture in Nineteenth-Century Spain* (Louisiana: Louisiana State University Press, 2011), 21.
11 The role of ambassadors should not be understated. Consumption by ambassadors is linked to luxury, fashion, art and parade. Corinne Thépaut-Cabasset, 'Princely Wardrobe and International Network: The Case Study of Bavaria in the 1680s', in *Royal Wardrobes: Visual Culture, Material Culture*, eds Isabelle Paresys and Natacha Coquery (Lille: CRHEN-O, 2011), 177–193; Henri Bedarida, *Parme et la France de 1748 à 1789* (Paris: Champion, 1928).
12 Richard Cantillón, *Essay on the Nature of Trade in General* (New York, 1734, reprint 2015), 43.
13 Mary Douglas and Baron Isherwood, *The World of Goods: Towards an Anthropology of Consumption* (New York and London: Routledge, 2002), 59; Corinne Thépaut-Cabasset, 'Présents du Roi: An Archive at the Ministry of Foreign Affairs in Paris', *Decorative Arts* 1 (2007), 4–18.
14 Nadia Fernández-de-Pinedo, 'Tax Collection in Spain in the 18th Century: The Case of the "Décima"', in *Taxation and Debt in the Early Modern City*, eds Jose Ignacio Andrés and Michael Limberger (London: Pickering and Chatto, 2010), 101–11.
15 *Copia de la instrucción dada, en consecuencia de lo que mandó S. M. por el Ilustrísimo Señor Don Joseph del Campillo, a todos los Superintendentes del Reyno, para la cobranza del Diez por Ciento*, BNE, Mss. 11.259 (39) Aranjuez, 31 May 1741.
16 For more details about the tax see Fernández-de-Pinedo, 'Tax Collection'.
17 In the case of barley, straw, wine, oil and soap, bacon/lard (pork), salted ham and chorizo, the source only collected the total amount introduced per day but does not specify who introduced it. These products are not included in the 450 products analysed.
18 There are 3,822 people but three records do not name the persons who introduced the merchandise because they were seized as contraband. *Ambassadors, Charitable Foundations, Church* and *Crown* represents the 1.4 per cent. The Crown and the Church were exempt from paying the tax; however, occasionally goods that were introduced by them were recorded although they did not pay the tax. *Upper Middle Class* includes the gentry. All the people noted in this category have the 'Don/Doña' distinction. Although uncertain, this denotes certain social and

economic criteria. Traders, merchant bourgeoisie, officials of the Administration, senior officials or property owners might belong to that category.

19 Pérez-García, '*Vicarious Consumers*', 179–80.

20 Dobado-González, García-Hiernaux and Guerrero-Burbano, 'West versus Far East'.

21 See also Ilja Van Damme, 'Middlemen and the Creation of a "Fashion Revolution": The Experience of Antwerp in the Late Seventeenth and Eighteenth Centuries', in *The Force of Fashion in Politics and Society: Global Perspectives from Early Modern to Contemporary Times*, ed. Beverly Lemire (London: Ashgate, 2010), 21–40.

22 Nadia Fernández-de-Pinedo and Emiliano Fernández de Pinedo, 'Distribution of English Textiles in the Spanish Market at the Beginning of 18th Century', *Revista de Historia Económica – Journal of Iberian and Latin American Economic History* 31 (2013), 253–84.

23 Pérez-García, '*Vicarious Consumers*'.

24 Daniel Roche, *The Culture of Clothing: Dress and Fashion in the Ancien Régime* (Cambridge: Cambridge University Press, 1996), 5.

25 José Sempere y Guarinos, *Historia del Luxo y de las leyes suntuarias de España*, 2 (Madrid: Imprenta Real, 1788), 142; see also Álvaro Molina and Jesusa Vega, *Vestir la identidad, construir la apariencia: La cuestión del traje en la España del siglo XVIII* (Madrid: Ayuntamiento de Madrid, 2004), 89–119.

26 Bruno Blondé and Jon Stobart, 'Introduction: Selling Textiles in the Eighteenth Century: Perspectives on Consumer and Retail Change', in *Selling Textiles in the Long Eighteenth Century: Comparative Perspectives from Western Europe*, eds Jon Stobart and Bruno Blondé (Basingstoke: Palgrave Macmillan, 2014), 5.

27 Lesley E. Miller, 'Material Marketing: How Lyonnais Silk Manufacturers Sold Silks, 1660–1789', in *Selling Textiles in the Long Eighteenth Century: Comparative Perspectives from Western Europe*, eds Jon Stobart and Bruno Blondé (Basingstoke: Palgrave Macmillan, 2014), 88.

28 Thépaut-Cabasset, 'Marie-Louise d'Orléans Queen of Spain'; Juana Natividad de Leon Salmeron Africa de Diego y González, *Compendio de indumentaria española* (Madrid: Imprenta de San Francisco de Sales 1915), 175.

29 The *golilla* was finally prohibited in 1701 after an attempt of Philip V to wear it. Alfred Morel-Fatio, 'La golille et l'habit militaire', *Bulletin Hispanique* 2 (1904), 114–42. The *golilla* stimulated the importation of bayette from England one of the reasons why M. Anisson advised the king of France to suggest Philip V to avoid the *golilla* in Spain and promoted French fashion. Arthur Michel de Boislisle, *Correspondance des contrôleurs généraux des finances avec les intendants des*

provinces, publiée par ordre du ministre des finances d'après les documents conservés aux Archives nationales, 2 (Paris: Imprimerie nationale, 1699–1708), 483.

30 Sempere y Guarinos, *Historia del Luxo*, 146.

31 See Marie-Catherine Le Jumel de Barneville Aulnoy, *La cour et la ville de Madrid vers la fin du XVIIe siècle: Mémoires de la cour d'Espagne*, 2 (Paris: E. Plon, 1874), 474; Thépaut-Cabasset, 'Marie-Louise d'Orléans Queen of Spain.'

32 Roche, *The Culture of Clothing*, 6; see also Natacha Coquery, 'Luxury and Revolution: Selling High-Status Garments in Revolutionary France', in *Selling Textiles in the Long Eighteenth Century: Comparative Perspectives from Western Europe*, eds Jon Stobart and Bruno Blondé (Basingstoke: Palgrave Macmillan, 2014), 181; Pérez-García, *'Vicarious Consumers'*, 75.

33 Philip Mansel, *Dressed to Rule: Royal and court costume from Louis XIV to Elizabeth II* (New Haven: Yale University Press, 2005); Jon Stobart, *Spend, Spend, Spend! A History of Shopping* (Stroud: History Press, 2008), 73.

34 Keeping in mind also that the military were trendy due to the wars in Italy and the War of Succession. See Molina and Vega, *Vestir la identidad, construir la apariencia*, 27.

35 Corinne Thépaut-Cabasset, *L'Esprit des modes au Grand Siècle* (Paris: Éditions du CTHS, 2010).

36 Felipe V, *Pragmática sanción que su Magestad manda observar, sobre trages, y otras cosas*. Traditional society is going to react against foreign influence at the end of the century with the project of the establishment of a national dress and the stereotype of the *petrimetre* with negative connotations about everything related to foreign fashions. *Discurso sobre el lujo de las señoras, y proyecto de un traje nacional*; see also Johanna Ilmakunnas, 'La mode française en Finlande au XVIIIe siècle et au début du XIXe siècle,' paper presented at the seminar 'Le tournant de 1914: Deux siècles d'interculturalité franco-finlandaise', Paris 12 November 2014, 6; Johanna Ilmakunnas, 'Careers at the Courts: Noblewomen in the Service of Swedish and Russian Royals, c. 1750–1850', *Women's History Magazine* 72 (2013), 4.

37 'It is made with 8 varas (jacket) but can be done with only 4' ['*hácense con 8 varas de tela (casacas) pudiéndose con 4 . . .*'] Sempere y Guarinos, *Historia del Luxo* (2), 146.

38 Amalia Descalzo, 'El Traje Francés en la Corte de Felipe V', *Anales del Museo Nacional de Antropología* 4 (1997), 205.

39 Michèle Cohen, *Fashioning Masculinity: National Identity and Language in the Eighteenth Century* (New York: Routledge, 1996), 'Introduction'.

40 Giorgio Riello, 'Fabricating the Domestic: The Material Culture of Textiles and the Social Life of the Home in Early Modern Europe', in *The Force of Fashion in Politics and Society: Global Perspectives from Early Modern to Contemporary Times*, ed. Beverly Lemire (Burlington: Ashgate, 2010), 64.

41 Jacques Savary Des Bruslons, *Dictionnaire universel de commerce,* (A–E), vol. 1, 922.

42 Riello, 'Fabricating the Domestic', 63.

43 Luis Fernández, *Tratado instructivo y práctico sobre el arte de la tintura* (Madrid: Imprenta de Blas Roman, 1778), 177.

44 Complaints were recurrent in the contemporary writings, see Gerónimo de Uztáriz, *Theorica y práctica de comercio y de marina en diferentes discursos* (Madrid: s.n. 1724), 339.

45 Bezon, *Dictionnaire général des tissus anciens et modernes* . . . . 1:1:XX.

46 'Pour la confection des draps, les producteurs languedociens se procurent en Espagne les laines ordinaires et les primes de Ségovie destinées aux qualités supérieures; ils agissent directement ou par l'intermédiaire de marchands espagnols ou toulousains spécialisés dans ce commerce.' Gilbert Buti, 'Des goûts et des couleurs: Draps du Languedoc pour clientèle levantine au XVIIIe siècle,' *Rives méditerranéennes* 29 (2008), 6.

47 Pérez-García, '*Vicarious Consumers*', 119.

48 Savary Des Bruslons, *Dictionnaire universel de commerce,* F–Z, 2, 857; Jacques Heers, 'La Búsqueda de Colorantes', *Historia Mexicana* 11 (1961–1962), 1–27; Marichal, 'Mexican Cochineal and European Demand for a Luxury Dye, 1550–1800', in *Global Goods and the Spanish Empire, 1492–1824: Circulation, Resistance and Diversity*, eds Bethany Aram and Bartolomé Yun-Casalilla (Basingstoke: Palgrave Macmillan, 2014); Sánchez Silva and Suárez Bosa, 'Evolution of Cochineal World Production and Marketing, XVIth-XIXth Centuries', *Revista de Indias* 66 (2006), 473–90.

49 Savary Des Bruslons, *Dictionnaire universel de commerce,* F–Z, 2, 924

50 Alain Becchia, *La draperie d'Elbeuf (des origines à 1870)* (Rouen: Publication Université de Rouen, 2000), 184.

51 Liveries were often made of coarser materials and bright colours. Sarah C. Maza, *Servants and Masters in Eighteenth-Century France: The Uses of Loyalty* (Princeton: Princeton University Press, 1983), 119.

52 Fernández-de-Pinedo and Fernández de Pinedo, 'Distribution of English Textiles'.

53 Fernand Braudel, *Capitalism and Material Life, 1400–1800* (London: Weidenfeld and Nicolson, 1967), 192.

54 Cruz, *The Rise of Middle-Class*, 26.

55 Roche, *The Culture of Clothing;* Savary Des Bruslons, *Dictionnaire universel de commerce*, F–Z, 2: Laval.

56 Roche, *The Culture of Clothing;* Savary Des Bruslons, *Dictionnaire universel de commerce*, F–Z, 2: Laval.

57 We have included shirts and handkerchief from Fabrics as they were ready-to-use and could be consider for personal use.

58 Pérez-García, '*Vicarious Consumers*', 196.

59 Clare Haru Crowston, *Fabricating Women: The Seamstresses of Old Regime France, 1675–1791* (Durham: Duke University Press, 2001).

60 Braudel, *Capitalism and Material Life,* 126.

61 Brian William Cowan, 'New Worlds, New Tastes: Food Fashions after the Renaissance', in *Food: The History of Taste*, ed. Paul H. Freedman (Berkeley: University of California Press, 2007), 219.

62 Aulnoy, *La cour et la ville de Madrid* (1874), 1, 479.

63 Mercier, *Tableau de Paris* (1788), 9, 73

64 Aileen Ribeiro, 'Fashion in the Eighteenth Century: Some Anglo-French Comparisons', *Textile History* 22 (1991), 331; see also Rebecca Haidt, *Women, Work and Clothing in Eighteenth-Century Spain* (Oxford: Voltaire Foundation, 2011).

65 Maria Angeles Pérez Samper, 'The Early Modern Food Revolution', in *Global Goods and the Spanish Empire, 1492–1824*, eds Bethany Aram and Bartolomé Yun Casalilla (Basingstoke: Palgrave Macmillan, 2014), 193.

66 Frank Trentmann, 'Crossing Divides: Consumption and Globalization in History', *Journal of Consumer Culture* 9 (2009), 198.

67 See among others Coady and Wright, *Chocolate*; Coe, *America's First Cuisine*s; Coe and Coe, *The True History of Chocola*te; Robertson, *Chocolate, Women and Empi*re; Young, *The Chocolate Tree: A Natural History of Cacao, Revised and Expanded Edition*; Stobart, *Sugar and Spice*; McCabe, *A History of Global Consumption*; Braudel, *Capitalism and Material Life*, 178.

68 Vicente Palacio Atard, *La alimentación de Madrid en el siglo XVIII y otros estudios madrileños* (Madrid: Real Academia de la Historia, 1998), 35.

69 Also, design starts to play an important role. See Giorgio Riello, Glenn Adamson and Sarah Teasley, *Global Design History* (Abington: Routledge, 2011).

70 For complaints see Gerónimo de Uztáriz, *Theorica y práctica de comercio y de marina en diferentes discursos*, 339, that pledged to favour dyers with exemptions in the Crown of Castile; see also Savary Des Bruslons, *Dictionnaire universel de commerce*, A–E, 1: 923.

71 About taste see John Styles and Amanda Vickery, 'Introduction', in *Gender, Taste and Material Culture in Britain and North America, 1700–1830*, eds John Styles and Amanda Vickery (New Haven: Yale University Press, 2006); Riello prompts that 'for most people, the accumulation of textiles remained a function of their income'. Riello, 'Fabricating the Domestic', 51.

12

French Fashions: Aspects of Elite Lifestyle in Eighteenth-Century Sweden

Johanna Ilmakunnas

In eighteenth-century Sweden, the lifestyle of elites was strongly influenced by France and French culture. Indeed, it has been argued that French cosmopolitan culture dominated elite lifestyles throughout eighteenth-century Europe.[1] However, the paradigm of a French Europe has been significantly nuanced by recent scholarship, which stresses the multiculturalism of the eighteenth century.[2] Pierre-Yves Beaurepaire argues that, contrary to what has been affirmed in previous research, Europe did not assimilate to France, but acculturated, negotiated and enriched French influences in local conditions.[3] In Sweden, French influences were especially visible amongst the aristocracy and titled nobility, who considered France as another cultural fatherland. This influence spanned from: education and the use of French language in social occasions and correspondence; military and diplomatic careers in France; styles of clothing, architecture and interior decorations; commissioning luxury goods from Paris; and employing French servants.

Charlotta Wolff stresses the significance of political alliance between Sweden and France, and Swedish aristocrats' personal interest in France, French language and French culture as key factors in forming close connections between the two countries.[4] Many Swedish aristocrats spent years in France, living in between two cultures, transferring and adjusting French cultural codes to their own use while in France and elsewhere in Europe, as well as when returning to Sweden.[5] The lifestyle and consumption of French aristocracy were the ideal image of a tasteful, elegant and fashionable lifestyle.[6] However, admiration of France and French culture was not uncritical. Swedish aristocrats were conscious of tensions that consumption of French luxuries and adaptation of French culture created in Sweden: it was a necessity for maintaining a certain lifestyle, but it was also considered morally and economically problematic.[7] Furthermore, Swedish aristocrats travelled throughout Europe, bringing back to Sweden influences from Italy, the German states, Holland and England. For mercantile elites, connections to and thus influences from the last three were more important than France or Italy, as Ulla Ijäs demonstrates in her chapter in this volume. Artists, craftsmen and architects studied in France, but also in Italy and Holland, transferring and accommodating their influences to the Swedish context. Therefore, albeit dominant and widely diffused, French fashions, taste and luxuries were not exclusive aspects of aristocratic lifestyle in eighteenth-century Sweden.

During the eighteenth and early nineteenth century, luxury was vehemently debated in Sweden, as elsewhere in Europe. However, in Sweden the debate concentrated more on the middling sorts than the elites, worrying the effect of opulence and luxury on social order, which would be disrupted by unnecessary luxury consumption.[8] Concern over luxury amongst middling sorts characterizes luxury debates in many countries, whereas a certain level of luxury was expected, and thus accepted, from the aristocracy in the *ancien régime* court society, where the outer appearance manifested rank, respectability and reliability of individuals. Even though luxury was a necessity for the aristocratic lifestyle, it eludes exact definitions, and its drifting connotations made it difficult to define for contemporaries. Count Hans Axel von Fersen epitomized the essence of aristocratic lifestyle, taste and luxury, when he wrote to his father about his expensive purchase of horses and bridles in 1779: 'I wish neither to shine, nor to be ridiculous, I only wish to be decent'.[9]

In Sweden, as elsewhere, luxury debates included a critique of the Frenchified aristocracy and elites' travels to France. Luxury was also criticized by aristocrats who themselves had close connections to France.[10] Their argument was not to ban luxury altogether, but to restrict the ostentatious display of luxury, which was considered tasteless and non-noble. A certain level of luxury and French fashions was vital for elite lifestyle and acted as a positive status symbol. However, flamboyant and conspicuous luxury consumption turned against the aristocracy, evoking negative perceptions.

This chapter offers new readings of luxury and taste amongst aristocracy in eighteenth-century Sweden. It explores different aspects of the aristocratic lifestyle, thus creating a more nuanced understanding of the variety of French influences in Sweden. It focuses on three key areas: clothing and outer appearance, strongly influenced by French fashion across Europe; genre paintings, demonstrations of their collector's taste, but also visualizations of aristocratic lifestyle, taste and material culture; and the employment of French servants, most importantly governesses and cooks. These influences, whether cultural or political, were primarily distributed to Sweden by Swedish diplomats, officers, architects and artists who had close connections to France. Swedish elites were connected through family relations, kinship and friendship, and the ties between those who had sojourned in France were remarkably strong, easing the flow of information, influences and goods. This chapter therefore draws mainly on elite correspondence and genre paintings, as well as objects such as clothes in museum collections, but account books of elite families also have been examined for information on French servants.

Clothing and outer appearance

In eighteenth-century court culture, clothing and outer appearance were key to elite respectability. For Swedish elites, Paris was the iconic shopping venue, from where luxury goods, amongst them clothes and accessories, were steadily bought either on location or by proxy.[11] Meanwhile, the Swedish state tried, through sumptuary legislation, to reduce the consumption of foreign (chiefly French) luxury and fashion goods, which were regarded as morally corrupting and harmful for the national economy. However, the benefits of the fashion industry for boosting the economy were acknowledged and the state strongly favoured domestic production.[12] In making the garments the elites commissioned, Swedish tailors and seamstresses followed French fashions, occasionally using materials imported or smuggled from France and Italy.[13] In 1778, Gustav III established a national uniform, which broke the hegemony of French clothing fashion and evoked both praise and criticism.[14] Despite the elites' awareness of the argued negative impact of foreign luxury trade on the Swedish economy, the aristocrats were less inclined to follow the official politics of favouring domestic production than were the lesser nobility and the mercantile and administrative elites.

Swedish diplomats sent from Paris to Sweden suits and gowns, lavish fabrics, ribbons and laces, swords, walking sticks, snuffboxes, fans, gloves and toiletries. Two suits that the then envoy, Count Gustav Philip Creutz, commissioned for Crown Prince Gustaf of Sweden (from 1772 Gustav III) in 1766 and 1777 are illustrative of French luxury clothing commissions to Sweden. Their acquisition is well documented in diplomatic correspondence and as objects.[15] In Sweden, the future king's attire acted as a model for French taste and exclusivity in clothes. Moreover, commissioning the suits gave Creutz an occasion to display in France the exquisite taste of Swedish royalty. The suit from 1766 was displayed in Paris before being shipped to Sweden, and it evoked wide admiration amongst French political elites who called on the Swedish envoy in order to see it.[16] Much of the admiration of Paris society fell on Creutz, whose taste in elegant clothing had guided the commissioning of the crown prince's garments from Parisian merchants.

Scholars have, in innumerable studies, stressed the importance of appearance in *ancien régime* court societies.[17] Clothing was an essential part of politeness and sociability, distinguishing the aristocracy from other elite groups and sovereigns from their subjects.[18] Although women and their consuming passions were often criticized and caricatured, men's clothing was at least as luxurious.[19] This is visible in the wardrobes of Swedish aristocrats. Hans Axel von Fersen's taste, judging from his diaries and correspondence with his father, was expensive and fashionable. In the 1780s he socialized in Paris and Versailles in the same circles as Ambassador Creutz and was a close friend of Queen Marie-Antoinette. Also from the 1780s dates a richly embroidered silk suit that Fersen wore in Paris.[20] The coat is made of grey and blue striped silk, with roses, leaves and small flowers embroidered in ivory, green, yellow and rose tones. The ivory waistcoat is embroidered with similar patterns to the coat, whereas the breeches are unadorned black silk. The relative simplicity of the suit and its new-modelled frock-coat, which was adapted from England, accentuated in a fashionable way Fersen's lean figure. Exquisite, high-quality and bright-coloured embroidery highlights the simplicity and elegance of the suit. In Parisian high society and at the court in Versailles, it was more effective for a Swedish nobleman to distinguish himself through simplicity than through lavish appearance, since French aristocrats would always be higher-ranking and richer than any Swedish aristocrat.

Those aristocrats who did not have the opportunity to buy luxury goods themselves in France, had to trust on the refinement of their peers' taste, as did royals, who – as we have already seen – entrusted diplomats to acquire French luxuries for them. Detailed instructions were given and received, as in 1743 when Baroness Charlotta Sparre, while commissioning gloves, stockings and jewellery, advised the then Swedish envoy, Count Clas Ekeblad, to ask for help in shopping from Marquise de Broglie, because she was 'a person who [has] good taste'.[21] Hans Axel von Fersen took care of a number of luxury commissions on behalf of his parents, Axel von Fersen and Hedvig De la Gardie.[22] In 1774, while in Wismar, Northern Germany, Hedvig De la Gardie commissioned dresses from Paris. She opened the boxes to examine whether the gowns were as desired, but found that her purchases were a disappointment: 'I do not find them [the dresses] being of the taste so much sought after, the spring grey dress is not at all as I commissioned it, and it is of most ugly cloth.'[23] The famous French taste represented for Hedvig De la Gardie the desirable quality of fashionable attire, but reality did not always meet the expectations of the commissioner.

Paintings as luxury objects and transmitters of French fashions

Art and books have long been considered as part of the eighteenth-century world of consumption and luxury.[24] Art collections, natural history collections or collections of books and rare manuscripts were an essential part of elite lifestyle and display of taste and knowledge,[25] and were bought or commissioned from across Europe. Nevertheless, it would be too simplistic to argue that the influences travelled primarily in one direction.[26] For instance, Swedish-born artists Gustaf Lundberg and Alexander Roslin made influential careers in mid-eighteenth-century Paris, while the artist Elias Martin was similarly successful in English art markets in the late eighteenth century, before they all in their turn returned to Sweden, continuing their careers there.[27]

While paintings can be read as representations of cultural values and norms, they can also be analysed as representations of elite culture and lifestyle.

Moreover, paintings can be seen – and certainly were seen by contemporaries – not only as works of art, but also as a luxury commodity, which could be commissioned, distributed and consumed, and which had a negotiable price. In genre paintings, artists did not depict the everyday life and interiors of European elites as they were in reality, but rather created an illusion: an image of cultivated, gracious and comfortable lifestyle. Thus, elite interiors in genre paintings by François Boucher, Jean Baptiste Siméon Chardin, Jean-Honoré Fragonard, Nicolas Lancret and Jean-François de Troy, among others, are very much metaphors of French luxury and the comfort of urban leisured milieus. The wealthy urban elites also represented one of the most important groups of buyers of these paintings.

One of the collectors and patrons of contemporary French artists was Count Carl Gustaf Tessin, Swedish ambassador in Paris 1739–1742. Patron of Boucher, Chardin and Lancret, Tessin was a well-known connoisseur of contemporary art in Paris. He bought art for his own collections and for royal collections in Sweden.[28] His taste for the material and intellectual delights of everyday life, his generosity, and his knowledge of French court society and French contemporary art made him invaluable as a transmitter of French aristocratic lifestyle to Sweden.

Two paintings, one by François Boucher, painted in the 1740s and another by Pehr Hilleström, painted in the 1770s or 1780s, with the same motive, a milliner and her female customer, visualize and concretize French taste and luxury, French influences in, and their adaptation to, Sweden.

François Boucher signed *The Milliner* (*La marchande des Modes*) or *Morning* in 1746 (see Figure 12.1).[29] An elegant and fashionable woman clad in a powdering mantel sits by her dressing table, examining a green ribbon; the milliner, just as fashionably clothed is seated by an open box of ribbons, holding a linen cap in her hand. The room is furnished and decorated after the latest fashion and, through a large window on left, morning light falls on the women, their faces and dresses. The theme and subject of the painting came from the commissioner, the Crown Princess of Sweden Lovisa Ulrika, sister of Frederic II of Prussia, who was the most important collector of contemporary French art in Sweden, along with Carl Gustaf Tessin.[30] *The Milliner* was to be the first of four genre paintings, depicting the four moments and typical feminine occupations of the day. Through Tessin and Swedish envoy Carl

Figure 12.1 François Boucher, *The Milliner* (*Morning*), 1746. Oil on canvas, 64 × 53 cm. NM 772.
Nationalmuseum, Stockholm. Photo Cecilia Heisser. CC BY-SA 4.0.

Fredric Scheffer, the princess gave detailed instructions to Boucher on what she wished the painting to depict.[31] This underlines Lovisa Ulrika as a self-confident consumer of French luxury goods, among them art and paintings as objects. However, Boucher waited months before painting *The Milliner* and never executed the other three, although in April 1750 Scheffer was still reporting that Boucher intended to deliver the missing three paintings as soon as possible. The reasons why Boucher did not fulfil the commission are not revealed by the extensive diplomatic correspondence recording the commission and its partial execution,[32] but it caused a rift between the painter and his former patron and friend Tessin.[33]

In eighteenth-century Paris, the morning toilette, as depicted in ideal and fictional form by Boucher, was an essential element of urban elites' sociability.[34] The habit diffused throughout Europe to the highest echelons of society. In Stockholm, it was a widespread mode of the aristocratic lifestyle.[35] The morning toilette represented female leisure and consumption of luxury goods. Furthermore, the woman and the milliner are fashioned as luxury objects themselves. A milliner on a morning call to a customer is the very embodiment of luxury trade in eighteenth-century Paris.[36] Even though the three other commissioned paintings were never executed, Boucher's *Milliner* alone was a significant demonstration of French taste for luxury transplanted to Sweden, where is was added to the collections of Lovisa Ulrika and to be seen by Swedish aristocracy and courtiers.

A Swedish counterpart and adaptation of Boucher's *Milliner* is Pehr Hilleström's painting, also called *The Milliner* (*Modehandlerska*), painted in the 1770s or 1780s (see Figure 12.2).[37] The central figure is a woman, sitting by a table while examining semi-luxuries presented to her by a milliner, who stands by the table. The woman holds in her hand a straw hat, while the milliner presents feathers for decorating it. Only one candle lights the room and the faces of the two women. Whereas Boucher's painting bathes in morning light, Hilleström examines the light of one candle in his and its reflections on the women, their clothes and in the gildings which decorate the room. The women's clothes are more unpretentious than the silk gowns worn in Boucher's painting and the colourings of these two paintings are different. Hilleström uses soft blues in the dress of the customer and the ribbon on her cap, and temperate greenish grey tones for the interior of the room. Whereas in Boucher's painting, the strong morning light irradiates bright reds, greens and blacks. Examining the light of a single candle was typical for Hilleström and his small-scale candle-lit interiors were sought-after paintings in Swedish art markets, always finding eager customers wanting them to decorate their salons and drawing rooms.[38]

The two *Milliners* by a French and a Swedish painter, some thirty years apart, offer us a French and a Swedish visual interpretation of a small-scale, but important luxury trade. Boucher's *Milliner* is unquestionably a French rococo

Figure 12.2 Pehr Hilleström, *The Milliner*. Oil on canvas, 79.5 × 65.5 cm. NM 3382. Nationalmuseum, Stockholm. CC BY-SA 4.0.

painting, visualizing an opulent luxury trade, whereas Hilleström's *Milliner* is equally unquestionably a Swedish version of luxury markets. Hilleström adapted the theme to less lavish Swedish interiors and clothing. Moreover, and more importantly, Hilleström also used artistic means he himself was interested in, artificial light and its reflections in an interior. Presumably Hilleström, who was appointed as royal painter in 1776, knew Boucher's painting, in the collections of the then Dowager Queen Lovisa Ulrika. Moreover, in 1757 Hilleström, who began his artistic career as a weaver, studied weaving techniques at the Royal Gobelins Manufactory, headed by Boucher. Boucher invited Hilleström to study painting in his atelier at the Royal Academy of Art, which gave Hilleström an impulse to aspire as a painter, an ambition which bore fruit in the 1770s.[39]

Mikael Ahlund argues that, in eighteenth-century art markets individual collectors, patrons, customers and broader audiences of art all had an impact on the shaping of the subjects of paintings.[40] While Boucher's production, clientèle and reception has been mapped,[41] more research is needed to form a broader picture of who commissioned and bought paintings from Pehr Hilleström, apart from his work as royal painter. However, judging from Hilleström's enormous productivity and his notes on selling his paintings, it is clear that his genre paintings, which adapted French ideals to Swedish art, had no problem finding buyers. Also, and more importantly, Hilleström created an expression of his own in his small paintings.[42]

Both Boucher's and Hilleström's works are linked to luxury, taste, consumption and the distribution of French cultural trends outside the borders of France in multiple ways. As paintings, they were at the same time artefacts, images and metaphors of French luxury, or rather French fashion and luxury adapted to Sweden. Through commissions and detailed instructions to the artists, aristocratic patrons were active consumers of luxury artefacts such as art works. In their turn, the paintings represented and pictured French luxury goods, material culture and everyday comfort. Furthermore, paintings existed in a physical space and place: an elite home or a royal residence. For their viewers, the paintings depicted the life lived in the spaces in which the paintings were hung. In eighteenth-century Sweden, architecture and interior designs were French, or French ideals adapted to Swedish context,[43] bringing paintings and domestic interiors into a dialogue which spoke of the complex relations between luxury objects, visual representations of luxury and national taste.

French servants

Servants were key agents in maintaining aristocratic lifestyle. The significance of servants for elites' lifestyle lay particularly in three fields: the number of servants employed in a household; the education of servants; and the nationality or language skills of the servants. Well-educated servants such as cooks or governesses were high-ranking in the hierarchy of the household. A French cook was an ultimate proof for the aristocratic taste and comfort in everyday life, while a French-speaking governess was regarded as a necessity in the most aristocratic circles. Indeed, French-speaking governesses were iconic for the European elites' home education well into the twentieth century. Governesses were vital both in terms of educating the children to francophone cultural norms and as status symbols.[44] In eighteenth-century Sweden, sumptuary legislation regulated the employment of foreign tutors and governesses.[45] At the Diet (*riksdag*) of 1765/6 the nobility as an estate opposed the prohibition and fees for employing foreign governesses, tutors and language teachers. Axel von Fersen, one of the representatives of the nobility in the Diet, defended the nobility's right to employ foreign tutors and governesses, arguing that those who wished their children to learn foreign languages should not be punished by any fees or regulations.[46] Being able freely study foreign languages at home (for boys also at the university), taught by native speakers, was at the very core of elite lifestyle and ideals of cosmopolitan European elite education.

In the 1760s, Carl von Fersen and Charlotta Sparre's five daughters were instructed by the French woman, Mademoiselle Liegeon. After the von Fersen girls had completed their education and entered high society, Mademoiselle Liegeon made a notable career in the theatre as one of the most admired actresses at the Swedish court.[47] In the 1750s and 1760s, Carl von Fersen's sister-in-law, Hedvig De la Gardie had a French maid, Barbe Hassé, who taught French and other feminine accomplishments to the von Fersen children.[48] Furthermore, in the 1760s, Axel von Fersen and Hedvig De la Gardie employed a governess, Mademoiselle Domér, whose yearly salary was 900 silver *dalers*, equivalent to middle-ranking civil servants and thus significant proof of her high status amongst the household staff. Significantly, there is no mention in the von Fersens' account books of any fines being paid for employing a foreign governess.[49] It is possible that these were never charged, because the nobility was often exempted from indirect fees and taxes, in addition to direct ones, such as tithe and state taxation. Nonetheless, it is important to note that governesses were employed despite possible taxes or fines and relatively high salaries. Equally important is the fact that, despite the sources noting 'French' governesses, the majority of the governesses and tutors, even in the most high-ranking aristocratic families, were neither foreign nor French. One of the most important reasons for this was religion. For the Swedish Lutheran aristocracy, employing a Catholic governess was problematic,[50] yet they were willing to pay substantial sums in order to employ French-speaking governesses, who played a key role in educating children about French culture and language. Probably the French governesses the von Fersen family employed were French Huguenots or the attributions 'French' and 'Mademoiselle' in the account books simply refer to their language skills, not to their origin.

French cooks and Swedish cooks educated in France were also essential for the elite lifestyle. They were responsible for everyday comfort and a pleasant life in terms of culinary pleasures in elite households. Moreover, cooks created gastronomic experiences for festivities, banquets and intimate dinner parties, essential for elite sociability. Several Swedish aristocrats either employed a French cook or sent their Swedish cooks to France to learn French gastronomy and cooking. Again, Swedish envoys in France played a key role, offering the members of Swedish elites the opportunity to send their cooks to be apprenticed in France.

In early-modern diplomacy, the display of wealth and taste through gastronomy, silver plate and festivities was vital for envoys, because a country's diplomatic and political power was weighted according to its diplomats' socializing and the meals he offered.[51] Consequently, Swedish diplomats in France employed a French cook while in France and often brought him to Sweden after their assignment in France was completed. In August 1741, envoy Carl Gustaf Tessin wrote from Paris to his wife Ulla Sparre in Sweden: 'I tried to find a cook, which is, as you know, the most difficult thing in the world. Especially presently, when everyone needs one for their country [houses].'[52] At the end of September 1741 Tessin could write that he had found a cook, who would travel to Sweden and work for the Tessins. The cook had been earlier employed by Count de La Marck, French ambassador in Madrid.[53] In April 1741 Tessin's niece Charlotta Sparre reported that the cook had arrived in Sweden together with furniture, books and paintings that Tessin had sent home from Paris. She wrote that the cook was the politest man in the world, even though he wanted to rearrange the whole kitchen from floor to ceiling. However, the cook's gastronomic skills were praised by the polite society

Countess Tessin had invited for dinner.[54] A cook's experience from other aristocratic and elite houses was an important recommendation. Tessin personally knew Count de La Marck, who had been French ambassador in Stockholm 1717–1719. Thus, the name of de La Marck and the cook's employment in his household acted as an extra assurance of the cook's skills in the eyes of Tessin.

In the early 1770s, Count Axel von Fersen and Count Erik Sparre af Söfdeborg sent their cooks to Paris, their progress being reported back to Sweden by envoy Gustav Philip Creutz. The cooks stayed at the Swedish residence, where Creutz's butler supervised their education. Fersen's cook, Eric Lindgren, prepared, alongside the staff at the diplomatic residence, dishes for feasts given by Creutz. He stayed almost two years in Paris, before his skills in gastronomy were polished to perfection.[55] After returning home, both cooks created exquisite meals for the guests of their masters, as was the custom in Stockholm high society. For instance, right after his arrival in Sweden in 1776, Count Hans Henrik von Liewen's French chef cooked a festive meal which was given for the king, queen and courtiers.[56]

In 1776, Axel von Fersen sent another cook to Paris and again it was Creutz who organized the apprenticeship. The cook was first sent to a confectioner and then served in Creutz's kitchen. Later Creutz sent him to the kitchen of Princess de Guéménée, whose chef was regarded as one of the best in Paris. The cook's apprenticeship cost to von Fersen was 800 *livres* a year, into which subsistence for accommodation and food was added. Creutz's good connections to French aristocracy and possibly also the connections Axel von Fersen himself had created while in France in the 1730s and 1740s, not only opened the doors to the kitchens of Mme de Guéménée but did so in October instead of the customary January.[57] The dominance of French gastronomic culture among the Swedish aristocracy was not complete, however: two years later, the same cook travelled to England, where the Swedish envoy in London, Baron Gustav Adam von Nolcken, found him an appointment at an English aristocratic house, where his skills were honed further.[58]

Indeed, not all foreign cooks in Sweden were French. In December 1740, the future admiral Carl Tersmeden, when returning to Stockholm after years in Germany, Portugal, Holland and England, brought with him a Portuguese servant named Le Clou. 'Born French, raised Portuguese, hairdresser and cook in profession, has been with me since August 1734',[59] explained Tersmeden to his astonished family, listening to Tersmeden and Le Clou discuss in Portuguese. Tersmeden explained to his sister that, whether she wished her hair fashioned after the latest English style or her meals prepared after English or French fashion, Le Clou would do all that. Again, both French and British fashions were adapted and shaped into Swedish context. The culinary skills of Le Clou were widely admired in Stockholm society and several members of the Tersmeden family borrowed him to cook while they gave dinner parties where they wished either to impress their peers or let them taste refined gastronomy and enjoy the pleasures of life.[60]

Conclusion

The three aspects through which this chapter has explored the aristocratic lifestyle in eighteenth-century Sweden stress the importance of French taste. In many ways 'French taste' was a construction, an adaptation of a variety of features regarded as French by the Swedish aristocracy, transplanted and shaped to a Swedish context. However, French taste did not dominate amongst the aristocracy; English novelties, fashions and manners were also important. In transmitting French tastes and fashions to Sweden, Swedish diplomats and aristocrats in France had a key role. They acted on behalf of their families, friends and sovereign, when orchestrating commissions of clothing and paintings or apprenticeships of cooks in the kitchens of French aristocracy. In clothing and outer appearance French fashion dominated high society throughout Europe, despite fashionable English, Polish or Turkish attires. In Sweden, the dominance of French or other foreign luxury in the form of garments and clothing was restricted through sumptuary laws. The aristocracy saw the political and economic importance of favouring domestic production, and much of its consumption was of domestic products; but this did not prevent those who desired luxury goods from buying or commissioning their clothing from France or elsewhere. French quality, taste and fashion were considered supreme, and a true aristocratic elegance was French.

Another aspect of French taste which diffused to Sweden was genre paintings, an essential part of any elite home interior. Like François Boucher's

Milliner, commissioned from the artist by Crown Princess Lovisa Ulrika through envoy Carl Fredrik Scheffer, paintings distributed in physical and metaphorical form French luxury in France and outside its borders. Boucher's *Milliner* is more of an imaginary representation of urban elite luxury and comfort in eighteenth-century Paris than faithful reproduction of a certain interior. This was understood by contemporaries, who could read paintings and their narration of luxury goods. However, Boucher's genre paintings depict in detail those French luxury goods that were so sought after by elites, both in France and abroad. All its connotations were reproduced, reworked and adapted to Swedish context by Pehr Hilleström in one of his genre paintings, also called *The Milliner*.

French servants were essential for an elite lifestyle. The importance of educating children in elite cosmopolitan culture and French language was achieved most thoroughly through French-speaking governesses. Certain circles within the Swedish aristocracy willingly invested considerable sums to educate their children, but also to apprentice their Swedish cooks in France or to employ French cooks. Cooks acted as proof of the status and refined taste of their employers, but also added considerably to pleasure and comfort in elites' everyday life. Here again, the aristocracy balanced national taste and French taste.

It has to be stressed that other aspects of aristocratic lifestyle could have been chosen for similar outcome: architecture and interior designs; intellectual and literary culture; or high military careers in the service of France or German states could serve as examples. The influence of France and French culture traversed the elite lifestyle in eighteenth-century Sweden, to such an extent that it is not easy to point to any aspects of aristocratic lifestyle not influenced by French taste. However, Swedish elites could never compete with their French counterparts in the field of luxury and ostentatious display (probably they did not even wish to), which led to adaptation, acclimatization and transformation of French taste for luxury to more discreet and simplistic Swedish tastes.

Notes

1 Classic studies on French 'radiance' in Europe include Pierre Chaunu, *La civilisation de l'Europe des Lumières* (Paris: B. Arthaud, 1971); René Pomeau,

L'Europe des Lumières: Cosmopolitisme et unité européenne au XVIIIe siècle (Paris: Éditions Stock, 1966); Louis Réau, *L'Europe française au siècle des Lumières* (Paris, 1938).

2 *Multilinguisme et multiculturalité dans l'Europe des Lumières - Multilingualism and Multiculturalism in Enlightenment Europe: Actes du Séminaire international des jeunes dix-huitiémistes 2004 - Proceedings of the International Seminar for Young Eighteenth-Century Scholars 2004*, eds Ursula Haskins Gonthier and Alain Sandrier (Paris: Éditions Honoré Champion, 2007).

3 Pierre-Yves Beaurepaire, *Le mythe de l'Europe française au XVIIIe siècle: Diplomatie, culture et sociabilités au temps des Lumières* (Paris: Éditions Autrement, 2007), 7–8; see also Kerry Bristol's, Alida Clemente's, Kristof Fatsar's, Nadia Fernandez de Pinedo and Corinne Thépaut-Cabasse's and Michael North's chapters in this volume.

4 Charlotta Wolff, 'L'aristocratie suédoise et la France dans la séconde moitié du XVIIIe siècle', *Histoire, économie & société* 29 (2010), 56–67; Charlotta Wolff, 'The Swedish Aristocracy and the French Enlightenment circa 1740–1780', *Scandinavian Journal of History* 30 (2005), 259–270, doi:10.1080/03468750500279632.

5 See e.g. Elisabet Hammar, *'La Française': Mille et une facon d'apprendre le français en Suède avant 1807* (Uppsala: Acta Universitatis Upsaliensis, 1991); Johanna Ilmakunnas, 'The Luxury Shopping Experience of the Swedish Aristocracy in Eighteenth-Century Paris', in *Luxury and Gender in European Towns, 1700–1914*, eds Deborah Simonton, Marjo Kaartinen and Anne Montenach (New York and London: Routledge, 2014), 116–17; Johanna Ilmakunnas, *Ett ståndsmässigt liv: Familjen von Fersens livsstil på 1700-talet* (Helsingfors and Stockholm: Svenska litteratursällskapet i Finland and Atlantis, 2012); Marie-Christine Skucke, 'Un prince suédois auteur français: L'éducation de Gustave III, 1756–1762', *Studies on Voltaire and the Eighteenth Century* 296 (1992), 123–63; Charlotta Wolff, *Vänskap och makt: Den svenska politiska eliten och upplysningstidens Frankrike* (Helsingfors: Svenska litteratursällskapet i Finland, 2005)

6 Ilmakunnas, *Ett ståndsmässigt liv*.

7 Ilmakunnas, 'The Luxury Shopping Experience'; Ilmakunnas, *Ett ståndsmässigt liv*, passim; Wolff, *Vänskap och makt*, passim.

8 Karin Hassan Jansson, 'When Sweden Harboured Idlers: Gender and Luxury in Public Debates, c. 1760–1830', in *Sweden in the Eighteenth-Century World: Provincial Cosmopolitans*, ed. Göran Rydén (Farnham: Ashgate, 2013); Leif Runefelt, *Att hasta mot undergången: Anspråk, flyktighet, förställning i debatten om konsumtion i Sverige 1730–1830* (Lund: Nordic Academic Press, 2015).

9 Hans Axel von Fersen to Axel von Fersen 29 June 1779. Axel von Fersen d.ä.:s arkiv vol. 8. Stafsundsarkivet, Riksarkivet, Stockholm (henceforth RA). 'je Veux point briller, ni etre ridicule, je Veux seulement etre decemment.'

10 Wolff, *Vänskap och makt*, 301–7.

11 Ilmakunnas, 'The Luxury Shopping Experience'.

12 Marjatta Rahikainen and Kirsi Vainio-Korhonen, 'Manlig och kvinnlig lyx: Överflödsförordningar och modeartiklar', in *Det svenska begäret: Sekler av lyxkonsumtion*, eds Paula von Wachenfeldt and Klas Nyberg (Stockholm: Carlssons, 2015); Carolina Brown, 'Den vita lyxen: Spetsar i 1700-talets visuella och materiella kultur', in *Det svenska begäret: Sekler av lyxkonsumtion*, eds Paula von Wachenfeldt and Klas Nyberg (Stockholm: Carlssons, 2015), 76.

13 Riitta Pylkkänen, *Kaksi pukuhistoriallista tutkielmaa. I: Miehen muotipuku Suomessa 1700-luvulla* (Helsinki: Suomen muinaismuistoyhdistys, 1984); Riitta Pylkkänen, *Säätyläisnaisten pukeutuminen Suomessa 1700-luvulla* (Helsinki: Suomen muinaismuistoyhdistys, 1982; Pernilla Rasmussen, *Skräddaren, sömmerskan och modet: Arbetsmetoder och arbetsindelning i tillverkningen av kvinnlig dräkt 1770–1830* (Stockholm: Nordiska museet, 2010).

14 On the Swedish national dress, see Lena Rangström, *Kläder för tid och evighet: Gustaf III sedd genom sina dräkter* (Stockholm: Livrustkammaren, 1997), 165–77; Aileen Ribeiro, *Dress in Eighteenth-Century Europe, 1715–1789* (New Haven and London: Yale University Press, 2002), 196–201.

15 Rangström, *Kläder för tid och evighet*, 65–75, 155–63.

16 Gustav Philip Creutz to Crown Prince Gustaf, 19 August 1766, in *Le Comte de Creutz, Lettres inédites de Paris, 1766–1770*, ed. Marianne Molander (Gothenburg: Acta Universitatis Gothoburgensis, 1987), 36–38.

17 See e.g. Kimberly Chrisman-Campbell, *Dress at the Court of Louis XVI and Marie-Antoinette* (New Haven and London: Yale University Press, 2015); Ribeiro, *Dress in Eighteenth-Century Europe*; Daniel Roche, *La culture des apparences: Une histoire du vêtement XVIIe–XVIIIe siècle* (Paris: Fayard, 1989).

18 See Bernard Hours, *Louis XV et sa cour: Le roi, l'étiquette et le courtisan* (Paris: Presses Universitaires de France, 2002), 39–40.

19 Roche, *La culture des apparences*, 98–9, 134–40, 177–93.

20 A man's suit, coat and waistcoat of embroidered silk, made in France c. 1785. Belonged to Hans Axel von Fersen. NMA 0052207, NM 0154745A-C, Nordiska museet, Stockholm. https://digitaltmuseum.se/011013849815?query=fersen&pos=8&count=28; https://digitaltmuseum.se/legacy/S-NM/NM.0154745A-C

21 Charlotta Sparre to Clas Ekeblad, undated letter, f. 14–5. E 3564 Ekebladska samlingen, RA. 'une personne de bon gout.'

22 Ilmakunnas, 'Luxury Shopping Experience'.

23 Hedvig De la Gardie to Axel von Fersen 2 June 1774, 6 June 1774. Axel von Fersen d. ä.:s arkiv vol. 7. Stafsundsarkivet, RA. 'je ne Les trouve pas d'un gout fort recherché, La Robe grise de printen, n'est pas du tout telle que je La demandois, et elle est d'une trai vilaine etoffe.'

24 *Women and Material Culture, 1660–1830*, eds Jennie Batchelor and Cora Kaplan (Basingstoke: Palgrave Macmillan, 2007); *The Consumption of Culture, 1600–1800: Image, Object, Text*, eds Ann Bermingham and John Brewer (London: Routledge, 1995); John Brewer, *The Pleasures of Imagination: English Culture in the Eighteenth Century* (Chicago: Chicago University Press, 1997).

25 Beth Fowkes Tobin, *The Duchess's Shells: Natural History Collecting in the Age of Cook's Voyages* (New Haven: Yale University Press, 2014); Merit Laine, *'En Minerva för vår Nord': Lovisa Ulrika som samlare, uppdragsgivare och byggherre* (Stockholm: [Merit Laine], 1998).

26 Cf. Charlotta Wolff's argument on how the Swedish diplomats actively participated the cosmopolitan intellectual sociability in the salons in Paris, instead of merely transmitting ideas of French Enlightenment to Sweden. Wolff, 'The Swedish Aristocracy and the French Enlightenment'.

27 Mikael Ahlund, *Landskapets röster: Studier i Elias Martins bildvärld* (Stockholm: Atlantis, 2011); Merit Laine and Carolina Brown, *Gustaf Lundberg 1695–1786: En porträttmålare och hans tid* (Stockholm: Nationalmuseum, 2006); *Alexander Roslin*, ed. Magnus Olausson (Stockholm: Nationalmuseum, 2007).

28 *Carl Gustaf Tessin och porträttkonsten* (Stockholm: Nationalmuseum, 1995); Pontus Grate, *French Paintings II: Eighteenth Century* (Stockholm: Swedish National Art Museum, 1994), *passim;* Jan Heidner, 'Carl Gustaf Tessin – en samlare och konstförmedlare', in *Carl Gustaf Tessin: Kulturpersonen och privatmannen, 1695–1770* (Stockholm: Atlantis, 1995), 21–40; Patrik Reutersward, 'Aveds Tessinporträtt', in *Carl Gustaf Tessin: Kulturpersonen och privatmannen, 1695–1770* (Stockholm: Atlantis, 1995), 57–74.

29 François Boucher, *The Milliner (Morning)*, 1746. Oil on canvas, 64 x 53 cm. NM 772, Nationalmuseum, Stockholm. http://collection.nationalmuseum.se/eMuseumPlus?service=ExternalInterface&module=collection&objectId=17775&viewType=detailView

30 Merit Laine, *'En Minerva för vår Nord': Lovisa Ulrika som samlare, uppdragsgivare och byggherre* (Stockholm, 1998); Paula Rea Radisich, 'Lovisa Ulrike of Sweden, Chardin and Enlightened Despotism', in *Women, Art and the Politics of Identity in Eighteenth-Century Europe*, eds Melissa Hyde and Jennifer Milam (Hampshire: Ashgate, 2003), 46–63.

31 *Carl Fredrik Scheffer: Lettres particulières à Carl Gustaf Tessin 1744–1752*, ed. Jan Heidner (Stockholm: Kungl. Samfundet för utgivande av handskrifter rörande Skandinaviens historia vol. 7, 1982), 103–4, 120, 122, 124–5, 132, 144, 154, 176–7, 200, 212, 214, 216, 253–4.

32 The history behind the painting is well known, documented and explored by art historians and historians. See e.g. Colin B. Bailey, 'François Boucher, *The Milliner (Morning)*', in *The Age of Watteau, Chardin, and Fragonard: Masterpieces of French Genre Painting*, ed. Colin B. Bailey (New Haven and London: Yale University Press, 2003), 226; Colin B. Bailey, 'Surveying Genre in Eighteenth-Century French Painting', in *The Age of Watteau, Chardin, and Fragonard: Masterpieces of French Genre Painting*, ed. Colin B. Bailey (New Haven and London: Yale University Press, 2003), 14–15; Ilmakunnas, 'Adelsdamen som konsument på 1700-talet', 89 (2004) *Historisk Tidskrift för Finland*, 117–34; Alastair Laing, 'Catalogue des peintures, La marchande de modes (Le matin)', *François Boucher 1703–1770*, dir. Alastair Laing, J. Patrice Marandel and Pierre Rosemberg (Paris: Éditions de la Réunion des musées nationaux, 1986), 226–30.

33 Laing, 'La marchande de modes (Le matin)', 228.

34 Kimberly Chrisman-Campbell, 'Dressing to Impress: The Morning Toilette and the Fabrication of Femininity', in *Paris: Life & Luxury in the Eighteenth Century*, ed. Charissa Bremer-David (Los Angeles: The Paul J. Getty Museum, 2011), 53–73.

35 Carolina Brown Ahlund, 'Mode och skönhet', in *Signums svenska kulturhistoria: Gustavianska tiden*, ed. Jacob Christensson (Stockholm: Bokförlaget Signum, 2007), 401, 406; Ilmakunnas, *Ett ståndsmässigt liv*, 266–8.

36 On luxury trade in eighteenth-century Paris, see e.g. Natacha Coquery, *L'Hôtel aristocratique: Le marché du luxe à Paris au XVIIIe siècle* (Paris: Publications de la Sorbonne, 1998); Natacha Coquery, *Tenir boutique à Paris au XVIIIe siècle: Luxe et demi-luxe* (Paris: CTHS histoire, 2011); Jennifer M. Jones, *Sexing La Mode: Gender, Fashion and Commercial Culture in Old Regime France* (Oxford and New York: Berg, 2004); *Luxury Trades and Consumerism in Ancien Régime Paris: Studies in the History of the Skilled Workforce*, eds Robert Fox and Anthony Turner (Aldershot: Ashgate, 1998); Carolyn Sargentson, *Merchants and Luxury Markets: The Marchand Merciers of Eighteenth-Century Paris* (London: Victoria and Albert Museum, 1996).

37 Pehr Hilleström, *The Milliner*. Oil on canvas, 79,5 x 65,5 cm. NM 3382, Nationalmuseum, Stockholm. http://collection.nationalmuseum.se/eMuseumPlus?service=ExternalInterface&module=collection&objectId=20435&viewType=detailView

38 On light in Hilleström's paintings, see Mikael Ahlund, *Att se vardagen: 1700-talet i blickpunkten* (Helsingfors: Konstmuseet Sinebrychoff, 2014), 56, 60, 62–75; On

Hilleström on the Swedish art market, see Mikael Ahlund, 'Konsten att försörja sig som konstnär: Pehr Hilleström och konstmarknaden i 1700-talets Stockholm', in *Kulturens finansiering i Stockholm 1750–1850*, ed. Klas Nyberg (forthcoming).

39 Ahlund, 'Konsten att försörja sig som konstnär', 32–3.

40 Ahlund, *Landskapets röster*, 9, 174–239.

41 See, e.g. Melissa Hyde, *Making up the Rococo: François Boucher and his critics* (Los Angeles: Getty Research Institute, 2006); *Rethinking Boucher*, eds Melissa Hyde and Mark Ledbury (Los Angeles: Getty Research Institute, 2006).

42 Ahlund, *Att se vardagen*; Johanna Ilmakunnas, 'Naisten työt ja arkielämä Pehr Hilleströmin maalauksissa 1770-luvulta 1810-luvulle,' *Historiallinen Aikakauskirja* 113 (2015), 339–60.

43 Gösta Selling, *Svenska herrgårdshem under 1700-talet* (Stockholm: Albert Bonniers, 1937); Rose-Marie Söderström, *Bostadskultur, informationsflöden och hantverkare 1740–1820 med utgångspunkt i Bålby (Närke) och Skottsbergska gården (Blekinge)* (Lund: Sekel, 2009); Bo Vahlne, *Frihetstidens inredningar på Stockholms Slott: Om bekvämlighetens och skönhetens nivåer* (Stockholm: Balkong 2012); Anne-Sophie Michel, 'Une communauté d'artistes et d'artisans français à l'étranger: Le cas ds sculpteurs au château royal de Stockholm au XVIIIe siècle,' *Sjuttonhundratal: Nordic Yearbook of Eighteenth-Century Studies* 12 (2015), 117–31. DOI: 10.7557/4.3528

44 Hammar, *'La Française'*.

45 Ilmakunnas, *Ett ståndsmässigt liv*, 68.

46 *Sveriges ridderskaps och adels riksdagsprotokoll från och med år 1719*, vol. 24–6 (1765–66) (Stockholm: P. A. Nordstedt and Son, 1958–1960), 412–13.

47 Hammar, *'La Française.' Mille et une façons d'apprendre le français en Suède avant 1807* (Uppsala: Uppsala universitet, 1991), 19; Ilmakunnas, *Ett ståndsmässigt liv*, 68, 433n120.

48 Ilmakunnas, *Ett ståndsmässigt liv*, 313–4.

49 Axel von Fersen's account books 1762–3. Axel von Fersen d.ä.:s arkiv vol. 41–2. Stafsundsarkivet, RA.

50 On Swedish aristocracy and Catholicism, see Wolff, *Vänskap och makt*, 288–94.

51 On how Swedish envoys entertained in Paris, see Wolff, *Vänskap och makt*, 129–39.

52 *Tableaux de Paris et la cour de France 1739–1742. Lettres inédites de Carl Gustaf, comte de Tessin*, ed. Gunnar von Proschwitz (Paris: Jean Touzot, 1983), 192. 'Je verrai a trouver un Cuisinier, c'est comme vous savés, la chose du monde la plus difficile, surtout a present, que chaqu'un en a besoin pour sa Campagne.'

53 *Tableaux de Paris*, 215.

54 Charlotta Sparre to Carl Gustaf Tessin 30 April 1742. Autografsamlingen vol. 196. Eriksbergsarkivet, RA.

55 Gustav Philip Creutz to Axel von Fersen 8 September 1771, 14 October 1771. Axel von Fersen d.ä.:s arkiv vol. 7. Stafsundsarkivet, RA.

56 Ehrensvärd, Gustaf Johan, *Dagboksanteckningar förda vid Gustaf III:s hof*, vol. I, ed. E. V. Montan (Stockholm: P. A. Norstedt and Söners Förlag, 1877), 9.

57 Gustav Philip Creutz to Axel von Fersen 30 June 1776. G 360. Uppsala universitetsbibliotek.

58 Hans Axel von Fersen to Axel von Fersen 17 August 1778. Axel von Fersen d.ä.:s arkiv vol. 8. Stafsundsarkivet, RA.

59 *Amiral Carl Tersmedens memoarer, vol. III, I Fredrik I:s Sverige*, ed. Nils Erdman (Stockholm: Wahlström and Widstrand, 1916), 21. 'Född fransos, uppfödd portugis, hårfrisör och kock till profession, har han varit hos mig alltsedan augusti 1734.'

60 *Amiral Carl Tersmedens memoarer*, 21–2, 36–9, 51, 67.

13

English Luxuries in Nineteenth-Century Vyborg

Ulla Ijäs

In August 1802, Johan Friedrich Hackman, a prominent merchant of Vyborg in present-day Finland,[1] wrote to his fellow merchant Mr Bruun, who at that time was staying in St Petersburg: 'My wife asks to send to her, from the English shop, a large English damask-silk fashion fabric, preferably orange with white or orange with brown.'[2]

Most studies discussing luxury focus on the situation in English-speaking countries or in France. The aim of this chapter is to illustrate some of the geographical variations in the concept of luxury by looking beyond these places to Europe's spatial margins.[3] Based on previous research on the Russian-Finnish Vyborg merchant elite, it seems that the material culture of Vyborg high society was much the same as that described by Maxine Berg in her studies.[4] There was a desire for so-called new luxuries, i.e. recently invented, more available, yet expensive and high-quality goods: Wedgwood china, mahogany furniture, carpets, gilded mirrors, timepieces, and so on. In Vyborg, a great many of these goods were imported from Britain.

In this chapter, I discuss luxury, taste and conspicuous consumption in late eighteenth- and nineteenth-century Vyborg, exploring the kinds of new English luxuries that were available and how these luxury goods were used in the identity building practices of Vyborg's commercial elite. Purchases of English luxuries were motivated very clearly by the taste of the consumer or purchaser (a commission agent) of these goods. Quality, modernity and fashion were important factors in shaping decisions, but luxury was not a term used by contemporary consumers to describe these goods.

During the time period studied here, Vyborg was under Russian rule, Peter I having captured the town and a large part of the surrounding territories from Sweden in 1710. After the establishment of the Grand Duchy of Finland in 1812, Vyborg was the third-largest town in Finland. In the nineteenth century, its population grew from 3,500 to slightly over 7,000 inhabitants, but it remained a very small place; over the same period St Petersburg's population grew from 200,000 to 860,000. The main activity in Vyborg was the export of timber, but a garrison of 200–300 soldiers also lived in the town.

The writer of the letter cited above, Mr Hackman, belonged to the German merchant elite in Vyborg. In 1818, the German population in the town was 362 people, but their political and economic power was much greater than their numbers suggested. The German merchants dominated trade, their main business being the sale of timber to England, Germany, France and Spain. Beside this, they imported mainly salt but also colonial goods, owned manufactories and saw mills, and were involved in local administration. Their social position was much of the same as the *brukspatrons* in Sweden, described by Steinrud in her chapter in this volume. Usually, these merchants had quite modest backgrounds and can be described as nouveau riche, though some of them gained a noble title.[5] The social groups in Vyborg were much the same as in the northern German cities and the consumption pattern and taste of the economic bourgeoisie (*Wirtschafsbürger*) and the administrative elite were also similar. Therefore, as Michael North has argued, there was not a particular middle-class consumption culture, nor did fashionable dress or luxury furniture in its own right form an access ticket to genteel society, as Berg argues was the case in Britain.[6] In Vyborg, the commercial elite, the Baltic nobility and officials mingled because they all spoke the same language, German. In a small community, group identity can be based on different premises than in a community where all either speak the same language (as in Britain) or where there is a vast cultural or economic gap between the social groups or classes (as in metropolises such as St Petersburg or London).

People in Vyborg lived only two days' journey away from the hustle and bustle of St Petersburg, established by Peter I in 1703 and the centre of Russian business, culture and fashion.[7] Anthony Cross briefly discusses British luxuries in St Petersburg in his study about the British community in the city. He writes that 'The St Petersburg British . . . were also on the spot to cater for the material needs that accompanied Russian anglophilia, to provide those luxury goods that became indispensable to the Russian elite'.[8] Britain had enjoyed a strong connection with Russia ever since the sixteenth century, when the English merchants of the Muscovy Company obtained the monopoly of trade in Russia. During the reign of Catherine II, British power in Russia was undoubtedly at its highest, but the larger picture of luxury production and import in eighteenth- and nineteenth-century Russia remains under-researched; scholars have not studied, for example, smuggling, which also accounted for a large proportion of luxury products available in Vyborg.[9]

English consumer goods were important social markers not only among the Russians but also among the Vyborg Germans, who were tied through business transactions, and later family ties, to British families in St Petersburg and Britain. The importance of these trade relations cannot be underestimated. Michael North, in his chapter in this volume, illustrates the importance of the British fashion to the middle class of north German cities, who, like their Vyborg contemporaries, were tied by business connections with Britain. More recently, Ragnhild Hutchinson has shown in her study of the timber trade between Britain, Norway and the Baltic that Britain's negative balance of trade brought profits and British goods to Baltic States (Prussia and Russia). She is the first scholar to link the timber trade directly with the availability of consumer goods.[10] In Vyborg, Britain was an important trading partner for most of the eighteenth and nineteenth centuries. However, the Napoleonic Wars, Russia's participation in the continental system in 1806–1810, and the Crimean War in the 1850s all had negative impacts. In addition, Britain began seeking timber from its own colonies, diminishing the trade with the Baltic, including Vyborg. Despite these negative outcomes, Vyborg merchants did not lose their connections with British merchant houses.[11]

The analysis presented here focuses on the Hackman family, who lived in Vyborg and owned the most prominent timber export business in the town, in particular the first three generations of the family, *c.* 1790–1890. The luxury consumption of the Hackman family has been traced from the letters and account books, written and kept both for business and private purposes. The Hackman family had strong connections with Britain in business and on a personal level, since two generation of sons were educated in Britain and the continuous business relationships with the British timber markets has lasted into the twenty-first century. In addition to the family archives, newspapers have been used to illustrate the concept of luxury and to widen the picture about the availability of the British luxury goods in Vyborg and St Petersburg. The newspapers published in Vyborg and St Petersburg have been studied from 1804 through to the 1890s.

Luxury and its definitions in Vyborg

In order to illustrate the social and geographical impact of the concept of luxury, it is essential to define how luxury was understood in a specific time and place. As in other European countries following mercantilist policies, the Russian authorities wanted to limit the import of luxury goods as a part of a policy to limit ostentatious living and the outflow of capital. The Commission of Commerce defined that superfluous luxury goods should bear high duties or be prohibited altogether. The central government preferred equivalent luxury goods, which were made in Russia and therefore induced foreign artisans and merchants to establish themselves in Russia. By the end of the eighteenth century, therefore, some luxury goods could be manufactured domestically.[12]

As in every other place and time, luxury was socially constructed. The state authorities, the aristocracy, the German merchants and the common people did not share the same ideas of luxury. Naturally, luxury was a mechanism of social distinction. To those with few financial resources, goods which were bought with real money were luxuries. To those with a better financial situation, luxury might have been a more clearly defined concept. It separated them from those who had no access to certain goods, although it appears that more important than social distinction was the overarching character of luxury among a certain social group. Defining luxury with the same attributes, such as taste, fashion and quality, was an expression of group identity.[13]

Discovering exactly what people viewed as luxury is by no means straightforward, as it seems that using the term 'luxury' was not socially acceptable. In the Hackman's letters the word is mentioned only once. In 1862, Emmy Cedercreutz wrote to her father J. F. Hackman Jr that her younger brother Julius wanted a crystal chandelier for a Christmas present. Mrs Cedercreutz thought that the chandelier was an unnecessary luxury article (*ein unnöthiger Luxus Artikel*) and the present should be something practical (*etwas Praktisches bester muß!*).[14] The letter gives the impression that the chandelier is a luxury in this context; typical Christmas presents were small, inexpensive pieces of jewellery, keepsakes, or prints.[15] On the other hand, the letter reveals that luxury was something unnecessary and even excessive in size, price or style. Hence, who would have liked to admit that she or he had purchased luxury goods? The better attributes for newly bought goods were taste and fashion, which will be discussed later in this chapter.

Between the 1850s and 1870s, the local newspapers *Wiborg* and *Wiborgs Tidning* discussed luxury and how society should regard common people's search for luxury goods.[16] These newspapers were mainly read by the middle class; they were published in Swedish which was the official language at the time. Some Finnish newspapers were published from the 1830s, aimed at those among the common people who were literate and the intelligentsia, who were interested in Finnish nationalism. In the 1830s, there were also German language newspapers in Vyborg, and German papers published in St Petersburg were read in Vyborg. The latter were especially aimed at the German middle class, who also preordered newspapers and magazines published in Germany.[17]

The discussion in the Swedish language press recognized that luxury was something that was socially and historically constructed, and it also refers to conspicuous consumption, though not explicitly. Since Thorstein Veblen, conspicuous consumption usually refers to the mechanism of communicating wealth, status and power by ostentatious consumption and is often given negative connotations.[18] In Vyborg newspapers, luxury was defined with the words *lyx* (luxus), *överflöd* (abundance) and *högfärd* (grandiosity) or *ylpeys* (pride), and people's desire to imitate (*efterapa*) others is recognized. In addition, luxury was defined with words such as *modet* (mode), *façon* (fashion), *vackert* (beautiful) and *köpt med pengar* (bought with money). Luxury goods were expensive, they were made of precious materials or they were imported from overseas. Hence, luxury was something excessive and unnecessary, even sinful. Goods would have been particularly unnecessary luxuries if they were bought instead of producing them at home. The unknown author(s) gave many examples, most of them concerning clothing. Clothes bought from St Petersburg or made in factories were especially dangerous, as they would lead the common people to forget their simple homemade dresses and the skills involved in making them, and to dream about rising socially, thus disrupting the social order. The authors also reflect state policies, in which economic self-sufficiency was the main goal. Importantly, these warnings did not apply to the German elite, but rather to the Finnish commoners and their spending habits.

In the Finnish context, Vyborg might be the place where people valued luxury more than in any other town. In 1812, when the new authorities from the Swedish side of the recently established Grand Duchy of Finland arrived, they were amazed and shocked by the 'Asiatic luxuries', fine horses and carriages that they met in Vyborg. The social and cultural gap between the cosmopolitan elite and the common people was clearly greater than in western Finland.[19] With this background, the authorities were not prepared for the Vyborg elite's lifestyle, which was inspired by or even imitated the life of St Petersburg's high society and wealthy merchants.[20] Here, once again, the word 'luxury' is used in a negative sense.

If luxury carried negative connotations of uselessness, abundance and ostentation, it is no wonder that the people in Vyborg did not use the word in their correspondence. Instead, they preferred the word 'taste'. For example, in a letter from 1801, Marie Hackman paid compliments to Madame Sievers about her taste when choosing fabric for Marie Hackman. The following year, J. F. Hackman wrote to Thomas Zagel in St Petersburg and asked if he could send him an overcoat, a cocked hat, and fashionable flowers for his wife; 'I shall trust your taste and friendship', he closed his letter.[21] In the Hackman letters, the word 'fashion' or other similar words (modish, *à la mode, Mode, modig*) are used even more often than taste. In 1830, for example, the Hackmans requested from Garbutts 'a dozen waistcoats of the most fashionable patterns',[22] and in 1801 Marie Hackman commissioned white feathers 'as the fashion is' (*so wie jezt Mode sind*).[23]

In the newspapers, taste was discussed as 'the public taste' of theatre visitors and in the context of sociability, and was used to promote goods and products of different kinds.[24] Taste was also discussed together with luxury in 1856 when an unknown author highlighted cultivated taste (*bildade smaken*) with cultivated luxury (*bildade lyx*).[25] In short, taste was something common for a certain social group and it was something that could be learned through social intercourse. However, the word 'fashion' (*mode, muoti*) was only discussed in the Finnish-language newspaper *Ilmarinen* in Vyborg from 1876.[26] Before that, fashion was used to promote local 'fashion shops' (*modemagazin*) and to promote the latest fashion (*neuesten Mode*), but only in Swedish and German newspapers.[27] *Ilmarinen*'s article was based on a public talk given by a member of the local Finnish language and literature society. The speaker, who was obviously a young man, equated fashion with femininity and beauty, and recognized its changing nature. The forward-looking speaker highlighted the fact that fashion expressed the *zeitgeist* and therefore should not be condemned. However, he was also aware that fashion might corrupt society in the same way as luxury; hence, fashion and luxury were combined.

English luxuries in Vyborg

As illustrated above, luxury was seldom discussed in everyday situations when purchasing new or fashionable objects, largely because of its negative connotations, including pride and ostentation. When conceptualizing luxury in this chapter, it is therefore understood in the same way as Maxine Berg: novel and often newly invented, quality products which, however, did not compete on price.[28] In Vyborg, these goods were often English, either by origin or style, so it is no surprise that, when J. F. Hackman commissioned a scarf from St Petersburg, he asked his friend to shop in the English shop.

In the latter part of the eighteenth century, Russia and much of the rest of Europe entered a period of Anglomania. As North makes clear in his chapter in this volume, in German-speaking areas, especially amongst the citizens of the northern German towns, English luxuries held a particular allure.[29] The bourgeoisie of these towns, as well as Vyborg's elite and middle class, found the English lifestyle and material culture more appealing than aristocratic French luxuries.[30] They used the term 'English' when shopping for goods that were made in England or Britain, bought from the English shops in St Petersburg or simply manufactured according to English taste and style – a broad definition that reflects Swedish conceptions of 'French', as Ilmakunnas discusses in her chapter. Importantly, this label not only distinguished them from French or German styles, for example, but also from goods coming from Scotland and Ireland.[31]

England was an important timber trading partner for the Hackmans despite the Napoleonic Wars and British-Russian trading policies which hindered the timber trade.[32] When J. F. Hackman Jr was sent abroad to finish his education in trade, he headed to England after staying some time in his father's hometown.[33] After this visit, he travelled to England at least once more and his sons were sent to study there. The family also welcomed the sons of English merchant families to stay and learn the trade in Vyborg.[34] The family kept alive their connections with English culture by reading English novels and newspapers. Their knowledge of English fashion, taste and luxury was perhaps better than any other family in Vyborg, since they knew the language and they could not only find information about the latest luxuries quickly, but also order these products directly from England via returning ships or homecoming family members. Naturally, the Hackmans were not the only family in Vyborg involved with the timber trade with Britain. Both the connections based on this trade and the wealth that it produced facilitated the luxury trade. Hence, we may argue that luxury consumption was dependent on geopolitics, time and place. As seen in Ilmakunnas's chapter, the politics of eighteenth-century Sweden turned the Swedish aristocracy towards France; in Vyborg, trade politics connected local elites to Britain.

The letters in the Hackman archive were not written solely to commission goods; the main reason to communicate with Englishmen was the timber trade. Indeed, the Hackmans commissioned goods via letters only when the personal relationship with the receiver of the letter was intimate enough. The letters that included commissions were sent to trading houses or merchants deeply involved in the Baltic timber trade. For example, the friendship ties between Robert Garbutt and his wife Ann and J. F. and Julie Hackman were maintained after the Hackmans visited them in 1832, and the Garbutts' nephew learned his trade in Vyborg in the 1850s. In such instances, personal friendship and business were inseparable. These ties also spread knowledge of English luxury products and fashion in Vyborg. For example, in 1834 Ann Garbutt sent an 'Oriental Annual, or Scenes in India' to Mrs Hackman, who was an enthusiastic painter and therefore would be inspired by the engravings in the book.[35] Thus, the British Empire, its Asian colonies and Vyborg merchants were intertwined. This also widens the concept of 'English' luxury; it might be called 'English' by contemporaries, but in reality, it included all sorts of luxury products from the British Empire. The print media helped to spread the idea of luxury and the British Empire extended its influence on the edges of Europe by spreading information about its colonies, inventions, luxuries and genteel lifestyles. This was possible not only because of the growing print media but also the private correspondence and individual relationships that nourished British cultural hegemony in Europe.[36]

The Hackmans also had trade partners in French port towns, especially Montpellier merchants who bought their timber, and the returning ships brought Mediterranean salt to Vyborg. J. F. and Julie Hackman visited France in the 1830s, their children spent winters on the Côte d'Azur and their son, Julius Hackman, lived in Nice for decades. Despite these connections, wine was the only consumption good commissioned from France via letters. Language was no barrier as both J. F. and Julie Hackman spoke French, yet hardly any objects are described as 'French' in the correspondence. It seems that either the bourgeois elite in Vyborg did not like French goods or they purchased them directly when visiting the country. That said, the Hackmans visited England and also commissioned goods from there, so there is no reason to assume that they would not have done the same with France and French products if they had chosen to. It might be that French products were considered too aristocratic, flamboyant or expensive; more likely, the Hackmans did not have sufficiently intimate connections with French merchants to feel able to burden them with their commissions. Hence, merchant ties, personalities and personal relationships, and in the Hackmans' case, religion, all guided luxury consumption. Both the Garbutts and the Hackmans supported evangelical missionary movements in their respective home towns; spirituality and charity were close to their hearts. Catholic French business partners might have had different views, making close ties to French merchant families harder to secure.

In addition to its association with general forms of taste and fashion, the word 'English' was often used to describe specific objects. Thus, 'not an ordinary, an English [straw hat]' (*nicht ordinaire, ein englischer*) was commissioned in the summer 1800.[37] However, we should not consider English in this context as strictly national; besides the origin of the product, 'English' might also refer to its style.[38] In Vyborg, 'English' was the adjective mentioned most often, together with those referring to taste, fashion and quality. Several times 'English' was used as an epithet of good quality, fashion and implicit luxury: in 1813, Marie Hackman smuggled into Vyborg English fabrics and cutlery, 'all of the very finest and best quality' and in 1820 'beautiful' (*schön*) English cotton and the best

English soap.[39] Even in those letters when 'English' was not spelled out, the product brands such as Wedgwood revealed that the writer was looking for English luxury consumer goods.

In St Petersburg, some English goods were available in the 'English shops'. According to Anthony Cross, these shops sold cloth, books, prints, statues, watches, stockings, hats, buttons, keys, tea and coffee machines, beer and all sort of haberdashery.[40] These were the typical 'English' goods that the Hackmans purchased from the Russian metropolis. However, during the course of the nineteenth century, there were increasing opportunities to purchase English goods in Vyborg itself, as is apparent from advertisements carried in the local press. Newspapers published in St Petersburg and later those in Vyborg often used the attribute 'English'. In 1804, the *St Petersburgische Zeitung* promoted 'white English' (*weiße englische*) visiting cards, 'the best English flowers' (*beste englische Blumen*) and 'a good English fortepiano' (*ein gutes englisches Fortepiano*).[41] In the 1820s and 1830s, the *Wiburgs Wochenblatt* and *Kanawa* carried notices for 'a strong modern English chaise' *(eine starke moderne englische Chaise*), English straw hats and English socks – all being sold in the local shops.[42] The Vyborg elite could write their letters on 'English *coleurt* [*sic*] post paper with golden sides' (*Engelskt Couleurt Post-Papper, med [. . .] Gold snit*).[43] Many of the advertised English goods were novelties or new inventions, the high-tech consumer goods of the time; things such as the English wall clock, which was sold in the local auction house, or the 'telescopes of the English work' (*Teleskoper auf [. . .] Engelskt arbete*), advertised in 1844.[44] English colonial products and newly invented canned foods, pickles and 'English biscuits' such as 'Royal Dessert, Sugar Wafers, Cocoa Nuts, and Nic Nac Fancies' were also known in Vyborg, where these type of imported delicacies were seen as luxurious.[45]

The word English combined modernity, good quality and fashion, according to the newspaper advertisements. However, the articles or advertisements only seldom made explicit the link between luxury or taste and Englishness. Only once, in 1888, *Wiborgsbladet* published a news report from England where the reporter noted that it had become very modern (*ytterst modern*) in England to decorate the piano (*taffelpiano*) with excessive amounts of fruits and flowers. He further observed that this luxury (*lyxen*) had prevented frugal (*sparsamma*) housewives from arranging dinners since the cost of flowers and fruits was too high.[46] In this case, as in most of the cases when luxury was discussed, English luxury and lifestyle was something that people in Vyborg should avoid.

Between the years 1799 and 1837, purchases from England or English products purchased from St Petersburg were mentioned in thirty-seven of the Hackman letters as being fashionable, modern or the latest fashion.[47] At least ten of these letters included instructions about smuggling the products safely to shore. These purchases included silver buckles for shoes, clothes and fabrics, shoes and boots, hats, table napkins, cutlery, Cheshire cheese, beers, china (typically Wedgwood), 'English health chocolate', pens and papers, and equipment for horses such as 'an English carriage' discussed in the 1830s. Apart from these, the Hackmans requested that they be sent 'an English dog a few months old and of a high race' and rosebushes and 'garden seeds'. Only for those products which were commissioned from St Petersburg or Germany is the attribute English mentioned. When sending commissions to England, the implicit idea of the desired products was that they were English and not from France or elsewhere in Europe. One particular English luxury good which reveals the importance of the lifestyle of the English bourgeoisie to their Vyborg counterparts is an English coal-burning fireplace in Hackman's country house.[48] Using an imported coal-burning stove in a country where fire wood was inexpensive and easy to get was pure luxury. Owning and using modern English goods was an important part of the Hackmans' lifestyle and illustrates the possibility of following and emulating English taste into the realms of vanity.

The variety of English products was quite large, from living animals to table napkins, but many were meant for socializing – a key attribute of 'new luxury'. The china, cutlery, coffee, beers and cheeses were put on display and enjoyed at social gatherings; they were central to genteel sociability. The English fashion in clothing, furniture and cutlery – or generally the whole genteel lifestyle with country houses, English landscape gardens, hunting parties, horses and dogs – was followed in Vyborg, and British hegemony was thus spread over Europe.[49] But, in some ways, luxury would not be luxury if no one saw it. It seems that conspicuous consumption was in many cases implicit for these English goods. However, as we have already noted, luxury as conspicuous consumption was not often written about in letters. Only once, in 1801, did Mr Hackman write that his wife 'wanted to show her new clothes in a certain society'.[50]

Only certain English products could satisfy the consumers in Vyborg; they knew the latest patterns and the places to shop. For example, in February 1815 the Hackmans ordered a porcelain service, which should be 'Queens patent best blue' and in June 1832 they commissioned a water filter from Lipscomb and Co. in London. The writer of the letter, J. F. Hackman Jr, knew that these could be purchased from No. 93 Regent Street at a price of 18 shillings. This kind of knowledge could not be possible without personal visits to London or by reading newspapers and advertisements printed in Britain. Following fashion demanded knowledge of the language and good connections in order to purchase these English goods – something which is apparent from many of the contributions to this volume, including those by North, Bristol and Steinrud.

Conclusion

Discussions of luxury in eighteenth- and nineteenth-century Vyborg, which was situated only 150 kilometres from St Petersburg, was limited to its negative effects. In the newspaper columns published in St Petersburg and Vyborg, luxury and conspicuous consumption were criticized heavily. These articles were aimed at a wide audience and the tone was patronizing; a growing literate working class and lower middle class should not get involved with the luxurious lifestyle of their superiors – a familiar message heard time and again in luxury debates. Lavish consumption of ready-made clothes, for example, would destroy the social order where dress could indicate its wearer's social rank (see also Pajur's chapter in this volume). This kind of discussion, however, was not conducted in the letters of the local commercial elite; although they admitted that certain objects were luxurious, it was only the context – a chandelier for a Christmas present – that made the object too lavish and ostentatious. Given these negative connotations, other attributes were used to describe the most desirable goods: taste, fashion, modernity, quality and Englishness were discussed and advertised repeatedly. Hence, it would be anachronistic to call certain objects categorically luxurious, if contemporaries used words such as tasteful or modish when purchasing them.

The merchant elite in Vyborg clearly communicated their status, networks and even wealth through their consumption choices. This behaviour can be called conspicuous consumption, but was seldom discussed as such. By praising the quality or style of the products or the taste of the commission agent, luxury goods and conspicuous consumption became socially acceptable. In this context, one of the attributes which was often combined with tasteful and fashionable goods was their Englishness. Both in letters and newspaper advertisements, an English origin was a positive association. Those who shopped for English goods knew that they received fashionable and good quality products at a reasonable price. In Vyborg, there was a growing audience for these types of goods; waged labour gave even common people an opportunity to purchase imported consumer goods. They had an opportunity to imitate the consumer choices of their superiors, who had preferred English goods for decades.

Taste and fashion were ways to articulate cultural capital, as Jon Stobart, in his previous studies, has illustrated.[51] By commissioning fashionable goods, Vyborg's German merchant elite showed that they not only knew and had access to the latest fashion and taste, but that they were connected with the St Petersburg Germans or the English commercial elite. By praising the taste of German merchants and their wives in St Petersburg, the German elite of Vyborg helped to develop the cultural capital of the German community and connect this community with the English commercial elite and their fashionable luxury goods. By acquiring fashionable, high quality goods directly from England, often with the help of their English partners, or by buying English luxury items from St Petersburg shops, the Vyborg German merchant elite made clear their need for cultural, social and economic capital. According to Maxine Berg, British goods reflected liberty and commerce which were greatly valued in eighteenth-century Britannia.[52] The discussions in private letters or newspapers in Vyborg does not, however, reveal any traces of such ideology. If English luxury goods were preferred, it was not the nationalistic character that was important but their intrinsic entailed style and quality, and the cultural and social capital they embodied.

Notes

1 I have chosen to use the name Vyborg, when referring the town of Vyborg/Wyborg/Viborg/Wiborg/Wijborg/Wybourg/Viipuri/Выборг. The town, during its long history, had had many official and unofficial languages. The archival sources

which I have used were mostly written by German-speaking people, who used the name Wiborg. Nowadays, the town's name is spelled Vyborg, when referring to its English name.

2 'Meine Frau bittet Sie richte sehr ihr aus dem Englischen Magazin ein groβes Englisches damastenes seidenes Mode Tuch, am liebsten orange mit Weiß, oder orange mit Braun . . .', 19 August 1802, Bruun, St Petersburg, B 16, Hackman and Co., The National Archives of Business Records (henceforth ELKA).

3 Only recently has there been an attempt to widen geographically the concept of luxury in Europe. See *Luxury and Gender in European Towns, 1700–1914*, eds Deborah Simonton, Marjo Kaartinen and Anne Montenach (New York and London: Routledge, 2014); Michael North, *'Material Delight and the Joy of Living': Cultural Consumption in the Age of Enlightenment in Germany.* Trans. by P. Selwyn (Aldershot and Burlington VT: Ashgate, 2008), 170; Maxine Berg, *Luxury and Pleasure in Eighteenth Century Britain* (Oxford: Oxford University Press, 2005).

4 Berg, *Luxury and Pleasure,* 3–4; see also the chapter by Marie Steinrud in this volume.

5 Tapio Hämynen, 'Viipurin läänin väestönkehitys autonomian ajalla', in *Viipurin läänin historia V. Autonomisen Suomen Rajamaa*, eds Yrjö Kaukiainen, Risto Marjomaa and Jouko Nurmiainen (Karjalaisen kulttuurin edistämissäätiö, 2014), 144–93, here 146, 149; Antony Cross, *By the Banks of the Neva: Chapters from the Lives and Careers of the British in Eighteenth-century Russia.* (Cambridge: Cambridge University Press, 1997), 16; J. W. Ruuth and Erkki Kuujo, *Viipurin kaupungin historia IV* (Torkkelin säätiö, 1981), 41.

6 See also Michael North's chapter in this volume; North, *'Material Delight',* 170; Ulla Ijäs, 'Favourites of Fortune: The Luxury Consumption of the Hackmans of Vyborg, 1790–1825', in *Luxury and Gender in European Towns, 1700–1914*, eds Deborah Simonton, Marjo Kaartinen and Anne Montenach (New York and London: Routledge, 2014), 190–205; Ulla Ijäs, *Talo, kartano, puutarha. Kauppahuoneen omistaja Marie Hackman ja hänen kulutusvalintansa varhaismodernissa Viipurissa.* (Turku: Annales Universitatis Turkuensis, Turku, 2015). (Published PhD thesis with an English abstract.)

7 Christine Ruane, *The Empire's New Clothes. A History of the Russian Fashion Industry, 1700–1917* (New Haven: Yale University Press, 2009), 10; Christine Ruane, 'Clothes shopping in Imperial Russia: The Development of a Consumer Culture', *Journal of Social History* 28 (1995), 765–82; Berg, *Luxury and Pleasure,* 6.

8 Roger P. Bartlett, *Human Capital, The Settlement of Foreigners in Russia 1762–1804* (Cambridge: Cambridge University Press, 2009); Cross, *By the Banks of the Neva,* 14–17, 44–5.

9 Herbert H. Kaplan, *Russian Overseas Commerce with Great Britain during the Reign of Catherine II*. Memoirs of the American Philosophical Society Held at Philadelphia for Promoting Knowledge. Vol. 218. (Philadelphia: America Philosophical Society, 1995), 33; for example, George E. Munro in his study *The Most International City: St Petersburg in the Reign of Catherine the Great* (Cranbury: Rosemont Publishing and Printing Corp., 2008), 192, 195, refers to a report which states that 'foreign influence [i.e. foreign artisans] had so developed a domestic luxury goods industry toward the end of the [eighteenth] century that certain items did not have to be imported at all, including embroidered cloth, millinery, coaches and carriages, furniture, stoves, porcelain, glassware, tapestries, and jewelry.'

10 North, *Material Delight*; Ragnhild Hutchison, 'The Norwegian and Baltic timber trade to Britain 1780–1830 and its interconnections', *Scandinavian Journal of History* 37 (2012), 578–99.

11 Markku Kuisma, *Metsäteollisuuden maa: Suomi, metsät ja kansainvälinen järjestelmä 1620–1920*, 2nd edn (Helsinki: Suomalaisen Kirjallisuuden Seura, 2006), 84–6, 151–2, 192–201, 233.

12 Kaplan, *Russian Overseas Commerce*, 33; compare with Murhem and Ulväng in this volume.

13 I have discussed these themes in Ijäs, 'Favourites of Fortune', 190–205. See also Marjo Kaartinen, Anne Montenach and Deborah Simonton, 'Luxury, Gender and the Urban Experience', in *Luxury and Gender in European Towns, 1700–1914*, eds Deborah Simonton, Marjo Kaartinen and Anne Montenach (New York and London: Routledge, 2014), 1–15. See also Ulväng's chapter in this volume.

14 3 December 1862, Emmy Cedercreutz to J. F. Hackman Jr, HH 25, Handelshuset Hackmans arkiv, Åbo Akademis Library (henceforth ÅA).

15 See the letter of 29 December 1872 from Emmy Cedecreutz to Julie Hackman, HH 25, Handelshuset Hackmans arkiv, ÅA.

16 So far, I have had an opportunity to search the year 1804 from *St Petersburgische Zeitung* and years 1823–1890 from Vyborg's newspapers *Östra Finland, Otawa, Kanawa, Sanan Saattaja Wiipurista, Wiborgs Annonce Blad, Wiborgsbladet, Wiborgs Tidning, Wiburgs Mancherley* and *Wiburgs Wochenblatt*, at the National Library of Finland's Digital Collections, http://digi.kansalliskirjasto.fi/sanomalehti [accessed 20 August 2015].

17 For example, the *Journal des Luxus und der Moden* was preordered in the household. Hence, the findings of Michael North's chapter in this volume can be applied, to some extent, in Vyborg. In this article, however, the focus is not on the German newspapers and magazines but the local prints.

18 Conspicuous consumption is discussed by several historians over the decades. A recent study, referencing luxury and conspicuous consumption is Jon Stobart and

Mark Rothery, 'Fashion, Heritance and Family: New and Old in the Georgian Country House', *Cultural and Social history* 11 (2014), 385–406; see also the chapter by Marie Steinrud in this volume.

19 In the so-called Old Finland, i.e. those counties that were annexed to Russia in 1721 and 1743, in many cases, the peasants did not own their land but instead hired it from the crown or an owner of a donation (a Russian aristocrat, who had got the land from the emperor as a reward). They were not serfs, however. There were only two towns, Turku and Helsinki, which could compete with Vyborg.

20 Yrjö Kaukiainen, 'Viipurin lääni palaa Suomeen – Suomi tulee Viipurin lääniin,' in *Viipurin läänin historia V: Autonomisen Suomen Rajamaa*, eds Yrjö Kaukiainen, Risto Marjomaa and Jouko Nurmiainen (Karjalaisen kulttuurin edistämissäätiö, 2014), 12–35, here 17–18.

21 'Seÿn Sie so gefällig für mich einen Modefarben Surtout nachdem neuesten Schnitte gemacht, einen feinen modernen dreÿecktigten Huth und einige Blumen für meine Frau zu besorgen . . . Ich verlasse mich in allen auf Ihre Geschmack u Schnelligkeit.' 25 March 1802, Zagel, St Petersburg, B 15, Hackman and Co., ELKA.

22 17 January 1803, Garbutt, Hull, B 59, Hackman and Co., ELKA.

23 29 March 1801, Bruun, St Petersburg, B 12, Hackman and Co., ELKA. See also Berg, *Luxury and Pleasure,* 6; about fashion (*mode*) in German context, see North's chapter in this volume.

24 *Wiborg*, 14 April 1869; 'Vårt sällskapslif,' *Wiborgs Tidning*, 26 April 1865; for example, a silversmith used taste (*smak*) in his advertisement. *Wiborgs Annonce Blad* 29 January 1842.

25 'Lyx och folkupplysning,' *Wiborg,* 12 December 1856.

26 'Muoti ja ajan henki,' *Ilmarinen*, 15 March 1876.

27 'Flechten . . . nach der neuesten Mode etc.' *Sanan Saattaja Wiipurista*, 17 January 1835; 'Modemagasin,' *Otawa*, 2 October 1863.

28 Berg, *Luxury and Pleasure,* 195; Maxine Berg, 'In Pursuit of Luxury: Global Origins of British Consumer Goods in the Eighteenth Century', *Past and Present* 182 (2004), 98–9.

29 See also North, *'Material Delight'*, 48–54. In this volume Anglomania is also touched on by Clemente and Coquery.

30 The aristocracy in Vyborg and St Petersburg, as in Sweden, appear to have preferred French luxury in the manner illustrated by Ilmakunnas in her chapter in this volume; but we lack detailed studies of these preferences.

31 In their letters, the Hackmans once commissioned a Scottish rug, and several times 'Irish linens'. On one occasion, they wrote: 'Be pleased to send us by one of Your ships a carpet worked of wool to cover a rooms floor, of modish colours black, high red & green or yellow about 6 Yards long and 6 Yards broad not

exceeding 20 £ in price, we get them formerly very nice from Scotland.' 15 January 1816, Oxley, English and Oxley, Lyn R[egi]s, B 33, Hackman and Co., ELKA.

32 Kuisma, *Metsäteollisuuden maa*, 192–204; Sven-Erik Åström, *From tar to timber: Studies in Northeast European Forest Exploitation and Foreign Trade 1660–1860* (Helsingfors: Societas Scientarum Fennica, 1988).

33 See the letters of 1821 in B 39, Hackman and Co., ELKA.

34 For example, Henry Eeles Dresser, the son of bank manager Henry Dresser, and his wife Eliza Ann Garbutt from London, spent two years in Vyborg in the 1850s.

35 'You made great progress in the Art. I have sent you by the providence a little momento [*sic*] of which I beg your kind assistance – It is a new work called the *Oriental Annual* – we consider the Engravings very good!' 14 April 1834, Ann Garbutt to Julie Hackman, HH 25, Handelshuset Hackmans arkiv, ÅA.

36 See also Michael North's chapter in this volume and North, *'Material Delight'*, 48.

37 17 July 1800, Bruun, St Petersburg, B 11, Hackman and Co., ELKA.

38 North, *'Material Delight'*, 75.

39 6 July 1813, Bourne and Co., Liverpool, B 30, Hackman and Co., ELKA; 16 January 1820, Neuman, Liverpool; 7 May 1820, Leigh and Co., Liverpool, B 39, Hackman and Co., ELKA.

40 Berg, *Luxury and Pleasure*, 195; Cross, *By the Banks of Neva*, 3, 10, 18; T. S. Willan, *The Early History of the Russia Company, 1553–1603* (Manchester: Manchester University Press, 1956). See also Ijäs, 'Favourites of Fortune'.

41 *St Petersburgische Zeitung*, 12 January 1804, 16 February 1804, 29 January 1804.

42 *Wiburgs Wochenblatt*, 31 July 1824, 3 June 1837; *Kanawa*, 8 February 1845.

43 *Wiborgs Annonce Blad*, 15 January 1842.

44 *Wiburgs Wochenblatt*, 11 September 1824; *Wiborgs Annonce Blad*, 10 February 1844. See also *Wiborgs Annonce Blad*, 22 September 1838.

45 *Wiborgs Tidning*, 20 September 1871; *Wiborgs Tidning*, 4 December 1877; *Wiborgs Tidning*, 12 August 1879.

46 *Wiborgsbladet*, 30 March 1888.

47 I have gone through the entire collection of the letter copies (*Brief Copey Buch*) from 1790 to 1837. From the copies, I have picked the letters which included commissions of goods or which referred to consumption of any kind.

48 The archives of a fire insurance company Suomen palovakuutuskonttorin arkisto, year 1822, Viipurin pitäjä, National Archives of Finland (henceforth NA) hold the fire insurance of the Herttuala manor. In the main building, there were several English coal stoves (*Engelsk kohl Camin af sjutit järn med koppar skärm*) beside the normal tiled wood burning fireplaces (*kakelugn af posslins kakel och*). In 1819, 40 Roubles was used for coals. 'Für steinkohlen 40 Rbl.' May 1819, G 20 V, Hackman and Co., ELKA.

49 Berg, 'In Pursuit of Luxury', 98–9; North, *'Material Delight'*, 76–95, 167.

50 5 April 1801, Bruun, St Petersburg, B 12, Hackman and Co., ELKA. '*Sie wollte gerne sich in einer gewißen Gesellschaft mit einem neuen Kleide produciren*'.

51 Stobart and Rothery, 'Fashion, Heritance and Family,' 385–406; Michael North discusses taste in his book *'Material Delight and the Joy of Living'*, but without further conceptualizing the notion of 'taste'.

52 Berg, *Luxury and Pleasure*, 9.

14

Luxury Goods Beyond Boundaries: The Parisian Market During the Terror

Natacha Coquery

Shopkeepers played a crucial role in revolutionizing consumption habits, the geographic setting for trade, and spreading novelties to broader segments of society. Coffee, tea and sugar – luxury goods in the late seventeenth century – had become staples a hundred years later: for the Sans-Culottes in Year II, these were questions of subsistence, much to Robespierre's dismay.[1] What became of luxury, one of the cornerstones of the French economy and a sector that had long enjoyed a vibrant international reputation, during the French revolutionary period? To reiterate the question raised in the introduction to this book, what happens to established notions of luxury and taste when society, politics and economics are transformed through revolution? I adopt the point of view of an historian of consumption and material culture, and as a specialist in economic agents that have not been studied substantially (at least not in French historiography), namely, shopkeepers.[2] My aim is to compare and contrast urban commercial practices with political and economic power during the revolutionary period. In other words, how did the Revolution transform the Old Regime's economic sociology of interests?[3] Thus, I will touch on the overall question of the relationship between economics and politics in times of crisis. I share Charles Walton's view that 'historians tend to think about politics and the economy as separate spheres.'[4] By studying how the economy works in times of crisis, we can measure how the market is transformed and adapts to political decisions, and analyse how economic agents attempted to be political agents as well. The revolutionary political class – Sieyès, Roland, Condorcet, Dupont de Nemours, and so forth – were all well-read in political economy and placed the circulation of goods at the heart of economic activity, but they were divided into dirigistes and liberals on the question of the primacy of politics.[5] In her material history of the assignats, Rebecca Spang has shown the extent to which the balancing act between liberalism and regulation weighed on monetary policy.[6] I intend to assess the lobbying and entrepreneurial strategies deployed under the new regime in order to grasp the relations between the political and economic spheres. Also relevant is the question of what happened to the retailers' profits when traditional consumers disappeared or changed their spending habits; when trade faced increasing barriers, and when the Revolution caused the collapse of the centuries-old institutional framework in which the merchant aristocracy had made its place. This entails observing transformations, detours, transgressions and successes.

Markets, revolution and luxury: an incomplete history

Researchers of the French Revolution generally favour political, intellectual, cultural or social questions, rather than economic ones. There are two major exceptions to this rather blanket statement: rural history[7] and, more recently, Atlantic history, which has given renewed impetus to the historiography of revolutions and trade by raising questions on a larger spatial and temporal scale without neglecting the micro-historical angle.[8] That said, most Anglo-Saxon or French research has explored consumption within an historical perspective that was chiefly intellectual and political, whereas the history of the French Revolution is an active field for research in France and the US. As rightly noted in a collaborative article about the market during revolutions, published in the journal *Annales Historiques de la Révolution Française*, combining the history of markets and the history of political revolutions is no easy task, even though both topics have opened up to global history in the past few years. Two completely separate historiographic approaches coexisted for a long time: an industrial and economic history focused on England, and a political history focused on France and the Americas.[9] As a result, French historians of the Revolution have paid little attention to the history of material culture. This can be seen, for instance, in the last ten years' issues and the website of *AHRF*.[10] A recent conference (2013) and two collective works (2005 and 2011) have confirmed French historians' interest in the political aspects of the French Revolution.[11] In contrast, the question of political revolution has received only modest attention from British historians of material culture, who are mainly focused on England or, since the global turn, on exchanges between the West and the East.[12] In his thought-provoking thesis, Manuel Covo combines historiographies: colonial history, history of the French and Haitian Revolutions, and history of the early American Republic. By studying commercial networks, flows and traffic on a transnational scale, he casts light on the role of the Atlantic trade in the transformation of political entities during the revolutionary period.[13]

When the question of luxury in the French or American Revolutions is raised, it is viewed through the lens of cultural history by historians of political culture or art historians. The French historian Audrey Provost has looked at luxury from a literary standpoint, based on essays, treatises, *libelles* and pamphlets published between 1762 and 1791 in an era when sumptuary laws had fallen into disuse.[14] In two thought-provoking books, American historians John Shovlin and Paul Cheney place political economy and its eighteenth-century representation into context. Both authors, as historians of ideas, reflect on the ties between science, politics, morals and economics.[15] Luxury is viewed from the perspective of moral economy and fashion interpreted as an array of symbols.[16] In the French historiography, art historians have studied the connection between art, luxury and Revolution, but economic historians have not.[17] However, there has been no historical research of the debate surrounding luxury in the context of political revolution. There is substantial work to be done because there are numerous archives to study, since the subject requires calling on economic as well as political and legal history. Hence this is a work in progress and I can only present its initial findings.

Economics and politics: the fate of luxury during revolutionary upheaval

The luxury market is a fluctuating one, highly competitive nationally and internationally and a source of substantial profits. Yet it is a fragile market because it is intrinsically linked to fashion, to the imperative for the ephemeral, to goods recognized as social markers, intended for consumption by social elites, such as the royal court. One might think that the revolutionary events caused a wave of panic in the retail sector. Of course, exile, bankruptcy and even death occurred, such as Quatremère who was guillotined in January 1794, accused of being 'the accomplice of unfaithful suppliers' by the Market Committee (*Comité des Marchés*).[18] But the luxury market survived, even during the darkest days of the Terror. Supported by the circulation of second-hand objects, the luxury market boasted an almost insolent vitality, as proven by the press of the time, to which we will turn shortly.[19] As noted by Beverly Lemire, the link between second-hand and luxury goods had long existed,[20] but in France it grew much stronger because of the Revolution. This is the key point of my chapter: the Revolution, far from encouraging market segmentation (as promoted in political speeches and laws), actually made the market more fluid. The boundaries of the luxury market shifted. Daniel Roche has written that 'not enough attention has been paid to the redistributive effect caused by the disorganisation of the market, auction sales, or even the violent confiscation of goods.'[21] I will demonstrate this by working on one type of source: the advertisements and legal notices published in the daily newspaper, *Affiches de Paris*. First, I will briefly present the newspaper, the political context, and some relevant legislation. Then, I will study advertisements to show that, despite – or rather because of – the dominance of the political sphere, which sought to regulate the economy by controlling the currency, prices, products and trade, the circulation of luxury goods revealed the porosity of social and political borders.[22] However, to show this, I must begin by talking about crisis and poverty.

Affiches, advertisements and reports

The *Affiches*, lists of miscellaneous property, administrative, commercial, and cultural advertisements and announcements, grew popular following the initial liberalization of the press in the early 1750s. Created in around fifty towns, the *Affiches* were largely dedicated to business and trade.[23] The *Affiches, annonces et avis divers, ou Journal général de France* was the first long-standing Parisian periodical, published from 13 May 1751 onwards.[24] It was intended to facilitate commercial transactions, announcements being included gratis: 'We shall continue to insert free of charge in the *Gazette*, or in these present Pages, all Notices that appear appropriate & interesting. We recommend that they should be written very legibly, & so as to leave no doubt as to proper names'.[25] The sections were more or less the same over time: land for sale, houses for sale, houses or flats for rent, sales of movable property and effects, sales of horses and carriages, lost and found effects, divorce or death notices, classified advertisements ('*Annonces Particulières*'), various notices ('*Avis Divers*'), requests, theatre playbills and the like. The importance initially given to science and literature disappeared in the late 1770s to the benefit of advertisements and became a favoured venue for retail shops which filled virtually the entire paper. Each issue had a supplement and additions. The number of pages published annually increased significantly in the second half of the century: 800 pages in 1752, when the paper appeared twice weekly, then 372 pages in July 1790 alone, after the paper had become a daily. The number of pages continued to increase during the 1790s: 448 pages in July 1793, 504 in Germinal (21 March–19 April) 1794.[26] I chose to study 1793 and 1794 to see how far the newspaper could reflect the difficulties of the time and its links with a potential luxury market. Taking the first ten days of July 1790, July 1793, Germinal 1794 (i.e. 21–30 March) and Nivôse 1794 (i.e. 21–30 December), I have noted all the advertisements and legal notices published during these periods, apart from property advertisements, which are very numerous and cannot be studied without a spatial analysis.

In 1792, 1793 and 1794, the national and international contexts changed dramatically. In Appendix 1, I recall some of the main events to bear in mind when reading advertisements from this period: the ever-present backdrop of war, drastic control of trade and prices (prohibitions, the General Maximum), the fight against hoarding, the subsistence crisis. The liberal period of 1789–1791 came to an end; dirigiste legislation was passed in spring 1793 (the first taxation of prices, the 'Law of the Maximum', was dated 4 May), and continued until December 1794.[27] Reports by secret agents of the Minister of the Interior and inspectors confirm the difficulties of the time. The authors constantly insisted on supply difficulties and the scarcity and cost of basic necessities.[28] They noted that 'meat is sold in the Saint-Roch district at 18 sous a pound, making many citizens grumble'[29] and that 'basic necessities are still overpriced [. . .]. There is no longer much or any meat in butcher's shops. What shall we do then, what will become of us if this misery, or rather famine continues?'[30] The blame was sometimes placed at the door of retailers: 'the ordinary people of the Faubourg Saint-Marceau complain considerably that the merchants no longer follow the Maximum. Sugar is becoming very scarce.'[31] Indeed, retailers were even seen as scaremongers, exacerbating people's worries about shortages:

> Commodities are at an exorbitant price; a cabbage costs 14, 15 or 16 sous, beans 18 and 20 sous a quart [litron], peas 30 sous a quart [litron], lentils 1 livre 4 pence, butter 36, 40 and 45 sous a pound, milk 12 sous a pint [pinte]: still not worth anything and it cannot be found. Finally, everything is overpriced and, to make matters worse, merchants still have the infamy of constantly repeating that there will soon be nothing left in Paris.[32]

On occasions, the agents expressed their dismay, even despair, noting that:

> Merchants [. . .] are increasing the prices of their goods every day [. . .]; linen shirting is very expensive, as are canvas paintings; all hosiery is at an unreasonable price; finally, all the most necessary things are increasing day by day at the whim of merchants. The people urge us to prevent this harassment.[33]

Particular concern was shown about the black market in luxury or semi-luxury goods, carried out by various types of intermediaries such as merchants and paupers. One agent noted that 'There is considerable speculation with Watches of all kinds at exorbitant prices in cafes and among wine merchants at the Marché des Innocents. Water carriers and labourers are solely occupied with this trade.'[34] They also denounced the development and activity of auction houses which became central to the dynamic luxury market during this period, as we will see in the next section.[35]

The contradictions between politics and economics: auctions of aristocratic goods, a driver for the luxury market

So what story was being told by advertisements in the *Affiches* at this time? Contrary to the reports mentioned above, there are no signs of crisis or poverty; even during the harshest years, there was no decline in the number of advertisements which remained considerable between 1790 and 1794, at roughly 200 per ten-day period (see Table 14.1). There were, however, different trends in the various categories of announcements. The most significant changes were the reduction in advertisements for horses and carriages, from 34.5 per cent in July 1790 to 7.5 per cent in December 1794, and the increase in the 'Sales of Goods and Effects', from 35 per cent in July 1790 to 66.5 per cent in July 1793. The former were typical aristocratic products, an important component of the Parisian luxury market, especially with the rise of Anglomania among courtiers since the 1770s – a feature also noted by Clemente for Naples and North for Germany. In Paris, this trend was evidenced by the activities of the Counts of Lauragais and Artois, the Dukes of Lauzun and Chartres, the Marquis de Voyer and Conflans, and the Duke of Coigny, first squire of the king, the Duke of Fitz-James, amongst many others.[36] The post-Revolution decline in advertisements for horses and carriages is unsurprising: the dangers of owning such an obvious symbol of aristocratic status was compounded by emigration of elites and the requisitioning of many luxury horses by the army, especially after March 1793.[37] And yet, in July that year, advertisements continued to announce the sale of a 'beautiful English horse', 'a pretty carrick', 'a pretty coach made in London', 'a new whiskey', 'a harness in the latest fashion', and so on. There was clearly still a market for these goods and, even with England as public enemy No.1, the traditional equestrian Anglomania continued as if nothing had happened. However, by December 1793, the term 'English' and words with an English resonance had disappeared from the advertisements because, from October of that year, the import, sale or advertisement of English products was formally prohibited.[38]

The 'Sales of Goods and Effects' section, as well as the '*Annonces Particulières*' (or classified advertisements), included other areas of consumption, such as textiles, furniture, interior decoration, or even foodstuffs, especially wines. Auctions are a very old means of exchange and the years 1760–1780 saw the opening of places devoted to auctions (the hotels Aligre, Louvois, Bullion and Lubert, amongst others); the affirmation of a 'public space of taste', and the new importance of the figure of the amateur, all of which signal the increasing commercialization of the arts.[39] Merchants played a fundamental role in the new market; they used public auctions to disperse private collections, to sell their stocks, but also to buy, both for a client or for themselves.

In 1793 and 1794, at the height of the political crisis (see Appendix 1), sales of furniture and effects list large amounts of luxury goods, notably in the textile sector: English muslins, muslin ties, Indian *Nankin*, satin from the Levant, silk handkerchiefs from India, etc. The furniture and decoration sector was very dynamic and offered long lists of highly luxurious objects: mahogany furniture, canopy beds, cabinet furniture, backgammon and gaming tables, silver candlesticks, silver tableware, gold clocks, 'a Superb Cartel by *Houchard*, Watchmaker of the former King at Versailles,'[40] alabaster vases, golden chandeliers, porcelain cabarets, paintings and prints, etc. In the foodstuffs sector, offered for sale were wines, Champagne, spirits, rum, coffee and brown sugar, as well as 'fine wines and fine liquors from America . . .'[41] Jewellery was also for sale in the *Affiches*: necklaces, rings, earrings, watches, all in gold. Yet this profusion of luxury goods came about precisely because the crisis was at its peak.

This is a fundamental paradox that calls into question conventional ideas on luxury, the French Revolution, and modernity. The French Revolution, a new regime that embodied modernity and the abolition of an inegalitarian ideology and order, far from completing this evolution, appears to have helped strengthen traditional values and luxury. This occurred through practices that, because of the revolutionary crisis, grew on an extraordinary scale: auction sales and supply of used goods.[42] What was different was that these traditional practices were used to disperse goods after emigration or death sentences, events that could be expressed as 'felt under the sword of the law'.[43] The sale of the goods of émigrés (Condé, Conti, Montmorency and so on), which has not been studied significantly in the urban context despite the availability of abundant source materials, triggered frenzied activity in auction houses and fuelled the market for second-hand luxury goods.[44] If merchants suffered from the emigration of their aristocratic clientele, many others took advantage of the sale of their goods by positioning themselves in the auction market as auction organizers, buyers for French or foreign collectors, or by buying to resell on the Parisian market or farther afield. Among others, Jacob and Riesener, cabinet makers, acquired furniture from the Palace of Versailles, sold between 25 August 1793 and 11 August 1794.[45]

Table 14.1 Trend in the number of ads per section: *Affiches, annonces et avis divers, ou Journal général de France*, 1790–1794

1–10 July 1790

Day	Annonces particulières (classified ads)	Various notices	Horses and carriages	Goods and effects	Daily total
1	4	3	9	11	27
2	2	1	4	7	14
3	3	2	6	8	19
4	3	5	9	7	24
5	6	3	9	8	26
6	3	3	5	2	13
7	3	3	7	6	19
8	4	1	7	9	21
9	4	2	4	9	19
10	9	2	14	8	33
Total	41 (19%)	25 (11.5%)	74 (34.5%)	75 (35%)	215 (100%)

1–10 July 1793

Day	Annonces particulières (classified ads)	Various notices	Horses and carriages	Goods and effects	Daily total
1			4	10	14
2	7	2	2	15	26
3	1		1	12	14
4	3	1	3	7	14
5	3	1	3	15	22
6	4	2	4	17	27
7		1	1	8	10
8		1	1	12	14
9	4		6	21	31
10	6	1	3	11	21
Total	28 (14.5%)	9 (4.5%)	28 (14.5%)	128 (66.5%)	193 (100%)

(*Continued*)

Table 14.1 (*Continued*)

1–10 Nivôse Year II (end of December 1793)

Day	Annonces particulières (classified ads)	Various notices	Horses and carriages	Goods and effects	Daily total
1	6	2	3	13	24
2	6	1	1	11	19
3	8	2	2	11	23
4	1	1	1	11	14
5	3	3	2	9	17
6	23	2	2	8	35
7	1	1	1	18	21
8	12	2	2	20	36
9	2	1	2	8	13
10	10	3	1	11	25
Total	72 (31.5%)	18 (8%)	17 (7.5%)	120 (53%)	227 (100%)

1–10 Germinal Year II (end of March 1794)

Day	Annonces particulières (classified ads)	Various notices	Horses and carriages	Goods and effects	Daily total
1	3		2	9	14
2	3	1	1	12	17
3	2		1	8	11
4	8	1	4	12	25
5	5	1	5	19	30
6	4	1	4	10	19
7	15	1	11	7	34
8			3	16	19
9		1	1	9	11
10	5	1	3	16	25
Total	45 (22%)	7 (3.5%)	35 (17%)	118 (57.5%)	205 (100%)

Many sales were carried out in the house of the deceased or émigré, but others took place at an auction house, the Bullion House ('Maison Bullion', the former 'Hôtel Bullion') or in an auction room at the 'Maison Égalité' (the former Palais-Royal). Such advertisements begin in a way that links the goods to their previous owner and explains the reason for the sale: '[...] the Sale of Furniture, Carriage and Wines of the émigré *Maillebois* and his wife, Rue de Grenelle . . .';[46] 'In the name of the French Republic. Sale [...] at the House of the Revolution, previously the Palais Bourbon, following the emigration of

Bourbon *Condé* . . .'.[47] The sale of the former Princess of Lamballe's goods shows the extraordinary variety and richness of the items offered, with a special mention for the '3,856 bottles of dessert wines of various sorts'.[48]

Through traders' agency, these sales fuelled the market for second-hand luxury goods. In the '*Annonces Particulières*' section, luxury goods are listed in announcements made by merchants, retailers or wholesalers. These may concern the same products as those already mentioned, but also many others which are not necessarily luxury goods per se, but which, in the context of scarcity where everything was lacking, could nevertheless be viewed as luxuries. This is a matter that will have to be debated much more fully: what is luxury in a context of scarcity? For now, let us focus on the products mentioned above. Finding advertisements for the same luxury goods as those sold at auctions, during a period of scarcity, means that merchants had bought them at auction for later resale. Indeed, these tradesmen played a crucial role in connecting markets, a connection made explicit in advertisements. In several cases, this connection is expressed clearly, as in these advertisements: 'Two chaises [. . .] **from the former Countess of** *Artois*' or 'Two Drawings and ten Prints by the best Masters [. . .] **from the sale of the émigrée Kinski**: in all, 400 livres. Call (mornings) at *Au Prix Fixe*, No. 39 in Rue de Tracy near Rue Franciade, formerly Denis, near Chaumont'.[49]

Studying this crucial connecting role, which is the true agency of traders, gives us new perspectives on the processes of acquiring objects and on the link between taste, luxury and identity, when society was transformed through revolution. What must one do, how must one appear, to be a fashionable citizen? This was the existential question of the urban bourgeoisie: how to recover the aristocratic distinction? By acquiring the goods of émigrés and victims of the guillotine and, in doing so, join the aristocratic good taste?[50] Some words, often cited for many goods, are worth noting in these advertisements: 'for sale or barter', 'second-hand', 'like new'. One could think that many of these goods belonged to émigrés or those sentenced to death, and were purchased at auctions to end up in shops. More than ever, thanks to the Revolution, retailers sold second-hand luxury items. The role of retailers during the Revolution in spreading the luxury production of the former royal manufactures – Sèvres, Gobelins, Savonnerie – should also be emphasized.[51] Hence some well-known luxury traders continued to move merchandise as they had before the Revolution, but with new clients; such traders included Daguerre and Lignereux, art dealers located in Rue Saint-Honoré (and London) who advertised the 'Sale [. . .] of a considerable share of new PORCELAINS and products of choice, from the National Manufacture de Sève [. . .] Rue S. Honoré [. . .] house of Daguerre and Lignereux'.[52]

Thus, luxury products were still announced in 1793 and 1794, and in the same places that had been fashionable in the 1780s, such as the former Palais-Royal and Rue Saint-Honoré, a luxury centre before the Revolution. Importantly, this covered not simply durable goods, but also those for immediate consumption. We thus see notices that: 'Lozzaro, at Equality House, glass gallery No. 224, has received from Italy various qualities of CHOCOLATE, with vanilla, for good health, or with cinnamon, all at the right price',[53] and that 'Citizen Velloni [. . .] will open [. . .] his new STORE at the Garden of Equality, stone gallery No. 65 [. . .] you will find daily complete assortments of shaped Ice and Chocolate by the cup and pound'.[54] It was even possible to acquire 'DRAGÉES FROM MECCA. [at] 24 livres for a box of a dozen, with a print that shows the use'.[55] Advertising chocolates, ice cream or *dragées* (sweets) still had to be done, even in 1793 and 1794.

Conclusions

It is fascinating and revealing to explore the apparently blatant contradiction between luxury and revolutionary ideals, political decisions, economic crisis and wars; to see how auction sales, property advertisements and classified advertisements in the daily press show that the luxury market not only continued to exist, but even flourished despite (or thanks to?) the revolutionary context. As the Revolution swept across the country, this market continued to handle the same goods, although its participants were different (at least partly). The reasons for this must be sought in the very dynamics of the Revolution; in its political, economic and social stakes. The period is interesting precisely because it makes this paradox visible. The new egalitarian ideology helped to maintain hierarchies and traditional consumption practices. Social practices appear to have defied the ideological framework of the Revolution; so does this mean that revolutions are doomed to failure?

To continue our investigation and to understand how the revolutionary period thought about and determined policy related to the luxury market, parliamentary archives and minutes from commercial committee meetings will prove crucial sources. Such thought and policy was not devoid of hesitations, ambiguities or even contradictions – and therein lies the value of this research. Through these documents, historians can discover the debates, draft legislation and laws concerning the definition and regulation of luxury goods, taxes on luxury and wealth, as well as the debate between commercial freedom versus trade restrictions, between shutting down manufacturers of Old Regime luxury goods that had fallen into disgrace versus the suffering of workers forced into poverty, and so on. These debates and this legislation were inseparable from the national and international context and the balance of powers between various politicians and political factions. This field of research is just beginning to open up.

Appendix 1: a short chronology of the French Revolution, 1792–1795

11 July 1792: '*La Patrie en Danger*': Declaration by the French Assembly

2 September 1792: Émigrés' goods confiscated and sold

12 September 1792: Export of all livestock, war animals or other munitions prohibited

13 September 1792: Goods of émigrés confiscated

21 September 1792: Abolition of the monarchy (death of Louis XVI on 21 January 1793)

9 October 1792: The National Convention orders the sale of a large portion of the royal furniture of the Palace of Versailles

23 October 1792: Émigrés permanently banished from the territory of the Republic

1 February 1793: Declaration of war against Holland and England, against Spain on 7 March

February 1793 onwards: The anti-French coalition led to a proactive policy of state control of politics and the economy. The interventionist legislation would last until January 1795

19 February 1793: Prohibition of imports and exports (imports of all products made or manufactured in the countries with which France was at war; exports of any livestock, horses, mules, grains and forage, butter, leather of any sort, raw cork, sludge or ash from gold and silversmiths, potatoes, chestnuts and other vegetables or starchy fruits)

10 March 1793 to 27 July 1794: The Revolutionary Court judged counter-revolutionary crimes without appeal or recourse (only acquittal or death); a decree ordered that the property of those sentenced to death would be seized by the French Republic

Spring 1793: It all goes wrong: the Girondists (moderate wing of the left) were executed; the Vendée revolt began; successive defeats were suffered; General Dumouriez defected to the Austrian side. The Committee of Public Safety (*Comité de Salut Public*) was established in April; this was the collective forum (body) of the Government (lasting until July 1794). Prices were also fixed: the General Maximum lasted from 4 May 1793 until 24 December 1794

19 May 1793: A decree confirmed that the death sentence in cases determined by law included the confiscation of property

3 June 1793: A decree of the National Convention ordered the sale of land of émigrés

26 July 1793: A decree against hoarders of food and basic commodities (death and confiscation of property)

5 September 1793: The Terror was added to the agenda by the National Convention

29 September 1793: Subsistence crisis, famine and price increases related to speculation and the depreciation of the assignats; the General Maximum froze prices and wages: grains, meat, butter, oil, wine, cider, wood, candles, salt, honey, wool, linen, shoes, tobacco, etc.; decree on the arrest of suspects (with the definition of who were 'suspects')

10 October 1793: The National Convention proclaimed that the government must be 'revolutionary until peace', known as the Reign of Terror. In October, rationing was established: 750 grams of bread a day, then 500, then 250 (in 1794); this meant queuing for hours, not only for bread

February 1794: Vote for the sequestration of assets of suspects and their distribution to the needy; threat of famine

10 June 1794 (22 Prairial): Law on the Revolutionary Tribunal that ushered in the Great Terror (abolished on 1 August)

27 July 1794 (9 Thermidor): Fall of Robespierre

15 November 1794: The Emigrants Act: émigrés were banished for life and their property was seized by the French Republic

3 November 1795: Beginning of the Directory

Notes

1 'The people of Paris should rise up not to get sugar, but to lay low the bandits', Robespierre said in a speech to the National Convention on 25 February 1793, when the rise in sugar prices had prompted mobs against shopkeepers. Quoted by Colin Jones in Lorna Auslander, Charlotte Guichard, Colin Jones, Giorgio Riello and Daniel Roche, 'Regards croisés: Les révolutions à l'épreuve du marché', *Annales Historiques de la Révolution Française* 370 (2012), 178; see Colin Jones and Rebecca L. Spang, 'Sans-culottes, sans café, sans tabac: Shifting realms of necessity and luxury in eighteenth-century France', in *Consumers and Luxury: Consumer Culture in Europe 1650–1850*, eds Maxine Berg and Helen Clifford (Manchester: Manchester University Press, 1999), 37–62.

2 Natacha Coquery, *L'hôtel aristocratique: Le marché du luxe à Paris au XVIIIe siècle* (Paris: Publications de la Sorbonne, 1998); Natacha Coquery, *Tenir boutique à Paris au XVIIIe siècle: Luxe et demi-luxe* (Paris: Éditions du Comité Historique et Scientifique, 2011); *Retailers and Consumer Changes in Early Modern Europe: England, France, Italy and the Low Countries*, eds Bruno Blondé, Eugénie Briot, Natacha Coquery and Laura Van Aert (Tours: Presses Universitaires François-Rabelais, 2005).

3 In so doing, I join Charles Walton, with a slightly different approach, in his investigation of the politics of liberal political economy and his call 'for integrating the problem of *interests* into the analysis of Revolutionary politics'. In the light of the 2008 financial crisis, Walton investigates how political and economic power related to each other in the French Revolution: 'How did contemporaries think these forms of power should relate to each other? 'And how did those forms of power actually relate to each other in practice? That is, how was the Old Regime's political sociology of interests transformed by the Revolution? [. . .] Texts have been privileged over the rough and tumble of the street . . .' Charles Walton, 'French Revolutionary Studies: Challenges and Potential Ways Forward,' in *New Perspectives on the French Revolution*, eds Alex Fairfax-Cholmeley and Colin Jones (e-France, 4, 2013), 7–8.

4 Walton, 'French Revolutionary Studies', 8.

5 For a discussion of what happened in a city with a heavily regulated economy, see also the chapter by Murhem and Ulväng in this volume.

6 Rebecca L. Spang, *Stuff and Money in the Time of the French Revolution* (Cambridge: MA: Harvard University Press, 2015); François Crouzet, 'La logique libérale de la Révolution française', *Contrepoints*, 29 March 2011 (section: *Histoire du libéralisme*): http://www.contrepoints.org/2011/03/29/19182-la-logique-liberale-de-la-revolution-francaise

7 Noelle Plack, *Common Land, Wine and the French Revolution: Rural Society and Economy in Southern France, c.1789–1820* (Farnham: Ashgate, 2009); Gérard Béaur, *Histoire agraire de la France au XVIIIe siècle: Inerties et changements dans les campagnes françaises à la fin de l'époque moderne (jusqu'en 1815)* (Paris: SEDES, 2000); Bernard Bodinier, Eric Teyssier and François Antoine, *L'événement le plus important de la Révolution: La vente des biens nationaux, 1789–1867, en France et dans les territoires annexés* (Paris: Société des Études Robespierristes, CTHS, 2000); Gérard Béaur, 'Révolution et redistribution des richesses dans les campagnes: mythe ou réalité?', *Annales Historiques de la Révolution Française* 352 (2008), 209–39.

8 Kevin H. O'Rourke, 'The Worldwide Economic Impact of the French Revolutionary and Napoleonic Wars, 1793–1815', *Journal of Global History* 1 (2006), 123–49; Silvia Marzagalli, 'Establishing Transatlantic Trade Networks in Time of War: Bordeaux and the United States, 1793–1815', *Business History Review* 79 (2005), 811–44; Silvia Marzagalli, *Bordeaux et les États-Unis (1776–1815): Politique et stratégies négociantes dans la genèse d'un réseau commercial* (Geneva: Droz, 2015); *The Routledge Companion to the French Revolution in World History*, eds Allan Forrest and Matthias Middell (Oxford: Routledge, 2016).

9 Auslander et al., 'Regards croisés', 165–90.

10 http://ahrf.revues.org/

11 Conference 'Les Révolutions: Un Moment de Relecture du Passé: La Rupture Politique par l'Argumentation Historique (XVIIIe-XXIe Siècle)', Lille, 5–6 December 2013, http://ser.hypotheses.org/1076; *La Révolution à l'œuvre: Perspectives actuelles dans l'histoire de la Révolution française*, ed. Jean-Clément Martin (Rennes: Presses Universitaires de Rennes, 2005); *La Révolution française au miroir des recherches actuelles*, ed. Cyril Triolaire (Paris: Société des Études Robespierristes, 2011).

12 I would refer here to a historiographic overview, mainly of Anglo-Saxon sources, that I recently published: Natacha Coquery, 'La diffusion des biens à l'époque moderne: une histoire connectée de la consommation', *Histoire Urbaine*, 'Consommation et exotisme, XVe-XVIIIe siècles', no. 30 (April 2011): 5–20. See

also Maxine Berg's well-known research on luxury; Frank Trentmann, 'Crossing. Divides: Consumption and Globalization in History', *Journal of Consumer Culture*, 29 (2009), 187–220; Frank Trentmann, *Empire of Things: How We Became a World of Consumers, Fifteenth Century to the Twenty-First* (London: Penguin Books, 2016).

13 Manuel Covo, 'Commerce et révolutions dans l'espace atlantique: États-Unis-Saint-Domingue. 1784–1806' (PhD thesis, École des Hautes Études en Sciences Sociales, Paris, 2013).

14 Audrey Provost, *Le luxe, les Lumières et la Révolution* (Seyssel: Champ Vallon, 2014).

15 John Shovlin, *The Political Economy of Virtue: Luxury, Patriotism and the Origins of the French Revolution* (Ithaca and London: Cornell University Press, 2006); Paul Cheney, *Revolutionary Commerce: Globalization and the French Monarchy* (Cambridge MA and London: Harvard University Press, 2010).

16 Aileen Ribeiro, *Fashion in the French Revolution* (London: B. T. Batsford Ltd, 1988); *Modes et Révolutions 1780–1804: Exposition, Musée de la Mode et du Costume, Palais Galliéra, 8 February–7 May 1989* (Paris: Éditions Paris-Musées, 1989); Richard Wrigley, *The Politics of Appearances: Representations of Dress in Revolutionary France* (Oxford and New York: Berg, 2002); Kate Haulman, *The Politics of Fashion in Eighteenth-Century America* (Chapel Hill: University of North Carolina Press, 2011).

17 Michel Beurdeley, *La France à l'encan, 1789–1799: Exode des objets d'art sous la Révolution* (Paris: J. Tallandier, 1981); *Collections et marché de l'art en France 1789–1848*, eds Monica Preti-Hamard and Philippe Sénéchal (Rennes: Presses Universitaires de Rennes-INHA, 2005); *La circulation des œuvres d'art 1789–1848: The Circulation of Works of Art in the Revolutionary Era 1789–1848*, eds Roberta Panzanelli and Monica Preti-Hamard (Rennes: Presses Universitaires de Rennes, 2007); Emily Jane Richardson, 'Unlikely Citizens? The Manufacturers of Sevres Porcelain and the French Revolution, 1789–1804' (PhD thesis, University College London, London, 2007); Cécilie Champy, *'Curieux idolâtres et acheteurs de statues': Le marché de la sculpture sous la Révolution et l'Empire à Paris* (PhD thesis, École Nationale des Chartes, Paris, 2008); Anne Perrin Khelissa, 'De l'objet d'agrément à l'objet d'art: Légitimer les manufactures d'État sous la Révolution (Sèvres, Gobelins et Savonnerie)', in *Le commerce du luxe: Production, exposition et circulation des objets précieux du Moyen Âge à nos jours*, eds Alain Bonnet and Natacha Coquery (Paris: Éditions Mare et Martin, 2015).

18 *Journal de Paris*, 2 Pluviôse Year II (21 January 1794), 1568.

19 See an initial approach to this question in Natacha Coquery, 'Luxury and Revolution: Selling Textiles in Revolutionary France', in *Selling Textiles in the*

Long Eighteenth Century: Comparative Perspectives from Western Europe, eds Jon Stobart and Bruno Blondé (Basingstoke: Palgrave Macmillan, 2014), 179–92.

20 Beverly Lemire, 'Developing Consumerism and the Ready-Made Clothing Trade in Britain, 1750–1800', *Textile History* 15 (1984), 21–44; Beverly Lemire, 'Consumerism in Preindustrial and Early Industrial England: The Trade in Secondhand Clothes', *Journal of British Studies* 27 (1988), 1–24.

21 Roche, 'Regards croisés: Les révolutions à l'épreuve du marché', 188; my translation.

22 For a discussion of blurred and permeable boundaries between social groups and consumer patterns, see also the chapter by Blondé and De Laet in this volume.

23 See Gilles Feyel's research on the topic, notably: 'Négoce et presse provinciale en France au 18e siècle: Méthodes et perspectives de recherches', in *Cultures et formations négociantes dans l'Europe moderne*, eds Franco Angiolini and Daniel Roche (Paris: Éditions de l'EHESS, 1995), 438–511; Feyel's articles in *Dictionnaire des journaux 1600–1789*, ed. Jean Sgard (Paris: Universitas, 1991); and *Dictionnaire de la presse française pendant la Révolution 1789–1799*, eds Gilles Feyel et al. (Ferney-Voltaire: Centre International d'Études du XVIIIe siècle, 2005).

24 See notice 49 written by Philip Stewart in *Dictionnaire des journaux*, ed. Jean Sgard, http://c18.net/dp/dp.php?no=49; the newspaper was initially published twice weekly, then it was issued daily from 22 December 1778. Until the 1770s, each issue contained 8 pages (120 x 200 mm). From the early 1760s, 4-page supplements were frequent, then in 1777, to combat competition from the new *Journal de Paris*, each issue could be up to 16 pages; 'Additions' (8 pages of advertisements) also increased the volume. The subscription price, for Paris, went from 18 *livres* to 24, 30 then 36 in 1794.

25 *Affiches*, Notice No. 1, 3 January 1752.

26 Newspaper issues were 8 pages long in 1752, 8 pages plus a 4-page 'Supplement' in July 1790, 8 pages plus a 4-page 'Supplement' in July 1793, with 8-page 'Additions' on some days (on the 9, 18, 23, 25 and 28 of the month), then 8 pages plus a 4-page 'Supplement' in Germinal Year II (1794) (a single issue, on 2 Germinal, contained 'Additions').

27 Dominique Margairaz, 'Les institutions de la République jacobine ou la révolution utopique', in *Révolution et République: L'exception française, Actes du colloque tenu en Sorbonne en septembre 1992* (Paris: Kimé, 1993), 237–51; with Philippe Minard, 'Marché des subsistances et économie morale: Ce que "taxer" veut dire', *Annales Historiques de la Révolution Française* 2 (2008), 53–99.

28 Pierre Caron, *Paris pendant la Terreur: Rapports des agents secrets du Ministre de l'intérieur* (Paris: Picard and Sons, 1910–1964); Alphonse Aulard, *Paris pendant la*

réaction thermidorienne et le Directoire: Recueil de documents pour l'histoire de l'esprit public à Paris (Paris: Le Cerf, 1898–1902).

29 Report by Le Harivel, in Caron, *Paris pendant la Terreur,* vol. 2, 4 January 1794, 178.

30 Report by Le Harivel, in Caron, *Paris pendant la Terreur,* vol. 2, 12 January 1794, 322.

31 Report by Bacon, in Caron, *Paris pendant la Terreur,* vol. 2, 3 January 1794, 151.

32 Report by Mercier, in Caron, *Paris pendant la Terreur,* vol. 2, 11 January 1794, 310.

33 Report by Pourvoyeur, in Caron, *Paris pendant la Terreur,* vol. 2, 31 December 1793, 109.

34 Report, in Aulard, *Paris pendant la réaction thermidorienne,* vol. 1, 3 October 1794, 145.

35 For a discussion of the link between the increased importance of auctions as means of distribution, and consumption restrictions, see also the chapter by Murhem and Ulväng in this volume.

36 Nicole de Blomac, *La gloire et le jeu: Des hommes et des chevaux, 1766–1866* (Paris: Fayard, 1991), and *Voyer d'Argenson et le cheval des Lumière* (Paris: Belin, 2004); Coquery, *L'hôtel aristocratique.*

37 There was abundant legislation on the requisition of luxury horses following the insurrection of 10 August. On 10–12 and 15 August, by decree, the horses that served the royal guard and those of émigrés were placed at the disposal of the nation, while those of the former court were at the disposal of army generals and officers. The Decree of 19 March 1793, virtually contemporaneous with the *Affiches* cited, 'places the horses of émigrés at the disposal of the Ministry of War' and calls for the 'sale of horses of émigrés that cannot be used in the armies.' Note that in early February, France went to war against a coalition of European monarchies organised by English Prime Minister William Pitt; in early March, the Vendée revolt began. 'The National Convention calls up 300,000 men who will join the Republican Armies as quickly as possible' (Decree of 23 February 1793).

38 Article 5 of the Decree of 9 October 1793 banned from French soil 'all merchandise made or manufactured in England, Scotland, Ireland, and in all the countries subject to the British government': 'All notices, signs and banners written in the English language, or indicating stores of English merchandise, or bearing English symbols or words, as well as any newspapers announcing or publishing the sale of such merchandise, are prohibited, with a penalty of 20 years in iron shackles for the authors and owners of said notices, signs, banners and newspapers.' http://frda.stanford.edu/fr/catalog/bg262qk2288_00_0293

39 Charlotte Guichard, *Les amateurs d'art à Paris au XVIIIe siècle* (Paris: Seyssel, Champ Vallon, 2008); Patrick Michel, *Le Commerce du tableau à Paris dans la*

seconde moitié du XVIIIe siècle: Acteurs et pratiques (Lille: Presses Universitaires du Septentrion, 2007).

40 *Affiches*, 8 July 1793.

41 *Affiches*, 8 July 1793.

42 I thank Bruno Blondé in helping me to reflect on this question.

43 Note that to respond to foreign invasions by European powers and domestic uprisings by royalists, an extraordinary criminal tribunal was established on 10 March 1793; it judged counter-revolutionary crimes without possibility of appeal or recourse; the accused were not allowed a defence or prior interrogation.

44 Under the Terror, legislation against émigrés grew harsher: their goods were sequestrated and sold; on 27 March 1793, the aristocrats and enemies of the Revolution were made outlaws; former nobles and émigrés were again the target of the Decree of 17 September on the arrest of suspect people.

45 Michel Beurdeley, *La France à l'encan, 1789–1799*, 97.

46 *Affiches*, 22 March 1794.

47 *Affiches*, 21 March 1794.

48 'Sale of Furniture and Effects from the Estate of the Former Princess of Lamballe', *Affiches*, 22 March 1794.

49 *Affiches*, 17 January 1794; 28 March 1794, 'Additions' – emphasis added.

50 For a discussion of luxury consumption and taste, and of the correspondence between boundaries of luxury and boundaries of social order, see the chapter by Pajur in this volume.

51 See Perrin Khelissa, 'De l'objet d'agrément à l'objet d'art'. The author examines the discourse on royal factories and their future through surveys, memoranda and draft decree reports.

52 *Affiches*, 2 July 1793.

53 *Affiches*, 3 July 1793.

54 *Affiches*, 27 March 1794.

55 *Affiches*, 9 July 1793.

Select Bibliography

Allerston, Patricia, 'Consuming Problems: Worldly Goods in Renaissance Venice', in *The Material Renaissance*, eds Michelle O'Malley and Evelyn Welch. Manchester: Manchester University Press, 2007.

Andersson, Gudrun, 'A Mirror of Oneself: Possessions and the Manifestation of Status among a Local Swedish Elite, 1650–1770', *Cultural and Social History* 3 (2006).

Auslander, Leora, *Taste and Power: Furnishing Modern France*. Berkeley: University of California Press, 1996.

Batchelor, Jennie and Kaplan, Cora (eds), *Women and Material Culture, 1660–1830*. Basingstoke: Palgrave Macmillan, 2007.

Barczewski, Stephanie, *Country Houses and the British Empire, 1700–1930*. Manchester: Manchester University Press, 2014.

Beaurepaire, Pierre-Yves, *Le mythe de l'Europe française au* XVIII*e siècle: Diplomatie, culture et sociabilités au temps des Lumières*. Paris: Éditions Autrement, 2007.

Berg, Maxine and Clifford, Helen (eds), *Consumers and Luxury: Consumer Culture in Europe 1650–1850*. Manchester: Manchester University Press, 1999.

Berg, Maxine and Eger, Elizabeth (eds), *Luxury in the Eighteenth Century: Debates, Desires and Delectable Goods*. London: Palgrave Macmillan, 2003.

Berg, Maxine, *Luxury and Pleasure in Eighteenth-Century Britain*. Oxford: Oxford University Press, 2005.

Bermingham, Ann and Brewer, John (eds), *The Consumption of Culture, 1600–1800: Image, Object, Text*. London: Routledge, 1995.

Berry, Christopher, *The Idea of Luxury: A Conceptual and Historical Investigation*. Cambridge: Cambridge University Press, 1994.

Blondé, Bruno and Ryckbosch, Wouter, 'In "Splendid Isolation": A Comparative Perspective on the Historiographies of the "Material Renaissance" and the "Consumer Revolution"', *History of Retailing and Consumption* 1 (2015).

Blondé, Bruno, 'Conflicting Consumption Models? The Symbolic Meaning of Possessions and Consumption Amongst the Antwerp Nobility at the End of the Eighteenth Century', in *Fashioning Old and New: Changing Consumer Preferences in Europe (Seventeenth-Nineteenth Centuries)*, eds Bruno Blondé et al. Turnhout: Brepols, 2009.

Blondé, Bruno, Briot, Eugénie, Coquery, Natacha and Van Aert, Laura (eds), *Retailers and Consumer Changes in Early Modern Europe: England, France, Italy and the Low Countries*. Tours: Presses Universitaires François-Rabelais, 2005.

Bonnet, Alain and Coquery, Natacha (eds), *Le commerce du luxe: Production, exposition et circulation des objets précieux du Moyen Âge à nos jours*. Paris: Mare et Martin, 2015.

Bourdieu, Pierre, *Distinction: A Social Critique of the Judgement of Taste*. Translated by Richard Nice. Oxford: Blackwell, 1984.

Bremer-David, Charissa (ed.), *Paris: Life & Luxury in the Eighteenth Century*. Los Angeles: J. Paul Getty Museum, 2011.

Brook, Timothy, *Vermeer's Hat: The Seventeenth Century and the Dawn of the Global World*. London: Profile Books 2009.

Burke, Peter, 'Res et verba: Conspicuous Consumption in the Early Modern World', in *Consumption and the World of Goods*, eds John Brewer and Roy Porter. London and New York: Routledge, 1993.

Calaresu, Melissa and Hills, Hellen, eds, *New approaches to Naples c. 1500–c.1800: The Power of Place*. Aldershot: Ashgate, 2013.

Cheney, Paul, *Revolutionary Commerce: Globalization and the French Monarchy*. Cambridge MA and London: Harvard University Press, 2010.

Chorley, Patrick, *Oil, Silk and Enlightenment: Economic Problems in Eighteenth Century Naples*. Naples: Istituto italiano per gli studi storici, 1965.

Chrisman-Campbell, Kimberly, *Dress at the Court of Louis* XVI *and Marie-Antoinette*. New Haven and London: Yale University Press, 2015.

Clemente, Alida, *Il lusso 'cattivo': Dinamiche del consumo nella Napoli del Settecento*. Rome: Carocci, 2011.

Coquery, Natacha, *L'Hôtel aristocratique: Le marché du luxe à Paris au* XVIII*e siècle*. Paris: Publications de la Sorbonne, 1998.

Coquery, Natacha, 'Shopping Streets in Eighteenth-Century Paris: A Landscape Shaped by Historical, Economic and Social Forces', in *The Landscape of Consumption: Shopping Streets and Cultures in Western Europe, 1600–1900*, eds Jan Hein Furnée and Clé Lesger. Basingstoke: Palgrave Macmillan, 2014.

Coquery, Natacha, *Tenir boutique à Paris au* XVIII*e siècle: Luxe et demi-luxe*. Paris: Éditions du Comité Historique et Scientifique, 2011.

Cornforth, John, *Early Georgian Interiors*. New Haven: Yale University Press, 2004.

Daloz, Jean-Pascal, *The Sociology of Elite Distinction: From Theoretical to Comparative Perspectives*. Basingstoke: Palgrave Macmillan, 2010.

De Laet, Veerle, 'At Home in Seventeenth-Century Brussels: Patterns of Art and Luxury Consumption in Private Households', in *Embracing Brussels: Art and*

Culture in the Court City, 1600–1800, eds Katlijne Van der Stighelen et al. Turnhout: Brepols, 2013.

De Laet, Veerle, *Brussel binnenskamers: Kunst- en luxebezit in het spanningsveld tussen hof en stad, 1600–1735, Studies Stadsgeschiedenis*. Amsterdam: Amsterdam University Press, 2011.

De Vries, Jan, 'Luxury and Calvinism/Luxury of Capitalism: Supply and Demand for Luxury Goods in the Seventeenth-Century Dutch Republic', *The Journal of the Walters Art Gallery* 57 (1999), 73–85.

De Vries, Jan, 'Luxury in the Dutch Golden Age in Theory and Practice', in *Luxury in the Eighteenth Century: Debates, Desires and Delectable Goods*, eds Maxine Berg and Elizabeth Eger. Basingstoke: Palgrave Macmillan, 2003.

De Vries, Jan, *The Industrious Revolution: Consumer Behavior and the Household Economy, 1650 to the Present*. Cambridge: Cambridge University Press, 2008.

Del Donna, Anthony, *Opera, Theatrical Culture and Society in Late Eighteenth-Century Naples*. Aldershot: Ashgate, 2012.

Dobado-González, Rafael, García-Hiernaux, Alfredo and Guerrero, David, 'West versus Far East: Early Globalization and the Great Divergence', *Cliometrica, Journal of Historical Economics and Econometric History* 9 (2015).

Elias, Norbert, *The Court Society*. Translated by Edmund Jephcott. Oxford: Blackwell, 1983.

Fatsar, Kristóf, 'Átváltozások: Eszterháza nagy parterjének vázlatos története', in *MM XC: Tanulmányok és esszék a 90 éves MŐcsényi Mihály tiszteletére*, ed. Kristóf Fatsar. Budapest: BCE Tájépítészeti Kar, 2009.

Fatsar, Kristóf, 'European Travelers and the Transformation of Garden Art in Hungary at the Turn of the 19th Century', *Studies in the History of Gardens and Designed Landscapes* 36 (2016).

Ferenc, David, 'Nicolaus Jacoby(?): Eszterháza, Erweiterungsplan des Schlosses Eszterháza, 1774', in *Arte Venustas: Studies on Drawings in Honour of Teréz Gerszi*, ed. Andrea Czére. Budapest: Museum of Fine Arts, 2007.

Fernández-de-Pinedo, Nadia, 'Tax Collection in Spain in the 18th Century: The Case of the "Décima"', in *Taxation and Debt in the Early Modern City*, eds Jose Ignacio Andrés and Michael Limberger. London: Pickering and Chatto, 2012.

Fernandez-de-Pinedo, Nadia and Emiliano Fernández de Pinedo, 'Distribution of English Textiles in the Spanish Market at the Beginning of 18th Century', *Revista de Historia Económica – Journal of Iberian and Latin American Economic History* 31 (2013).

Finn, Margot, 'Men's Things: Masculine Possessions in the Consumer Revolution', *Social History* 25 (2000).

Forrest, Allan and Middell, Matthias (eds), *The Routledge Companion to the French Revolution in World History*. London: Routledge, 2016.

Fox, Robert and Turner, Anthony (eds), *Luxury Trades and Consumerism in Ancien Régime Paris: Studies in the History of the Skilled Workforce*. Aldershot: Ashgate, 1998.

Furnée, Jan Heine and Lesger, Clé, 'Shopping Streets and Cultures from a Long-term and Transnational Perspective', in *The Landscape of Consumption: Shopping Streets and Cultures in Western Europe, 1600–1900*, eds Jan Hein Furnée and Clé Lesger. Basingstoke: Palgrave Macmillan, 2014.

Gates-Coon, Rebecca, *The Landed Estates of the Esterházy Princes: Hungary during the Reforms of Maria Theresia and Joseph II*. Baltimore and London: Johns Hopkins University Press, 1994.

Gilles, Feyel et al. (eds), *Dictionnaire de la presse française pendant la Révolution 1789–1799*. Ferney-Voltaire: Centre International d'Études du XVIIe siècle, 2005.

Greig, Hannah, *The Beau Monde: Fashionable Society in Georgian London*. Oxford: Oxford University Press, 2013.

Guichard, Charlotte, *Les amateurs d'art à Paris au XVIIIe siècle*. Paris: Seyssel, Champ Vallon, 2008.

Harris, Eileen, *The Genius of Robert Adam: His Interiors*. New Haven and London: Yale University Press, 2001.

Hassan Jansson, Karin, 'When Sweden Harboured Idlers: Gender and Luxury in Public Debates, c. 1760–1830', in *Sweden in the Eighteenth-Century World: Provincial Cosmopolitans*, ed. Göran Rydén. Farnham: Ashgate, 2013.

Haulman, Kate, *The Politics of Fashion in Eighteenth-Century America*. Chapel Hill: University of North Carolina Press, 2011.

Hayward, Maria, *Rich Apparel: Clothing and the Law in Henry VIII's England*. Farnham: Ashgate, 2009.

Horányi, Mátyás, *The Magnificence of Eszterháza*. Translated by András Deák. London: Barrie and Rockliff, 1962.

Hours, Bernard, *Louis XV et sa cour: Le roi, l'étiquette et le courtisan*. Paris: Presses Universitaires de France, 2002.

Hunt, Alan, *Governance of the Consuming Passions: History of Sumptuary Law*. Basingstoke: Palgrave Macmillan, 1996.

Ilmakunnas, Johanna, 'The Luxury Shopping Experience of the Swedish Aristocracy in Eighteenth-Century Paris', in *Luxury and Gender in European Towns, 1700–1914*, eds Marjo Kaartinen, Anne Montenach and Deborah Simonton. London and New York: Routledge, 2015.

Ilmakunnas, Johanna, *Ett ståndsmässigt liv: Familjen von Fersens livsstil på 1700-talet*. Helsigfors and Stockholm: SLS and Atlantis, 2012.

Imbruglia, Girolamo (ed.), *Naples in the Eighteenth Century: The Birth and Death of a Nation State*. Cambridge: Cambridge University Press, 2000.

Jacobsen, Helen, *Luxury and Power: The Material World of the Stuart Diplomat, 1660–1714*. Oxford: Oxford University Press, 2012.

Jones, Jennifer M., *Sexing La Mode: Gender, Fashion and Commercial Culture in Old Regime France*. Oxford and New York: Berg, 2004.

Kaiser, Gerhard R. and Seifert, Siegfried (eds), *Friedrich Justin Bertuch (1747–1822): Verleger, Schriftsteller und Unternehmer im klassischen Weimar*. Tübingen: Niemeyer, 2000.

Körner, Stefan, '"Evviva il nostro prence, che il mondo fa stupir!": Esterházy I. Miklós követsége II. József 1764: évi frankfurti koronázásán: szertartásrend, ünnepségek, mütárgyvásárlások', in *KŐ kövön: Dávid Ferenc 73. születésnapjára*, vol. II, eds Edit Szentesi, Klára Mentényi and Anna Simon. Budapest: Vince, 2013.

Mansel, Philip, *Dressed to Rule: Royal and Court Costume from Louis XIV to Elizabeth II*. New Haven: Yale University Press, 2005.

Marshall, Peter, *East Indian Fortunes: The British in Bengal in the Eighteenth Century*. Oxford: Oxford University Press, 1976.

Masseau, Didier, *Une histoire du bon goût*. Paris: Perrin, 2014.

Mathiassen, Tove Engelhart et al. (eds), *Fashionable Encounters: Perspectives and Trends in Textile and Dress in the Early Modern Nordic World*. Oxford: Oxbow Books, 2014.

McCabe, Ina Baghdiantz, *A History of Global Consumption: 1500–1800*. London and New York: Routledge, 2015.

McCants, Anne E. C., 'Exotic Goods, Popular Consumption, and the Standard of Living: Thinking about Globalization in the Early Modern World', *Journal of World History* 18 (2007).

Memoirs of the Life of the Late Mrs. Catharine Cappe, written by herself, ed. Mary Cappe. London, 1822.

Miller, Leslie, 'Material Marketing: How Lyonnais Silk Manufacturers Sold Silks, 1660–1789', in *Selling Textiles in the Long Eighteenth Century*, eds Jon Stobart and Bruno Blondé. Basingstoke: Palgrave Macmillan, 2014.

Modes et Révolutions 1780–1804: Exposition, Musée de la Mode et du Costume, Palais Galliéra, 8 February–7 May 1989. Paris: Éditions Paris-Musées, 1989.

Moe, Nelson, *The View from Vesuvius: Italian Culture and the Southern Question*. Berkeley: University of California Press, 2002.

Möller, Håkan, *Lyx och mode i stormaktstidens Sverige*. Stockholm: Atlantis, 2014.

Müller, Leos, 'The Swedish East India Trade and International Markets: Re-exports of Teas, 1731–1813', *Scandinavian Economic History Review* 51 (2003).

Müller, Leos, *The Merchant Houses of Stockholm, c. 1640–1800: A Comparative Study of Early-Modern Entrepreneurial Behaviour*. Uppsala: Uppsala University, 1998.

Murhem, Sofia, Ulväng, Göran and Lilja, Kristina, 'Tables and Chairs Under the Hammer: Second-Hand Consumption of Furniture in the Eighteenth and Nineteenth Centuries in Sweden', in *Modernity and the Second-Hand Trade: European Consumption Cultures and Practices, 1700–1900*, eds Jon Stobart and Ilja Van Damme. Basingstoke: Palgrave Macmillan, 2010.

North, Michael, *'Material Delight and the Joy of Living': Cultural Consumption in the Age of Enlightenment in Germany*. Translated by P. Selwyn. Aldershot: Ashgate, 2008.

Panzanelli, Robert and Preti-Hamard, Monica (eds*), La circulation des œuvres d'art 1789–1848: The Circulation of Works of Art in the Revolutionary Era 1789–1848*. Rennes: Presses Universitaires de Rennes, 2007.

Pérez-García, Manuel, *'Vicarious Consumers': Trans-National Meetings between the West and East in the Mediterranean World (1730–1808)*. London: Ashgate, 2013.

Pietsch, Ulrich and Banz, Claudia (eds), *Triumph of the Blue Swords: Meissen Porcelain for Aristocracy and Bourgeoisie, 1710–1815*. Leipzig: E. A. Seemann, 2010.

Preti-Hamard, Monica and Sénéchal, Philippe, eds, *Collections et marché de l'art en France 1789–1848*. Rennes: Presses Universitaires de Rennes-INHA, 2005.

Purdy, Daniel L., *The Tyranny of Elegance: Consumer Cosmopolitanism in the Era of Goethe*. Baltimore: Johns Hopkins University Press, 1998.

Raikes, Sophie and Knox, Tim, *Nostell Priory and Parkland*, 6th edn. Swindon: National Trust, 2009.

Reinert, Sophus A., *Translating Empire: Emulation and the Origins of Political Economy*. Cambridge MA: Harvard University Press, 2011.

Ribeiro, Aileen, *Dress in Eighteenth-Century Europe, 1715–1789*. New Haven and London: Yale University Press, 2002.

Roche, Daniel, *The Culture of Clothing: Dress and Fashion in the Ancien Regime*. Translated by Jean Birrell. Cambridge: Cambridge University Press, 1994.

Rublack, Ulinka. *Dressing Up: Cultural Identity in Renaissance Europe*. Oxford: Oxford University Press, 2010.

Runefeldt, Leif, *Att hasta mot undergången: Anspråk, flyktighet, förställning i debatten om konsumtion i Sverige 1730–1830*. Stockholm: Nordic Academic Press, 2015.

Said, Edward, *Orientalism*. New York: Vintage Books, 1994; orig. 1978.

Saisselin, Rémy G., *The Enlightenment against the Baroque: Economics and Aesthetics in the Eighteenth Century*. Berkeley: University of California Press, 1992.

Sargentson, Carolyn, *Merchants and Luxury Markets: The Marchand Merciers of Eighteenth-Century Paris*. London: Victoria and Albert Museum, 1996.

Savage, M., 'Status, lifestyle and taste', in *The Oxford Handbook of the History of Consumption*, ed. Frank Trentmann. Oxford: Oxford University Press, 2012.

Schama, Simon, *The Embarrassment of Riches: An Interpretation of Dutch Culture in the Golden Age*. New York: Random House, 1987.

Sekora, John, *Luxury: The Concept in Western Thought, Eden to Smollett*. Baltimore: Johns Hopkins University Press, 1977.

Sewell, William H., 'The Empire of Fashion and the Rise of Capitalism in Eighteenth-Century France', *Past and Present* 206 (2010).

Shovlin, John, *The Political Economy of Virtue: Luxury, Patriotism and the Origins of the French Revolution*. Ithaca and London: Cornell University Press, 2006.

Simonton, Deborah, Kaartinen, Marjo and Montenach, Anne (eds), *Luxury and Gender in European Towns, 1700–1914*. London: Routledge, 2015.

Sirén, Osvald, *China and Gardens of Europe of the Eighteenth Century*. New York: The Ronald Press Company, 1950.

Smith, Woodruff, *Consumption and the Making of Respectability, 1600–1800*. London and New York: Routledge, 2002.

Sombart, Werner, *Luxury and Capitalism*. Translated by W. R. Dittmar. Ann Arbor: University of Michigan Press, 1967.

Somfai, Lászl6, 'Haydn at the Esterházy Court', in *The Classical Era: From the 1740s to the end of the 18th century*, ed. Neal Zaslaw. Houndmills and Basingstoke: Macmillan, 1989.

Spang, Rebecca L., *Stuff and Money in the Time of the French Revolution*. Cambridge, MA: Harvard University Press, 2015.

Stobart, Jon and Hann, Andrew (eds), *The Country House: Material Culture and Consumption*. Swindon: Historic England, 2016.

Stobart, Jon and Rothery, Mark, *Consumption and the Country House*. Oxford: Oxford University Press, 2016.

Stobart, Jon, 'Luxury and Country House Sales in England, c. 1760–1830', in *The Afterlife of Used Things: Recycling in the Long Eighteenth Century*, eds Ariane Fennetaux, Amélie Junqua and Sophie Vasset. London: Routledge, 2015.

Stobart, Jon, 'Status, Gender and Life Cycle in the Consumption Practices of the English Elite: The Case of Mary Leigh, 1736–1806', *Social History* 40 (2015).

Stobart, Jon, 'The Language of Luxury Goods: Consumption and the English Country House, c. 1760–1830', *Virtus* 18 (2011).

Styles, John and Vickery, Amanda (eds), *Gender, Taste, and Material Culture in Britain and North America 1700–1830*. New Haven and London: Yale University Press, 2006.

Styles, John, 'Product Innovation in Early Modern London', *Past and Present* 168 (2000).

Szentesi, Edit, 'Eszterháza 18. századi leírásai,' in *KŐ kövön: Dávid Ferenc 73. születésnapjára*, vol. II, eds Edit Szentesi, Klára Mentényi and Anna Simon. Budapest: Vince, 2013.

Thépaut-Cabasset, Corinne, 'Marie-Louise d'Orléans Queen of Spain', in *Spanish Fashion at the Courts of Early Modern Europe*, eds J. L. Colomer and Amalia Descalzo Lorenzo. Madrid: CHEE, 2014.

Thépaut-Cabasset, Corinne, *L'Esprit Des Modes Au Grand Siècle*. Paris: Éditions du CTHS, 2010.

Todd, Christopher, 'A Swiss Milady in Yorkshire: Sabine Winn of Nostell Priory', *Yorkshire Archaeological Journal* 77 (2005).

Trentmann, Frank, 'Crossing Divides: Consumption and Globalization in History', *Journal of Consumer Culture* 9 (2009).

Trentmann, Frank, *Empire of Things: How We Became a World of Consumers, Fifteenth Century to the Twenty-First*. London: Penguin Books, 2016.

Ulväng, Göran, *Herrgårdarnas historia: Liv, arbete och bebyggelse på Uppländska herrgårdar*. Uppsala: Hallgren and Björklund, 2008.

Veblen, Thorstein, *The Theory of the Leisure Class: An Economic Study in the Evolution of Institutions*. New York: Macmillan, 1899.

Vickery, Amanda, 'Women and the World of Goods: A Lancashire Consumer and her Possessions, 1751–81', in *Consumption and the World of Goods*, eds John Brewer and Roy Porter. London and New York: Routledge, 1993.

Vickery, Amanda, *Behind Closed Doors: At Home in Georgian England*. New Haven: Yale University Press, 2009.

Von Wachenfeldt, Paula and Nyberg, Klas (eds), *Det svenska begäret: Sekler av lyxkonsumtion*. Stockholm: Carlssons, 2015.

Welch, Evelyn, 'Public Magnificence and Private Display: Pontano's "De Splendore" and the Domestic Arts', *Journal of Design History* 15 (2002).

Wolff, Charlotta, 'The Swedish Aristocracy and the French Enlightenment circa 1740–1780,' *Scandinavian Journal of History* 30 (2005), doi:10.1080/03468750500279632.

Wilson, Richard and Mackley, Alan, *The Building of the English Country House, 1660–1880: Creating Paradise*. London: Hambledon Continuum, 2000.

Wurst, Karin, *Fabricating Pleasure: Fashion, Entertainment, and Cultural Consumption in Germany, 1780–1830*. Detroit: Wayne State University Press, 2005.

Index

Page numbers in *italics* refer to illustrations.

www.ingramcontent.com/pod-product-compliance
Lightning Source LLC
LaVergne TN
LVHW050301210926
848481LV00014BA/296